Spanish Erotic Cinema

Spanish Erotic Cinema

Edited by Santiago Fouz-Hernández

For Ralf and for Kiki, el amor se hace

Edinburgh University Press is one of the leading university presses in the UK. We publish academic books and journals in our selected subject areas across the humanities and social sciences, combining cutting-edge scholarship with high editorial and production values to produce academic works of lasting importance. For more information visit our website: edinburghuniversitypress.com

© editorial matter and organisation Santiago Fouz-Hernández, 2017
© the chapters their several authors, 2017

Edinburgh University Press Ltd
The Tun – Holyrood Road
12 (2f) Jackson's Entry
Edinburgh EH8 8PJ

Typeset in 11/13 Monotype Ehrhardt by
Servis Filmsetting Ltd, Stockport, Cheshire

A CIP record for this book is available from the British Library

ISBN 978 1 4744 0047 3 (hardback)
ISBN 978 1 4744 0048 0 (webready PDF)
ISBN 978 1 4744 2418 9 (epub)

The right of the contributors to be identified as authors of this work has been asserted in accordance with the Copyright, Designs and Patents Act 1988 and the Copyright and Related Rights Regulations 2003 (SI No. 2498).

Contents

List of Figures vii
Acknowledgements ix
Notes on the Contributors xi

Introduction: One Hundred Years of Sex 1

1 The Colour of Kisses: Eroticism and Exoticism in Spanish Film Culture of the 1920s and '30s 19
  Eva Woods Peiró
2 Impressions of Africa: Desire, Sublimation and Looking 'Otherwise' in Three Spanish Colonial Films 37
  Brad Epps
3 The *Desarrollismo* Years: The Failures of Sexualised Nationhood in 1960s Spain 55
  Annabel Martín
4 Sexual Horror Stories: The Eroticisation of Spanish Horror Film (1969–75) 74
  Antonio Lázaro-Reboll
5 Undressing Opus Dei: Reframing the Political Currency of *Destape* Films 92
  Jorge Pérez
6 Middlebrow Erotic: Didactic Cinema in the Transition to Democracy 109
  Sally Faulkner
7 Revisiting Bigas Luna's *Bilbao*: The Female Body-Object 125
  Carolina Sanabria
8 The Male Body in the Spanish Erotic Films of the 1980s 139
  Alejandro Melero

9	Sonorous Flesh: The Visual and Aural Erotics of Skin in Eloy de la Iglesia's *Quinqui* Films *Tom Whittaker*	154
10	Masochistic Nationalism and the Basque Imaginary *Rob Stone*	169
11	Erotohistoriography, Temporal Drag and the Interstitial Spaces of Childhood in Spanish Cinema *Sarah Wright*	187
12	Sex After Fifty: The 'Invisible' Female Ageing Body in Spanish Women-authored Cinema *Barbara Zecchi*	202
13	Boys Interrupted: Sex between Men in Post-Franco Spanish Cinema *Santiago Fouz-Hernández*	219
Index		239

Figures

I.1 and I.2	Trailer for *Kiki, el amor se hace*/*Quickie, Love is So*	7
1.1	'Besos cinematográficos', *La Pantalla*	20
1.2	'La ciencia del beso', *La Pantalla*	26
1.3	'Desde América', *Cine Popular*	31
2.1	*Misión blanca*/*White Mission*	39
2.2	*¡Harka!*	41
3.1	*Noche de verano*/*Summer Night*	66
3.2	*Los felices sesenta*/*The Happy Sixties*	69
4.1	*El asesino de muñecas*/*Killing of the Dolls*	85
4.2	*El asesino de muñecas*/*Killing of the Dolls*	87
5.1	*La trastienda*/*The Backroom*	95
5.2	*La trastienda*/*The Backroom*	98
6.1	*El diputado*/*Confessions of a Congressman*	118
6.2	*El diputado*/*Confessions of a Congressman*	119
7.1	*Bilbao*	130
7.2	*Bilbao*	131
7.3	*Bilbao*	134
8.1	*Profesor Eroticus*/*Professor Eroticus*	142
8.2	*Deseo carnal*/*Desire of the Flesh* aka *Carnal Desire*	144
9.1 and 9.2	*El pico*/*Overdose*	161
10.1 and 10.2	*Akelarre*/*Witches' Sabbath*	181
11.1 and 11.2	*Cría cuervos*/*Raise Ravens*	192
12.1	*¡Vámonos, Bárbara!*/*Let's Go, Barbara!*	206
12.2	*De tu ventana a la mía*/*From Your Window to Mine*	214
13.1	*Segunda Piel*/*Second Skin*	227
13.2	*Fuckbuddies*	231
13.3	*Los amantes pasajeros*/*I'm So Excited*	233

Acknowledgements

This book originated in a series of workshops and conference panels where most of the contributors to this book presented this work for the first time. First and foremost I wish to thank the contributors for accepting my invitations to those events and then for expanding their work for this collection. They have been extremely generous and cooperative throughout the process. The British Academy funded the first workshop at Harvard University in October 2012 and also my stay there for one semester, which allowed me to start work on this project. I am grateful to Brad Epps (now at Cambridge University) for his role in facilitating my stay and the workshop at Harvard, and also to Isolina Ballesteros (Baruch College, The City University of New York) for being a model respondent at the event. Durham University hosted and sponsored two further workshops in February 2013 and March 2014. At Durham I am also grateful to the School of Modern Languages and Cultures and the Faculty of Arts and Humanities for kindly funding my trips to the Society for Cinema and Media Studies (SCMS) in Boston (March 2012) and in Atlanta (March 2016), where I coordinated two panels on Spanish erotic cinema which served as bookends to the project. I would also like to thank Dan O'Neill (University of California, Berkeley) for his invitation to spend a semester at Berkeley in 2015 so that I could complete research for my own contribution to this book. At Berkeley I had the pleasure of attending some of Linda Williams' and Mary Ann Doane's lectures, which helped me shape up ideas for the Introduction.

At Edinburgh University Press I am indebted to commissioning editor Gillian Leslie, who encouraged me to submit a proposal for this book after the SCMS panel at Boston and for being extremely supportive of this project ever since. Richard Strachan was also tremendously helpful throughout the editing process and Eddie Clark in the final stages of production. My thanks also to Rebecca Mackenzie (project manager) and Emma Rees (marketing) for their generous help and support with the cover design and promotion of the book respectively. Victoria Bernal at Egeda processed the necessary copyright permissions for the cover image. Thanks also to Betty Bigas for putting me in touch with Egeda and Video Mercury Films, S.A.U., and to Christian Mieves for the original concept for the cover.

On a more personal note I would like to thank my husband Christian (Kiki), and all my family and friends for their continued love, support and confidence in me.

Editor's note – All translations of foreign-language sources are the authors' own, unless otheerwise indicated.

Notes on the Contributors

Brad Epps is Professor of Spanish and Chair of Spanish and Portuguese at the University of Cambridge and former professor of Romance Languages and Literatures and Studies of Women, Gender and Sexualities at Harvard University. He has published over a hundred articles and chapters on modern literature, film, art, urban studies, queer theory, and immigration from Spain, Latin America, Catalonia, the United States and France. He is the author of *Significant Violence: Oppression and Resistance in the Narratives of Juan Goytisolo* (1996); and co-editor of *Spain Beyond Spain: Modernity, Literary History, and National Identity* (2005); *Passing Lines: Immigration and Sexuality* (2005); *All About Almodóvar: A Passion for Cinema* (2009); a special issue of *Catalan Review* on Barcelona and modernity; and a special issue of *GLQ* on lesbian theorist Monique Wittig. He has taught as visiting professor or scholar in Spain, Germany, France, Chile, Cuba, the Netherlands, Sweden and the People's Republic of China. He is currently preparing two books: *Barcelona and Cinema* and *El cine como historia; la historia como cine*.

Sally Faulkner is Professor of Hispanic Studies and Film Studies at the University of Exeter, where she is Head of Modern Languages and Founder-Director of the College of Humanities Centre for Translating Cultures. She has published widely on Spanish audiovisual culture and Film Studies. Her books include *Literary Adaptations in Spanish Cinema* (2004), *A Cinema of Contradiction: Spanish Film in the 1960s* (Edinburgh University Press, 2006), *A History of Spanish Film: Cinema and Society 1910–2010* (2013), forthcoming in Spanish translation in 2017, and, as editor, *Middlebrow Cinema* (2016). In 2013 she won the Philip Leverhulme Prize for Modern Languages and Literatures.

Santiago Fouz-Hernández is Reader in Hispanic Studies at Durham University. He is author of the book *Cuerpos de cine. Masculinidades carnales en el cine y la cultura popular contemporáneos* (2013), co-author of *Live Flesh: The Male Body in Contemporary Spanish Cinema* (2007), editor of *Mysterious Skin: Male Bodies in Contemporary Cinema* (2009) and co-editor of *Madonna's Drowned Worlds: New Approaches to Her Cultural Transformations* (2004) and *Rethinking Identities: Cultural Articulations of Alterity and Resistance in the New Millennium* (2014). He has been visiting scholar at the University of Queensland in Australia (2002, 2005), and at CUNY Graduate Center (2010), Harvard (2012), University of California, Berkeley and Pittsburgh (2015) in the USA. He is an editorial board member for the journal *Studies in Spanish and Latin American Cinemas*. He is currently completing a monograph on director Bigas Luna and coordinating a series of international tribute events to celebrate the work of the late filmmaker.

Antonio Lázaro-Reboll is a Senior Lecturer in Hispanic Studies at the University of Kent. He is the author of *Spanish Horror Film* (Edinburgh University Press, 2012) and the co-editor (with Andrew Willis) of *Spanish Popular Cinema* (2004). His research interests are in Spanish cultural studies and film studies, especially Spanish popular film, the development of film cultures in Spain (reception, consumption and fandom), and the cross-cultural dialogue between Spain and other world cinemas (international traditions of the horror genre, global psychotronic culture). He is currently working on the emergence of subcultural modes of production, reception and consumption in Spain in the 1970s across different media (film, comics, magazines) and their relation to two key moments of recent Spanish history – late Francoism and the Transition.

Annabel Martín is an Associate Professor of Spanish, Comparative Literature, and Women's, Gender and Sexualities Studies, and the director of The Gender Research Institute at Dartmouth College. Working within the field of cultural studies and with a particular interest in nationalism, her research and publications pay special attention to the narratives of cultural and gender identity in contemporary Spanish culture. She is the author of the book *La gramática de la felicidad: Relecturas franquistas y posmodernas del melodrama* (2005) on mass culture and its multiple political readings from early Francoism to the more contemporary period. Currently she is studying the cultural context surrounding the end of ETA terrorism in Spain and the role the arts play in processes of reconciliation in her manuscript *Rest in Peace: The Basque Political Contours of the Arts*, a collaborative project with Basque artists Bernardo Atxaga, Julia Otxoa, Ricardo Ugarte, Luisa Etxenike and Helena Taberna, among others. She is also a member of a research team at the Universitat de València (Spain) studying tourism and national identity and a member of a research group studying the importance of gender studies in higher education with other faculties from the Universidad de Deusto (Spain) and Boston College.

Alejandro Melero is Assistant Professor at the Universidad Carlos III in Madrid. He has published several articles on the representation of sex onscreen, as well as queer and gender theory. He has contributed to books including *Gender and Spanish Cinema* (2004) and *Spanish and Lusophone Women Filmmakers* (2013). His books *Placeres ocultos. Gays y lesbianas en el cine español de la Transición* and *Guía ilustrada del cine europeo* were published in 2010. He is the co-editor of *Performance and Spanish Film* (2016).

Jorge Pérez is Professor of Iberian Cultural Studies at the University of Texas, Austin. He is the author of *Cultural Roundabouts: Spanish Film and Novel on the Road* (2011) and *Confessional Cinema: Religion, Film and Modernity in Spain's Development Years* (2017); and co-editor of *The Latin American Road Movie* (2016). He has published several book chapters as well as articles on Spanish cinema, novel and queer culture in journals such as *ALEC*, *Arizona Journal of Hispanic Cultural Studies*, *España Contemporánea*, *Revista de Estudios Hispánicos*, *Revista Canadiense de Estudios Hispánicos* and *Studies in Hispanic Cinemas*. He has also co-edited a special issue of the *Journal of Spanish Cultural Studies* on the topic of Spanish popular music.

Carolina Sanabria obtained her PhD in Audiovisual Communication from the Universitat Autònoma Barcelona. She is a full Professor in Film Studies at the University of Costa Rica. She has published widely in the field of literature and communication. Her books include *Bigas Luna, El ojo voraz* (2010), *Contemplación de lo íntimo. Lo audiovisual en la cultura contemporánea* (2011) and *Adaptaciones subliminales. Tres obras maestras de Alfred Hitchcock* (2013).

Rob Stone is Professor of Film Studies at the University of Birmingham, where he directs B-Film: The Birmingham Centre for Film Studies. He is a fellow of the Leverhulme Trust, Associate Research Professor at the University of Deusto in the Basque Country and co-editor of the annual Screen Arts issue of *Hispanic Research Journal*. He is the author of *Spanish Cinema* (2001), *Flamenco in the works of Federico García Lorca and Carlos Saura* (2004), *Julio Medem* (2007), *Walk, Don't Run: The Cinema of Richard Linklater* (2013; 2nd edition 2017), co-author of *Basque Cinema: A Political and Cultural History* (2015), and co-editor of *The Unsilvered Screen: Surrealism on Film* (2007), *Screening Songs in Hispanic and Lusophone Cinema* (2012), *A Companion to Luis Buñuel* (2013) and *Screening and European Heritage* (2016). He has published widely on Spanish, Basque, Cuban and independent American cinema.

Tom Whittaker is Senior Lecturer in Film and Hispanic Studies at the University of Liverpool. He is the author of *The Films of Elías Querejeta: A Producer of Landscapes* (2011) and co-editor of *Performance and Spanish Film* (2016) and *Locating the Voice in Film: Critical Approaches and Global Practices* (2017), as well as a wide range of articles on Spanish, Latin American and British cinema. He is presently working on a monograph entitled *Deviant Noise: Quinquis, Criminality and Sound in Spanish Film*.

Eva Woods Peiró is an Associate Professor in Hispanic Studies at Vassar College. She has directed and has taught in the programmes of Media Studies, Latin American and Latino Studies and currently teaches and mentors in Women's Studies and International Studies. Her books include *White Gypsies: Race and Stardom in Spanish Musicals* (2012), *Visualizing Spanish Modernity* (co-edited with Susan Larson, 2005) and the forthcoming, collaborative *Cinema and the Mediation of Everyday Life: An Oral History of Cinema-Going in 1940s and 1950s Spain*. At present she is researching representations of technology in Spanish silent film.

Sarah Wright is Reader in Hispanic Studies at Royal Holloway, University of London, and author of the books *The Trickster-Function in the Theatre of García Lorca* (2000), *Tales of Seduction: The Figure of Don Juan in Spanish Culture* (2007) and *The Child in Spanish Cinema* (2013), as well as articles on Spanish theatre, film and cultural studies. She is also co-editor of *Locating the Voice in Film: Critical Approaches and Global Practices* (2017).

Barbara Zecchi is Professor in the Department of Languages, Literatures and Cultures and in the Interdepartmental Programme in Film Studies at the University of Massachusetts Amherst. She has taught at several universities in Spain (Universitat de València, Universidad Carlos III de Madrid, Universidad de Cádiz) and in the United States (UCLA, California State University and Johns Hopkins). Her research focuses on Gender Studies, Filmology, Feminist Film Theory, Adaptation Theory, Videographic Criticism and the Digital Humanities. In these fields she has published numerous articles and the books *Sexualidad y Escritura: 1850–2000* (2002, co-editor); *La mujer en la España actual ¿Evolución o involución?* (2004, co-editor); *Teoría y práctica de la adaptación cinematográfica* (2012, editor); *Gynocine* (2013, editor), *Desenfocadas: Cineastas españolas y discursos de género* (2013) and *La pantalla sexuada* (2014) among others. She currently directs the Digital Humanities project 'Gynocine: History of Spanish Women's Cinema' funded by the University of Massachusetts.

Introduction: One Hundred Years of Sex

Santiago Fouz-Hernández

SEX AND SPANISH CINEMA FROM THE SCREEN TO ACADEMIA

Sex and sexuality have permeated Spanish cinema scholarship for the last three decades or so. With few exceptions, however, eroticism has only been considered as part of studies on other issues such as gender (for example, the collection by Marsh and Nair 2004), the body (Fouz-Hernández and Martínez-Expósito 2007), queer cinema (Perriam 2013a) or in the context of the work of specific directors known for the sexually explicit content of their films – Pedro Almodóvar, Vicente Aranda, Luis Buñuel or Bigas Luna, for example. Understandably, discussions on eroticism have tended to revolve around the so-called *destape* (literally 'uncovering'/'undressing') films of the late 1970s and early 1980s.[1] This distinctively erotic genre of films that burgeoned after the abolition of Francoist censorship at the end of 1977 has often been dismissed by critics and scholars alike for its weak and often sexist plotlines, debatable aesthetic value and in some cases poor acting performances.[2] More recently, however, the films have experienced a critical re-evaluation on the basis of their socio-historical interest, but also for their significance in terms of gender and sexual politics in the context of the Transition. This volume aims to extend that re-evaluative effort to cover erotic content in Spanish cinema from the silent period until today.

It is worth noting that, although not focusing explicitly on eroticism, the work of Pilar Aguilar (1998), Isolina Ballesteros (2001), Barbara Zecchi (2014) or Susan Martin-Márquez (1999) has been essential in building a feminist perspective on studies of sex and the erotic image in the history of Spanish film. Lengthy studies by Alejandro Melero Salvador (2010), Alberto Mira (2004) or Perriam (2013a) have been equally important from GLBT and queer standpoints. Indeed, Melero Salvador has been a key voice in the critical re-evaluation of erotic films of the Transition more widely: see, for example, Melero Salvador 2010, 2011, 2014 and his contribution to this book. Yet, despite the inescapable presence of the erotic in writings about Spanish cinema, work focused solely on Spanish erotic films is rare. This is all the more surprising when we consider that, as Xavier Mendik notes, 'recent years have witnessed an explosion of critical interest in the pervasive influences of the erotic image' and 'the study of the "cine-erotic" has emerged as one of the most significant and subversive aspects of film cultural studies' (2012: 1). Much of this work has been focused on pornography and inspired by Linda Williams' influential *Hard Core. Power, Pleasure, and the Frenzy of the Visible* (1999). Williams' edited collection *Porn Studies* followed in 2004, leading the way for countless other edited volumes, including Lehman (2006) or Hines and Kerr (2012). Porn Studies is now a well-established discipline with its own journal and several international conferences and panels devoted to the field. Monographs published within the last ten years or so by Linda Ruth Williams (2005), Tanya Krywinska (2006) or Linda Williams (2008) and Mendik's edited collection (2012) have discussed eroticism and depictions of sex on the screen beyond the realm of pornography. In Spain, Gubern's (1989) pioneering study of the pornographic image has been equally influential. More recent work on pornography includes the monograph by Barba and Montes (2007) and some of the theoretical essays produced in the context of queer studies. These writings, however, rarely focus on Spanish primary material. Books by José Ponce (2004), Tomás Pérez Niño (2011) or Aguilar García (2012) provide useful overviews of national erotic productions, but with very little critical analysis. Ponce's book is mostly a collection of visual materials such as posters and press cuttings covering the Transition period, Pérez Niño provides encyclopedic entries on a selection of one hundred Spanish erotic films that the author considers most representative of the Spanish erotic genre, while Aguilar García's book is a more journalistic discussion of the stars of the *destape* films.

If there is something that the various writings on aspects of eroticism in Spanish films reveal it is that it is impossible to understand the history of Spanish cinema without paying some close attention to the erotic. As Melero Salvador has shown, it is commonplace, especially outside of Spain, to associate post-Franco Spanish cinema with explicit sexual imagery (2014: 179). Numerous studies have demonstrated that such an association is not a cliché and that the erotic element of Spanish films is by no means exclusive to post-Franco productions. Indeed, sex and eroticism were important elements of some Spanish films since the silent period, starting from around 1916 with the short films produced for the private enjoyment of King Alfonso XIII that have been attributed to the Baños brothers and their Barcelona production company Royal Films (Gubern 2005: 9). Eva Woods Peiró has established that many films of the 1920s were the 'product of the popular erotic novel'

(2012: 83), while Leigh Mercer has worked on some fascinating materials that would seem to form the basis for an early history of sex and pornography in Spanish cinema (2016 and in preparation). Even films produced during the most unlikely times, the 1950s and '60s, become all the more interesting to study due to the existence of 'double versions' for co-productions and exports: one censored for Spanish audiences and one uncensored with extra or longer scenes and different wardrobe for foreign, more liberated markets. The relatively recent availability of uncensored versions on foreign DVDs proves the significance of eroticism in the cinema of that period. The repressed erotic content that was already present in the cuts, fades to black, silences and wardrobe choices in the Spanish versions, has become visible. The production of double versions had always been denied by Franco's administration, but there was anecdotal evidence that proved otherwise: in January 1973 a film theatre in Santiago de Compostela (Cines Yago) exhibited the uncensored version of Rafael Moreno Alba's *Las melancólicas/Exorcism's Daughter* (1971) by mistake, drawing in unprecedented numbers of delighted spectators and becoming the talk of the town until a local authority investigated the case and corrected the error (see Alonso Tejada 1977: 141–3).

FORTY YEARS WITHOUT SEX?

One of the most entertaining (albeit problematic) critiques of the double standards of the Franco regime in relation to sex and eroticism is Juan Bosch's sketch-based satirical film *Cuarenta años sin sexo/Forty Years without Sex*. The film, released in 1979 – shortly after the abolition of censorship – unambiguously points the finger at the Catholic Church and the State as instigators of a damaging sexual repression with long-lasting effects. Under a thick layer of comedy, the film ridicules absurd laws and regulations imposed by the Francoist Ministry of the Interior, such as the 1950s legal requirement to cover up at the beach.[3] The film also highlights the responsibility of the Church for its disparaging teachings on masturbation, sexist views on the 'holy' marriage or condemnation of homosexuality. Some of the comedy sketches are introduced by more reflexive and direct criticisms recited by an actor who talks directly into the camera. These direct attacks on the Church and the State underscore the didactic message of the stories: 'for centuries the Church has been the big administrator of sex for all Spaniards'; 'in these forty years more than four thousand super large families were rewarded with small change and a diploma ... some of these cases were a clear example of sex put at the service of the homeland'. A number of sketches blame priests, in their role as preachers, teachers and confessors, for the widespread existence of sexless marriages, homophobia and sexism. The stories illustrate their role in brainwashing women and children, interfering with family life and sex education, sometimes leading to tragedy. In one of the sketches a fascist man commits suicide after being informed by a priest/teacher that his child has been expelled from school because they suspect he might be gay. Importantly, the film also debunks the *macho* myth and draws attention to the sexism embedded in marriage laws. It culminates with a long sketch where an adulterous man sets up his wife to commit an act of adultery herself, so that he has a legal reason to separate and live with his lover. It becomes clear that the law is fully behind the man, and would even protect him if he were to kill his wife on the basis of adultery. Even while critiquing the oppression of the dictatorship years, Bosch's film is itself oppressive and exploitative in other ways. The markedly male-centred narrative is emphasised through the pervasive male voiceover that threads the stories together, as well as the male actors who introduce some of the sketches or the overtly dominant male gaze. Despite some male nudity, the gaze is very much focused on the female bodies on the screen. This was characteristic of the *destape* films – although, as Jorge Pérez and Alejandro Melero Salvador show in their contributions to this collection, there are notable exceptions.

ANOTHER FORTY YEARS OF SEX

The years following the abolition of censorship saw the introduction of new film classifications mostly determined by the explicit depiction of sex and violence. The 'S' classification ('S' stands for sensitivity) was a financially successful and hugely popular product. According to Pérez Niño, the so-called 'S' films (*películas S*) accounted for 25 per cent of all films produced in Spain between 1980 and 1982, with a total of 127 produced between late 1977 and 1983 (when the stronger 'X' category and purpose-built X theatres were introduced) (2011: 56). The popularity of X theatres with audiences previously targeted for 'S' films and, as Jordan and Morgan-Tamousunas note (1998: 66), other factors including rising production costs, introduction of the Miró film reforms and increased circulation of erotic films on videotape, resulted in the rapid decline of a group of films of considerable interest for this volume, as we shall see.

The aforementioned renewed interest in the 'S' films is perhaps best illustrated in the popularity of contemporary films that pay homage to them nostalgically, notably *Los años desnudos (clasificada S)/Rated R* (dirs. Dunia Ayaso and Félix Sabroso, 2008) and *Torremolinos 73* (dir. Pablo Berger, 2003), films that Melero Salvador has studied in a recent essay (2014). As he argues, these films demonstrate the importance of the Transition as 'a landmark in the exploration of sexual discourses' (2014: 187). There were, of course, other types of film during the Transition (and since) that placed sex at the very centre of their narratives. If Fernando Colomo's debut film *Tigres de papel/ Paper Tigers* (1977) became iconic for its depiction of the freedoms (not just sexual) afforded to the newly liberated post-Franco youth, years later Chus Gutiérrez's documentary *Sexo oral/Oral Sex* (1994) was also ground-breaking in making a point not only about the need to talk about sex openly and freely (the playfully deceiving title in Spanish refers to 'talking' sex, not just 'oral sex') but also in having a woman behind (and at times in front of) the camera. By filming and interviewing people about their sexual preferences, she is also making a point about taking active control of a narrative centred in a topic traditionally reserved for men – and, importantly, also taking charge of the gaze.

Needless to say, eroticism continues to be a major ingredient of many Spanish films. Besides the names mentioned at the start of this introduction, directors like Manuel Gómez Pereira and Julio Medem have also become famous for their sexually explicit material. In the case of Gómez Pereira, titles like *¿Por qué lo llaman amor cuando quieren decir sexo?/Why do They Call it Love When They Mean Sex?* (1993), *Boca a boca/Mouth to Mouth* (1995) or *Entre las piernas/Between Your Legs* (1999) speak for themselves, while some scenes in Medem's *Lucía y el sexo/Sex and Lucia* (1999) or *Habitación en Roma/Room in Rome* (2010) push the limits between eroticism and pornography – a distinction that I will return to below. Both directors have also made the most of utilising a certain erotic cachet and strong screen presence of their stars. Many became famous precisely for their sex appeal. These include Jorge Sanz, Javier Bardem, Victoria Abril and Aitana Sánchez Gijón in Gómez Pereira's films or Paz Vega and Elena Anaya in Medem's.

As these examples show, while comedy might be the prevailing genre for erotic narratives in Spanish cinema, eroticism is also at the centre of melodramas (in many Almodóvar films, for example), period dramas (Aranda's *Juana la loca/Mad Love* (2001) or Bigas Luna's *Volaverunt* (1999) are good examples), musicals (see Perriam 2013b) or even documentaries, as we saw in the case of Chus Gutiérrez.[4] Indeed, as exemplified in the international notoriety of Jess Franco, eroticism has been an important factor for the global success of Spanish horror films, despite critics' disapproval of this combination when it started to emerge in the early 1970s, as Lázaro-Reboll has shown (2012: 167–8).

Let us return briefly to the 'S' classification, as I believe it can function as a useful way to draw the sometimes blurry line between eroticism and pornography. This interesting category served the double purpose of promising some sexually explicit content while preventing the alienation of audiences who may not yet be ready to watch porn, at least not in a public space. Importantly, this type of film offered what Linda Ruth Williams describes as 'a promise of effect': 'If the film contains erotic scenarios', she argues, 'it ought to produce an erotic response in its viewer' (2005: 25). This appeal to the viewer is one of the premises that, as we shall see in contributions in this volume by Fouz-Hernández, Whittaker or Zechhi, has become crucial for the study of sex on the screen: the affective and haptic quality of the erotic image, as informed by the work of Linda Williams (1991), Laura Marks (2000), Sobchack (2004) or Barker (2009), among others.

KIKI: SEX THROUGH THE SENSES

In that sense, the recent and enormously popular *Kiki, el amor se hace/Quickie, Love is So* (dir. Paco León, 2016) becomes the latest example of a film sold very much on the basis of its sexual narrative and some nudity, but that in fact leaves much to the imagination. It also presents a set of themes, aesthetic concerns, performances and ideas that make it a fitting case study that helps to draw out some conclusions about the erotic tradition in Spanish cinema and to introduce some of the main concerns of this volume. The tagline 'Una comedia erótico festiva' – literally 'a merry erotic comedy' (see Figure I.2) – used in the intensive promotional campaign in Spain is a conscious effort to link the film with the *destape* tradition and the 'S' cinema, since many people would informally refer to those films as '*erótico festivos*'. The extra-diegetic soundtrack of some of the sex scenes also draws out this comparison – in particular in the culminating ménage-a-trois between Paco, Ana and Belén – by using the kind of music that became a common feature of the *destape* genre, drawing on a range of commercial musical styles, here most notably bossa nova, and French and German popular song from the late 1960s, thereby referencing an 'international' style common to much European erotic film from the period. As Julio Arce (2014) – informed by Linda Williams (2008) – has shown, this 'musical sexual interlude' was common in post-Code Hollywood cinema. Williams explains that this interlude provided an element of affective control of the explicit sexual imagery presented on the screen and made it more palatable, as opposed to hearing the diegetic sounds of the sex act (see Williams 2008: 83).[5] Yet, in sharp contrast to the backward Spanish society represented in *Cuarenta años sin sexo*, León's film (almost forty years later!) presents a much more sexually liberated, permissive society that is happy to discuss openly its increasingly sophisticated sexual preferences. Importantly, if, in *Cuarenta años sin sexo*, women seemed subjugated by their husbands and, in some cases, apparently non-orgasmic, women in *Kiki, el amor se hace* appear to be utterly in control of their sexuality, well-informed about various practices, open-minded and confident in their pursuit of their preferences and desires.

Female orgasm becomes an important driving force in the narrative from the first scene where, shortly after sex, Natalia (Natalia de Molina) confesses to her partner that she experienced a very intense sexual climax when she

Figures I.1 (upper) and I.2 (lower) Natalia de Molina and Álex García in a trailer for *Kiki, el amor se hace/Quickie, Love is So*, directed by Paco León. Spain: ICAA, Mediaset España, Telecinco Cinema, Vértigo Films, 2016.

was mugged at a petrol station the previous week. Harpaxophilia (becoming sexually aroused by a burglary or robbery) is the first of many paraphilias and fetishes presented in the film as the main narrative thread between five loosely interconnected stories: María Candelaria (Candela Peña), a fairground worker, is sexually aroused by sobbing (dacryphilia); Ana (Ana Katz) is married to Paco (played by the director Paco León), but attracted to bisexual Belén (Belén Cuesta) with whom the couple eventually enter into a polyamorous relationship; cosmetic surgeon José Luis (Luis Bermejo) finds in somnophilia a way to rekindle his sex life with his differently-abled wife Paloma (Mari Paz Sayago); while Sandra (Alexandra Jiménez) is slightly deaf, has a lactose resistance and a fetish for certain textile materials.[6]

The casting of Candela Peña is, in my view, a crucial part of this film's conscious effort to firmly place itself into the long tradition of erotic Spanish cinema. This is arguably Peña's first major role in a Spanish film since she famously admitted to having serious financial problems during her Goya Award acceptance speech in 2013, openly asking for work in several television chat shows thereafter. Interestingly, two of her most recent important roles in Spain were in the aforementioned erotic-nostalgic comedies *Torremolinos 73* and *Los años desnudos (clasificada 'S')*, while one of her most iconic performances (for which she received a Goya Award) was in the role of a sex worker in León de Aranoa's *Princesas/Princesses* (2005). While it would not be fair, nor particularly productive, to establish comparisons between Peña and the stars of the *destape* films, it is worth pointing out that Peña's sexually explicit roles and her performances in nostalgic comedies set in the Transition in particular, further underscore this film's symbolic re-inscription into that tradition.

There are at least three other issues that make this film particularly fascinating for the study of sex and eroticism on the Spanish screen. Firstly, the film establishes a clear tension between the primal, animalistic aspects of sex and the need to rationalise, perform, mediate and sometimes pay in order to make erotic fantasies come true. The opening credit sequence superimposes images of the first sex scene between Natalia and Álex (Figure I.1) with footage of wild animals on heat or breeding, sometimes combining the two so that the faces or body parts of the characters are replaced with the heads or equivalent body parts of the animals. From the outset, then, the film makes a point of blurring the distinction between animal and human sexuality. One of the main tenets of Bataille's theory of eroticism is that it is '[an] aspect of the inner life of man', that human sexual activity is only erotic 'whenever it is not rudimentary and purely animal' (2012: 29). Thus, for him, the creation of taboos is a crucial aspect of human evolution and part of what differentiates us from animals. The sense of animal abandonment that characterises the opening moments of *Kiki* rapidly gives way to the characters' 'inner life'. Natalia can't stop thinking about what caused her unexpected orgasm when she was robbed at the petrol station. This inexplicable, almost primal reaction is thus hastily rationalised, humanised. Álex, wishing to give his girlfriend a sexual thrill, will attempt to recreate the robbery in an underground parking lot. In contrast with the spontaneity of the unexpected first incident, however, a lot of planning, props and, importantly, financial investment will go into this re-enactment. Not only will Álex pay actors to perform the robbery attempt, he will also dress up as a robber to become part of the enactment after the foreplay provided by the actors. The plan goes horribly wrong, but the scene introduces two more points of interest: the performativity and the commodification of sex.

This performance of sex within a film *about* sex draws attention to the fact that what we are seeing, throughout the film, is a performance – a fact that the film seems interested in foregrounding in other ways, for example by giving most of the characters the real names (or similar) of the actors who play them. The fake robbery scene also demonstrates that, as Krywinska has argued, we should 'be sceptical about any putative dividing line between the constructed, the natural and the real, particularly as sex and sexuality in life are themselves performative, grounded in the imagination, often staged and involving roleplay and fantasy' (2006: 6). In other words, the performativity of the robbery and of sex in film more generally are but reflections of the performative nature of sex also in the lives of those who are watching. The commodification of sex underlies the whole film and becomes particularly obvious in the references to the sex industry implicit in the nature of Belén and José Luis' jobs. The fetish parties in Belén's club involve both performativity and a series of financial transactions: costumers have to pay an entrance fee and, once inside, consume drinks. For special parties they will also need to rent or buy pricey outfits to adhere to specific sexual dress codes. José Luis buys her maid's silence (she knows that he secretly sedates his wife in order to have sex with her) with ever-increasing discounts for the breast implants that she wants. Meanwhile, José Luis' assistant at the clinic is worried about her daughter, who has started selling her used underwear online. The business of sex is, of course, best symbolised in the film product itself. Outselling Almodóvar's long-awaited *Julieta* by three to one in the Spanish box office in the first four months of theatrical exhibition (both films were released within a week of each other) and arguably resurrecting Peña's career, *Kiki* proves Krywinska's point about 'the allure of erotic sensationalism' at times of crisis in the industry (2006: 13–14), something that also applies more widely to the erotic films of the Transition.[7]

The role of technology as mediator of sexual desire is also evident in Sandra's job as a sign language interpreter. She falls in love with one of her clients who calls requesting that she interprets a call to a telephone sex line. In a complex incitement to the spectator's senses, Sandra becomes the visual and language mediator between her client Rubén (David Mora) and the erotic female voice that he can't hear. In a further turn of the screw that is reminiscent of the humorous dubbing scene at the start of Almodóvar's *La ley del deseo/Law of Desire* (1987), we see the real person at the other end of the phone. The lady pretending to be a hot 'heterosexual blonde' is in fact a rather unglamorous and business-oriented person multitasking at home. She is holding the phone with one hand and waxing her facial hair with the other, while also keeping an eye on the stove. Her very unsexy appearance resulting from the *real* circumstances once again draws attention to the performativity of sex – already implicit in the context of the paid act – while at the same time highlighting the role of technology, capital and the senses in this multiply mediated exchange. The scene cleverly plays out its affective appeal by emphasising specific senses in different characters. Rubén, as a 'super consumer' (he pays the sex-line worker and the interpreter), relies on his gaze to filter sensations conveyed by Sandra. Sandra, who also relies on a sometimes malfunctioning hearing aid, depends on her hearing in order to interpret the conversation with the telephone sex worker – while at the same time becoming aroused herself with the vision of handsome Rubén on her screen. The telephone sex worker draws attention to the senses of touch and smell: not only is she painfully waxing her facial hair, at one point she has to put out a fire in the kitchen. The inescapable hapticality of this scene is further enhanced by Sandra's fetish for fabrics. In an earlier scene she had an intensive orgasm in a metro station after frenziedly touching the shirt of an anonymous fellow passenger as she alighted the train.

The senses of touch, smell and taste are, of course, essential in most paraphilias, and this highly sensual film emphasises them unambiguously through the fetishes of the main characters and some secondary ones, as seen in a golden shower scene or in the references to the used-underwear traffic. Talking about what she calls the 'body genres' (melodrama, horror, pornography), Linda Williams argues that 'the success of these genres seems a self-evident matter of measuring body response' (1991: 5). Although this erotic comedy would not quite fit any of the genres identified by Williams, the emphasis placed on bodily fluids (tears, blood, sperm, urine), smells (used clothing, food), sounds (and their interruption by a malfunctioning hearing aid), textures (fabrics, skin), flavours (food, bodies) and, of course, provocative imagery is remarkable.

By reinserting the human sensorium into the critical frame and emphasising such degraded categories as 'feeling' and 'intensity', this study of Spanish erotic cinema seeks to contribute to the current tendency in Film Studies of doing theory through the senses. One of the main premises of this book's approach to erotic cinema is informed by Williams' work on embodied ways of experiencing sex in films and, in particular, Benjamin's concept of *innervation*. As Williams argues, in watching bodies engaged in sexual acts, the spectator 'is solicited sexually too' (2008: 19). The studies that follow combine the more established approaches to socio-historical contextualisation and interpretation of the films with analysis informed by cutting-edge film and cultural theories, with a view to making room within the analytical trajectory for the auteurs, the texts, their contexts, the stars, the industry and, importantly, the audiences.

THIS BOOK

The main aim of this book is to use the erotic as a prism through which to study and better understand important aspects of Spanish cinema and Spanish society as wide-ranging as age, class, gender, modernity, national identities, race religion or sexualities. To that end, and while not claiming comprehensive historical coverage, the chapters are presented chronologically (on the basis of the main case studies discussed) in an attempt to reveal the evolution of what we may understand as 'erotic' in the Spanish cinema production of the last hundred years or so. The thirteen chapters included in this collection offer a detailed overview of a wide range of aesthetics, genres, directors and styles.

Genres discussed include the crusade film (Epps), comedy, horror (Lázaro-Reboll), melodrama and religious film (Pérez), as well as some specifically Spanish genres, including *cine con niño* (Wright), *cine quinqui* (Whittaker) and, or course, *destape* (especially Pérez and Melero Salvador). The stars discussed include household names such as Alfredo Mayo (Epps), María José Cantudo (Pérez), José Sacristán (Faulkner), Silvia Munt (Stone), Ana Torrent (Wright), Amparo Soler Leal (Zecchi), Bardem or Banderas (Fouz-Hernández), but also some lesser-known figures including Pisano (Sanabria), Jorge Rivero and Tony Fuentes (Melero Salvador), or José Luis Manzano (Whittaker). The list of directors is too long to enumerate here, but it ranges from Benito Perojo in the silent period to Almodóvar, Paula Ortíz or Paco León today. Eloy de la Iglesia deserves a special mention, as this book, suitably, celebrates his erotic film production in almost half of the contributions (Lázaro-Reboll, Pérez, Melero Salvador, Fouz-Hernández – and whole chapters by Faulkner and Whittaker).

Starting in the silent period, Eva Woods Peiró explores the erotic allure of the kiss in 1920s Spanish films, paying special attention to discussions about the cinematic kiss in the Spanish specialised press at the time. Her research reveals an obsessive fascination with the technological mediation of the Hollywood kiss on the one hand and, on the other, a highly racialised discourse about Japan's prohibition on kissing, used by the Spanish printed media to present a comparatively modern image of 1920s Spain – despite the shortage of Japanese films shown in domestic theatres at the time. If Woods Peiró ends her chapter by referring to the renewed emphasis on racialised erotic discourses in 1990s Spanish cinema, where foreign bodies are often exoticised, Brad Epps starts his essay by connecting those 1990s postcolonial film narratives to the 'jumbled conflux of the exotic and the erotic' in the three 1940s Spanish films set in Africa that he examines: *¡Harka!* (dir. Carlos Arévalo, 1941), *¡A mí la legión!/Follow the Legion* (dir. Juan de Orduña, 1942) and *Misión blanca/White Mission* (dir. Juan de Orduña, 1946). In his chapter, Epps argues that the films use desiring subjects as a propagandistic vehicle of Spain's imperial ventures that are put at the service of the Nationalist cause. While the decidedly homosocial colonial military setting has inspired a number of homoerotic readings focused on the strong male friendships celebrated by the films, Epps critiques the misogynistic and racialised nature of those relationships. The very sublimation of desire implied in the 'masculine mystique' promoted in the narratives inspires in this case a different and innovative kind of queer reading.

Concerned with a different kind of exoticism, that which was motivated by the new influx of mass tourism in the *desarrollismo* years, Annabel Martín explores the transformative power of the then newly introduced neoliberal economic policies. In her study of 1960s films (especially Jaime Camino's *Los felices sesenta/The Happy Sixties* and Jorge Grau's *Noche de verano/Summer*

Night), Martín teases out the tensions that the films establish between the allure of capitalism, consumerism or the potential for social upward mobility on the one hand, and erotic frustration on the other. Moreover, while the films suggest a certain sexual liberalisation both of the characters and 1960s Spanish cinema and Spanish society more widely, they also commodify bodies. In the new neoliberal regime, bodies become consumers as well as consumer objects. This preoccupation with the objectification of the body also underlies Lázaro-Reboll's chapter on 1970s erotic horror films. His essay reveals how the Spanish film press became highly critical of what it perceived as an exploitative commercialisation of eroticism and sexuality in what it appropriately called *erotismo de consumo*. Rather than focusing on the well-trodden territory of the objectification of female bodies in horror cinema, Lázaro-Reboll turns his attention to the male body and the camp aesthetics of Miguel Madrid's (aka Michael Skaife) *El asesino de muñecas / Killing of the Dolls* (1975) and, in particular, to the body of David Rocha as spectacle.

Jorge Pérez's essay on filmic depictions of the Opus Dei opens a section of five chapters that explore different aspects of eroticism in the films of the Transition. To an extent, all five chapters explore the political potential of the erotic content of these films. Focused on the *destape* films, Pérez and Melero Salvador make important contributions to the aforementioned re-evaluation of this often scorned genre from two different perspectives, while Sanabria, Faulkner and Whittaker propose new readings on the work of two crucial directors of the period, Bigas Luna and Eloy de la Iglesia.

Pérez's revealing analysis of the Opus Dei in Grau's *La trastienda / The Backroom* (1976), Yagüe's *Cara al sol que más calienta / Facing the Warmest Sun* (1977), and Berlanga's *La escopeta nacional / The National Shotgun* (1978) demonstrates the political value of these films in their different approaches to the depiction of the secretive religious organisation. In *La trastienda*, for example, the casting of Czech-born actor Frederick Stafford helps associate the Opus Dei elites with modern European democracies. The other two films offer more direct criticisms of the organisation, exposing the perverse effects of the sexual repression that it fosters. The potential of the erotic as political critique is also at the centre of Sally Faulkner's essay. Adapting her original concept of 'middlebrow cinema' (Faulkner 2013) to Spanish erotic cinema – what she calls 'the middlebrow erotic' – her chapter examines how, after the abolition of censorship in 1977, eroticism 'extended beyond subject matter and became the very grammar by which a new film language was constructed'. In turn, that new language was used to express the new freedoms afforded by democracy. She illustrates this theory with a fresh reading of an important film of this period, Eloy de la Iglesia's *El diputado / Confessions of a Congressman* (1978), demonstrating how the erotic is used to didactically explain previously forbidden political and sexual tendencies and, indeed, how these go hand in hand with each other. Carolina Sanabria's chapter focuses on another iconic film of the Transition, Bigas Luna's *Bilbao*, released in the same year as *El diputado* and causing a similar uproar – but for very different reasons. After reclaiming the importance of this controversial film as 'a foundational text of Spanish sex-cinema' and an essential testament of the Transition, Sanabria reveals that despite the film's reputation as sexually provocative and overtly erotic, *Bilbao* is in fact an abstract tale about the disenchantment with the body, which is quite literally turned into a lifeless, undesirable and *anti*-erotic object.

Returning to the *destape* comedies, Melero Salvador proposes a different focus to what we are used to in work on this genre by turning attention to the male star system. In this sense, his chapter joins forces with Pérez, but also with Epps, Lázaro-Reboll, Faulkner, Whittaker and Fouz-Hernández's discussions of masculinities and male bodies in this and other genres and periods elsewhere in this book. Melero Salvador studies the performances of Tony Fuentes in two popular *destape* films: *Deseo carnal/Desire of the Flesh* aka *Carnal Desire* (dir. Manuel Iglesias, 1978) and *Jóvenes viciosas/Dirty Young Ladies* (dir. Manuel Iglesias, 1980), as well as the evolution of Fuentes' star persona. The analysis reveals both how the films projected onto the actor's body stage some of the social anxieties of the time, and how, in turn, these and other historical traces are carried forward into his roles in other films. The male body and another male star are also the focus of Tom Whittaker's discussion of Eloy de la Iglesia's *quinqui* films. Informed by senses-receptor-based film theories, as previously discussed, his chapter reflects on the importance of the visual erotics of touch and skin, using the body of de la Iglesia's *actor fetiche* José Luis Manzano as a productive and very fitting case study. The chapter proposes that the aesthetic roughness, the post-synch sound and the delinquent narratives characteristic of this type of film, make it ideal to illustrate the kind of visual immediacy that sensually engages the viewer with the image on the screen. Manzano's skin is often shown in close-up, pierced and tattooed. Through his work in de la Iglesia's *quinqui* films, the actor became iconic of a genre fascinated with 'the fragile glamour of male youth' as a memorable example of what the press at the time referred to as the *estética de calzoncillo*, as Whittaker notes.

As the book reaches beyond the Transition, into the democratic period, the last four chapters show how eroticism in contemporary Spanish cinema continues to be used as a tool to draw attention to social anxieties of the times: national and nationalist identities, gender equality, ageing and sexuality. In his chapter, Rob Stone sets out to investigate the curious absence of erotic content in Basque cinema (Julio Medem's feature films are the obvious exception), an absence that, as he says, extends well into the democratic period and therefore cannot be blamed on censorship or Catholic repression. His research shows that the explicit content of Basque films often revolves around contexts of torture, revealing a certain fascination with masochist narratives that could be suggestive of nationalist martyrdom. This is explored in his Deleuzian analysis of his two main case studies, *Estado de excepción/State of Emergency* (dir. Iñaki Núñez, 1977) and *Akelarre/Witches' Sabbath* (dir. Pedro Olea, 1984), and of a segment of Medem's documentary *La pelota vasca: la piel contra la piedra/The Basque Ball: Skin Against Stone* (2003), among many other examples throughout the history of Basque cinema. This noticeable absence of erotic narratives could be part of a revolutionary intent to distance Basque cinema both from the erotic narratives of the Barcelona School and from the *destape* films associated with Madrid, but also a nationalist commitment to sacrifice individualistic desires and pleasures in the service of more collective aims.

Sarah Wright studies the child figure as 'the conduit for the exploration of the trauma and loss of the Spanish Civil War and its aftermath of dictatorship in Spain' in well-known films including *El espíritu de la colmena/The Spirit of the Beehive* (dir. Víctor Erice, 1973), *Cría cuervos/Raise Ravens* (dir. Carlos Saura, 1976), *Secretos del corazón/Secrets of the Heart* (dir. Montxo Armendáriz, 1997) and *Pa negre/Black Bread* (dir. Agustí Villalonga, 2010). In an analysis informed by queer theory, and in particular by Lee Edelman's concept of reproductive futurism and Elizabeth Freeman's erotohistoriography, Wright focuses on sequences of intense intimacy (between mother and child, for example), transgressive kids' games and some traumatic events witnessed by children, to explore the potential of the child figure to queer the films' version of history. If Wright focuses on the child, Barbara Zecchi puts the spotlight at the other end of the age spectrum to discuss the figure of the ageing female character as a sexual being in a wide selection of films directed by women filmmakers, including Cecilia Bartolomé, Isabel Coixet, Pilar Miró, Josefina Molina or Paula Ortíz, among others. Zecchi usefully identifies a number of sometimes opposing strategies that serve to organise the films into three distinctive categories. Some films actively spectacularise the body of the mature and sexually active woman, while others do the opposite and use the portrayal of the unglamorous older female body as a means to draw attention to and denounce the expectations set by the youth-obsessed mainstream film and media that displace mature women, making them invisible. Finally, she identifies a third group of films with 'affirmative ageing' discourses. In ways that closely link this chapter to Whittaker's, Zecchi explains how this last group of films actively encourages the spectator's sensual engagement with the erotic experiences of the older women on the screen.

In the chapter that closes the collection I investigate why so many erotic scenes involving sex between men are often interrupted. While these interruptions are perhaps to be expected in erotic – as opposed to pornographic – films, the frequency and sometimes violence with which they occur is intriguing and troubling. The chapter identifies different strategies of interruption that go from the classic ellipsis with fades to black to literal concealment achieved with distance, poor lighting or visual obstructions such as doors, window blinds or props. In some other cases, other characters enter the scene. These include family members (often female – wives, girlfriends, mothers) but also (often male) strangers that halt the sex act quite suddenly and aggressively midway. Importantly, these *violent* interruptions prevent the kinds of pleasurable identification that are often encouraged in heterosexual erotic scenes, even when the sex act is left to the spectators' imagination. The study revisits some classic and well-known films by directors including Pedro Almodóvar, Cesc Gay, Eloy de la Iglesia or Gerardo Vera, as well as more recent and lesser-known work, including Juanma Carrillo's short film *Fuckbuddies* (2011). The analysis of the final case study, Almodóvar's *Los amantes pasajeros/I'm So Excited* (2013), suggests that, as demonstrated in other contributions in this collection, the erotic content of films can sometimes be hidden (and found) in surprisingly conspicuous places.

NOTES

1. The erotic content of Spanish films is also often discussed with reference to later productions that may have experienced classification or distribution problems in foreign markets due to their sexually explicit content. Almodóvar's *¡Átame!/Tie Me Up! Tie Me Down!* (1991) is often cited as an example (see, for example, Jordan and Morgan-Tamousnas 1998: 112).
2. Kowalski's succinct account of the poor critical reception of the *destape* films in Spain is as accurate as it is revealing (2004: 203).
3. Shaha Pack's study of European tourism in Franco's Spain provides an excellent context for this important trope often revisited in Spanish films of the 1960s and '70s (2006).
4. In her book *Sex Radical Cinema*, Carol Siegel refers to some scenes in another Chus Gutiérrez film, *El Calentito* (2005), as 'sex radical cinema at its most powerful' (2015: 125).
5. Virginia Sánchez Rodríguez (2013) has written an excellent analysis of the soundtrack in 1960s Spanish cinema from a Gender Studies perspective.
6. Belén's job in a nightclub that organises fetish parties provides the perfect excuse to introduce a whole set of other paraphiliac and fandoms, including furries and swingers.
7. As of 11 August 2016, *Kiki* made 6,192,817 euros at the Spanish box office, becoming the second most successful Spanish release of the year since opening on 1 April. In comparison, Almodóvar's most recent film, *Julieta* (2016) – third in the year ranking – released only a week later on 8 April, made 2,120,527 euros in Spain. Source: Spanish Ministry of Education, Culture and Sport: http://www.mecd.gob.es/cultura-mecd/dms/mecd/cultura-mecd/areas-cultura/cine/datos-industria-cine/taquilla/agosto2016/cine-espanol-acumulado-11-agosto16.pdf (last accessed 11 August 2016).

REFERENCES

Aguilar García, José Antonio (2012), *Las estrellas del destape y la transición: el cine español se desnuda*, Madrid: T&B Editores.
Aguilar, Pilar (1998), *Mujer, amor y sexo en el cine español de los 90*, Madrid: Fundamentos.
Alonso Tejada, Luis (1977), *La represión sexual en la España de Franco*, Barcelona: Luis de Caralt Editor S.A.
Arce, Julio (2014), 'Con "S" de Sexo. Representaciones musicales en el cine erótico de la transición', *Quaderns*, 9, 97–105: https://rua.ua.es/dspace/bitstream/10045/41183/1/Quaderns-de-Cine_09_11.pdf (last accessed 30 July 2016).
Ballesteros, Isolina (2001), *Cine (ins)urgente: Textos fílmicos y contextos culturales en la España postfranquista*, Madrid: Fundamentos.
Barba, Andrés and Javier Montes (2007), *La ceremonia del porno*, Barcelona: Anagrama.
Barker, Jennifer M. (2009), *The Tactile Eye: Touch and the Cinematic Experience*, Berkeley and Los Angeles: University of California Press.
Bataille, Georges (2012), *Eroticism*, trans. Mary Dalwood, London: Penguin.
Faulkner, Sally (2013), *A History of Spanish Film: Cinema and Society (1910–2010)*, New York: Bloomsbury.
Fouz-Hernández, Santiago and Alfredo Martínez-Expósito (2007), *Live Flesh: The Male Body in Contemporary Spanish Cinema*, London and New York: I. B. Tauris.
Gubern, Román (2005 [1989]), *La imagen pornográfica y otras perversiones ópticas*, Madrid: AKAL Comunicación.
Hines, Claire and Darren Kerr (eds) (2012), *Hard to Swallow. Hard-Core Pornography on Screen*, London and New York: Wallflower Press.
Jordan, Barry and Rikki Morgan-Tamosunas (1998), *Contemporary Spanish Cinema*, Manchester: Manchester University Press.
Kowalsky, Daniel (2004), 'Rated S: Softcore Pornography and the Spanish Transition to Democracy, 1977–1982', in Antonio Lázaro-Reboll and Andrew Willis (eds), *Spanish Popular Cinema*, Manchester: Manchester University Press, pp. 188–208.
Krzywinska, Tanya (2006), *Sex and the Cinema*, London and New York: Wallflower Press.
Lázaro-Reboll, Antonio (2012), *Spanish Horror Film*, Edinburgh: Edinburgh University Press.
Lehman, Peter (ed.) (2006), *Pornography: Film and Culture*, New Brunswick, NJ: Rutgers University Press.
Marks, Laura (2000), *The Skin of the Film: Intercultural Cinema, Embodiment and the Senses*, Durham, NC: Duke University Press.
Marsh, Steven and Parvati Nair (eds) (2004), *Gender and Spanish Cinema*, Oxford and New York: Berg.
Martin-Márquez, Susan (1999), *Feminist Discourse and Spanish Cinema: Sight Unseen*, Oxford: Oxford University Press.
Mendik, Xavier (2012), 'Introduction. Perversive Peeping: New Ways to Survey the Cine-Erotic', in Xavier Mendik, *Peep Shows, Cult Film and the Cine-Erotic*, London and New York: Wallflower Press, pp. 1–24.
Melero, Alejandro (2010), *Placeres ocultos. Gays y lesbianas en el cine español de la Transición*, Madrid: Notorious Eds.
Melero Salvador, Alejandro (2011), 'Armas para una narrativa del sexo. Transgresión y cine "S"', in Manuel Palacio (ed.), *El cine y la transición política en España (1975–1982)*, Madrid: Biblioteca Nueva, pp. 127–44.
Melero Salvador, Alejandro (2014), 'New Bodies, New Sounds: Rediscovering the Eroticism

of the Transition', in Duncan Wheeler and Fernando Canet (eds), *(Re)viewing Creative, Critical and Commercial Practices in Contemporary Spanish Cinema*, Bristol: Intellect, pp. 177–89.
Mercer, Leigh (2016), 'Sexual Technophilia: Vernacular Modernism in Spain's Early Pornographic Film History', unpublished conference paper, *Society for Cinema and Media Studies*, Atlanta (1 April 2016).
Mercer, Leigh (in preparation), *An Incoherent Voyage: Spanish Cinema Pioneers, Between Technophilia and Technophobia*.
Mira, Alberto (2004), *De Sodoma a Chueca: una historia cultural de la homosexualidad en España en el siglo XX*, Madrid: Egales.
Pack, Sasha D. (2006), *Tourism and Dictatorship. Europe's Peaceful Invasion of Franco's Spain*, New York: Palgrave Macmillan.
Pérez Niño, Tomás (2011), *Cine erótico español: los cien mejores títulos*, Madrid: Cacitel, S.L.
Perriam, Chris (2013a), *Spanish Queer Cinema*, Edinburgh: Edinburgh University Press.
Perriam, Chris (2013b), 'Contemporary Musical Comedy, Sex and Gender', in Jo Labanyi and Tatjana Pavlović (eds), *A Companion to Spanish Cinema*, Chichester: Wiley-Blackwell, pp. 217–21.
Ponce, José María (2004), *El destape nacional. Crónica del desnudo en la transición*, Barcelona: Ediciones Glenat.
Sánchez Rodríguez, Virginia (2013), 'La banda sonora musical en el cine español (1960–1969). La recreación de identidades femeninas a través de la música de cine en la filmografía española de los años sesenta', PhD thesis, Universidad de Salamanca: http://gredos.usal.es/jspui/handle/10366/123048 (last accessed 14 August 2016).
Siegel, Carol (2015), *Sex Radical Cinema*, Bloomington and Indianapolis: Indiana University Press.
Sobchack, Vivian (2004), *Carnal Thoughts: Embodiment and Moving Image Culture*, Berkeley: Los Angeles and London: University of California Press.
Williams, Linda (1991), 'Film Bodies: Gender, Genre and Excess', *Film Quarterly* 44:4 (Summer), 2–13.
Williams, Linda (1999), *Hard Core: Power, Pleasure, and the 'Frenzy of the Visible'*, Berkeley: University of California Press.
Williams, Linda (ed.) (2004), *Porn Studies*, Durham, NC: Duke University Press.
Williams, Linda (2008), *Screening Sex*, Durham, NC and London: Duke University Press.
Williams, Linda Ruth (2005), *The Erotic Thriller in Contemporary Cinema*, Edinburgh: Edinburgh University Press.
Woods Peiró, Eva (2012), *White Gypsies: Race and Stardom in Spanish Musicals*, Minneapolis: Minnesota University Press.
Zecchi, Barbara (2014), *La pantalla sexuada*, Madrid and Valencia: Cátedra.

FILMOGRAPHY

¡Átame!/Tie Me Up! Tie Me Down!, film, directed by Pedro Almodóvar. Spain: El Deseo, 1991.
Boca a boca/Mouth to Mouth, film, directed by Manuel Gómez Pereira. Spain: Bocaboca Producciones, Sogetel, Sogepaq, Star Line TV Productions S.L., 1995.
Cuarenta años sin sexo/Forty Years without Sex, film, directed by Juan Bosch. Spain/Belgium: 2000 Productions, Producciones Zeta, 1979.

El Calentito, film, directed by Chus Gutiérrez. Spain: Telespan 2000, Studios Picasso, Canal + España, ICAA, 2005.
Entre las piernas/Between Your Legs, film, directed by Manuel Gómez Pereira. Spain/France: Bocaboca Producciones, Aurum Producciones, DMVB Films, 1999.
Habitación en Roma/Room in Rome, film, directed by Julio Medem. Spain: Morena Films, Alicia Produce, Canal + España, Instituto de Crédito Oficial, ICAA, Intervenciones Novo Film 2006 Aie, TVE, Wild Bunch, 2010.
Juana la loca/Mad Love, film, directed by Vicente Aranda. Spain/Italy/Portugal, France: Canal + España, Enrique Cerezo Producciones Cinematográficas S.A., Eurimages, Pedro Costa Producciones Cinematográficas S.A., Production Group, Sogepaq, Take 2000, 2001.
Julieta, film, directed by Pedro Almodóvar. Spain: El Deseo, TVE, Canal + France, Ciné +, 2016.
Kiki, el amor se hace/Quickie, Love is So, film, directed by Paco León. Spain: ICAA, Mediaset España, Telecinco Cinema, Vértigo Films, 2016.
La ley del deseo/Law of Desire, film, directed by Pedro Almodóvar. Spain: El Deseo, Laurenfilm, 1987.
Las melancólicas/Exorcism's Daughter, film, directed by Rafael Moreno Alba. Spain: Dauro Films, 1971.
Los años desnudos (Clasificada S)/The Naked Years (Rated S), film, directed by Dunia Ayaso and Félix Sabroso. Spain: Antena 3 Films, Little Giraffe Producciones, 2008.
Lucía y el sexo/Sex and Lucia, film, directed by Julio Medem. Spain/France: Alicia Produce, Canal + España, Sogocine, Sogepac, StudioCanal, TVE, 1999.
¿Por qué lo llaman amor cuando quieren decir sexo?/Why do They Call it Love When They Mean Sex?, film, directed by Manuel Gómez Pereira. Spain: Audiovisuales Nebli, Cristal Producciones Cinematográficas S.A., 1993.
Princesas/Princesses, film, directed by León de Aranoa. Spain: Reposado Producciones, Mediapro, Antena 3 Televisión, Canal + España, 2005.
Sexo oral/Oral Sex, film, directed by Chus Gutiérrez. Spain: Kaplan S.A., Muac Films, Stico Producciones, 1994.
Tigres de papel/Paper Tigers, film, directed by Fernando Colomo. Spain: La Salamandra Producciones Cinematográficas, S.L., 1977.
Torremolinos 73, film, directed by Pablo Berger. Spain, Denmark: Estudios Picasso, Mama Films, Nimbus Film Productions, Telespan 2000, 2003.
Volaverunt, film, directed by Josep Joan Bigas Luna. Spain/France: Mate Producciones, M.D.A. Films S.L., UGC YM, UGC International, MEDIA programme of the European Union, Eurimages, TVE, Vía Digital, Canal +, 1999.

CHAPTER 1

The Colour of Kisses: Eroticism and Exoticism in Spanish Film Culture of the 1920s and '30s

Eva Woods Peiró

In a 1922 issue of *Cine Popular* (Barcelona), the fan magazine writer calling himself 'Aurello' asks the question on every reader's mind: 'what would the cinema be without kisses?' 'The kiss', he explains, 'belongs to the cinema as do punches, cowboys and pistol shots' (Aurello 1922: 1). Fourteen years later in *Cinegramas* (1936), a writer used the same analogy: 'the authentic kiss was, well, something as consubstantial to romance movies as was "the real pistol" to Westerns' (De la Rosa 1936). Like the pistol, kissing endowed the medium with its 'final mark', its seal of identity: 'In cinematography [the kiss] is like a seal, a stamp, the postscript finale' (De la Rosa 1936). Fans eagerly awaited, and expected, kissing with its symbolic and haptic compensation. And for good reason. Cinema's sensuous, erotic impact was carried not only by corporeal violence – punches or pistols – but also bodily ecstasy experienced in the vision of two mouths coming together and the gesture, and later sound, of an ecstatic breath (Aurello 1922). As one magazine writer put it, 'let's not forget the very special case of the gasps of breath after a kiss that would every now and then spark revolution in the movie' (Billoch 1935: 22).

Kissing was germane to cinema. Getting to the heart of this matter was thus a mission of many Spanish film magazines as early as 1921 and still drew attention in 1936, which marked the end of the so-called Silver Age of Spanish cinema. Magazine articles on '*los besos*' (kisses) were as ubiquitous as beauty secrets, star marriages, divorces and the wonders of technology. Articles about, as well as, photo montages and drawings of '*los besos*' were repurposed and recycled in a range of cinema publications: *Arte y Cinematografía*, *El Cine*, *Cinegramas*, *Cine Popular*, *Cine Sparta*, *Films Selectos*, *La Pantalla* (see Figure 1.1), *Popular Film*, *Proyector* and *Tarari*. Reproductions of film posters and theatre listings in these magazines testified to the abundance of cinema content featuring a kiss. Filmgoers who had never left their towns were inundated with kissing scenes from Hollywood, French, German and other national cinemas.

Figure 1.1 Source: Carlos Fernández Cuenca (1928), 'Besos cinematográficos', *La Pantalla*, 42:14, October 1928, p. 679.

Viewers were sharing what Monica Dall'Asta calls an 'international-popular culture' (2000: 302), a global vernacular that local viewers could make sense of even though its scope was transnational. In modes both imitative and strikingly original, then, kisses entered the climaxes and titles of Spanish film. Apart from overtly pornographic films such as *El confesor* or *Consultorio de señoras/The Confesor* or *Ladies' Appointment* (dir. anonymous, 1920s), the kiss had played an important role in films in the teens: *El beso de la muerte/The Kiss of Death* (dir. Alberto Marro, 1916, dirs. Fructuoso Gelabert and Alberto Marro, 1917), *El beso fatal/The Deathly Kiss* (dir. Julio Roesset, 1916) and *El Golfo/The Scoundrel* (dir. José de Togores, 1917). By the twenties the cinema kiss was a well-established feature of Spanish films as well as the Spanish branches of Fox or Paramount, which produced *Un beso en un taxi/A Kiss in a Taxi* (dir. Clarence G. Badger, 1927) or *El precio de un beso/The Price of a Kiss* (dir. James Tinling, 1930), which was filmed in Barcelona.

By no means is this above list of films about kissing or the promise thereof exhaustive, as a study of this topic in US or other national cinemas has yet to be done. That said, we know with certainty that films schooled generations of Spanish spectators in the lessons of love. Magazines responded not only by educating viewers about the kiss, but also by reinforcing demand and expectations for kisses according to a set of interwoven logics that framed kisses as erotic, exotic and simultaneously technological. Visually and textually framing kisses within this rhetoric allowed viewers to identify with a normative gendered and racial subject position while encouraging more cosmopolitan understandings of themselves. In order to claim a stake in modernity, eroticism and kissing could not be entirely repressed; thus, magazines negotiated censorship by setting the boundaries of acceptability. Magazines also reiterated in sociological and commercial terms the psychology of the cinematic kiss. If the 'psychological quest' of eroticism, as Bataille understood it, was to re-establish the wholeness of and communication with the other that is discontinued through birth and death (1987: 11, 12) and thereby overcome our fundamental 'discontinuity' (13–14) with otherness, the cinematic kiss simulated the achievement of wholeness, performing an essential psychological function.

Yet how did spectators experience the erotic when the screen kiss happened in a different racial and cultural scenario or among individuals not considered? As I will argue at the beginning of this chapter, the kiss was an erotic object, but it was also a technological one, created by camera and filmic technology, the awareness of which mediated the intimate experience of the kiss while paradoxically making it feel more immediate. Through increasingly perfected techniques of technological reproduction, magazine readers could minutely examine and even touch the exotic image while film viewers might *feel* as if they were touching it. Proximity and distance also underlay the commodification of the kiss in cinema culture. Ironically, consuming these idealised and commodified images allowed viewers to inhabit what Rita Felski terms a 'transcendent sublime', which enabled utopian fantasies of enraptured surrender to otherworldly and ineffable structures of feeling (1995: 120, 139–40). As I will demonstrate throughout the remainder of the chapter, the exigencies of cultivating eroticism as a market force were bound up with teaching taste. Visually and textually framing kisses within this rhetoric allowed viewers to identify with a normative gendered and racial subject position while encouraging more cosmopolitan understandings of themselves. To claim a stake in this cosmopolitan modernity, however, room had to be made for eroticism and kissing; magazines thus negotiated the censorship of kisses by setting the boundaries for an acceptable eroticism. Cinema fan magazines were highly aware of their role in this push and pull dynamic, playfully, even gleefully seducing the reader as they simultaneously set radicalised and gendered parameters around who could kiss whom.

Magazines are essential for filling in the gaps of an extant and accessible body of Spanish film, of which 10 to 15 per cent survives. More importantly, they are also key to understanding the dynamic context of Spanish cinema between 1910 and 1936, by which time over fifty cinema publications were in circulation in the peninsula (Hernández Eguíluz 2009: 25). Cinema had arrived in Spain by 1896, and by 1910 narrative film, magazines and wide networks of distribution and projection were in place. Spain's economy struggled, yet through much of the century it boasted the highest number of cinemas in Europe per capita. The average Spaniard could never dream of owning a car, but cinema and magazines were inexpensive and readily available. During the Second Republic (1931–6), they reached even the most remote regions of Spain. For a nation of spectators roughly 40 per cent illiterate, cinema magazines, serial-novelised cinema, posters and collectible cards were literacy guides, teaching viewers how to watch and think about film. Feminist film historians have encouraged a shift in focus from the content of early films to early cinematic culture, that unlike the study of film content alone, encompasses 'a wide range of film experiences such as stardom, fandom cults, theatre architecture, and fashion' (Zhen 2002: 506). Cinema magazines provided a forum for conversation between critics, spectators and professionals about all aspects of the film industry. Despite their mass-culture sheen, this form of media housed some of the most vanguard ideas about cinema. Hispanists have not always agreed. In his book on vanguard Spanish writers and poets inspired by the cinema, C. B. Morris singled out articles on kissing like 'La ciencia del beso' ('Kissing Science') as noteworthy for the 'pretentious absurdity' of their 'infantile' titles. He concludes, however, that 'happily, the responses of Spanish writers and critics to the cinema went far deeper than the foolish question "Would you know how to kiss for the screen?"' (1980: 11).[1]

But Spanish magazines probed deeper than a mere spectacularisation of kissing. Embedded in the frivolous language of edutainment we find a series of concerns ranging from technological mediation to hyper-mediacy, revealing awareness about the kiss as a technology. That is, a recognition that the machinic apparatus was what made spectators feel even more human. Already in 1921, the article 'Cómo se besa en el cine' (How to Kiss in the Cinema) makes what will become a standard set of claims about cinema kisses: they are realistic beyond comparison with the theatre, painting or literary kisses (*Cine Popular* 1921b: 6). What makes kissing in movies even more real is that the photographer and the camera can intrude upon intimate moments, surprise lovers in the act, capture the kiss unmediated, so to speak, returning the aura to the kiss: 'Here is Alice Joyce whom the photographer has surprised in a moment of intimacy' (*Cine Popular* 1921b: 6). The conceit is that this mediated moment is what most moves the spectator *and* what also emotionally impacts the actors, those 'happy mortals' who 'not only earn fabulous sums for playing their roles, but who also enjoy the caresses of the most splendid beauties in the world'. The article 'El cine como escuela de amantes' ('Cinema as a school for lovers') recognises the debt owed to cinema for 'our new way of loving [and] our selective behaviour in the highly trafficked terrain of making love' (*Cine español* 1936). And in 'Alone, at last', written in 1936, pulling back the curtain on the kiss had become a branded feature of magazines:

> Fifteen hundred meters to get that shot; the lovers looking for the moment when the pact of love will be sealed with a kiss, and with a cinematographic kiss, which is a much more serious thing. [...] Fantasies soar! Yet the pure and simple truth is the one we see here. The cameraman focusing his lens on their heads, the assistants filming, and the director, very serious, giving instructions: 'Press a bit more, man; turn your eyes, woman. Make it really clear that you are alone, that you are savoring this moment you've so desired.' Meanwhile, in the cinema, three thousand ingénues are emotionally moved for real. What a foolish joke! (*Cine Sparta* 1935: 17)

Here the marketing strategy is both titillating and admonishing the reader if she has ever fallen for the ruse, despite its magnetic realism.

Indeed, film magazines promoted a morally ambiguous rhetoric. This magazine doublespeak was both a marketing ploy and the means for containing or liberating the erotic body. Editors and writers provided erotic written descriptions, photos, drawings or stories but delivered them with a morally ambivalent style that teetered between playful, wry, delicious insinuation and authoritative admonition. Like silent cinema's global reach, this contradictory vernacular was popular from Hollywood to Spain. It resembled US magazines published between 1910 and 1930 like *Ladies' Home Journal*, as described by Jennifer Scanlon: 'The appeal to the sexual imagination of young women formed an aspect of the magazine that permeated not only the fiction but also the advertisements, and occasionally, the advice' (1995: 29).

Spanish film magazines addressed both male and female readers through gender-differentiated content, although women were sometimes targeted by direct address – '*queridas lectoras*' ('dear female readers') – that invited them to enjoy yet be mindful in mixed-message fashion. In a Chinese film of the same period, Zhen Zhang shows how *Amorous History* (1931) promised women both 'liberation and social mobility as well as the lure and risks of a new kind of commodification of the body by film technology' (2002: 503). Felski and, in the context of Spain, Lou Charnon Deutsch show us that the formation of this ambivalent rhetoric aimed at the female body was a residue of the nineteenth-century novel and illustrated magazine which fought for women's hearts, minds and pocketbooks (Charnon Deutsch 2011: 204). Magazines offered a 'schizophrenic notion of ideal femininity' that was demonised as irrational yet 'simultaneously [...] seen as modern because it was a managed desire', calculated and rationalised in the interests of profit (Felski 1995: 62). Cinema magazines were ideal and idealising spaces, if not one of the birthplaces of the merging of eroticism and commercialisation of pleasure through 'erotically saturated' and 'enticing visual displays of commercial abundance' that focused on self-gratification (Felski 1995: 65).

Over the span of this decade, virtually all fan magazines began to frame spectacular eroticism within the grammar of exoticism which had spread virally throughout a range of media. Like *films exóticos* (films produced in the West about the East), an established genre since the late teens, exoticism was evident in storified or novelised films; (*Cine Popular* 1921a); reviews of exotic films; film ads such as *Las Indias negras/The Black Indian Women* (dir. René Éclair, 1917), *El misterioso Dr Wang/The Vermilion Pencil* (dir. Norman Dawn, 1922) (*Cine Revista*, 1922: 1), *El Árabe/The Arab* (dir. Rex Ingram, 1925) (*El mundo cinematográfico*, 1925: 6), *The Sheik* (dir. George Melford, 1921) (*El mundo cinematográfico*, 1921: 1), *El negro que tenía el alma blanca/The Black Man with a White Soul* (dir. Benito Perojo, 1927) (*La Pantalla*, 1927: 46) and *La Venenosa* (dir. Roger de Lion, 1928); and ads for products designed in an orientalist vein. Of the three dominant varieties of exoticism named above, I focus here on East Asian exoticism. In an ad for Gong perfume, for example, published in *Proyector* (1936a: back page) the caption reads: 'To perfume oneself with Gong is to travel with your senses through countries of dream and fantasy.' A few months later the same magazine ran an ad featuring Anna May Wong, the Chinese-American star, who, like other actors of Asian descent, was type-cast in caricatured Asian roles. In an ad for Dermasol products she may be modern but, true to stereotype, remains silent: 'Use Dermasol's Beauty Products to Enhance Your Beauty' (*Proyector* 1936b). Although frequently employed in ads for beauty products, Asian exoticism, as I will later show, would be strategically employed in discourse on the cinematic kiss.

To maximise profit and pleasure, the exoticised object was viewed from a safe distance, marked as different, yet readable and therefore navigable and knowable. Although Wendy Chun works in the context of the Internet's digital interface, her interpretation resonates with magazine reading practices. Her point is that the spectacle seduces by offering the reader-viewer spaces or spatialised information that are strange yet reducible to accessible content, 'navigable yet foreign, readable yet cryptic' (Chun 2002: 250). The entire back cover of *Fotogramas* of June 1926 features a traditional Chinese theatre mask, with no explanation or mediating border. In reality it is an ad for *El velo de la dicha/The Veil of Happiness* (dir. Édouard-Émile Violet, 1923), about a blind man in China who recovers his sight.[2] The film is reviewed in this issue, but as the cover can function separately as a displayable commodity-cum-collector's item on a table or wall, it becomes an accessory, unanchored from the film and simply gratuitous as an isolated image, pleasurable yet disturbing. Specialising (and fetishising) the exotic object on the back cover, divorcing it from the intimate interior content (its history), the magazine's physical layout enacts both distance and closeness, illustrating how eroticism engaged the exotic.

Magazine content on kissing brought racial and cultural difference into the heart of sexual fantasy (Felski 1995: 139) and this packaging was, as Felski argues, a central part of modern cosmopolitan sensibility (140). Readers' understanding of themselves as modern and cosmopolitan (and racially and culturally worthy subjects) had to be nurtured. Magazines took their mentorship role very seriously, and being literacy guides it was paramount to teach the different classes of kisses – and of course, who was kissable. In ways both earnest and coy, articles on the kiss offered a balanced dose of quasi-scientific information and erotic descriptions of kissing. In 'La ciencia del beso' (see Figure 1.2) the author indulges the memory of pleasure while seeking to intellectualise the different species of kiss:

> after a long look during which one anticipates the kiss, nose against nose remain intertwined, in that interminable kiss, in that anonymous, impersonal way in which almost all films end. There exists *another* variant, introduced to the screen by the 'vamps' and the 'perfect lovers': it's the soft and slow caress, illustrated on this page by Joan Crawford, which is the prelude to the tempestuous, absorbing, brutal kiss of unleashed passion. (*La Pantalla* 1928: 141 – emphasis mine)

Describing the variations between 'the impersonal and anonymous kiss' and the 'tempestuous and brutal' one was a common strategy in prose devoted to kissing. In an authoritative-sounding classificatory scheme, kisses were

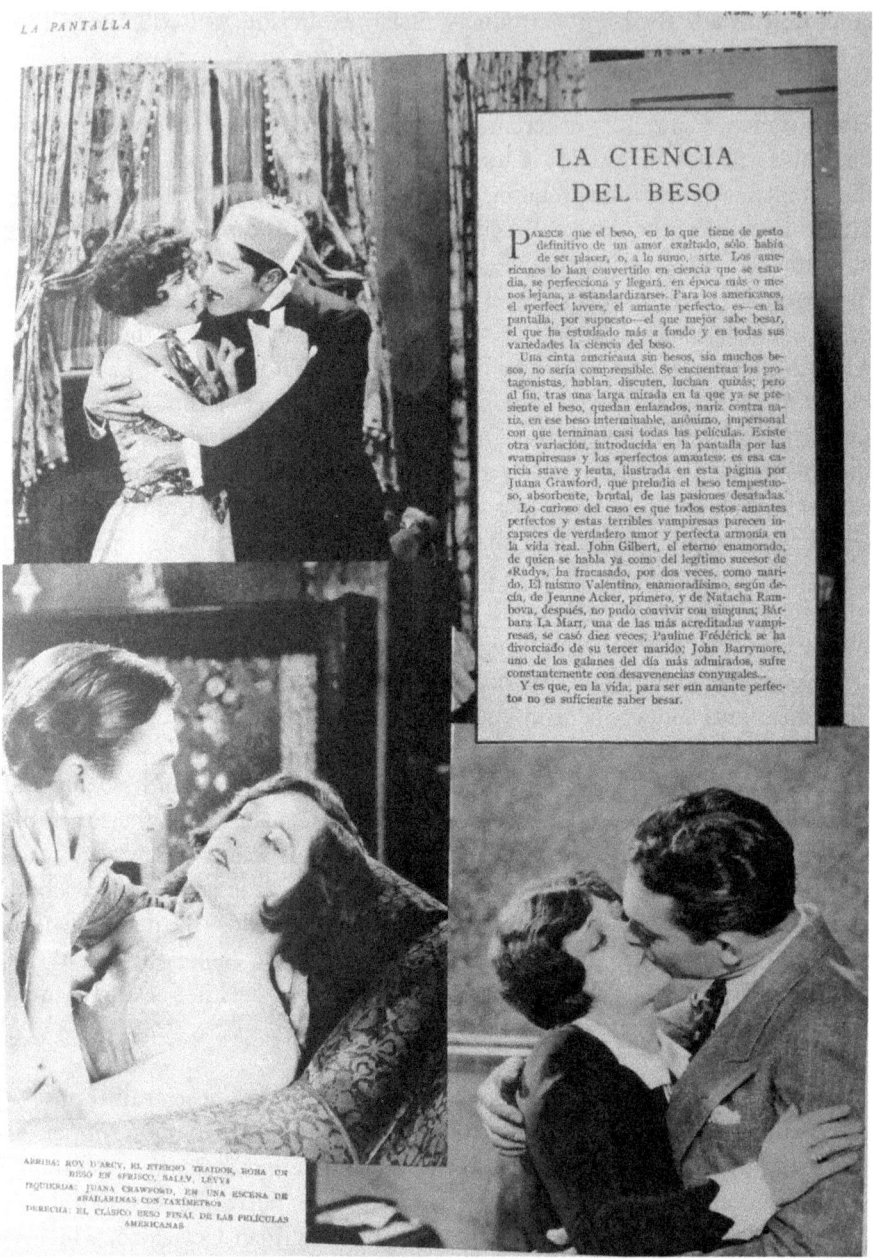

Figure 1.2 Source: 'La ciencia del beso', *La Pantalla* 9, 24 February 1928, p. 141.

differentiated according to gendered and racial ideas implicit in references to *'vampiresas'* (vamps), an exotic invention of 1920s cinema culture incarnated by actresses coded as exotic such as Theda Bara, Pola Negri or Spain's Raquel Meller. The vamp is traditionally heartless, calculating, wilful, intelligent. She threatened both white identity and class stability by destroying 'not only a man's discipline and will by feeding off him', but also 'depriving him of home, money, and social status' (Staiger 1995: 150). But as the author of another magazine article clarifies, '[o]f course, there are kisses, and then there are *kisses*' (Aurello 1922).

Lessons on the classification of kisses could double as a criticism of moralisers and an incentive to study the valuable art of kissing. Given the difficulty of realistically filming and performing a cinema kiss, however, spectators should be savvy enough to know the difference between a decent and an overly suggestive kiss. The 1935 article '¿Sabría Ud. besar para el celuloide?' ('Would you Know How to Kiss in a Film?') teaches about these variations:

> against what those inflexible people say, far from being a school of impudence, the kiss is in the majority of cases merely the natural expression of a tender and serene love [...] this is why the kiss is such a difficult undertaking in the cinema. Because one has to say a lot without revealing anything; because one must avoid invoking turbulent feelings in the spectator and not induce her to think beyond a good, clean happiness. [...] If it's not that way, one couldn't maintain on the screen those long and fundamental kisses, upon which those terrible and diabolical vamps have an exclusive patent and that seem to test the public on purpose and justly distinguish between the educated spectator and the doubly shameful trashiness of a spiritual coarseness. (Billoch 1935: 22)

As this quote ambivalently shows, spectators who crossed the line were called out as 'vulgar and impolite', while at the same time, it is disingenuously implied, what else can one do when those vamps have cornered the market on kissing?

Such resignation underlay the claim that for better or for worse, the cinema is a 'school for lovers'. In another article published in *Cine español* in 1936, 'El "cine" como escuela de amantes', the author states:

> Cinema is the great illuminated book that with its images shows us such exquisite and delicious training [...] Today any woman will be able to brag of getting attention and affection from her chosen man if she knows how to put in practice a candid look à la Norma Shearer, or, mysteriously, promising à la Marlene Dietrich. [...] And later she [the female spectator] will know how to kiss, she will kiss completely and deliciously,

like *they* kiss, and languish like they languish in the arms of their leading men; and kindle the fire of male hearts with their gestures, poses, their femininities, whether ingénues or vamps. (*Cine español* 1936)

Women of all types ('*cualquier mujer*') could observe stars as professional tutors and revel in this kiss-a-thon that was the cinema. Even male authors felt confessional in light of such positive educational effects: 'I confess that I didn't know how to kiss until I became a cinema fan ...' (Aurello 1922).

But what happens when the stars who model the most intimate of gestures are subjects deemed taboo? As early as 1922, a subgenre of the kissing article had emerged that diverged from the mainstream. These articles on '*besos*' illustrated the kiss through the lens of foreignness, employing Asian ethnicity and concepts of racialised colour (white, black and yellow) to expound upon kissing. In other words, they used exoticism to perform the erotic. One of the first such articles is titled 'The Japanese Don't Want Kissing in the Movies' (Aurello 1922). The premise of the article is the recent declaration (the date is left unspecified) by the Japanese government to prohibit kissing in the cinema. In the usual exaggerated prose of fan magazines, the author (Aurello) reports:

> With true and genuine admiration we have read that the director of Japan's Department of Education, T. Kikuchi, has made a transcendental declaration regarding cinema in the Yellow land. The Yellow Wiseman says, 'the Japanese never kiss, thus we don't like kissing in the cinema'. We can already see the astonished faces of our readers, male and female fans of this inoffensive sport. (Aurello 1922: 1)

Repeatedly painting Japan and its intelligentsia with racist colour-slurs, and capitalising the word 'yellow' (in Spanish, adjectives are lower case), the author essentialises and distances Japanese subjects as irremediably other and out of reach. Historically speaking, the Home Ministry censors of Japan's Imperial State *did* ban the public presentation of cultural material containing representations of kissing in Tokyo in the 1920s (Abel 2012). According to Jonathan Abel, 'The public kiss was glossed in Japan during the 1920s and '30s as both the anarchic Western eroticism of ruthless capitalism and the cunning infiltration of Soviet-ism that could put the ruling classes in jeopardy' (2012). But it was more likely that this interpretation of the Japanese, ripped from Hollywood cinema magazines, merely exposed Spanish readers to anxieties about the Yellow Peril, a fraught discourse that acquired currency after Japan's victory over Russia in 1905 – its first-ever triumph over the West (Wang 2005: 163). Filtered through Hollywood, this exclusionary perception of East Asian identity pervaded Spanish cinema culture. Relatively few Asian films were distributed in Spain. Those that were constituted the exception to the rule and were mostly the equivalent of *españoladas*. These period-piece 'Asian' films recirculated stereotypes about the 'inscrutable' Oriental Other and either assuaged or stoked fears about the Yellow Peril. In effect, this media projected a political form of orientalism that translated into xenophobic social discourses and governmental practices (Wang 2005: 163).

Despite the lack of diplomatic or economic relations between Spain and Japan at this time, the (however understood) Japanese prohibition on kissing, in tandem with the profitable genre of film exoticism, perfectly suited the Spanish reader, who could now feel culturally and racially superior to the Japanese and more enlightened than upper-crust, outdated Spanish moralisers. Regardless of whether the reader was subject to social and moral constraints by her own family, city or province – and historical documentation tells us she was – Aurello nevertheless interpellates the reader as a modern, progressive and secular subject. Because these articles uniformly insist that kissing is inseparable from cinema, he can feign admiration for the Japanese, but then signal to the reader that she should feel surprise at such a prohibition. Given this popular connection between cinema and kissing, one might have wondered how there could possibly be a legitimate cinema industry, or an understanding of the medium, if one excised kissing? Then, impulsively changing tactics, Aurello claims he understands the Japanese prohibition, motivated as it is by a 'question of colour': 'But in the end, I found this [prohibition] even logical. It's a question of colour.' He launches into an attack on Spanish moralists as old-fashioned prudes who pass as modern yet are nevertheless sexually repressed, and therefore 'Yellow' like the Japanese:

> we confess that in Spain, without exaggeration, there are other 'Yellows' who wear Marie-Antoinette-type wigs and blush before mildly erotic scenes. (Aurello 1922: 1)

The Japanese were now merely a screen for projecting a critique of conventional moralisers, labelled 'Yellow' because of their associations with the Church and monarchy, but also for their inability to distinguish 'the innocent naughtiness of an infantile modern world from what has been termed ultra-futurist "pornography"' (Aurello 1922: 1). In other words, anti-modern Spaniards equal uneducated spectators who can't read the symbols of modern cinema culture (unlike the devoted fans who are reading this very magazine).

Aurello's article concludes by asserting the question of blood: the Japanese are incapable of being modern:

> But of course, the Japanese, even though they Europeanise themselves by cutting off their ponytail, erecting large factories, arming themselves

with formidable destroyers, and wearing a frock coat, are incapable of changing their blood. They are yellow and like other Chinese and Japanese without ponytails from the old and adored Iberia. (1922: 1)

Yet fixing the Japanese as a surrogate model for 'Old Iberia' allows an idea of at least half of Spain as a *moderately modern* country, somewhere in between Hollywood and Tokyo.[3]

Other articles would recycle the linking of kisses to the Japanese and also to the colours white and yellow. In 'Yellow love and White love', the topic is the Japanese film star Sessue Hayakawa, a precursor to Valentino and by the 1920s a millionaire who had already starred in dozens of films (Jack 1923). One of his most famous works, *The Cheat* (dir. C. B. DeMille, 1915), typecasts him as the villainous but dashing lead, a role that he would not be able to escape in his career in the USA.[4] The article (see Figure 1.3) shows two photos, one of Hayakawa in traditional Chinese dress with Chinese fortune sticks, and another of Rudolph Valentino lounging in modern Western clothes. The caption under the traditionally dressed Hayakaya reads: 'The enigmatic silhouette of the Japanese Hayakawa has also managed to awaken more than one sudden and engulfing passion.' The caption accompanying the image of Valentino states: 'But the hero in these questions, as the American chronicles preach, continues to be Rudolph Valentino, whom as you can see, reader, is quite a guy' (Jack 1923: 7).

The article is centrally concerned with the Asian heartthrob Hayakawa, yet the author refuses to allow the reader to imagine kissing him. While pushing the refrains of love as 'a many coloured rainbow' and 'love has no race', the author deflects attention from Hayakawa to his ethnicity and the vexed issue of mixed-race attraction. The 'problem' of mixed-race couples was an inevitable side-effect of the internationalism of silent cinema, here equated with the 'morphine of women's ambitions':

> to each her own [...] the 'marrying' type [...] dream about a movie-like Lohengrin. Women here, like everywhere else, dream about the impossible [...] but settle with a second-rate docile office worker. (Jack 1923: 7)

In nineteenth-century classificatory fashion, the author lists the different types of love, naming Italian, British and Spanish nationalities, yet reducing Asian love to simply 'a la amarilla'. Notwithstanding, if money is involved, it is implied, perhaps even 'yellow love' can be tolerated:

> There are ones who like love Italian style [...] ones who adore British coolness; while others chase a 'Spanish' passion, some are drawn to [love] 'a la Yellow'. The colours of the rainbow complement each other

Amor a «lo amarillo» y amor a «lo blanco»

Figure 1.3 Source: Jack (1923), 'Desde América', *Cine Popular*, 17 October 1923, p. 7.

as we can see with Antonio Moreno, the Italian Valentino or the Yellow Hayakawa [...] with this [attitude] gold and fame are made. (Jack 1923: 7)

The possibility of money and fame as colour-blind was a major theme of the immensely popular erotic novel, *El negro que tenía el alma blanca* ('The Black Man with a White Soul'), serially published in the weekly magazine *La Voz* (Insúa 1998: originally published in 1922), adapted to film by Benito Perojo in 1927 and remade in 1934. The 1927 filmic version tells the story of the tragic relationship between Peter Wald, a dark-skinned Afro-Cuban jazz dancer played by an Egyptian actor in blackface, and the lily-white Emma, played by Concha Piquer. In both the novel and the film, Peter possesses noble and heroic qualities – a 'white soul' – and achieves wealth and stardom as a result of his dancing talents. But his skin colour prevents him from attaining Emma's love. A provincial chorus girl, Emma is pushed by her entrepreneurial father into a business contract with Peter, with the justification that success 'always has the same colour, that of gold' (Insúa 1998: 96). Yet in all versions of this story cycle Peter's skin colour is the obstacle to their romantic relationship. In both the novel and the 1927 film, Emma is sickened by the thought of touching Peter throughout their relationship but is finally won over when Peter succumbs to a fatal lovesickness. On his deathbed, his impossibly perfect virtue and perseverance transcend his skin colour to become 'white as snow'. Emma can finally fall in love, as she can experience a 'transcendent sublime' through the mortification of Peter's body from a thriving athletic dancer to a sickly and pale spectre of his former self. Just as Emma is about to kiss him, however, she catches the eye of Peter's white servant whose presence inhibits her from touching Peter's lips. The ambivalent final message both critiques Spanish provincialism and sternly admonishes young women aspiring to cosmopolitan fashions and mores of 'love is a many coloured rainbow'.

Interest in the 'colour of kisses' continues through the late 1920s. A 1928 issue of *La Pantalla*, 'Besos Cinematográficos' by Carlos Fernández Cuenca, discusses 'white' kisses and once again returns to the deployment of Asianness – the Japanese prohibition on the kiss – to criticise Spanish censorship (Fernández Cuenca 1928: 679). Fernández Cuenca begins this piece by recounting a visit to a city in Northern Spain in which kissing was strictly prohibited with the following justification: 'It's not good that so many daughters of families who come here contemplate these unedifying scenes' (1928: 679). He proceeds to explain how 'in American cinema, kisses are always white. [ ] their kisses aren't steamy and passionate; they are naïve kisses, proper to a race to whom the cultivation of sports doesn't leave time for learning about the lessons of love' (679). If there are exceptions, he claims, kissers such as Antonio Moreno and Rudolph Valentino owed their fame to the 'southernness [that] lit their lips on fire' or southern influence, once again invoking the bio-racial explanation. However 'some countries are the enemies of cinematic kisses' (689). The Japanese explain their prohibition by asserting the intimacy and isolation necessary for a poetic embrace. Rather than ethical and aesthetic choice, Fernández Cuenca writes, this is a question of psychology and knowledge about love.

Here again the hollow praise of Japanese morality and erotic taste functions in the service of a post-imperial nostalgia that undermines Japanese modernity and (indirectly) Spanish traditionalism. The Japanese might be 'more advanced' in questions of love and kisses as they all seem to know how to kiss, 'perhaps by intuition', but in Europe and America, 'the White race, learns how to kiss well by learning the science of the kiss through practice, or at the very least, by visual instruction' or by watching it on the screen (Fernández Cuenca 1928: 679).

As we have seen, all of these articles emphasise the centrality of kissing to cinema and vice-versa – the reader gets the joke: the Japanese cannot know how to kiss by intuition. Knowing how to kiss by watching it on screens is evidence of technological modernity instantiated by cinema. As Ortega y Gassett wrote during this period, to be human is to be technological (1996: 41). Thus, by casting into doubt the Japanese restraint about kissing, and by linking it with the colour fetish, articles like this became, in effect, attempts to erase and distance Japan's modernity while the technology of kissing could be zoomed in and out in order to determine who was, or was not, kissable. Policing the kiss was not exclusively anti-Asian in character, as from the early twenties it applied generally to racialised bodies and aligned itself seamlessly with underlying ideologies of miscegenation and coloniality. As I have demonstrated, films such as *El negro que tenía el alma blanca*, or films and magazine content remediating the craze for the Valentino-as-Sheik fantasy thrived during this period. Yet despite the remarkable surge in interest in kissing in the twenties and thirties, after the Spanish Civil War and the beginning of Franco's cultural revolution, this ludic, cosmopolitan flirtation with the subject of kissing would be refiltered through the frameworks of honour, marriage, adultery or other lenses more palatable to National Catholic rhetoric. In the late thirties and forties, Spanish actresses in 'Gypsy-face' would seal with a kiss their love for a '*payo*' (non-'Gypsy') in Andalusian folkloric musical comedy films. Although light and rarely sensual, kissing was still obligatory in films such as *Morena Clara* (dir. Florián Rey, 1936), *Suspiros de España* (dir. Benito Perojo, 1939), *Oro y marfil* (dir. Gonzalo Delgrás, 1947), *Filigrana* (dir. Luis Marquina, 1949) and a plethora of others. The topic of (White Spanish) women kissing men of colour would not re-emerge in mass terms until after the democratic Transition. In several post-nineties films about North African, Sub-Saharan or Latin American immigration, the kiss between a Spanish woman and a man of colour constitutes the film's climax. Much excellent scholarship exists that closely reads kissing scenes in films such as *Las cartas de Alou/Letters from Alou* (dir. Montxo Armendáriz, 1990), *Saïd* (dir. Llorenç Soler, 1998) or *Tomándote/ Two for Tea* (dir. Isabel Gardela, 2000). What remains to be studied is the parallax history of eroticism and kissing, race and technology. For it is not only in the digital era that cyborgs, sex and race are urgent questions. As I hope to have shown, sophisticated articulations of eroticism, machines and race were already in play in the 1920s and '30s.

NOTES

1. Morris is referencing Billoch (1935).
2. It is worth noting that the film was based on the eponymous play by Georges Clémenceau, a French politician and avid collector of Asian objects.
3. I am grateful to my colleague, Jeffrey Schneider, for pointing this out.
4. According to Davidson, *The Cheat* was the inspiration for naming Barcelona's red-light district the '*barrio chino*' (2009: 104).

REFERENCES

Abel, Jonathan (2012), 'Kiss and Censor: Redactionary Aesthetics in Transwar Japan': www.personal.psu.edu/jea17/JEA/Jonathan_E._Abel/News/Entries/2012/3/2_Kiss_and_Censor.html (last accessed 14 May 2016).
Aurello (1922), 'Los japoneses no quieren besos en el cine', *Cine Popular* 55 (Barcelona), 15 March 1922, p. 1.
Bataille, Georges (1987), *Eroticism*, trans. Mary Dalwood, London: Marion Boyars.
Billoch, F. (1935), '¿Sabría Ud. besar para el celuloide?', *Cinegramas* 17, 6 January 1935, p. 22.
Charnon Deutsch, Lou (2011), 'What They Saw: Women's Exposure to and in Visual Culture in 19th Century Spain', in Xon de Ros and Geraldone Hazbun (eds), *A Companion to Spanish Women's Studies*, London: Tamesis, pp. 189–209.
Chun, Wendy (2002), 'Othering Space', in Nicholas Mirzoeff (ed.), *The Visual Culture Reader*, 2nd edn, London and New York: Routledge, pp. 243–54.
Cine español (1936), 'El "cine" como escuela de amantes', *Cine español*, February 1936, 24 n.p.
Cine Popular (1921a), 'Almas de Oriente: Drama cinematográfico en cuatro partes', *Cine Popular* 29, 14 September 1921, pp. 10–11.
Cine Popular (1921b), 'Cómo se besa en el cine', *Cine Popular* 32, 5 October 1921.
Cine Revista (1922), '*El misterioso Dr Wang*', *Cine Revista*, 7 October 1922, p. 1.
Cine Sparta (1935), 'Alone, at last ...', *Cine Sparta* 11, 3 January 1935, p. 17.
Dall'Asta, Monica (2000), 'Italian Serial Films and "International popular culture"', *Film History* 12, pp. 300–7.
Davidson, Robert A. (2009), *Jazz Age Barcelona*, Toronto: University of Toronto Press.
De la Rosa, Ruth (1936), 'De los Tiempos Románticos del Film: El Beso Cinematográfico', *Cinegramas. Revista semanal* 75, 16 February 1936, pp. 14–15.
El mundo cinematográfico (1921), '*The Sheik*' *El mundo cinematográfico* 3, 19 January 1921, p. 1.

El mundo cinematográfico (1925), '*El Árabe*' *El mundo cinematográfico*, 3 March 1925, p. 6.
Felski, Rita (1995), *The Gender of Modernity*, Cambridge, MA: Harvard University Press.
Fernández Cuenca, Carlos (1928), 'Besos Cinematográficos', *La Pantalla* 42, 14 October 1928, p. 679.
Fotogramas (1926), *El velo de la dicha*, June.
Hernández Eguíluz, Aitor (2009), *Testimonios en huecograbado. El cine de la 2.a República y su prensa especializada (1930–1939)*, Valencia: Ediciones de la Filmoteca.
Insúa, Alberto (1998 [1922]), *El negro que tenía el alma blanca*, Madrid: Clásicos Castalia.
Jack (1923), 'Desde America', *Cine Popular*, 17 October 1923, p. 7.
La Pantalla (1927), '*El negro que tenía el alma blanca*', *La Pantalla*, 2 December 1927, p. 46.
La Pantalla (1928), 'La ciencia del beso', *La Pantalla* 9, 24 February 1928, p. 141.
Morris, Cyril Brian (1980), *This Loving Darkness: The Cinema and Spanish Writers 1920–1936*, New York: Oxford University Press.
Ortega y Gasset, José (1996 [1939]), *Meditación de la técnica y otros ensayos sobre ciencia y filosofía*, Madrid: Alianza.
Proyector (1936a), back page.
Proyector (1936b), 'Use productos de belleza Dermasol', *Proyector* 6, 15 April 1936.
Scanlon, Jennifer (1995), *Inarticulate Longings: The Ladies' Home Journal, Gender and the Promise of Consumer Culture*, New Brunswick, NJ: Rutgers University Press.
Staiger, Janet (1995), *Bad Women: Regulating Sexuality in Early American Cinema*, Minneapolis: Minnesota University Press.
Wang, Yiman (2005), 'The Art of Screen Passing: Anna May Wong's Yellow Yellowface Performance in the Art Deco Era', *Camera Obscura* 20:3, 159–91.
Zhen, Zhang (2002), 'An Amorous History of the Silver Screen', in Jennifer M. Bean and Diane Negra (eds), *A Feminist Reader in Early Cinema*, Durham, NC: Duke University Press, pp. 501–29.

FILMOGRAPHY

El Árabe/The Arab, film, directed by Rex Ingram. USA: Metro-Goldwyn Pictures Corporation, 1925.
El beso de la muerte/The Kiss of Death, film, directed by Alberto Marro. Spain: Barcinógrafo, 1916.
El beso de la muerte/The Kiss of Death, film, directed by Fructuoso Gelabert and Alberto Marro. Spain: Barcinógrafo, Hispano Films, 1917.
El beso fatal/The Deathly Kiss, film, directed by Julio Roesset. Spain: Patria Films, 1916.
El confesor or *Consultorio de señoras/The Confessor* or *Ladies' Appointment*, film, anonymous. Spain, 1920s.
El Golfo/The Scoundrel, film, directed by José de Togores. Spain: Dessy Films, 1917.
El misterioso Dr Wang or *El Lápiz rojo/The Vermilion Pencil*, film, directed by Norman Dawn. USA: Robertson-Cole Pictures Corporation, 1922.
El negro que tenía el alma blanca/The Black Man with a White Soul, film, directed by Benito Perojo. Spain/France: Goya Producciones Cinematográficas and Production Française Cinematographique, 1927.
El negro que tenía el alma blanca/The Black Man with a White Soul, film, directed by Benito Perojo. Spain: Benito Perojo, Balart y Simó, 1934.
El precio de un beso/The Price of a Kiss, film, directed by James Tinling. USA: Fox, 1930.

El velo de la dicha / The Veil of Happiness, film, directed by Édouard-Émile Violet. France: unknown, 1923.
Filigrana / Filigree, film, directed by Luis Marquina. Spain: Manuel del Castillo, 1949.
Las Indias negras / Les Indes Noires / The Black Indies, film, directed by Michel Verne. France: Les Films Jules Verne, Edition Aubert, 1917.
La Venenosa / The Venomous Lady, film, directed by Roger de Lion. France: Plus Ultra Films, 1928.
Las cartas de Alou / Letters from Alou, film, directed by Montxo Armendáriz. Spain: Elías Querejeta Producciones Cinematográficas S.L., TVE, 1990.
Morena Clara, film, directed by Florián Rey. Spain: CIFESA, 1936.
Oro y marfil / Gold and Ivory, film, directed by Gonzalo Delgrás. Spain: Hidalguía Films, 1947.
Saïd, film, directed by Llorenç Soler. Spain: Centre Promotor Imatge, Institut del Cinema Català, TV3, TVE, 1998.
Suspiros de España / Sighs of Spain, film, directed by Benito Perojo. Spain / Germany: Hispano Filmproduktion, 1939.
The Cheat, film, directed by C. B. DeMille. USA: Jesse L. Lasky Feature Play Company, 1915.
The Sheik, film, directed by George Melford. USA: Paramount Pictures, 1921.
Tomándote / Two for Tea, film, directed by Isabel Gardela. Spain: Producciones Kilimanjaro, 2000.
Un beso en un taxi / A Kiss in a Taxi, film, directed by Clarence G. Badger. USA: Paramount, 1927.

CHAPTER 2

Impressions of Africa: Desire, Sublimation and Looking 'Otherwise' in Three Spanish Colonial Films

Brad Epps

In the 1990s, Africa returned to Spain – in the overlapping forms of mass immigration, ethno-racial diversity, global economic inequality, racism, xenophobia and a potent new variant of the protracted crisis of Spanish national identity. As the memory of past colonial projects, rife with militaristic and missionary zeal, was overshadowed by more secularised and ostensibly multicultural modes of late capitalism, a number of Spanish filmmakers, largely without leaving Spanish territory, set their sights on the stories of people who came from 'the other side' of the turbulent waters of the Strait of Gibraltar and the barbed-wire borders of Ceuta and Melilla. Though formally conventional, such thematically innovative and politically charged films as *Las cartas de Alou/Letters from Alou* (dir. Montxo Armendáriz, 1990), *Bwana* (dir. Imanol Uribe, 1996) and *Poniente/West* (dir. Chus Gutiérrez, 2002), all set in Spain, showcased the intolerance, ignorance, indifference, sexual objectification and violence that hound African immigrants as they strive to make a new life for themselves in an overwhelmingly white and historically Christian country.[1] Variously in tune with the dynamics of globalisation, these and other recent films nonetheless remit, almost certainly in spite of themselves, to prior cinematic endeavours such as *¡Harka!* (dir. Carlos Arévalo, 1941), *¡A mí la Legión!/Follow the Legion* (dir. Juan de Orduña, 1942) and *Misión blanca/White Mission* (dir. Juan de Orduña, 1946), all set in Africa, in which Spanish filmmakers working within the Francoist regime set their sights on the proverbial 'dark continent' in ways that were unabashedly in tune with the paternalistic politics of colonialism. In what follows, I shall examine how these three films, representative of two significant strands of Spanish colonial cinema, mobilise desiring subjects in order to propagate, in the form of entertaining and emotionally manipulative propaganda, imperial projects of power and identity that constitute the forgotten and disavowed prehistory of more contemporary postcolonial returns to the Iberian peninsula.[2] Interestingly, all three Franco-era films, with their jumbled conflux of the exotic and the erotic, allow for alternative or even 'resistant' readings (Labanyi 1997: 216) in which identifications are not necessarily 'straightforward' (Labanyi 2001: 27) and looks, in the fullest sense of the word, may be otherwise than intended or desired by the regime.

¡Harka! and ¡A mí la Legión! centre on intensely emotional relations between men in a theatre of military conflict in the Spanish Protectorate of Morocco before the Civil War.[3] Narratives of emphatic pronouncements (evident in the exclamation marks of their titles) and sublimated substitutions, they both star Alfredo Mayo and Luis Peña, whom David Bravo Díaz calls, respectively, the 'pet actor' – '*actor fetiche*', literally, the 'fetish actor' – and the second great actor of the early Francoist period (2012: 122). Dashingly handsome, the two actors, though especially Mayo, play characters who are enveloped in mystery and whose rough and ready arrogance is imbued with melancholy sensitivity. In ¡Harka!, Mayo's Santiago Valcázar, a seasoned officer who sports a fez and a djellaba in testimony to his *ostensible* assimilation into Moroccan culture, befriends Peña's Carlos Herrera, a younger officer fresh from the Spanish Legion – the organisation in which a young Francisco Franco first came to prominence. In ¡A mí la Legión!, Peña's Mauro, who has relinquished pomp and privilege as heir to the throne of the fictional land of Eslonia to enlist, incognito, in the Legion, rescues Mayo's Grajo, an older, more experienced Legionnaire wounded by an invisible indigenous sniper. In both films, the younger newcomer leaves the scene of military action for the comforts of Europe, only to renounce them and return to Morocco with a renewed determination and sense of purpose.[4] In ¡Harka!, his return takes place in the wake of the heroic death of his friend in battle, while in ¡A mí la Legión! his return takes place – after Grajo has twice saved his life, first from a firing squad in Morocco, where he had been falsely accused of murder, and then from a political assassin in Eslonia – while his friend, still very much alive, broods over his absence. For Alberto Elena, ¡A mí la Legión! functions as a 'remake' of sorts in which the sober and serious ¡Harka! is reworked into a relatively light-hearted romp (2010: 107); for Francisco Llinás, it constitutes 'a curious mixture of musical comedy, film of intrigue, and patriotic-military exaltation' that points to some of the director's later musicals (1998: 105), the most famous of which is *El último cuplé/The Last Torch Song* (dir. Juan de Orduña, 1957), and away, by and large, from the supposedly sublime suffering of ¡Harka! Significant as the tonal and stylistic differences are, the films are bound together not just by their colonial military setting but also by the intensity of the relationship between two men.

A no less intense relationship between men marks *Misión blanca*, which Elena calls the 'most relevant of all the fictions, literary or cinematographic' to address the 'evangelisation' of Spanish Guinea during the Francoist period

Figure 2.1 Manuel Luna and Julio Peña in *Misión blanca/White Mission*, directed by Juan de Orduña. Spain: Colonial AJE, 1946.

(2010: 175) and which María Dolores F.-Fígares calls 'the rejoinder to the military exaltation' of the films set in Morocco (2003: 256). That the two men at the centre of the film are father and son arguably heightens its paternalistic and protectionist charge, though, interestingly, the roles are reversed, generationally out of sync: it is the son, in the guise of a Catholic missionary abandoned as a young boy by his father, who serves as the spiritual father to his wayward biological progenitor.

The latter, who goes by the name of Brisco, is played by Manuel Luna, a prolific actor who appears as a haughty but compassionate commander in *¡A mí la Legión!*; the son, who is known simply as Padre Javier – or '*padrecito*', 'little father', by the two 'indigenous' leads – is played by the no less prolific Julio Peña (see Figure 2.1). Brisco is as ruthless, irascible and lecherous as Javier is steadfast, patient and chaste. Although it is revealed that Javier subsequently succumbs to yellow fever while ministering to the locals, it is Brisco, the victimiser, who falls victim to what Elena, building on the work of Robert Young (1995), calls 'colonial desire' (2010: 176), specifically, the 'sexual danger' of overcoming 'the prejudices of the white man' and of falling into 'the arms of ebony', as the veteran father Urcola (Jesús Tordesillas) puts it. It is surely not accidental that Brisco dies, redeemed, in the white-clothed arms of his son, Father Javier, who has also ensured that the indentured object of Brisco's desire, a young Guinean woman named Souka, is free to marry a young Guinean man. We shall return to the film's sexual and racial politics, but for the moment suffice it to say that *Misión blanca* enacts a filial redemption of the paternal body, and spirit, that resonates, allegorically, with the much-ballyhooed redemption of the fatherland by the dutiful 'sons' of the Nationalist cause. What is also redeemed is history, for like *¡Harka!* and *¡A mí la Legión!*, *Misión blanca* is set in a time shortly before the Nationalist rebellion that paved the way for Franco's dictatorship. The film's genealogical dynamics, conveyed as a veritable tangle of the biological and the spiritual, reverberate, in short, in deeply geopolitical ways.

Although *¡Harka!* nods to a paternal-filial quality in the relationship between the male protagonists – Peter Evans goes so far as to refer to Santiago as 'Carlos's mentor and homoerotically defined Oedipal father-figure' (1995: 218) – it is the fraternal that holds sway, in keeping with the vexed conception of Hispano-Moroccan brotherhood that is trumpeted, along with the 'imperial route' of Spain, at the very start of the film (see Figure 2.2). While the cross-national 'brotherhood' is so grossly uneven as to be little more than a colonialist ruse, the 'brotherhood' between the white European soldiers entails a reciprocal if overwrought emotionality that places the films in the field of an 'impure' melodrama. Diana Jorza, for instance, writes of a 'discursive mixture' (2012: 50) and a 'peculiar hybridity between war cinema and melodrama' (53) in *¡Harka!* and *¡A mí la Legión!*, while Rafael Nieto Jiménez declares that 'in *Misión blanca* melodrama is put in the service of a greater interest, to wit, the defence of the Catholic religion' (2014: 251). The melodramatic mode is conventionally associated with so-called 'women's pictures' or 'weepies' in which drama is inflamed by music, but here it is deployed in male-dominated contexts of conquest and conversion. Nowhere is the stirring potential of music more in evidence than in a scene in the otherwise buoyant *¡A mí la Legión!* in which Grajo cradles a dying soldier. As the young man calls out for his mother, his face bathed in half light and blood oozing from his mouth, Grajo holds him close and begins to recite a verse from one of the two official hymns of the Spanish Legion, 'El novio de la muerte' ('The Bridegroom of Death'): 'I am a man whom fortune wounded with the claw of a beast.' An extradiegetic choir continues where Grajo leaves off, singing tremulously: 'I am the bridegroom of death/who goes to join himself in a strong bond/with such a loyal companion.' The hymn continues, sung not by a choir but by a troop of Legionnaires, shown marching defiantly onward: 'When the fire was roughest and the fighting fiercest, defending his flag, the Legionnaire advanced.' Eminently melodramatic, the sequence compresses an entire ideological trajectory in which an individual, unknown soldier, fallen in battle, is comforted by a comrade-in-arms, purified in an act of post-mortem transcendence, and actively memorialised in the indefatigable movement of a military force.[5] If the first part of the

Figure 2.2 Alfredo Mayo in ¡Harka!, directed by Carlos Arévalo. Spain: Arévalo; Compañía Industrial de Film Español; UPCE, 1941.

sequence evokes what Emmanuel Le Vagueresse calls a '*pietà dégenrée*' (2010: 36), in which Grajo plays the part of the succouring Virgin, the last part evokes the 'National Movement' of the Francoist regime.

The result, as Jorza so nicely styles it, is a 'melodrama that has been ideally resignified towards a sort of military-patriotic mysticism' (2012: 53), a melodrama that, for Tatjana Pavlović, 'perfectly matches' the '[e]xcessive and romanticised Falangist vocabulary' (2003: 34) that colours, as we shall see, both *¡Harka!* and *¡A mí la Legión!* It is just this blend of melodrama and mysticism that figures, not surprisingly, in *Misión blanca*, the first film to depict the religious missions in the Spanish colonies (Nieto Jiménez 2014: 242, 245). Although the militant forgiveness that Father Javier espouses rings in highly paradoxical ways for a regime that pitilessly punished the 'vanquished' supporters of the Republic, it is consistent with the rhetoric, if not the reality, of the Church. The rhetoric of the Spanish Legion, founded in early 1920 by José Millán Astray, a general who recruited Franco to serve as his second-in-command during the Rif War, is likewise steeped with a mystically blind devotion that entails the renunciation of worldly ties. According to Susan Martin-Márquez, the Legion thus 'functions as a peculiar new form of religion' (2008: 188), one in which sexual attachments, especially of any emotionally enduring sort, are sublimated, renounced or belittled. What is promoted, in contrast, is a *masculine mystique* in which the enigmatic spiritualisation of the flesh is rendered all the more imposing by virtue of the 'enigmatic' and 'exotic' African settings. All three films mine to melodramatic effect the secretive pasts of their heroes, particularly Santiago, Grajo and Father Javier, the moral anchors of their respective vehicles.[6] Their pasts largely withheld, they function as quasi-blank slates onto which, in principle, other characters and the audience project a welter of desires. Of all these 'mystery men', none is more mysterious than Santiago Valcázar. Daniel Berjano Rodríguez observes that Santiago is surrounded by an atmosphere of awe and admiration that only accentuates his mystery (2014: 12). Described by one of his companions before he appears on screen as 'noble, loyal, detached to the point of exaggeration, brave to the point of temerariousness, but incomprehensible', Santiago epitomises, in Evans' estimation, 'Nietzsche's concept of the higher man' (1995: 218), but also evinces, as Fèlix Fanés notes, an acutely neurotic, self-punitive personality that also functions as 'the highest of military virtues' (1982: 49–50) and that recalls, we might add, the self-flagellation of certain religious disciplinarians.

Amidst all the mystery, melodrama and psycho-sexual implications, it is important to note that the largely monoracial and homosocial dynamics of the military films, *¡Harka!* and *¡A mí la Legión!*, set in Morocco and produced during the Second World War, dovetail the potentially interracial and heteronormative dynamics of the missionary film, *Misión blanca*, set in what is now Equatorial Guinea and produced after the Second World War, in ways that complicate monolithic perceptions of Francoist Spain even as they reinforce its reliance on highly codified hierarchies of race and gender. Whereas both *¡Harka!* and *¡A mí la Legión!* bear the imprint of the *Falange Española*, whose idealised aesthetics of male corporeality and masculine camaraderie approximate kitsch, at least in the eyes of Le Vagueresse (2010: 25), *Misión blanca* is in tune with the National Catholicism that came to the fore after the War. As Jo Labanyi remarks:

> in the wake of the Allied Victory in 1945, the Franco regime sought to disengage itself from its previous overt association with fascism, thus replacing the Spanish Fascist Party Falange Española in key government positions with Church appointees, whose moralising rhetoric offered a model of conservative nationalism that was civilian rather than militaristic. (2001: 27)

Whatever the differences between Falangism and National Catholicism, the politically motivated shift from military duty to religious devotion is by no means absolute, for both formations are defined by ideals of sacrifice, renunciation and redemption as well as by strategies of recruitment and proselytisation. Conscious of the propagandistic potential of cinema, they both strive, that is, to mobilise Spaniards in the pursuit of patriotic and pastoral objectives. Thus, while the postwar model of conservative nationalism was not as *explicitly* militaristic as the model of conservative nationalism that prevailed from the outbreak of the Spanish Civil War to the final period of the Second World War, it was civilian only in the most constrained of manners. Indeed, the consolidation of Catholic religious authority, most notably in the form of the Concordat of 1953 between the Spanish State and the Holy See, ensured that Spanish society was more confessional than civilian in any truly secular sense. Rather predictably, the State, in the person of the Caudillo, often addressed its citizens in spiritualised terms.

In its attempts to transcend internecine bellicosity and to replace civil strife with civil order, the Francoist regime turned to the Catholic Church for support, guidance and validation. Such religiously orientated films as *La mies es mucha/Great is the Harvest* (dir. José Luis Sáenz de Heredia, 1948), *Balarrasa/Reckless* (dir. José Antonio Nieves Conde, 1951) and *Marcelino, pan y vino/Miracle of Marcelino* (dir. Ladislao Vajda, 1955) contributed to the ascendancy of the image of a kinder, gentler form of dictatorial tutelage. Far from being merely an effect of the termination of the Second World War, however, the shift from Falangism to National Catholicism that is perceptible in the shift from colonial films centred on military conflict to colonial films centred on spiritual conciliation is also an effect of the initiation of the Cold War. The shift, which outstrips the timeframe of the three films examined here, occurs within a tense international context in which the precarious, isolated status of Spain is stabilised, if not resolved, by the Pact of Madrid, a military and economic agreement with the United States in 1953 that buttresses and supplements the Concordat with the Holy See, adopted scarcely a month earlier. The confluence of religious, moral, economic and military interests in the form of Pacts and Concordats complicates, however, any clear-cut timeline. Víctor Morales and Carmen Campuzano declare that as early as 1943, when offensives by Allied forces indicated that the course of the war was changing, the Spanish State began working to dispel its image of 'suspicious neutrality' (1993: 360), though, in fact, between June 1940 and September 1942, when ¡Harka! and ¡A mí la Legión! premiered, the regime had shifted from a position of neutrality to one of non-belligerence (Viscarri 2002: 411). Morales and Campuzano also affirm that it is not until 1956, when Morocco gains its independence, that the regime moves from a fascistic and autocratic model to an authoritarian and technocratic one (1993: 360). Martin-Márquez, for her part, notes that 'Spain's eagerly awaited acceptance into the United Nations had been imbricated with the concession of Moroccan independence' (2008: 283), both brokered in late 1955 and both building, at least indirectly, on the accords with the United States and the Vatican. The international scope of the United Nations bears more than a passing resemblance to the universal pretensions of the Catholic Church, whose special status in Spain as National Catholicism is borne out in the mixture of patriotic nationalism and religious supranationalism, in which, in the words of María Pilar Amador Carretero, '"Catholicism", seen through the prism of the Nation and the Fatherland, attains an absolute and totaling presence' (2010: 5) – one that, while tempering the values of Falangism, nonetheless weighs mightily on the reality and representation of gender, sexuality and eroticism.

Amador Carretero broaches the subject of National Catholicism in her examination of sexuality in early Francoist-era cinema. She is by no means alone in understanding the impact that a national ideology of religiously inflected sublimation had on cultural production. As Asunción Gómez points out, one of the aims and effects of National Catholicism is the reassertion of one-dimensional models of women (2002: 575) that both arrest and reverse the relative loosening of gender and sexual roles that was effected during the Republic. Under the cloak of Church doctrine, the regime aggressively recuperates patriarchal conceptions of society in which women largely fade from the public sector and appear on screen either as dangerous diversions or as exemplars of maternal or sisterly self-abnegation. If the presence of the former outstrips that of the latter in Spanish colonials films, it is in no small part because the government limited, often by law, the presence of women – Spanish women – in the Spanish colonial sphere. The restrictions were particularly sharp for Spanish Guinea, where, as Martin-Márquez remarks, the 'conceptualisation of the racial incommensurability of [white] Spaniards and [black] Guineans' was bolstered by 'the radically divergent religious status of the colony' (2008: 280). In *Misión blanca*, only two women have speaking parts, the wealthy Spanish wife of the renegade protagonist (Father Javier's mother) and his indentured Guinean servant. In *¡Harka!* and *¡A mí la Legión!*, only Spanish women appear, but they do so either sporadically or late in the diegesis. The dearth of women in the latter two films responds, in no small part, to the all-male status of the Harka and the Legion, which function, amongst other things, as what Bernard Bentley describes as 'a refuge away from women' (2008: 92). In *¡Harka!* the sense of an all-male refuge from women – though *not* from death – is particularly sharp, with Carlos leaving the service, and Santiago, to engage in what are presented as frivolous metropolitan pastimes with his fiancée, the symbolically named Amparo ('shelter'), only to return, as noted, to carry on fighting after Santiago's death. The relative invisibility of women is braced, more inexplicably, by the relative invisibility of the Moroccans – more inexplicably because the *harkas*, which Bentley neatly summarises as 'detachments of Berber recruits led by Spanish officers' (90), were primarily composed of Moroccans.

Although Moroccans figure prominently in *Romancero marroquí/Moroccan*

Ballad (dirs. Carlos Velo and Enrique Domínguez Rodiño, 1939), a dramatised documentary that Elena calls 'a remarkable forerunner of the cinema of colonial and military exaltation' (2010: 26),[7] and in *La canción de Aixa/Song of Aixa* (dir. Florián Rey, 1939), a fiction film shot in Germany during the Spanish Civil War and promoted at the time of its release as 'the first [cinematic] homage of Spain to its Moroccan Protectorate' (cited in Elena 2010: 22), they have a minor presence in the subset of post-Civil War films that comprise what Román Gubern has called 'crusade cinema'.[8] Then again, inasmuch as these films – of which *¡Harka!* is persistently deemed to be emblematic or essential (Martín Corrales 1999: 23; Elena 2010: 203) – are wrapped up in tendentious notions of Spanish imperial destiny, they partake of a militant Christianity of conquest and occupation that leaves little room for indigenous Muslim culture beyond quasi-ethnographic, quasi-touristic modes of 'local colour'. Christianity may not figure frontally in *¡A mí la Legión!* or *¡Harka!*, which is awash with non-Spanish signs such as the Seal of Solomon – or Star of David – that graces the promotional poster and the opening and closing credits, but it nonetheless informs any number of things, as Dionisio Viscarri notes, from the protagonist's name, Santiago (2002: 413), to the 'insinuated reference to the yoke and the arrows of the Catholic Monarchs, a fundamental piece of Franco-Falangist iconography' (2002: 404).[9] Although critics, as we shall see, have generally been more invested in fleshing out a putative homoerotic or even homosexual 'subtext' in *¡Harka!* and *¡A mí la Legión!* than in attending to their latent Christian imagery, there can be little doubt that, for all the differences between Falangism and National Catholicism, a shared if uneven sense of martial and spiritual fervour in 'other' places and vis-à-vis 'other' races links both films to *Misión blanca*, whose priestly protagonists a contemporaneous reviewer extolled as an 'army of missionaries' (cited in Nieto Jiménez 2014: 241). What also links the three films is the visual and narrative subordination, even inconspicuousness, of 'native' people, particularly in the films set in Morocco, in which, as Elena puts it, 'the Moors become obscure extras who relinquished their leading roles to the legionnaires' (2001: 33).

The 'obscurity' of the 'Moors' in these films is overdetermined. Produced at a time when the regime did not want to ignore its debt to its Africanist origins (Franco was stationed in Morocco and orchestrated the uprising from it) and yet also wanted, more pressingly, to rebuild the Spanish homeland, the films were averse to portraying Moroccans as enemies or even, it seems, as colonial subjects, largely forgotten during the Republic until it was too late (Martín Corrales 1999: 21). As Diez Puertas observes, the Francoist government maintained that Morocco should not be referenced as a colony (2003: 284), but as a Protectorate. Guinea, it almost goes without saying, was even less present in the consciousness of Spaniards, but it could at least be cited openly as a colony and, what is more, as a site of Catholic proselytisation. The status of Islam as a monotheistic Abrahamic religion, like Christianity, distinguished Morocco from the sub-Saharan colony in the Bight of Biafra, but so did geographic proximity and a history of cultural contact – at times violent, at times peaceful – that stoked the story of Hispano-Moroccan brotherhood. But while the reputation of Moroccan religious ardour spurred amongst some Spaniards what Martin-Márquez describes as 'a grudging respect' (2008: 205), and led others, after the Civil War, to propose granting citizenship to the Moroccans who fought for the Francoist cause (205–6), the reputation of Moroccan sexual ardour, part and parcel of an extensive orientalist tradition, generated considerable ambivalence and anxiety. Martin-Márquez, drawing on George Mosse's work on nationalism and sexuality, refers to a 'Mediterranean model' that 'suggested that homosexuality was not in the least at odds with virility' (188). The 'Mediterranean model', which tends to limit the 'stigma' of 'homosexuality' to so-called 'passive feminine' sexual acts and roles, recalls Sir Richard Burton's (1885–8) more sweeping and fluid 'Sotadic Zone', a torrid terrestrial swathe that, embracing the Mediterranean, the Middle East, Asia Minor, Mesopotamia, Afghanistan, Kashmir, Indo-China, China, Japan, the South Sea Islands, and the Americas, was supposedly a space of sensual permissiveness and gender bending.[10] However designated, it would appear that the much-vaunted 'brotherhood' between Spaniards and Moroccans harboured something deeply carnal.[11]

The notions of sexual permissiveness and gender fluidity that fleck the works of orientalists *and* their critics implicate another, more momentous, notion: miscegenation. Jo Labanyi, in her study of four missionary films of the Francoist period, claims that the imperial rhetoric that courses through them 'offers models that deviate significantly from the theorisation of race dominant in the Anglo-Saxon world' (2001: 26). For Labanyi, the Spanish colonial difference resides in practices of incorporation and assimilation of 'racial "others"' in which 'territorial and sexual conquest were [...] seen as two sides of the same process' (28). Though only one of the films she considers, *La mies es mucha*, 'illustrates the incorporation of the feminine through miscegenation' (30), Labanyi insists that 'this particularly Spanish male imperial fantasy' (29) of conquest and expansion through 'racial incorporation' is operant 'even when miscegenation or sexual activity of any kind are absent' (29). Leaving aside the paradoxes and possible inconsistencies in the argument (the Spanish Empire favoured miscegenation even when miscegenation is absent), *Misión blanca*, the only one of the four films set in an *ongoing Spanish colony*, is *not* an illustration of miscegenation or of 'racial incorporation', but rather of paternalistic segregation, and in ways that trouble the idea of some overarching Spanish 'difference' vis-à-vis the 'rest' of Europe, at least by the twentieth century.[12] By the time that Spanish officials, still reeling from the loss of their colonies in the Caribbean and the Pacific in the late nineteenth century, turned their attention to Guinea, attitudes had changed considerably. In the words of Martin-Márquez, 'gone were the days when a Spaniard might propose racial mixing as the surest path to civilizing the native inhabitants without destroying their culture' (2008: 279). In fact, as Elena notes, the Francoist authorities were deeply '*mixófobas*', suspicious and fearful of mixings, so much so that 'Hispano-Guinean *mestizaje* was practically inexistent' (2010: 179, 180). The aversion to racially mixed sexual relations implicates *both* Falangism *and* National Catholicism, which all but mandated the sublimation of desire in ways that would keep some bodies apart and bring others together in certain sanctioned marriages. These marital trajectories mark *Misión blanca* and ¡*Harka!*, but with a dramatic difference: in the missionary film, the couple sanctioned is comprised of a man and a woman of the same race; in the military film, the couple sanctioned is comprised of a man and death, eulogised in 'El novio de la muerte'.

Death, as the hallmark of sublime redemption, haunts all three films here under consideration as well as the subgenres of colonial military and missionary films with which they are associated. The mortal cast of the early Francoist-era military and missionary films, in which the protagonist-heroes confront everything from snipers to yellow fever, distinguishes them from the more popular folkloric musicals in which death, inasmuch as it has a place, is not tied to the organised endeavours of the armed forces and the Church. There is, in other words, something like an objective correlative that shadows the on-screen representation of death in these films, a sense, at least amongst the metropolitan audience, that 'over there', in the Spanish colonial sphere, men risk their lives, selflessly, for the greater glory of God and country. It is not, by any measure, that the films follow a principle of mimetic realism, for what matters is the symbolic import of the attitudes and acts so histrionically on display. With respect to the obvious and fairly clumsy use of make-up and costume to make the Spanish-Cuban actress Elva de Bethancourt and the Spanish actor Jorge Mistral 'appear' to be native Guineans in *Misión blanca*, Elena states that verisimilitude is clearly not the 'discursive scenario' that the film advances (2010: 180), an assessment that Nieto Jiménez corroborates by referring to a 'deficit of verisimilitude' in relation to the 'clearly distinguishable' difference between the exteriors shot on location in Guinea and those shot in Madrid's Casa de Campo, Aranjuez and elsewhere in Spain (2014: 244). A similarly cavalier approach to historical truth and material reality characterises not just the rather fantastical ¡*A mí la Legión!* but also the decidedly more solemn ¡*Harka!*, which incorporates segments from *Romancero marroquí* (Bentley 2008: 90; Viscarri 2002: 409). Viscarri argues that the recycling of documentary footage confers a certain exoticised veracity on the fiction film (409), but he also contends, more powerfully, that what prevails in ¡*Harka!* is an idealised, fetishised conception of the male body as voluptuously delivered unto death: '[i]n Fascist aesthetics, Thanatos … displaces Eros', and to such a degree that 'to die while serving the State becomes the supreme emotional moment of the human being, substituting sexual orgasm' (417).

What thus emerges, in a manner that is applicable, *mutatis mutandis*, to *Misión blanca*, is a form of 'sexual austerity' (415) that appears to have few proponents amongst contemporary critics, clearly more 'bent' on translating austerity into repression and on finding something queer – or rather something homoerotic and even homosexual – in so much masculine sacrifice and sublimation. Julio Pérez Perucha (1998), John Hopewell (1986), Fanés (1982), Evans (1995), Labanyi (1997; 2001), Gubern (2010), Navarrete-Galiano Rodríguez (2011) and Martin-Márquez (2008), amongst others, all see the homosocial relations between the 'brothers in arms' as shot through with erotic energy, with Evans arguing that Arévalo's film 'dramatises the return of the repressed' by which 'the love that cannot be named […] succeed[s] in gaining recognition' (1995: 219), and with Pérez Perucha arguing that it 'slips from civil epic into homosexual apology' (1998: 134). For the latter critic, the brief on behalf of homosexuality issues from Arévalo's treatment of 'the conflict between the two protagonists as if it were love quarrel seasoned with a generous dosage of misogyny' (134).[13] A scene in *¡Harka!*, in which an increasingly inebriated Santiago upbraids and insults a newly engaged Carlos, remits to a previous scene in which the two men exchange cryptic confidences by a campfire, their faces aglow, their eyes glistening, in extreme close-up (cf. Evans 1995: 219; Miranda 2010: 169) (see Figure 2.2). Labanyi offers a similar reading of the climactic encounter in *Misión blanca* between Brisco and Father Javier, 'their two faces […] framed in soft-focus close-up as they gaze at each other homoerotically' (2001: 33–4) (see Figure 2.1).[14] These emotionally charged encounters and exchanges between men exist, remember, against a backdrop of the repudiation or mistreatment of women; in other words, homoeroticism and homosexuality here come into being not 'in their own right' but couched in misogyny. Although all three films are brimming with sexism, for Gómez, 'the degree of misogyny is so pronounced that some scenes of *¡Harka!* verge on homoeroticism by positing that sexual and emotional needs have to be fulfilled by the sort of manly camaraderie characteristic of a military institution' (2002: 576). Although it is particularly manifest in Gómez's reading, the linkage of misogyny, homoeroticism and homosexuality courses through more than one of the relatively few critical studies on these films and puts the brakes on what might otherwise pass, uncomplicatedly, as a 'resistant' reading.

Martin-Márquez, for instance, declares that even as she highlights 'the presence of homosexually inflected tensions and practices within the Spanish Africanist milieu', she remains 'exceptionally wary of simply reifying the decades-old conflation of homosexuality with Nazism' (2008: 201) or other regressive ideologies. The worry that Martin-Márquez expresses is not without foundation. Or rather, its foundation is that slippery slope along which men's disdain for women allegedly fires their desire for other men. Teeming with stereotype and inattentive to the varieties of lived experience, the linkage of misogyny and homoeroticism parallels other assumptions that swirl as so many cues and clues to something homoerotic or homosexual, principal amongst which are the expression of emotion and the recourse to melodrama, both taken to connote femininity – and, it seems, homoeroticism – *tout court*. Labanyi, citing Evans, refers to 'a homoeroticism that frequently feminises the male through specularising camerawork normally reserved for female stars' (2001: 30), and repeatedly ties homoeroticism to 'a feminised model of masculinity that can express vulnerability and love' (33). Thus, the homoeroticism that Gómez links to misogyny, Labanyi, amongst others, links to femininity and feminisation. The upshot is an uneasy blend of femininity *and* its repudiation as pivotal to the appearance, and perhaps the experience, of male homoeroticism. Such formulations leave in the wings the linkage between misogyny and male heteroeroticism, a concept whose unfamiliarity, doubtless a function of its normative status as 'that which goes without saying' (and hence related, albeit not identical, to homosociality), shadows the ironically more familiar homoeroticism, suffused, historically, with 'that which cannot be said'. Heteroeroticism is most noticeably at play in *¡Harka!*, when Santiago demonstrates his ability, in the cantina in which he quarrels with Carlos, to have a woman, any woman, whenever he desires; scoffing at Carlos' professed need for a bit of tenderness, Santiago stands up, dashes his glass to the floor and wrenches a woman from her dance partner. It is also on display in Brisco's ogling of Souka and, much more subtly, in Father Javier's solicitous impassivity before the same young woman: proof that he, unlike his refractory parent, shall not fall into 'the arms of ebony'.

This is not to say that the films, which betray what Labanyi calls 'colonial ambivalence' (2001), are devoid of anything homoerotic. Such, however, appears to be the position of Diana Jorza, who claims that Peter Evans 'misreads' the 'emotional excess' (2012: 57) of *¡Harka!* and *¡A mí la Legión!*, heavy with melodrama, as homoerotic or homosexual. Although she herself misreads the sweep of what she calls a 'misreading' (Evans is neither the first nor the only critic to detect a homo-subtext), Jorza makes a compelling point when she states that the 'assignation of veiled homosexuality to *¡Harka!* and *¡A mí la Legión!* is the effect of a stereotypical vision of masculinity, which excludes the display of emotions, especially strong ones' (2012: 57). One might add that it is also the effect, in much of the criticism, of a stereotypical vision of homosexuality as a bundle of entrenched gynophobia and intermittent effeminacy, where effeminacy is the surfacing of emotion and gynophobia the bedrock of misogyny. If Tatjana Pavlović is right, as I believe she is, that 'the seemingly monolithic narratives of *Harka* [sic], *Raza*, and *A mí la legión* [sic] are fragmented, filled with lapses and illogical gaps' (2003: 35) – lapses and gaps that pepper a missionary film like *Misión blanca* as well – then it should not be surprising that the lapses and gaps cannot be paradoxically made good or stabilised through appeals to homosexual subtexts and homoerotic situations. Indeed, a rigorously *queer* take, in keeping with renewed interest in asexuality, might tarry with austerity, spiritualisation and sublimation as 'alternative' modes of desire – the desire not to desire, to desire differently – and not merely or only as 'repression'. It might also recognise the temporally and spatially contingent status of identity and relationality.[15] A number of the critics who 'look back' to the largely forgotten or disavowed cinema of the Francoist and colonialist past – buckled by its own forgotten or disavowed past – refer to 'contemporary viewers' as discerning something that few in the past discerned or, at least, could say that they discerned. In so doing, they suggest that the past can be re-represented, its mysteries resolved, its closets opened, its repressive returns articulated in identifiable terms and its blind spots clarified in a manner consistent with notions of progress and development – from dictatorship to democracy, from censorship to freedom, from intolerance to acceptance, from domination to resistance, from looking the same to looking otherwise. And yet, they also suggest, at their most searing and searching, that the politically and economically charged plays of gender, race and sexuality, religion, nationality and (neo)-colonialism remain, for all the 'progress', entangled indeed.

NOTES

1. For more on these films, see Santaolalla (1999), Ballesteros (2001), Gordillo (2006), Materna (2007), Daddesio (2009) and Parejo (2014).
2. Although the Francoist regime did not nationalise or control cinematic production directly, it exerted sufficient influence and pressure on it to make it reasonable to speak of Spanish colonial cinema and propaganda. As Amador Carretero puts it: 'the Spanish film industry, under state protectionism (films of National Interest) and the pressure of censorship, drew upon different genres through which it managed to transmit messages consistent with those of the regime that influenced the emotions, attitudes, opinions, value systems and behaviour of the citizenry' (2010: 6). This and all subsequent translations from the Spanish are mine.
3. The historical coincidence between the origins of the cinematograph and colonial conflict in Africa has prompted Martín Corrales to state that 'from the very first the camera was pointed in the same direction as Spanish rifles' (1999: 12). Francoist-era films set in Africa – particularly military films set in Morocco – build on these early twentieth-century endeavours, which were largely documentary and thick with propagandistic import.
4. In ¡*Harka!*, Carlos jilts his fiancée, depicted as mundane and metropolitan, in order to continue the spirit of self-sacrifice embodied by Santiago. The rupture with women, urbanity, leisure and the Peninsula is dramatically condensed at the very end of the film,

when Carlos rips a photograph of his fiancée into pieces and pledges renewed allegiance to the *harka*.

5. The image of a man in another man's arms is echoed, later on, in the initial encounter between Mauro and Grajo, when the former, wounded in battle, rescues the latter, clutching him close, speaking reassuringly to him, and then dragging him to safety. In contrast to the melodramatic tone of the previous scene, the tone is here upbeat, even jocular; the scene, which demonstrates both self-sacrifice and valour, ends felicitously, cementing a lifelong bond of loving friendship between the two men.
6. Interestingly, although the elderly Father Urcola states that 'for a long time, Guinea was something like a foreign Legion, where no one inquired into a person's background', the spectator actually receives more information about Brisco's past than about Father Javier's.
7. For more on *Romancero marroquí*, see Elena (1996, 2004).
8. For more on the '*cine de cruzada*' as well as an expert overview of the propagandistic charge and historical value of cinema under Franco, see Gubern (1986); for more on gender in 'crusade cinema', see Miranda (2010).
9. Viscarri (2002: 404–5) provides an excellent analysis of the multiple, politically laden meanings of the Semitic star.
10. Neither model accounts for the *shared* and *reciprocal* virile activity amongst the protagonists in *¡A mí la Legión!* or *¡Harka!*, where the difference in age and military experience is not enough to annul the senses of fraternity and friendship. That said, 'gender bending' in its more explicit mode does appear in *¡A mí la Legión!* in the highly codified form of a burlesque cross-dressed performance, played for laughs, by a secondary character, Curro (Miguel Pozanco), who also plays the stereotypical part of the Andalusian funny man; for more on this scene, see Le Vagueresse (2010: 36).
11. Susan Martin-Márquez, in one of the most insightful and well documented studies of modern Spanish culture, colonialism and Africa, speculates that 'any number of [Spanish] soldiers [...] may have eschewed the straight and narrow in their preference for going native, sexually speaking, that is, for "going queer"' (2008: 191).
12. The other two films that Labanyi examines are *La manigua sin Dios/The Godless Swamp* (dir. Arturo Ruiz-Castillo, 1949), set in eighteenth-century Paraguay, and *Cerca de la ciudad/On the City's Edge* (dir. Luis Lucía, 1952), set in a shantytown outside Madrid. In marked contrast to the notion of Spanish colonial miscegenation, Laura Miranda, in her reading of 'crusade films', argues that music is deployed to advance 'the segregationist ideas that these films implied' (2010: 163–4); Viscarri, more laconically, sees in *¡Harka!* a mode of 'aesthetic "apartheid"' (2002: 409).
13. Jo Labanyi is even more lapidary in her assessment: *¡Harka!* evinces 'a typically fascistic Nietzschean misogyny' (2002: 46).
14. In her reading of *Misión blanca*, Labanyi persuasively argues that 'the love plot between a female native sold into servitude and a male native who works for the Spanish mission is of interest only insofar as it throws into relief male–male relations' (2001: 33), which are also, I quickly add, Spanish–Spanish and white–white relations. Originally titled *Souka, o Souka, alma de Guinea* (Nieto Jiménez, 2014: 242), after the leading female character in the film, the definitive title of 'White Mission' not only underscores the racialist dimension of colonial proselytisation but also points to Father Javier's 'double mission': to bring the word of God to the native Guineans and, more pointedly, to his apostate biological father.
15. Le Vagueresse (2010), for instance, drawing on the work of Alberto Mira (1999: 335), refers to a *décalage* between the model of male interaction that *¡Harka!* showcases and the model already dominant by 1942.

REFERENCES

Amador Carretero, María Pilar (2010), 'La sexualidad en el cine español durante el primer franquismo', *Revista Científica de Cine y Fotografía* 1, 3–22.
Ballesteros, Isolina (2001), *Cine (ins)urgente: Textos fílmicos y contextos culturales en la España postfranquista*, Madrid: Fundamentos.
Bentley, Bernard P. E. (2008), *A Companion to Spanish Cinema*, Woodbridge: Tamesis.
Berjano Rodríguez, Daniel (2014), '*¡Harka!*: Del homoerotismo a la opresión de género y raza', *Revista Latino-americana de Geografia e Gênero* 5:2, 11–18.
Bravo Díaz, David (2012), '*¡A mí la legión!* La visión franquista del África española en la gran pantalla durante la postguerra civil', in Leandro Martínez Peñas, Manuela Fernández Rodríguez and David Bravo Díaz (eds), *La presencia española en África: Del 'Fecho de Allende' a la crisis de Perejil*, Valladolid: Asociación Veritas, pp. 119–29.
Burton, Sir Richard Francis (1885–8), *The Book of the Thousand Nights and a Night, with Introduction Explanatory Notes on the Manners and Customs of Moslem Men and a Terminal Essay Upon the History of The Nights*, London: Burton Club.
Daddesio, Thomas C. (2009), '*Poniente* and the Questioning of Spanish National Identity', *Cincinnati Romance Review* 28, 53–71.
Diez Puertas, Emeterio (2003), *Historia social del cine en España*, Madrid: Editorial Fundamentos.
Elena, Alberto (1996), 'Romancero marroquí: Africanismo y cine bajo el franquismo', *Secuencias: Revista de Historia del Cine* 4, 83–120.
Elena, Alberto (2001), 'Spanish Colonial Cinema: Contours and Singularities', *Journal of Film Preservation* 63, 29–35.
Elena, Alberto (2004), *Romancero Marroquí: El cine africanista durante la Guerra Civil*, Madrid: Filmoteca Española & Ministerio de Cultura.
Elena, Alberto (2010), *La llamada de África: Estudios sobre el cine colonial español*, Barcelona: Bellaterra.
Evans, Peter (1995), 'Cifesa: Cinema and Authoritarian Aesthetics', in Helen Graham and Jo Labanyi (eds), *Spanish Cultural Studies: An Introduction: The Struggle for Modernity*, Oxford: Oxford University Press, pp. 215–22.
Fanés, Fèlix (1982), *CIFESA, la antorcha de los éxitos*, trans. Enric Dobó, Valencia: Institución Alfonso el Magnánimo, D.L.
F.-Fígares Romero de la Cruz, María Dolores (2003), *La colonización del imaginario: Imágenes de África*, Granada: Universidad de Granada/Centro de Investigaciones Etnológicas Ángel Ganivet.
Gómez, Asunción (2002), 'La representación de la mujer en el cine español de los años 40 y 50: Del cine bélico al neorrealismo', *Bulletin of Spanish Studies* 79:5, 575–89.
Gordillo, Inmaculada (2006), 'El diálogo intercultural en el cine español contemporáneo: Entre el estereotipo y el etnocentrismo', *Comunicación* 4, 207–22: www.idus.us.es/xmlui/bitstream/handle/11441/11691/file_1.pdf?sequence=1 (last accessed 12 July 2016).
Gubern, Román (1986), *1936–1939: La guerra de España en la pantalla. De la propaganda a la historia*, Madrid: Filmoteca Española.
Gubern, Román (2010), 'La taquilla y la mirada homosexual', *El País*, 12 August 2010: www.elpais.com/diario/2010/08/12/revistaverano/1281564002_850215.html (last accessed 12 July 2016).
Hopewell, John (1986), *Out of the Past: Spanish Cinema after Franco*, London: British Film Institute.

Jorza, Diana Roxana (2012), 'Triunfalismo nacional y mística guerrera en ¡Harka! y ¡A mí la legión!', Bulletin of Hispanic Studies 89:7–8, 49–59.
Labanyi, Jo (1997), 'Race, Gender and Disavowal in Spanish Cinema of the Early Franco Period: The Missionary Film and the Folkloric Musical', Screen 38:3, 215–27.
Labanyi, Jo (2001), 'Internalisations of Empire: Colonial Ambivalence and the Early Francoist Missionary Film', Discourse 23:1, 25–42.
Labanyi, Jo (2002), 'Historia y mujer en el cine del primer franquismo', Secuencias: Revista de Historia del Cine 15, 42–59.
Le Vagueresse, Emmanuel (2010), 'Un "canon" peut en cacher un autre: Les ambigüités de la virile camaraderie militaire dans les films espagnols de guerre nationalistes à travers ¡Harka! (1941) de Carlos Arévalo et ¡A mí la Legión! (1942) de Juan de Orduña', Lectures du genre 7, 20–42: www.lecturedugenre.fr/lectures_du_genre_7/le vagueresse.html (last accessed 12 July 2016).
Llinás, Francisco (1998), 'Redundancy and Passion: Juan de Orduña at CIFESA', trans. Nicholas Spadaccini and Jenaro Talens, in Jenaro Talens and Santos Zunzunegui (eds), Modes of Representation in Spanish Cinema, Minneapolis: University of Minnesota Press, pp. 104–12.
Martín Corrales, Eloy (1999), 'Un siglo de relaciones hispano-marroquíes en la pantalla (1896-1999)', in E. Martín Corrales, J. R. Saiz Viadero et al (eds), Memorias del cine: Melilla, Ceuta y el norte de Marruecos, Melilla: Ciudad Autónoma de Melilla, pp. 10–32.
Martin-Márquez, Susan (2008), Disorientations: Spanish Colonialism in Africa and the Performance of Identity, New Haven: Yale University Press.
Materna, Linda (2007), 'Globalization and African Immigration in Spanish Film: Chus Gutiérrez's Poniente (West 2002)', in Ursula E. Beitter (ed.), Reflections on Europe in Transition, New York: Peter Lang, pp. 57–72.
Mira, Alberto (1999), Para entendernos. Diccionario de cultura homosexual, gay y lésbica, Barcelona: Libros de la Tempestad.
Miranda, Laura (2010), 'The Spanish Crusade Film: Gender Connotations during the Conflict', MSMI 4:2, 161–72.
Morales, Víctor and Carmen Campuzano (1993), 'Resistencia indígena, guerras de liberación, nacionalismo magrebíes', Filmhistoria 3:1–2, 359–65.
Mosse, George (1985), Nationalism and Sexuality: Respectability and Abnormal Sexuality in Modern Europe, New York: Howard Fertig.
Navarrete-Galiano Rodríguez, Ramón (2011), 'Conceptualización de lo queer en ¡A mí la Legión!: Relecturas de la filmografía franquista', Revista Icono 14:9, 345–60.
Nieto Jiménez, Rafael (2014), Juan de Orduña: Cincuenta años de cine español (1924–1974), Santander: Asociación Shangrila.
Pavlović, Tatjana (2003), Despotic Bodies and Transgressive Bodies: Spanish Culture from Francisco Franco to Jesús Franco, Albany: State University of New York Press.
Parejo, Nekane (2014), 'La representación de la migración y la figura del Otro en el cine español en la película Poniente (Chus Gutiérrez, 2002)', Observatorio 8:2, 143–53.
Pérez Perucha, Julio (1998), Antología crítica del cine español, Madrid: Cátedra.
Santaolalla, Isabel (1999), 'Racial Otherness in Imanol Uribe's Bwana', Bulletin of Hispanic Studies 76:1, 111–22.
Viscarri, Dionisio (2002), '¡Harka!: Representación e imagen del africanismo fascista', Revista de Estudios Hispánicos 36:2, 403–24.
Young, Robert J. C. (1995), Colonial Desire: Hybridity in Theory, Culture and Race, London: Routledge.

FILMOGRAPHY

¡A mí la Legión!//Follow the Legion, film, directed by Juan de Orduña. Spain: Compañía Industrial de Film Español; UPCE, 1942.

Balarrasa/Reckless, film, directed by José Antonio Nieves Conde. Spain: Aspa Producciones Cinematográficas, 1951.

Bwana, film, directed by Imanol Uribe. Spain: Aurum; Creativos Asociados de Radio y Televisión; Origen Producciones Cinematográficas, 1996.

Cerca de la ciudad/On the City's Edge, film, directed by Luis Lucía. Spain: Goya Producciones Cinematográficas; Exclusivas Floralva Producción, 1952.

El último cuplé/The Last Torch Song, film, directed by Juan de Orduña. Spain: Producciones Orduña Films, 1957.

¡Harka!, film, directed by Carlos Arévalo. Spain: Arévalo; Compañía Industrial de Film Español, 1941.

La canción de Aixa/Song of Aixa, film, directed by Florián Rey. Germany/Spain: Hispano Filmproduktion, 1939.

La manigua sin Dios/The Godless Swamp, film, directed by Arturo Ruiz-Castillo. Spain: Taurus Films, 1949.

La mies es mucha/Great is the Harvest, film, directed by José Luis Sáenz de Heredia. Spain: Chapalo Films, 1948.

Las cartas de Alou/Letters from Alou, film, directed by Montxo Armendáriz. Spain: Elías Querejeta Producciones Cinematográficas; Televisión Española, 1990.

Marcelino, pan y vino/Miracle of Marcelino, film, directed by Ladislao Vajda. Spain/Italy: Chamartín, 1955.

Misión blanca/White Mission, film, directed by Juan de Orduña. Spain: Colonial AJE, 1946.

Poniente/West, film, directed by Chus Gutiérrez. Spain: Amboto Audiovisual; Antena 3 Televisión; Euskal Irrati Telebista, Junta de Andalucía, Olmo Films S.L., Sociedad Kino Visión, Vía Digital, Yahoo! España, 2002.

Raza/Race, film, directed by José Luis Sáenz de Heredia. Spain: Consejo de la Hispanidad, 1942.

Romancero marroquí/Moroccan Ballad, film, directed by Enrique Domínguez Rodiño; Carlos Velo. Morocco/Spain/Germany: Alta Comisaría de España en Marruecos, C.E.A., Tobis Filmkunst, 1939.

CHAPTER 3

The *Desarrollismo* Years: The Failures of Sexualised Nationhood in 1960s Spain

Annabel Martín

Spain's *desarrollismo* years will be the focus of this chapter's probing into the historicity of the erotic in Spanish cinematography. It would seem fitting to link the writing of the erotic body (or its absence) on the screen in 1960s Spain to, of course, the Franco dictatorship and its special revision of desire through the ideology of National Catholicism. While the ideological fabric of the regime is, unquestionably, one of the foundational pieces of this cinematography in both regime-friendly films or the more evaluative Spanish New Wave in all of its diversity, this chapter places special attention on the culture of crisis that comes into being as Spanish society turns from an isolationist economy of autarchy to one of capitalist consumption.

Segments of Spanish society of the 1960s were invited to join Europe's consumer society and did so with a vengeance. The accumulation of goods, the habitus of the 'new' bourgeoisie, and the depoliticisation of the working classes through consumption (goods and tourism) was not 'Spanish' in intent but rather the necessary outcome of a model of early neoliberal modernisation grounded on the widespread decoupling of the economic sphere from all others in developed Western societies. The Franco regime might have been anachronistic in the limitations it secured in most political, social and cultural manifestations but it was, on the other hand, a model student in its installation of a societal state of affairs that placed capitalist market structures, the development of a new service sector centred on tourism, and the consumption of consumer goods at its core. In this new state of socio-economic affairs Spain proved itself a worthy European neighbour, given how the lack of political freedom or the repressive State discourses on cultural mores were overshadowed by rapid, market-driven and speculative economic development.[1]

Naturally, this process of modernisation and its profound effects on the social order, on models of subjectivity and of gender identity, were to be problematised in European cinematography of the period in the films of directors like Roberto Rossellini, Pier Paolo Pasolini, Jean-Luc Godard and Michelangelo Antonioni, directors who developed new filmic languages that brought to the forefront how the neoliberal turn produces, in sociological terms, a profound systemic crisis that affects our capacity to psychologically remain whole, for the promise of capitalist consumption functions as a chimera of sorts, a delusion that confuses market freedom with personal freedom, consumption of goods with happiness, futurity with the present. And, of course, this confusion has a direct implication in the way the body is imagined and lived.

Film scholars have historically grouped Spanish filmmaking of the 1960s addressing the rise of neoliberalism under the dictatorship into two broad categories: on the one hand, commercial filmmaking that supported in more or less overt ways the regime's project of modernisation; on the other, an auteurist cinematography that presented a much more uncomfortable stance with the effects of capitalism and its peculiar entanglement with the dictatorship.[2] Recent scholarship on cinematic works pertaining to either category has made it very clear that the business of support or critique does not transparently fall onto either group, or at least not exclusively.[3] Many Francoist-leaning films withhold important elements of cultural critique and many films within the auteurist tradition have more than questionable sexual and gender politics structuring their narrative framework. This is due, in part, to the ways films tell their story, to the genre that organises the cinematic aesthetic, and the meaning-making process of the films themselves.

When looking at the mass cultural imagining of the tourist industry in *desarrollismo* Spain, tourism becomes a trope for the commercialisation of national identity, a formulation that readers will readily recall as the domestic and international staging of a pastiche version of the romanticised 'Carmenesque' backwardness of Spain in the regime's capitalist quest for foreign capital. Spain was up for sale thanks to a clever marketing strategy that made political, cultural and social underdevelopment attractive through five-star vacation resorts, a special kind of luxury 'underdevelopment'. Despite its cleverness in offering a folkloric depiction of authenticity for the newly minted European and US working-class vacationers to consume on its beaches, this cultural and political backwardness resonates very differently at home, for this packaging of national identity only served as yet another source of frustration for those wishing to normalise Spain (and a vision of themselves) within the Europe of their time.

Regime-friendly films that address with some degree of comic removal this new staging of national identity through the economic filter of capitalist development tend to do so through several facile dichotomies in narrative terms. In films like *Pero, ¿en qué país vivimos?/But In What Kind of a Country Do We Live?* (dir. José Luis Sáenz de Heredia, 1967), *El turismo es un gran invento*/*Tourism is a Fabulous Concoction* (dir. Pedro Lazaga, 1968), *Amor a la española*/*Love Spanish Style* (dir. Fernando Merino, 1966) or *En un lugar de La Manga*/*In a Village of La Manga* (dir. Mariano Ozores, 1970), autarchy stands in amicable opposition to development, that is, a pre-capitalist, humane, community-centred, rural Spain fights to overcome a powerful, seductive, modernising, urban, instrumentalised and internationalist version of itself. Consumerism, glamour and masculine sexual freedom are put to the test with the visual pleasure of seeing parading foreign beach queens on the streets of beach towns in southern Spain or la Costa Brava, bikini beauties that are contrasted with the limitations of our '*don Juan turísticos*' (tourist-industry Don Juans) who feel entitled to underscore the superior manhood of *homo Hispanicus* if only to be out-tricked or ridiculed by the worldliness of the visiting foreign beauties, the beloved '*suecas*' (Swedes). The films characteristically end 'happily', equating heteronormative sexuality for men with a Spanish (conservative) version of modernity and success (traditional but different), and link the triumph of tamed National Catholic values for women (family, respectability, modesty, faithfulness), despite their sometimes unruly or feminist inclinations, with a better (Spanish) imagining of all things social. And at times, even an occasional queerness – think of the characters portrayed by José Luis López Vázquez in *En un lugar de La Manga* or *El turismo es un gran invento* – is even offered a space to breathe.[4] None of the gender or bodily thinking takes place, nevertheless, without the appropriate economic transformation that compensates in some way the backward social mores in these films. Hence the sale of ancestral family land to real-estate developers in *En un lugar de La Manga*, the huge accumulation of debt on behalf of rural villages wishing to partake in economic prosperity thanks to the promise of the economic miracle of resorts, supermarkets, or of bringing the sea to landlocked hamlets in *El turismo es un gran invento*, or the brilliant reading of mass culture, of the logic of instrumentalisation that a consumer society installs in *Pero, ¿en qué país vivimos?* Regime-friendly films are sophisticated cultural products that read their time with great insight despite proposing visual imaginaries that did little to unravel the deep social and personal dissatisfaction looming underneath the supposedly upward times of economic progress.

For a more comprehensive probing into the malaise of dictatorship and neoliberalism one needs to look elsewhere, to films like Basilio Martín Patino's *Nueve cartas a Berta*/*Nine Letters to Bertha* (1966), Luis García Berlanga's *El verdugo*/*The Executioner* (1963) or Antxon Eceiza's *El próximo otoño*/*Next Autumn* (1967), where the hypermasculine macho of Francoist tourist cinema is substituted by a masculinity in crisis that cannot attain the promise of development. In these films, the type of democratic freedoms the masculine figure desires is many times embodied in a chimerical foreign female character, asserting in a heteronormative way that under the dictatorship, the site of politics for the Spanish Left is almost always a space of frustrated heterosexual male desire, as was the case in most New Wave European cinema of the period as well. In this chapter, two Spanish films heavily inspired by Antonioni's work on modernity, space and neoliberal unhappiness will help us understand why, and complicate the gender and erotic presuppositions of this model: Jorge Grau's *Noche de verano/Summer Night* (1963) and Jaime Camino's *Los felices sesenta/The Happy Sixties* (1963).

THE NAGGING AESTHETICS OF THE INVISIBLE

In *The Shape of a Pocket* (2001) John Berger dedicates a short and exquisite chapter to the ways Italian master cinematographer Michelangelo Antonioni uses abstraction to bring to life the societal uneasiness and discontent embodied in his films from the 1960s, his masterpieces *L'avventura* (1960), *La notte* (1961), *L'eclisse* (1962) and *Il deserto rosso/Red Desert* (1964). The sociocultural malaise Antonioni portrays is, metaphorically, a kind of photographic filter that washes or tints reality not so much with a colour (although this actually is the case with *Il deserto rosso*) as with an infusion of dullness and confusion. In these films, Antonioni's characters, both male and female, embody a generalised state of anxiety and dissatisfaction that is hardly ever expressed head-on as a complaint or defiance; instead, his characters seem to be searching for a remedy that never seems to work, despite the best efforts (Berger 2001: 133). Antonioni never names; he prefers to push his characters through weblike mazes, through psychological entrapments that point with great subtlety towards the effects of the transformation of contemporary society at the hands of neoliberal economic policies: a state of affairs of unfulfilled promise built upon the plague-like, dehumanising effect of contemplating all things human through the logic of economic gain and efficiency. Antonioni's greatness lies in his capacity to bring the effects of this instrumental logic to life in the interstices of reality, in its wrinkles and silences, through a new filmic language that was to unequivocally resonate with Spanish directors like Jaime Camino and Jorge Grau, who welded onto neoliberal anomie the effects of dictatorship.[5]

Perhaps the influence Antonioni's filmmaking had on Spanish directors struggling with meek creative conditions under censorship owes much to his historical vision, to the ways he develops an aesthetic that indexes the structural underpinnings of our world, those parts of reality that can never be fully seen (Berger 2001: 135) for they exceed representative status. Hence, Antonioni develops a cinematic language whereby non-narrative elements are elevated to the status of characters, whereby architecture, angles, objects, cities, streets, point to the profound societal transformations that are taking place in the 1960s with the full-blown development of neoliberal, consumerist society, transformations which, of course, affect the human psyche in very acute ways.[6] His uncomfortable camera can linger on a character's compulsive repetition of gestures or on silence, that is, on long, non-narrative sequences of streets, objects, sidewalks, parks, empty apartment buildings, construction sites or blank, empty skies. This is a new kind of 'realism' that mimics in some way the state of crisis and loss underlying plots and storylines. In this cinematography the camera is no longer an invisible observer creating seamless narratives because the times are such that language (form) does not adhere to meaning (content) any longer (Pasolini 1988: 183). Pasolini saw this as a direct epistemological outcome of the 'cultural development of neocapitalism' (185), which, if it is to be clearly understood in its compulsive and dehumanising effects, requires an aesthetic medium that produces 'insane semantic deformations' (185).[7] This monstrosity of sorts can also be understood as a 'gap' that needs to be closed, an unbearable distance between the actual experience of life and the new public narratives that are offered to make it meaningful. Filmmakers like Antonioni and Pasolini in the case of Italy, or Ecieza, Martín Patino, Berlanga, Camino and Grau, among others, in Spain understood this fully and offered their audiences uncomfortable renditions of their times, placing their characters in existential crises but, nevertheless, rescuing them before they went mad.

Spanish cinematographers had the added complication of bringing to life a lie that would, if successfully rendered, point to the messy and comfortable linkage between economic transformation and dictatorship. And they will do so, much like Antonioni, through carefully crafted critiques of gender, through female visionaries who become societal litmus tests of sorts. But this is where the comparison stops. If Antonioni was able to be truthful to his revelation of the lie through the restlessness of his female characters, always searching, always unhappy, fearlessly breaking societal gender expectations concerning sexuality or the heteronormative family unit, Spain's context allowed for equally unhappy female protagonists but the times demanded resolutions of a very different nature.

NEOLIBERALISM, CONSUMERISM AND SUBJECTIVITY

As we look at the creative and political entanglements in the Spanish films, it might be helpful to spend some time thinking about the effects of neoliberalism on the configuration of social relations and their crossover into the realm of subjectivity and the erotic. The 1960s witnessed two important transformations that were to change contemporary society to the core, one economic, the other identitarian-epistemological. In regards to economic structure, the 1960s consolidated the road for neoliberalism to become the dominant theory of political and economic practice, a theory that proposes, in David Harvey's terms, that 'human well-being can best be advanced by liberating individual entrepreneurial freedoms and skills within an institutional framework characterised by strong private property rights, free markets, and free trade' (2). In his classic *A Brief History of Neoliberalism* (2005), Harvey explains that this new equivalence between well-being and entrepreneurial freedom turns the State into the guarantor of such practices at all costs, even if this means

> much 'creative destruction', not only of prior institutional frameworks and powers (even challenging traditional forms of state sovereignty) but also of divisions of labour, social relations, welfare provisions, technological mixes, ways of life and thought, reproductive activities, attachments to land and habits of the heart. (3)

It is these 'habits of the heart' that the films hinge upon for this economic takeover, this measuring of life predominantly through the logic of profit and gain, naturally yields a particular kind of subjectivity, ways of living embodiment and the erotic. They are products of a specific kind of epistemological turn.

Embedded within this 'new' society lies a mode of construction of the self based on a version of 'self-mastery' that channels the usual uncertainties that human existence faces into anxious, yet fruitful, activity (Harvey 2005: 10–11). In societal terms, this 'productivity' operates within a paradigm that haphazardly links reason, efficiency and freedom (Harvey 2005: 10) in the name of growth. This is a process that elevates economic activity over all other areas and that bases success on a psychological process that pauperises the individual for it paradoxically wraps us in a cloak of precariousness within abundance. Economic theorist Wendy Brown (2015) has pointed out quite convincingly in her study of the effects of neoliberalism on democracy, that this 'neurosis' of sorts stems, on a structural level, from the transformation of 'homo politicus' (prior centre of the social sphere) into that of 'homo oeconomicus' (9), or what Jean Baudrillard in *The Consumer Society* (1998 – originally published in 1970) termed '*homo consumens*' (99), forever locked in a chain of profit and gain. In this scheme of things, the traditional entanglement of the political, social, economic and cultural spheres collapses onto the economic.

Now, this structural transformation also embodies a new model of human subjectivity, one that reduces the ontology of the subject to its manifestation as human capital that is tasked, according to Brown, with improving and leveraging its competitive positioning and with enhancing its (monetary and non-monetary) portfolio value across all of its endeavours and venues (2015: 9). And this especially determines our bodily selves. 'Homo oeconomicus' is the outcome of the 'financialisation of daily life' (Martin 2002: 3) and of the self in that web. For Martin, this reduction of human activity to only its economic output has had the effect of transforming elements of the world of finance into domestic ones. In this type of economy, money is both a 'means and an ends of life' (2002: 3), whereby 'finance, the management of money's ebbs and flows is not simply in the service of accessible wealth, but presents itself as a merger of business and life cycles, as a means of acquisition of the self. The financialisation of daily life is a proposal for how to get ahead, but also a medium for the expansive movements of body and soul' (2002: 3).

In this scheme of things, human subjectivity construed as human capital becomes an 'obsessive' subjectivity, for it is persistently at risk of 'failure, redundancy, and abandonment through no doing of its own, regardless of how savvy and responsible it is' (Brown 2015: 37). As human capital, the subject is at once in charge of itself, responsible for itself, yet 'an instrumentalisable and potentially dispensable element of the whole' (37). While this might be true for neoliberal societies within democracies, the Spanish situation has its idiosyncratic complication. In the Italian case, like in most other Western nations, the equation of political freedom with economic freedom secured inequality because in this equivalence individuals are branded according to the market formulation of winners and losers instead of with the successful 'mastering of the conditions of life [...] or securing the demos' (Brown 2015: 41).[8] In the Spanish situation, the demos itself was lost and nowhere in sight.

However, one needs to wonder if this shift from non-instrumentalised dreams to the economic reality of the European democracies was also not equally shared by the dictatorship, or even favoured by it. If market logic and not political logic is what articulates this new society, then modernity is secured for the dictatorship as well, provided it follows the laws of profit and gain. Individuals who bear this process under dictatorship and do so with a blunt political imagination do not automatically link a change in political regime with the improvement of the conditions of life, for 'progress' is, for the most part, exclusively branded in economic terms. Spanish filmmakers who comfortably worked within the artistic restrictions of the Francoist policies were quick to point to this very significant erasure as part and parcel of the new visual regime that they gave form to in films such as those of the tourist genre. Regime-friendly renditions of a mass-marketed embodiment of Spain on the screen for Spanish audiences appealed to the neoliberal-*desarrollista* policies of expansive growth, of the development of the new service sector, and with it, in the case of tourism, merchandising national historic monuments, places and natural reserves for the freshly minted tourist/working classes of Europe. However, the national staging could never be too removed from the new sexual imaginary that capitalist development also needed to depict on the screen. Films like those mentioned above staged in more or less successful fashion how tourism achieved the packaging of a consumable identity for visitors and natives alike through a symbolic operation that erased the messiness and complexities of the real, and instead opted for facile oppositions based on national, gender and sexual stereotypes. In this logic of diversion, free-time and 'liberation from work' (inactivity) become the highest goals to achieve, given how they are the reward for participating in a system that tricks us into believing that economic gain is disassociated from its many class, family, gender, race or national entanglements. All one needs to do is understand the rules of the game and play with individual skill to succeed in the new economy. So the regime-friendly films imply as they make real-estate sales, entrepreneurship, advertising, commerce, the new service sector and a new imaginary for the body's capital the road to affluence for the poor and working classes.

If the new consumer economy is less about the usage and life of things and more about how individual and social identity is linked to goods and images, shouldn't we pause to ask if consumption means something different when performed from the space of poverty? To answer this question it might be helpful to compare two of Luis García Berlanga's films which address Spain's level of development in two different stages of neoliberal *desarrollismo*: his remarkable *¡Bienvenido, Míster Marshall!/Welcome Mr Marshall!* (1953) of the very early years of economic development and his later *El verdugo* (1963). Readers might recall that in the first film the townsfolk of downtrodden and backward Villar del Río get a chance to request one item from their Santa Claus-like mayor, who is staging a tourist version of the hamlet for the visiting US dignitaries of the Marshall Plan. The town will be artificially transformed into a tourist version of a completely different region of Spain (Andalucía) so that the Americans will identify Villar del Río with that particular folkloric and consumer version of the country ripe with bullfighters, flamenco dancers, serenading street singers, and so on. The promise of development will bring the much-needed railway station to the village and with it the dream of affluence and happiness. For starters, the 1,642 village folk are allowed one consumer wish each. And here lies the paradox, for their object of desire is not utilitarian but rather one of comfort and hope, the stuff of dreams: the hungry ask for clarinets; the illiterate for wristwatches; the toothless dream of chocolate; the farmer who needs fertiliser for his fields prefers an umbrella. The women dream about new mirrors, embroidered quilts or sewing machines so that they can adorn homes that have no running water, electricity or heat (Martín 2005: 188).

Baudrillard reminds us that consumer goods present themselves not as the products of labour but rather as the harnessing of power (1998: 33). Goods become a magic remedy of sorts that turn plenty into 'an effect of nature', into an 'inalienable right' (33), a natural right to abundance. Goods within the logic of consumerism are just that, a fragmentary example of that logic, not the product of a history, of labour, of class relations. They conjure away the real with a sign of the real, just like the complexities and layers of history get reduced and confused with signs of change (34). This has the effect of making consumption natural and the social relations within consumption natural as well. And while films that focus on the upper classes are correct to point to this epistemological violence, to this profound falsification and denial of the real as the cause of the deep anomie they portray, how do we reconcile the promise of hope that consumption does offer, no matter how ephemeral, to those in need? Could it just be so that the tranquillity (however violent in symbolic terms) that the distancing or disengagement from the real (the distancing from the world embedded in the process of the creation of object-signs) leads to a comforting in the poor while provoking a process of neurosis and anxiety (usually manifest in erotic terms) in those in not so dire circumstances?

The process of misrecognition (signs for the real) is lived differently in both situations, whereby the poor find in that misrecognition a brief respite from the brutality of the real, especially when that real weighs so much more within the parameters of dictatorship. If the more fortunate live this misrepresentation as an anxious inebriation of banality or as a 'violent' imposition of gender identity as outlined above, for the poor, as Berlanga so insightfully points out, consumerism withholds a promise of change, of hope, a momentary arrest of the difficulties of life brought about by the political and economic impossibilities that the working poor faced in Spain despite the economic boom of *desarrollismo*. There is, of course, a dark side to this. Let's not forget his film *El verdugo* (1963), quite possibly one of the most provocative critiques of the Franco regime ever screened, a film that presents with absolute normality how the violence of the dictatorship can comfortably coexist within consumer society through the life of the poor, in this case, that of an executioner. In this film, the workers of the world are now members of what one might call an International Leisure Class, workers turned vacationers who hide behind their sunglasses the ethical and moral concessions that such a state of affairs demands, especially for those belonging to the marginal poor of society like the young executioner (José Luis) who finds himself literally trapped, sequestered and complicit with the structures of the State in his aspiration to have employment, support his family and own the long-awaited apartment promised to his father-in-law by the State. In films like these, there is an underlying critique of how individuals and states evolve into projects of 'capital enhancement' (Brown 2015: 22), dominated by the economic framing of life that displaces the social into the logic of profit and gain. This is the socio-cultural backdrop of the profound anomie that drives the plot of films critical with this state of affairs, an anomie that is also linked to the tension between a less economised notion of the self (the promise of the erotic) and one of subjectivities and bodies conceived as projects of capital, frictions developed in *Noche de verano* and *Los felices sesenta*.

HOMO CONSUMENS AND THE PROMISE OF THE EROTIC

As we turn to *Noche de verano* and *Los felices sesenta*, we find that both Jorge Grau and Jaime Camino are particularly sensitive to how the new economic milieu relinquishes human identity to that of an unfortunate equivalence with a 'brand,' that is, with a cohesive external structure that transforms subjectivity into a 'dissociable totality' (Baudrillard 1998: 28). This collective vision of sorts is linked to a habitus that individuals strive to futilely embody or cloak into a promise of desire, a promise of identity. One only needs to recall the world of upper-class protagonists Carmen (Lidia Alfonsi) and Bernardo (Francisco Rabal) in *Noche de verano* or Mónica (Yelena Samarina) and Víctor (Jacques Doniol-Valcroze) in *Los felices sesenta*, and how both filmmakers carefully craft their dreams and desires through the world of goods and consumption. The two couples embody the 1960s version of the Spanish upper middle classes, of that special segment of Iberian society that could consume at the level of their European counterparts, and define happiness along the same terms. Both films share many documentary-like scenes where the habitus of the bourgeois class is chronicled at great length: homes, furnishings, clothing, cars, children, and social spaces and playgrounds, sites where many of the contradictions embedded in this world surface. Characters are defined by the designer label of their dresses, by the cars they drive, by the champagne that they drink, by their choice of language, by the man or woman at their side, and by the social spaces they inhabit, mapping out the city of Barcelona (*Noche de verano*) or the vacation town of Cadaqués (*Los felices sesenta*) along the lines of these class distinctions.

The films narrow in on the gestures that make these characters display neurotic identities whereby well-being is equated with affluence and affluence with 'the accumulation of signs' (Baudrillard 1998: 32) or stand-ins for happiness. If consumption demands the death of the object (of its history and labour) and a decoupling of that history from our own, it follows that, in this context, life becomes removed from a more cohesive real and that signs (abstractions) stand in its place. Hence, in *Noche de verano*, it makes sense for social identity (prestige and status) to be grounded on the ephemeral filters of material wealth for the bourgeois class (Bernardo and Carmen) or for it to be the shaky pillars of the dream of those seeking social mobility like Rosa and Miguel (played by Italian actors Rosalba Neri and Umberto Orsini). In *Los felices sesenta* the focus is a bit different, given how the contradictions within these spheres are displaced onto the physical world itself, like Antonioni would do in *L'avventura*. Inspired by the great master, Camino uses the setting of the maritime village and its landscape to defamiliarise a group of upper middle-class city dwellers from Barcelona and their chimeric and facile way of life. The camera contrasts an upper-class Mónica dressed in modern urban vacation garb (mini shorts) as she enjoys an existentialist stroll through the early morning village streets of Cadaqués, contrasting the authenticity (poverty) of the barren and dilapidated white walls of her surroundings with the world and preoccupations embodied in her. These are still the early days of tourism and development, times when one could still catch a glimpse of an older and less commodified way of life. Camino chooses this setting to create a hybrid context ('authentic' and yet speculatively capitalist) to highlight the torn interior world of two characters searching for a last moment of sincerity with each other and with themselves prior to being viciously swallowed by the weight of the expectations and compromises that are expected of them, a blunting of the imagination that has also invaded and colonised their interiority. The director places Mónica and Víctor in what are still non-instrumentalised places (the ruins of a monastery, on an island, in a boat at sea), with the hope that this physical displacement into a third space of sorts will also unshackle them from the expectations and logic that governs their lives as trophy wife or famed cardiologist living abroad in the US. Their profound unhappiness would seem to underscore the insufficiencies of consumer capitalism, given how success is framed as an engagement with a symbolic system that equates maximum separation from the real as life itself, an abstraction that supposedly offers a false index of security through accumulation (the cultural and economic capital of these characters) and a notion of the self that is likewise 'disembodied' or 'abstracted' from its inner complexities but anxiously attached to its 'things'.

While affluence is always the explicit backdrop in the films of the *desarrollismo* years, Spanish filmmakers critical with the regime have been very responsive to the different ways class structure, gender and sexuality resignify affluence and the tensions within.[9] In both films, eroticism and sexuality become the preferred markers of this tension, for consumer society bases its profit-making modus operandi on cultivating a narcissistic subjectivity in the individual, one that will identify consumption as a remedy to psychic and social precariousness but in gender-specific terms, an individual who is interpellated by consumerism but whom consumerism imagines as 'feminine' or feminised (at least in this period) through the 'myth' of Woman as a 'collective and cultural model of self-indulgence' (Baudrillard 1998: 96). If the films then wish to turn to the cultural critique of their time, it follows that they would pay special attention to the ways women and men consume signs of femininity and masculinity in order to develop a gendered understanding of the (im) possibilities of life. To be sure, this binary, heteronormative schema originates not in nature but rather in the 'differentiated logic of the system' (Baudrillard 1998: 97), for the relation of the 'Masculine and the Feminine to real men and women is relatively arbitrary' (97). And this, of course, implies addressing both men's and women's relationship with themselves and with others directly through the lens of the eroticised body.

It is illuminating to see how the erotic in both films leads down a path of dissatisfaction, of unfulfilled promise. In *Noche de verano*, Grau toys at first with having Bernardo, the lead bourgeois male of the film, the embodiment of hypermasculine predatory sexuality, be the figure defining the rules of the sexual (always on the hunt for a ration of female flesh), if only to displace this energy onto a notion of the erotic as a transgression of this model of masculinity (his patient, year-long wait from one festival of Sant Joan to the next to declare his love to one of his wife's closest friends). The opening scene of the film has Bernardo cruising the streets of Barcelona on the eve of the first Sant Joan, shouting out sexual platitudes from behind the wheel of his ridiculously expensive car to the late-night revellers out on the streets as the camera gives us a documentary-like depiction of the excess of the hyper-sexualised expression of human experience of Barcelona *la nuit*. The action quickly shifts and puts Bernardo back in his stiff, bourgeois terrain whereby he reconnects with his milieu in the bar of an elegant hotel and where Grau introduces the second storyline of the film: Rosa's dream of upward mobility grounded in the power of seduction that her youth, beauty and body command in this sexual market. As illustrated in Figure 3.1, following the voyeuristic rules of cinematic seduction, Grau will always have the camera emphasise Rosa's seductive capital through close-ups of her face or body. The two stories intersect briefly

Figure 3.1 Rosalba Neri in *Noche de verano / Summer Night*, directed by Jorge Grau. Spain-Italy: David Film, Domiziana Internazionale Cinematografica, 1963.

through flirtatious innuendo between the two, but sufficiently long for spectators to understand that the erotic is intimately tied to space, to class relations and to the commodification of the body, setting the stage for the contractual marriage between Rosa and Miguel, the frustrated romantic relationship between Miguel and Alicia (the intellectualised female character in the film played by Italian actor Marisa Solinas), or the sexless marriage of wealth and social position between Bernardo and Carmen.

In both films the erotic is less a site for transgression as it is almost one of abstract violence, for in many senses it is the spot that most blatantly makes us aware of how consumer society is both a society of solicitude and one of repression. The violence exerted here is of a symbolic and abstract nature but it is, nevertheless, experienced through the body, for there is no other way to move through life despite the abstractions (signs) consumerism imagines us in. In the films themselves, this symbolic violence finds a translation in narrative terms by emphasising fragility and sites of crisis, and by reminding us just how bodies are tamed and seduced through consumerism.[10] Under this logic, the taming that needs to take place demands self-abnegation or to shun what Audre Lorde would term the 'yes within ourselves' (57), our capacity for joy. In her classic 'The Uses of the Erotic' Lorde carefully lays out a theory of emancipatory (embodied) knowledge through a thinking of the erotic as a site of resistance to the makings of capitalist society and its rendering of life. By acknowledging the force of the human capacity for joy and satisfaction, Lorde undoes the logic of consumer instrumentalisation and its effects on identity. In her theorisation, the 'erotic' is shorthand for quite possibly our last connections with the real in consumer capitalist society. This turns an awareness of this joy into a dangerous and disruptive force, one to tame and to be made suspect, given how it can become a political tool of unstoppable emancipatory power. Yes, it is sexual, but it is also more.

The films provide a wise and accurate gendered portrayal of this state of affairs; one that accentuates just how subtly (or not) the domestication of the inner drive towards happiness operates. On the one hand, the process involves a profound re-elaboration of meaning, one that situates individuals and their search for systems of belief in a tautological realm governed, in this world of capitalist consumerism, by the logic of advertising, that is, by a paradigm that makes things 'true by saying they are so' (Baudrillard 1998: 129). In this world, it becomes increasingly more difficult to find answers to questions that deeply question the purpose of life, the content of identity, the possibility and conditions of freedom, or the quest for happiness. Individuals locked within the closed-circuit paradigm of truth based on the fetishisation of content, as so deemed by market realities, can no longer resort to an 'external' reality, to the quest of a lost 'original', that is, to a manifestly referential dimension, because *homo consumens* lives within the play of signs, 'truth' being a derivative of an internal (artificial) logic. Meaning-making operates at a mythological level here, self-referential, no longer verifiable outside of its circuit of origin and operation. And yet our filmmakers seem to suggest that the paradigm might not be as airtight as it is made out to be, that characters in these films set out to chase the dream of identity proposed by the lure of class mobility and class habitus and comfort but that they do so knowingly entrapped, harnessing and repressing the will to joy, relinquishing the most powerful instrument of resistance to this state of affairs they have: the promise of the erotic.

Both films portray a liberalisation of the Spanish screen during the 1960s in that the explicit treatment of sexuality both within and outside the confines of the heterosexual monogamous couple becomes central to understanding this state of affairs. In this sense *Noche de verano* and *Los felices sesenta* are children of their times in that consumer societies of this period were witnessing an end to the puritanical entrapment of the body and substituting the repressive physical, interpersonal and sexual mores with the omnipresence of a newly discovered bodily freedom. However, despite its new emancipatory energy, consumer society quickly turned the liberated body into a new site, perhaps *the* site, of capital, heavily investing in a new split, which, naturally, performed the body as a fetish or consumer object.

For the female characters looking for social mobility, this cultural malaise gets resocialised and embodied in the narcissistic needs of the bodies at stake, a movement that, on the one hand, turns beauty, seduction, desire into an 'investment of an efficient, competitive, economic type' (Baudrillard 1998: 132). This is clearly the character of Rosa in *Noche de verano* but it is also applicable to the bourgeois socialites in both films. The 'yield' of this beauty is measured in purely instrumentalised forms, ones that have a particularly acute gendered reading in this context. Given the logic of 'falsehood' in which they operate, they create the paradox of the overtly (de)sexualised body, of bodies that can offer sex but that no longer offer the erotic as a promise of truth, for this would imply a critique of the paradigm of consumption and instrumentalisation that governs this universe. In this framework, the body is not an autonomous (untamed) embodiment of the subject but rather 'a normative principle of enjoyment and hedonistic profitability' (Baudrillard 1998: 132); it is an 'enforced instrumentality that is indexed to the code and the norms of a society of production and managed consumption' (132). One handles the body as one might handle 'an inheritance; one manipulates it as one of the many signifiers of social status' (132).

Hence the disillusioned ending of both films, narrative resolutions that demonstrate that a truly erotic (liberatory) attachment within the confines of the social hypocrisy demanded of both men and women is impossible. In the case of *Una noche de verano*, the film comes full circle as we see Bernardo once again on the prowl, becoming 'himself' after he confesses his true feelings to

Inés (María Cuadra), one of his closest allies within his circle of friends, only to be romantically rejected by her given her strong attachment to husband and children. *Noche de verano* demonstrates in both subplots that a truly erotic (liberating) attachment within the confines of the social hypocrisy demanded of both men and women is impossible. It does not matter that lower-class women can be portrayed as unequivocally interested in their sexual satisfaction, or that other models of female identity are also possible like that of the university student interested in books, avant-garde films or writing. The film destroys any hope for 'truth' in its depiction of the close circuit of societal options that National Catholic Spain tattoos on the bodies of those resisting its forces. Likewise, although much more radical in its depiction of anomie and in the erotic as a source of liberation, *Los felices sesenta* also has its female protagonist Mónica making the round-trip back to Barcelona with husband and children after experimenting with the thought of a more focused and fulfilling life through the promise of the erotic. Given its formulation as an extra-marital affair, the road to failure and unhappiness was a given from the beginning. It was a brave pursuit but doomed to failure, for the trappings of bourgeois morality and social expectations were always barking at her heels. As her lover reminds her, 'It was too beautiful to last'. Mónica's saddened and resigned post-coital face (see Figure 3.2) speaks for itself. There is no illusion of a different kind of future.

Figure 3.2 Yelena Samarina in *Los felices sesenta / The Happy Sixties*, directed by Jaime Camino. Spain: Tibidabo Films, 1963.

The depiction of the *desarrollista* years on the screen demanded a special sensitivity towards the possibilities of the erotic as a counter-consumerist force. Much like cinematic melodrama, these films also wrestle with a hermeneutical strategy of 'excess' that destabilises Francoist cultural expectations. If *Noche de verano* is more sensitive to the effects of commodification on the body, in that it connects both upward mobility and the de-eroticisation of bourgeois life to this phenomenon, it would be fair to claim that *Los felices sesenta* is, in this regard, much more in line with exploring the power of the erotic as a counter-consumerist force, if only to fail. Grau and Camino focus on how the society of satisfaction, the society of promise and affluence, is actually a society built upon epistemological and psychic violence, for all things are glazed through a paradigm of value that is exclusively based on economic thinking. It is a painfully blind, rigid and schizophrenic society that uses consumption (the cause) as its paradoxical remedy. On the screen, it is a world where life aspirations and life disillusions are never remedied, where true happiness or self-fulfilment is always postponed, where the path to satisfaction is hinted at but always diverted, where joy is substituted for other 'psychological lubricants' (Baudrillard 1998: 178). In its place, characters are offered societal, family and personal identities that heavily rely on powerfully constrained models of desire, which in the Spanish case fit all too comfortably with the extra layer of restrictive social mores the dictatorship added to this state of affairs. If in other European films of the period that inspire the Spanish New Wave, the anomie felt by characters turns into a state of permanent flux, an abandonment of societal expectations, the inexplicable disappearance of characters or the unsatisfactory collapse of normative models of identity, the Spanish examples will follow this route but with moderation, always turning to a resolution that, unfortunately, neutralises and tames those same tensions and contradictions.

NOTES

1. Two excellent studies of the Spanish context are: Míguez and Castillo (1969) and Huerta and Sánchez (2014).
2. I refer readers to Heredero and Monterde (2003), Pavlović (2011) and Benet (2012). In *A History of Spanish Film* (2013), Sally Faulkner, British film scholar and contributor to this volume on erotic cinema, proposes a novel way of thinking about Spanish filmmaking of the period outside of the more conventional split that categorises the body of work of the decade according to its political positioning towards the dictatorship. Instead, Faulkner recuperates for Spanish filmmaking the notion of the 'middlebrow' and focuses on the ways the Spanish middle class becomes both a narrative theme in the actual films as well as the target audience for such reflections. In other words, Faulkner's approach is less interested in how successful the films actually are in destabilising conservative social and

political mores and more focused on how the values of the middle class push Spain closer to a project of modernity.
3. For example, my work on cinematic melodrama claims a bilingualism for the genre, for it can either sit in agreement with discourses of hegemony (Francoist or otherwise), given its 'manipulative' emotional universe, or be a celebrated narrative mode because that complicity is never quite total. For a detailed analysis of the contradictions within the filmmaking of the 1940s to the 1960s, see Martín (2005).
4. For more on this topic I refer readers to Martín (2016).
5. In his much-cited letter to Antonioni, Roland Barthes (dated 1980 – see Barthes 1997) distinguished his filmmaking as being preoccupied with formulating 'new questions' (63) that demand subtlety in order to capture the magnetism of a particular historical moment: 'For you, contents and forms are equally historical; dramas, you have said, are plastic as much as psychological. The social, the narrative, the neurotic are just levels [...] of the *world as a whole*, which is the object of every artist's work (63)' (emphasis original).
6. Pasolini found the situation so grave that he would remark in 'Cinema of Poetry' (1972) that the 1960s saw the birth of a new anthropological type, that of the ill bourgeois who is obsessively attached to the world (181).
7. In *The Shape of a Pocket* (2001) John Berger draws a genealogy of compassion in art and claims that it is compassion's lack of means and ends, its disinterestedness, that defies the natural order of things in our contemporary world. For Berger, closing this gap, overcoming this vertigo, has been the task of many artists from the late eighteenth century onwards beginning with Goya, artists who have keenly understood that the desolation of this experience resides in its being based on a 'lie', not so much with the facts of reality themselves (176).
8. Recall the unhappy writer (Giovanni) guiltily toying and succumbing to the new culture industry Marcello Mastroianni plays in *La notte*, the stock runner (Piero) Alain Delon embodies in *L'eclisse* always running after capital, always on the verge of collapse, unsure of himself and of his relationships, banal and superficial, or the lost architect (Sandro) in *L'avventura*, played by Gabriele Ferzetti, who remembers a time when he wished to build beautiful buildings and not work with balance sheets, profits and management of the bottom line.
9. For an analysis of how class structure is linked with consumer society in 1960s Spanish filmmaking critical of the regime, see Martín (2013).
10. In films like *Noche de verano* or *Los felices sesenta*, one could say that the 'tamed bodies' are, nevertheless, dominant ones, white, European, heterosexual bodies of privilege, bodies that suffer, of course, from capitalist instrumentalisation, but bodies whose legitimacy to happiness is never under question, its impossibility or frustration marking the narrative force and tension in the films themselves.

REFERENCES

Barthes, Roland (1997 [1980]), 'Dear Antonioni', in *L'avventura* by Geoffrey Nowell-Smith, London: British Film Institute.
Baudrillard, Jean (1998 [1970]), *The Consumer Society: Myths and Structures*, London: Sage.
Benet, Vicente (2012), *El cine español: Una historia cultural*, Barcelona: Paidós.
Berger, John (2001), *The Shape of a Pocket*, New York: Pantheon.

Brown, Wendy (2015), *Undoing the Demos: Neoliberalism's Stealth Revolution*, New York: Zone Books.
Faulkner, Sally (2013), *A History of Spanish Film: Cinema and Society (1910–2010)*, New York: Bloomsbury.
Harvey, David (2005), *A Brief History of Neoliberalism*, Oxford and New York: Oxford University Press.
Heredero, Carlos F. and José Enrique Monterde (eds) (2003), *Los 'Nuevos Cines' en España. Ilusiones y desencantos de los años sesenta*, Valencia: Institut Valencià de Cinematografía Ricardo Muñoz Suay.
Huerta, Pilar and Antonio Sánchez (2014), *El desarrollismo en la España de los sesenta*, Madrid: Creaciones Vicent Gabrielle.
Lorde, Audre (1984), *Sister Outsider: Essays and Speeches*, Freedom, CA: The Crossing Press.
Martin, Randy (2002), *The Financialisation of Daily Life*, Philadelphia: Temple University Press.
Martín, Annabel (2005), *La gramática de la felicidad: Relecturas franquistas y posmodernas del melodrama*, Madrid: Libertarias/Prodhufi.
Martín, Annabel (2013), 'El viaje sin retorno: Turismo y disidencia identitaria en el cine de los 60', in Antonia del Rey Reguillo (ed.), *Turistas de película*, Madrid: Biblioteca Nueva, pp. 65–90.
Martín, Annabel (2017), '¿Turismo "queer"?: La generación felpa o el cuerpo social del turismo', in Antonia del Rey Reguillo (ed.), *Viajes de cine. El relato del turismo en el cine hispánico*, Madrid: Tirant lo Blanch Humanidades.
Míguez, Alberto and J. Castillo (1969), *España: ¿Una sociedad de consumo?*, Madrid: Ediciones Castilla.
Pavlović, Tatjana (2011), *The Mobile Nation: España cambia de piel (1954–64)*, Bristol and Chicago: Intellect.
Pasolini, Pier Paolo (1988 [1972]), 'Cinema of Poetry', in Louise K. Barnett (ed.), *Heretical Empiricism*, Bloomington and Indianapolis: Indiana University Press, pp. 167–86.

FILMOGRAPHY

Amor a la española / Love Spanish Style, film, directed by Fernando Merino. Spain: Ágata Films, 1966.
¡Bienvenido, Míster Marshall! / Welcome Mr Marshall!, film, directed by Luis García Berlanga. Spain: Unión Industrial Cinematográfica, 1953.
El próximo otoño / Next Autumn, film, directed by Antxon Eceiza. Spain: Buch-San Juan, Elías Querejeta Producciones Cinematográficas, 1967.
El turismo es un gran invento / Tourism is a Fabulous Concoction, film, directed by Pedro Lazaga. Spain: Pedro Masó Producciones Cinematográficas, 1968.
El verdugo / The Executioner, film, directed by Luis García Berlanga. Spain: Naga Films, 1963.
En un lugar de La Manga / In a Village of La Manga, film, directed by Mariano Ozores. Spain: Arturo González Producciones Cinematográficas, 1970.
Il deserto rosso / Red Desert, film, directed by Michelangelo Antonioni. Italy/France: Film Duemila, 1964.
L'avventura, film, directed by Michelangelo Antonioni. Italy: Cino del Duca, 1960.
L'eclisse, film, directed by Michelangelo Antonioni. Italy/France: Cineriz, Interopa Film, 1962.

La notte, film, directed by Michelangelo Antonioni. Italy: Nepi Film, 1961.
Los felices sesenta / The Happy Sixties, film, directed by Jaime Camino. Spain: Tibidabo Films, 1963.
Noche de verano / Summer Night, film, directed by Jorge Grau. Spain/Italy: David Film, Domiziana Internazionale Cinematografica, 1963.
Nueva cartas a Berta / Nine Letters to Bertha, film, directed by Basilio Martín Patino. Spain: Eco Films, 1966.
Pero, ¿en qué país vivimos? / But, In What Kind of a Country do We Live?, film, directed by José Luis Sáenz de Heredia. Spain: Arturo González Producciones Cinematográficas, 1967.

CHAPTER 4

Sexual Horror Stories: The Eroticisation of Spanish Horror Film (1969–75)

Antonio Lázaro-Reboll

'To talk specifically about erotic cinema in Spain borders almost on the ridiculous', wrote *Nuevo Fotogramas*' film commentator Mr Belvedere (1969: 6) in an article entitled 'España 69: la lenta escalada del erotismo' ('Spain 69: the slow rise of eroticism').[1] At a time when erotic and pornographic films were becoming an important industrial trend and recognised genre category in film industries such as the sexploitation movie circuit in the US (Schaefer 1999, 2014) and the sex films in Scandinavian countries (Larsonn 2010), Mr Belvedere attempted to chart a provisional history of the erotic in Spanish films as a more liberal censorship was establishing itself. '[T]he slow rise of eroticism' therefore must be considered vis-à-vis the political and cultural *apertura* ('opening up') of the 1960s, which in the case of cinema was reflected in the changes to the censorship policies of the *Junta de Clasificación y Censura de Películas Cinematográficas* (Board of Classification and Censorship) in 1962 and in the screening of themes in domestic and international productions that were deemed to be morally controversial (for example, adultery).[2] What might be deemed erotic (or not) by Spanish audiences in late-1960s Spain, Mr Belvedere speculated? '[A] dazzling music hall starlet? An extreme close-up of [Sara] Montiel's lips while singing? Rita Hayworth removing her famous glove in *Gilda*? The ineffable "Helga" [in the 1967 German sex-documentary] giving birth amidst blood, sweat and tears?' (1969: 6). The examples offered by Mr Belvedere place female protagonists as the erotic objects of male desire, and, by extension, presume a male reader and spectator, though of course the forms of popular entertainment, the titles and the names invoked here also lend themselves to camp appropriations and readings. Mr Belvedere surveyed a body of erotic landmarks: before the 1960s, Juan Antonio Bardem's *Muerte de un ciclista*/*Death of a Cyclist* (1955) and *Calle Mayor*/*Main Street* (1956). These films told stories of adultery and sexual repression with foreign female leads (Italian Lucia Bosé in the former and American Betsy Blair in the latter).

The historic 1962 *Bahía de Palma/Bay of Palma* (dir. Juan Bosch) revealed for Spanish audiences the bikini-clad figure of foreign actress Elke Sommer. The works of young directors associated with the *Nuevo Cine Español* of the mid-1960s such as Miguel Picazo's *La tía Tula/Aunt Tula* (1964) and Carlos Saura's *Peppermint frappé* (1967) dealt with 'serious adult topics' (1969: 7). Above all, in the late 1960s the popular comedies of Manuel Summers, whose male protagonists embodied the prototypical 'Iberian repressed man, dazed by an attractive woman', physically and culturally associated with 'the variety show starlet stereotype' (1969: 8), came to epitomise the burgeoning *erotismo de consumo* (consumerist eroticism) (1969: 8) in cinema.[3] Atypical in relation to these trends were two unusual films, *Diferente/Different* (dir. Luis María Delgado, 1962) and *Algo amargo en la boca/Something Bitter in the Mouth* (dir. Eloy de la Iglesia, 1969), as well as two directors, Luis Buñuel and Jesús Franco – an unlikely coupling in histories of Spanish cinema – whose 'ability to handle in depth or at length the topic of the erotic' (1969: 6) represented a different mode of eroticism in contemporary productions. For Mr Belvedere, Delgado's *Diferente* was 'a shrewd film, calculatingly ambiguous, full of homosexual symbols and theses' (1969: 7); de la Iglesia's *Algo amargo en la boca* conveyed an 'omnipresent morbid eroticism' (1969: 7) which permeated the story of three sexually repressed women whose lives and relationships are disrupted when their young distant cousin arrives at their isolated house; Buñuel's *Belle de jour* (1967) was a masterpiece study of erotic fantasies which ought to be included in 'future histories of cinema and eroticism' (1969: 6); and Franco was reaching international audiences with his successful 'formula of comic-erotic-truculent cinema' (1969: 6). The article concluded with the following remarks:

> 1) the *apertura* of Spanish cinema towards eroticism rises slowly at national level, and is seeking the same pleasures pursued by contemporary Italian cinema [...]. 2) Our 'minipornography' is only 'mini' to the extent that nudity is still an insurmountable taboo [...]. 3) Adult topics, the rational approach to an 'eroticism' à la Spanish does not exist, and, for the time being, there are no signs that it is going to happen. (Belvedere 1969: 6)

If I have quoted at length from Mr Belvedere's account of the inclusion of erotic images and sexual storylines in Spanish cinema, it is because it serves here to extend the trends and patterns he identified across a variety of genres and films to the horror genre, which peaked production during the early 1970s. Furthermore, it locates the eroticisation of horror cinema in relation to wider cultural debates concerning the liberalisation of censorship, the commercial exploitation of the erotic in popular genres and the production of a cinema with adult content for Spanish audiences. As an example of contemporary discourses on eroticism in film criticism, 'España 69' shows how Spanish critics and audiences understood and attempted to define the 'erotic', and how the films, trends and names included in the magazine's survey presented differing manifestations of cinematic eroticism.

Initially, this chapter sketches general trends within the genre that blended eroticism and horror. Then, it moves to a discussion of the critical reception of Spanish horror films in the national daily press and in specialist genre magazine *Terror Fantastic* (1971–3) as specific sites where critics and journalists wrote about the eroticisation of the genre. For many cultural commentators (Gubern 1974; Vanaclocha 1974, 1975), the (dis)pleasures associated with the commercial exploitation of eroticism and sexuality in horror films were symptomatic of the repressive socio-cultural situation in Spain. But such readings, I argue, were reductive. The pleasures of horror, or even the pleasures of eroticism in horror, can be read differently if the exploitation and positioning of a film's erotic assets are considered as part of broader production and distribution strategies. Many films were promoted, sold and received not only as horror films but also as commercial vehicles for the erotic appeal of their female leads. Such was the case with *La corrupción de Chris Miller/The Corruption of Chris Miller* (dir. Juan Antonio Bardem, 1973), *Una vela para el diablo/A Candle for the Devil* (dir. Eugenio Martín, 1974) or *El asesino de muñecas/Killing of the Dolls* (dir. Miguel Madrid *aka* Michael Skaife, 1975), where the promotion of the films in the popular press relied on the star reputation of members of the cast.[4] While Marisol and Inma de Santis sought to reinvent themselves from child and teen stars to adult actresses for domestic audiences with *La corrupción de Chris Miller* and *El asesino de muñecas* respectively, Aurora Bautista and Esperanza Roy were involved in a cinematic project designed partly to revitalise their careers and open their work to new audiences. Their erotic appeal could be traced back to previous roles: Bautista as the repressed Aunt Tula in a compelling performance in Picazo's film of the same name, and Roy had been cast regularly in sex-comedies of the late sixties such as *¿Por qué te engaña tu marido?/Why Does Your Husband Deceive You?* (dir. Manuel Summers, 1969). Parallels were drawn in promotional material as well as in reviews with *What Ever Happened to Baby Jane?* (dir. Robert Aldrich, 1962), which had helped to resuscitate the careers of Bette Davis and Joan Crawford. In some instances the promotional tactics and paratexts surrounding a film fostered a plurality of pleasures for its viewers. *El asesino de muñecas* generated interest around the potential romance between Inma de Santis and the male lead David Rocha in popular women's magazines – 'The new couple in Spanish cinema' (*ABC* 1973: 76), announced *ABC* – as well as the pin-up appeal of Rocha for male and female audiences alike.[5] This, together with the controversial nature of the film's subject matter – 'El caso de la doble personalidad sexual'/'The case of the double sexual personality' – makes *El asesino de muñecas* an attractive case study for the exploration of desires. Michael Skaife's film is the object of close analysis in the final section of this chapter, with particular attention paid to the eroticisation of the male body and the inscription of a 'homosexual affect' (Smith 1992: 138) through narrative and stylistic strategies.

TRENDS AND RARITIES IN THE HORROR GENRE

After the commercial success of *La residencia/The House that Screamed* (dir. Narciso Ibáñez Serrador) in 1969 and *La noche de Walpurgis/Werewolf's Shadow* (dir. León Klimovsky) the following year, the horror genre reached its production peak between 1971 and 1975 with over fifty films being released.[6] The boom of the horror film coincided with the tightening of censorship under the directorship of Alfredo Sánchez Bella in the *Ministerio de Información y Turismo* from 1969 to 1974. Working in co-production partnerships with producers notorious for their exploitation of popular genres across Europe – German Adrian Hoven or British Harry Alan Towers – Jesús Franco tapped into commercially successful European industrial and generic trends, blending genres, trafficking in the erotic and confronting domestic and international audiences with active female sexuality. *El caso de las dos bellezas/Rotte Lippen Sadisterotica* and *Bésame, monstruo/Kiss Me, Monster*, both released in 1969, responded to the demand for spy-thrillers in the James Bond mould but featured two sexy female detectives, Diana (Janine Reynaud) and Regina (Rosanna Yanni), driving the narrative forward and resolving the kidnapping and murder of a fashion model. *Las vampiras* (1971), which was one of Franco's contributions to the female vampire subgenre coming out of France and Great Britain, explored the transgressive sexuality of a female vampire embodied in the figure of Franco's muse, Soledad Miranda. The references to lesbianism in the original title, *Vampyros Lesbos*, were censored along with nude scenes before the retitled *Las vampiras* could be exhibited in Spain in 1974. In fact, Franco's brand of horror encountered many problems with the Spanish censors. When Franco's films were distributed abroad, however, the explicit addendum of the erotic and related terms in the title as well as the insertion of soft-core and hard-core footage placed the product in specific exhibition circuits: *El caso de las dos bellezas* became *Rotte Lippen Sadisterotica* and *Las vampiras* was released as *Vampyros Lesbos* for the German market. Within the constraints of what could be shown for a home audience, Franco's products promised 'daring', 'forbidden' or 'taboo' subjects which were duly exploited in the marketing and the publicity. The tag-line for *El caso de las dos bellezas* was 'Two beautiful women who will disclose for you everything you want to see ... or almost all of it'. As for *Las vampiras*, advertising material traded on the eroticism of strip-tease scenarios and sadomasochistic iconography. These are just a few examples of Franco's prolific production, which was a trend in and of itself.

The *erotismo de consumo*, rampant in the comedy genre, soon penetrated the field of horror at the beginning of the 1970s. A range of representative films will suffice to illustrate the commercial exploitation and profitability of eroticism. Since my aim is to identify briefly their erotic dimension, no plot summaries are provided here. Such self-evident titles as *La orgía nocturna de los vampiros/The Vampires Night Orgy* (dir. León Klimovsky, 1973) and *La orgía de los muertos/Terror of the Living Dead* (dir. José Luis Merino, 1974) promised more than they delivered. The former presented some voyeuristic episodes in what was an otherwise conventional horror scenario: a coachload of people on their way to begin work at a stately home are stranded in a remote village, Tolnia, which they soon find is inhabited by the undead, living under the feudal rule of 'La Señora'; the latter film brings together a murder mystery, a mad scientist plot to reanimate the dead, and a gravedigger who is obsessed with death and sexually attracted to female corpses. Other films pitted the forces of tradition against a series of modern elements personified in the bold sexuality of young female characters as a way of introducing the spectacle of eroticism into the horror storyline. In *La noche del terror ciego/Tombs of the Blind Dead* (dir. Amando de Ossorio, 1972), for example, the love relationship between Virginia (María Elena Arpón) and Roger (César Burner) is disturbed by a chance encounter with Virginia's school friend Betty (Lone Fleming), with whom, as conveyed through a flashback, she has had a lesbian liaison; when Betty shows interest in Roger, Virginia gets off the train early and heads towards the abandoned ruins of a monastery where the horror story will start. In *Una vela para el diablo* two sexually frustrated middle-aged sisters, Marta and Verónica, run a guesthouse in a small Andalusian village. Their conservative and puritanical world is upset by young female tourists whose liberal appearance and outlook cross the line of moral (and sexual) decorum. Sexual tensions between characters and repressive environments were common narrative tropes in films that blended horror and eroticism, whether low-budget productions like *Los ojos azules de la muñeca rota/Blue Eyes of the Broken Doll* (dir. Carlos Aured, 1973) or films with considerable financial backing like *La corrupción de Chris Miller*. The former introduces the presence of new caretaker Gilles (Paul Naschy) in an isolated manor house inhabited by three sisters – Claude (Diana Lorys), wheelchair-bound Ivette (Maria Perschy) and Nicole (Eva León) – against the backdrop of a series of murders being committed in the vicinity. The latter, similarly, presents the arrival of a young male drifter, Barney (Barry Stokes), to an all-female household, at the same time that a spate of crimes troubles the region. The conflict between the stepmother (Jean Seberg as Ruth Miller) and her stepdaughter (Pepa Flores as Chris), whom she blames for the departure of her husband, intensifies when Barney becomes the sexual interest for both women. But Ruth sees Barney as another opportunity to destabilise an already psychologically damaged Chris, who is traumatised by her rape when she was younger, and as a means to execute her revenge. Believing that Barney is the killer terrorising the area, Ruth persuades Chris to help her to murder him. Ruth's sexual interest in Chris, as originally conceived by the scriptwriter Santiago Moncada, left the door open for the possibilities of lesbian desire, although Spanish audiences could only read between the lines since these scenes were excised by the censors.

Male chauvinism and machismo were the themes of *La novia ensangrentada/ The Blood Spattered Bride* (1972) by Vicente Aranda, a director associated with the School of Barcelona. Aranda's film is representative of the one-off incursions – not strictly a trend, arguably – of young filmmakers into the genre to provide a critique of the dominant social and sexual mores characteristic of Francoism within the generic and narrative conventions of the horror film. The film's tag-line was bold and risky: 'the first sexual encounter: matrimonial consummation or rape?', splashed in red lettering across the poster image of a bride dressed in virginal white. Of course, the work of Aranda was seriously mutilated by the censors: while the lurid title and the sensationalist tag-line were allowed, the image of the blood-spattered virginal bride and a total of seventeen minutes were cut from the final version, neutralising the sexual and gender dynamics proposed in the script. Another example is Claudio Guerín Hill, an up-and-coming graduate from the *Escuela Oficial de Cine*, who directed *La campana del infierno/Bell of Hell* in 1973, where a young male character confronts his family and the wider village community who clearly symbolise Francoist institutions. The plot establishes the following scenario: Juan (Renaud Verley), who has been kept in a mental institution since the death of his mother, seeks revenge against his aunt Marta (Viveca Lindfords), whom he believes has inherited his will, and his three cousins María (Christine Betzner), Teresa (Núria Gimeno) and Esther (Maribel Martín). Juan not only embodies liberal sexual mores but also uses his sexual allure to seduce and play the sisters against each other as part of his revenge.

The horror genre also allowed some directors to display distinct homosexual sensibilities in the late years of Francoism. Such was the case of Eloy de la Iglesia whose productions in the early 1970s upset Spanish censors and critics alike with his stories of sexual horror. In 'España 69' Mr Belvedere detected 'morbid eroticism' as a key aesthetic and thematic feature in de la Iglesia's *Algo amargo en la boca*, where the main protagonist César (Juan Diego) becomes the object of desire of two of his distant cousins (Clementina (Irene Daina) and Aurelia (Maruchi Fresno)) and their niece Ana (Verónica Luján), whom he visits one Christmas. César enters a claustrophobic and oppressive environment in which personal histories and sexual perversions define the repressions of the house's inhabitants: Aurelia fetishises the military uniform of her dead fiancé; Ana has left the convent and is rediscovering her sexuality; Clementina hides her nymphomaniac tendencies, which are left unsaid; and Jacobo (Javier de Campos), a mentally retarded family servant, spies at the women through keyholes. Through the desiring gaze and the active sexuality of the three women, de la Iglesia goes against the conventional representation of women as objects of desire, which populated the *erotismo de consumo* products, and transfers the objectification onto the body of César. César is the sexual temptation that needs to be banished in order to restore normality to the house. In the original script it is the women who kill César, but the censors demanded a different ending, whereby Jacobo becomes the executioner. De la Iglesia's crude and dark depictions of sex and violence, as well as those moments of visual pleasure in the eroticisation of the male body, would be trademark traits intensified in subsequent films: *El techo de cristal/The Glass Ceiling* (1971), *La semana del asesino/Cannibal Man* (1972), *Nadie oyó gritar/No One Heard the Scream* (1972) and *Una gota de sangre para morir amando/Murder in a Blue World* (1973) (see 'The Horror Cycle of Eloy de la Iglesia' in Lázaro-Reboll 2012: 127–55). As I will argue in my reading of *El asesino de muñecas*, Skaife displayed similar moments of visual excess in his juxtaposition of eroticism and violence.

'BLOOD, HORROR AND SEX': ROUTINISED CRITICAL HABITUS

Having sketched the dominant production trends which exploited eroticism through the lens of the horror genre, I now move to a discussion of the adverse critical reception of many films whose increasing blending of eroticism and horror did not meet the artistic decorum and expectations of reviewers and scholars. Elsewhere I have argued that the most frequent negative criticism levelled at horror films of this period is that they were 'mindless, repetitious fodder for the masses' (Lázaro-Reboll 2012: 25) and that the narratives ought to be read 'as reflections of social (read sexual) repression' (2012: 25). In the context of this volume devoted to Spanish erotic cinema, my interest in this chapter, however, is to zoom into the language and the images used by contemporary critics to describe and contend with the erotic in these films, and, more specifically, their exploitation of *erotismo de consumo*. Their discursive practices must be put into their wider cultural and historical context where this concept, that is, *erotismo de consumo*, circulated widely in different types of publications accounting for the exploitation of eroticism in the mass media. Medical experts and philosophers dwelled on the topic in books such as *Sexualidad y represión* (Carlos Castilla del Pino 1971), a Freudo-Marxist approach to understanding the mechanisms of sexual and social repression, and *Erotismo y liberación de la mujer* (José Luis Aranguren 1972), which argued that the forces of conservatism were using eroticism as a narcotic for the masses and presented the younger generation with a dilemma, either eroticisation or politicisation. The pervasiveness of erotic imagery in advertising and cinema became a burning topic in the editorials and the religion sections of the daily press, as a search in the digital archives of major dailies *ABC* and *La vanguardia española* for the period 1970 to 1975 reveals: in its coverage of the 1970 Spanish Episcopal General Assembly, *La vanguardia española* endorsed the words of Monsignor Morcillo censuring 'the surge of eroticism spattering our streets, soiling the world of advertising and swamping our entertainment industry' (*La vanguardia española* 1970: 7); *ABC*'s editorials in 1975 provided Cardinal Tarancón with a platform from which to wage his war against pornography ('Guerra a la pornografía'), declaring that 'the current displays of depravity place Spain at the border of a moral abyss [...] This is the time to contain the torrent of pornography affecting Spain, before it pollutes all spheres of our lives' (*ABC* 1975: 7). From a very different perspective, the Spanish weekly cultural and political magazine *Triunfo* contributed to shaping discourses around eroticism with a monograph on 'El erotismo y España' ('Eroticism and Spain') (September 1970). 'Interior repression, self-repression', noted the editorial, 'is the essential habit of Spanish eroticism' (*Triunfo* 1970: 24). The minds and bodies of Spaniards had been shaped – and continued to be shaped – by censorship and self-censorship, Catholic morals and traditions. *Triunfo* also published several articles on cinema and eroticism by film critics, among them Gubern (1974) and Vanaclocha (1975).[7] Concurrent to their contributions to *Triunfo*, these two authors would play a significant role in framing and fixing readings of *erotismo de consumo* in relation to contemporary popular genres in the volume *Cine de género, cine de subgéneros* (1974), Gubern authoring the 'Foreword' and Vanaclocha providing an analysis of contemporary sex-comedies.[8]

Reviews of *La noche del terror ciego* captured the themes that would be recurrent – almost formulaic – in descriptions and evaluations of horror products. Some reduced the formula to its basic constituents, as the *Pueblo* review subtitle did: 'Blood, horror and sex' (*Pueblo* 1972). The blending of horror and eroticism yielded a baffling 'mixing of bikinis and shrouds, monastic skeletons and sculptural women' (1972). *La vanguardia española* stated that the director de Ossorio had 'found the effective formula to attract contemporary viewers [to the genre]' by adding 'doses of eroticism' to the mix (Maso 1972: 46). *Nuevo Diario* criticised the 'excessive gratuitousness' (1972) in some of the episodes. It 'is one of those films', wrote *El Álcazar*, '[that] satisfies the appetites of a certain type of spectator who rummages for erotic scenes no matter where' (Martialay 1972). The forays of more reputable directors into the genre were also criticised along the same lines. Guerín Hill's *La campana del infierno* 'could have been a respectable horror and suspense film', according to *Ya*, but '[it] is full of truculence, sadism, blood and erotic aberrancies' (Cebollada 1973). Examples are copious, but these references are clearly indicative of the common 'habitus' of film critics, used here in the Bourdieuan sense of 'a set of dispositions which generate practices and perceptions' (Johnson 1993: 5).

Similar views are to be found in the pages of *Terror Fantastic*. The editors coined the term *sexi-terror-show* to describe those horror film products destined to be exported to international circuits of exhibition and consumption. *Terror Fantastic* showed its disapproval of censorship practices as well as the double standards of an industry exporting 'hot' versions in which 'the skin of our "stars" is exhibited in abundance through the most "artistic" poses and angles one can imagine' (1973a: 7). The *sexi-terror-show* brand of horror was leading to 'the gradual death of the horror film' and 'increasingly giving way to what is only a purely erotic cinema with horror titles' (1973b: 7). *Terror Fantastic* called for 'the use of an instructive eroticism, which justifies itself for clear artistic reasons' (1973b: 7) and condemned the unwarranted insertion of erotic content: 'gratuitous eroticism is unacceptable' (1973b: 7). The editorial did not shed light on what they understood by 'instructive eroticism'. One can only speculate and turn the gaze to foreign territories in which secular, liberal attitudes to eroticism and sexuality were being represented on screen, and not necessarily through the horror genre. The more 'literary' (and therefore respectable) sexual teachings associated with the filmic adaptations of *Emmanuelle* (Just Jaeckin 1974)? The sex-instructional films produced in Germany or Scandinavia? Or, simply, the possibility of representing narratives and characters free of the burden of repression?

It is not surprising that the first scholarly responses to the phenomenon of *erotismo de consumo* in popular genre production echoed the set of negative responses outlined above. The Equipo 'Cartelera Turia' (Company, de Mata Moncho, Vanaclocha and Vergara) co-authored the volume *Cine español, cine de subgéneros* (*Spanish Cinema, A Cinema of Subgenre Films*), which legitimated theoretically and ideologically such critical dispositions. In its 'Foreword' Gubern provided a framework for the chapters that followed on horror (*sub-terror hispano*), westerns (*spaghetti westerns*), musicals (*musical español*) and comedies (*cine sexy celtibérico*) to read the production and the consumption of these films symptomatically as sublimations of repressed and unsatisfied sexual needs, which had an exorcising and gratifying function. Popular genres, whether musicals or horror films, functioned as indexes of repressed social meaning. For Gubern,

> There is no difference between Manolo Escobar and Dracula apart from narrative contexts and conventions, since the *mitogenia* of these products

derives with mathematical precision from frustrated collective appetites, whereby the libido and the desire for power occupy a central role (replicating the real lacks of the viewer), disguised under protean masks (be it violence, dominance, social mobility, cruelty, sentimentalism). (1974: 15)

Gubern not only distanced himself intellectually from these products and their audiences but he also marked a physical detachment: '[I am]', he confessed, 'a very occasional consumer of Spanish subgenre products. [Only] the insistence of Terenci Moix has dragged me to the box-office. Terenci Moix adores these products because he submits them to a rigorously camp reading' (1974: 11). Moix had been giving voice to gay sensibilities in camp readings of international film stars – Barbara Steele, among others – in the pages of *Terror Fantastic* and 'the iconic stars of Hollywood and Spanish musicals and melodramas' (Triana-Toribio 2014: 459) in *Nuevo Fotogramas*. But Gubern himself closed down the potential for multiple readings and camp positions. What follows is a camp reading of *El asesino de muñecas*.

EL ASESINO DE MUÑECAS

Admittedly, camp is a notoriously problematic concept to determine. Tensions between 'camp as a product of queers' experiences and perceptions and camp as a discourse available to all' (Medhurst 1997: 279) have been central to its circulation as a critical discourse since the publication of Susan Sontag's 'Notes on Camp' (1964). Here it is understood as a stylistic strategy, 'that favors "exaggeration", "artificiality" and "extremity"' and that is 'affiliated with homosexual culture, or at least with a self-conscious eroticism that throws into question the naturalisation of desire' (Bergman 1993: 5). In 'Camp and the Gay Sensibility' (1977) Jack Babuscio observed that the horror genre 'is susceptible to a camp interpretation' (1993: 23), in particular those films which 'make the most of stylish conventions for expressing [...] subjective fantasies [...] instant feelings, thrills [...] outrageous and "unacceptable" sentiments' (1993: 23). The interaction between camp and horror is also noted by LaValley: 'Gays understand in horror films the duality of their own emotional lives, the straight social mask they are often compelled to wear and beneath it the illegitimate strong sexual desires that constitute their real self' (1995: 66). And, as Harry Benshoff reminds us in *Monsters in the Closet: Homosexuality and the Horror Film*, from the 1950s onwards the genre increasingly used the 'popular [...] construction of homosexuality as a psychiatric illness' (1997: 178).

El asesino de muñecas perplexed most contemporary critics. Martínez Tomás in *La vanguardia española* defined it as 'a tremulous, frustrating and excessive film', close at times to the 'the delirious and the spasmodic' (1975: 55). López Sancho, in a review entitled 'Surrealism and confusion' for *ABC*, concluded that *El asesino de muñecas* was an 'anxious film' whose plot was incongruous, 'a load of nonsense impossible to interpret' (1975). The language used by these critics conveyed not only their bafflement with Skaife's film but also the film's affective and excessive qualities.[9] What did critics find perplexing, then? And wherein laid the excess and the affect of the film? Counter to the formulaic nature of other low-brow products, Skaife used the genre as a vehicle to tell a different (sexual) horror story. Moreover, counter to the preponderance of heterosexual imagery and, at times, the male chauvinistic eroticism shown in many contemporary horror films, the film flaunted its camp sensibilities unashamedly and intimated a homosexuality that could not be openly conveyed in the narrative. The film's playful theatricality, its moments of spectacle (aestheticised violence, self-conscious eroticism and a musical number) and its generic artificiality lend themselves to a camp reading steeped in gay sensibility, both at the level of style and of spectatorial reception.

The film tells the story of a young man, Paul (David Rocha), traumatised by the memories of his childhood. After the death of his sister, his mother started to dress him as a girl and made him play with his sister's dolls. The trauma is manifested in his double personality condition. When Paul fails in his ambitions to become a heart surgeon, he returns to the stately home in Montpellier where his parents work as gardeners. As soon as he arrives, Paul attracts the attention of his parents' employer, Countess Olivia (Helga Liné), who will try to seduce him. But Paul falls for her daughter Audrey (Inma de Santis). Paul suffers recurrent psychotic episodes in which his 'other' personality takes control, changing him into a murderous criminal. As Paul the assassin, he dons a doll's mask, a wig and a doctor's scrub, and speaks in an effeminate voice (both the psychological disorder and elements of Paul's characterisation visibly mirror Norman Bates in *Psycho* (dir. Alfred Hitchcock, 1960)). From the opening sequences, the film makes clear that Paul is responsible for the murders being committed within the house grounds. His victims are young women who have trespassed the gardens to engage in sexual acts with their boyfriends. Paul's morbid obsessions with dolls and mannequins, the haunting reflections in the mirror of the sister as his alter ego,[10] and the apparitions of his mother in traumatic flashbacks, are constant reminders of his double personality. Unable to control his murderous impulses, he kills Audrey. The film ends with Paul in the midst of a delirious episode setting a mannequin on fire while the 'The End' credits disappear dramatically into his gaping mouth.

Like Hitchcock in the *Alfred Hitchcock Presents* TV series (CBS, 1955–65), or Narciso Ibáñez Serrador in *Historias para no dormir* (TVE, 1966–8), Skaife prefaced the horror story to be told in the pre-credit sequence. '*El asesino de muñecas*', observed Skaife talking directly to the camera after having methodi-

Figure 4.1 Michael Skaife in *El asesino de muñecas/Killing of the Dolls*, directed by Miguel Madrid (*aka* Michael Skaife). Spain: Huracán Films S.A, 1975.

cally dismembered a doll, 'is the self-analysis of a psychopath whose mental illness is based on one of the most common concerns of criminal psychopathology: the drama of the double personality'. As his name appears on the screen, 'Michael Skaife presenta' (see Figure 4.1), the camera pans to his right to focus on the theatrical opening of curtains, which disclose the lead actor David Rocha seated on a chair in a contemplative pose while holding a mannequin's head within a mannequins' workshop. The double personality motif is firmly established: Rocha as the director's alter ego, and the mannequin's head as an extension of the main character's self.

The cinematic portrayal of a psychotic killer perpetrating acts of sexualised violence in contemporary settings places Skaife's film in dialogue with the Italian *giallo*. Extreme psychological states of mind, masked criminals, creepy mannequins and baroque *mise en scène* were common conventions in the genre. But, unlike the psychotic killers who populated the *gialli*, the titular assassin in *El asesino de muñecas* is undraped from the very beginning. Like Norman Bates in *Psycho*, Paul is a character tormented by a domineering mother. Rocha's physique and performance may have reminded some viewers of Anthony Perkins. Further horror credentials were closer to home. Names in the cast and the technical crew, as well as the promotional material produced by illustrator Jano, well known for his visual contribution to many a horror poster of the period, linked *El asesino de muñecas* to other Spanish horror products.[11] But the cinematic lineage I am interested in drawing here is with Luis María Delgado's *Diferente*, which Mr Belvedere had described in his 'España 69' as an 'utterly remarkable erotic film' (1969: 7), and which could be regarded as a cinematic antecedent of *El asesino de muñecas* in its approach to eroticism and submerged homosexuality. There are a number of narrative and stylistic similarities between the two films. If choreographer Alfredo (Alfredo Alaría) stood symbolically for Delgado, Paul can be read as Skaife's alter ego. In terms of characterisation, Paul fails to fulfil the academic expectations of his parents in the same way that Alfredo is seen as a failure by his bourgeois family. Equally, the presence of young female characters as love interests has the same function in both films, that is, the heterosexual relationship as a 'cure'. 'I never found myself in a situation like this and I don't know how to act', says Paul when he is alone with Audrey in his room. Stylistically, *Diferente* is punctuated by dream-like scenes and the irruption of musical numbers in the diegesis, a strategy also deployed in Skaife's film. The intertwining of reality and fantasy illuminates the inner desires of the character. In contrast to *Diferente*, which 'avoids the pathological characterisation' (Mira 2004: 352) of Alfredo, *El asesino de muñecas* presents 'the case of double sexual personality', that is, homosexuality, as an illness or sexual disorder.

And yet, like *Diferente*, *El asesino de muñecas* did not deal explicitly with homosexuality, for this was not possible during the Francoist period. The inscription of a distinct homosexual affect operated through *mise en scène*, cinematography and editing. Rocha's acting style and performance characterised by emotional intensity, affectedness and androgynous qualities – accentuated by his outfits and his haircut – would have struck a chord with male viewers attuned to camp. When Paul sees Audrey for the first time, coming down a stately staircase, the camera stays with Paul while he is voluptuously drenched by a hose he is holding. In these scenes, as well as in other exterior shots, the colour film process used for the film, Gevacolor, produced an effect of intense saturation. Cinematographically, the film openly and repeatedly eroticised and sexualised Paul's (and Rocha's) body: close-ups and medium close-ups convey his state of mind and the photogenic qualities of the actor; the composition of shots and the framing of some scenes function as moments of spectacularisation of the desirable male body; and point-of-view shots convey a lingering gaze fetishising different parts of his body, as in the shower scenes (see Figure 4.2), which follow those episodes where Paul has committed a murder. The film's promotional posters also exploited Rocha's pin-up appeal with the tagline 'David Rocha (naked/reveals everything) in a case of double sexual personality'.[12] These are instances of a deliberate textual and stylistic construction on the part of Skaife to display the male body. In *El asesino de muñecas* the mustering of a camp aesthetic and the equation of a psychotic condition with homosexuality elucidate a gay sensibility.

This chapter set out to map the increasing eroticisation of the Spanish horror film between 1969 and 1975. The blending of horror and eroticism responded not only to the demands of an international market where more daring and

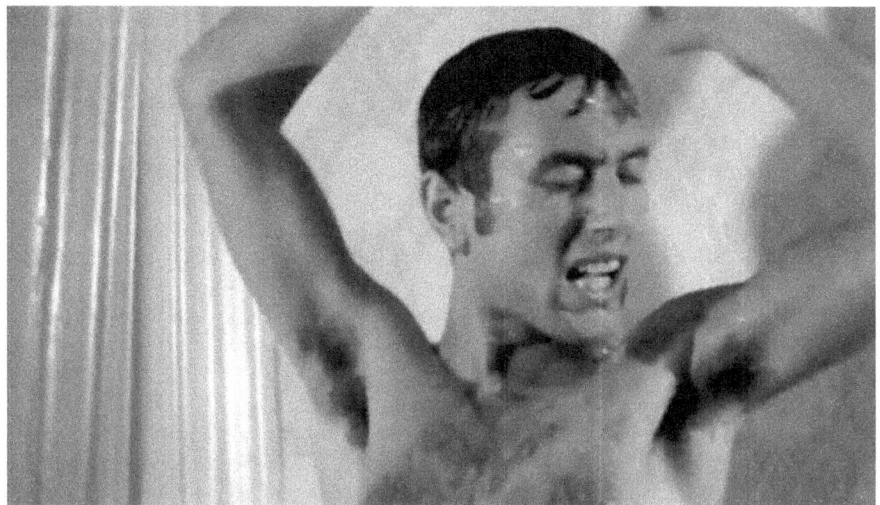

Figure 4.2 David Rocha in *El asesino de muñecas / Killing of the Dolls*, directed by Miguel Madrid (*aka* Michael Skaife). Spain: Huracán Films S.A., 1975.

explicit images of sex circulated in territories with more 'liberal' attitudes but also to the upsurge of *erotismo de consumo* in a country marked by the realities of the dictatorship – censorship, Catholic morality and repression – and by the socio-economic transformations of a fast-developing consumerist society. The *erotismo de consumo* as an economic and cultural phenomenon shaped production trends within the horror genre, as well as the critical reception of films in mainstream film criticism and pioneering studies. As a discussion of the critical habitus of reviewers has illustrated, repression came to epitomise the textual and ideological schema of local horror production. However, films like *El asesino de muñecas* confounded critics and exceeded their reading protocols. In Skaife's film the irruption of alternative meanings via textual and stylistic strategies and the unrestrained exhibition of the eroticised deviant body allow for the representation of and identification with other horror pleasures. As a proto-erotic precursor of films to come during the early years of democracy with the creation of the category 'S' and the emerging soft-core pornography films, *El asesino de muñecas* articulated *avant la lettre* erotic sensibilities whose direct treatment was unimaginable within contemporary Francoist structures of censorship and repression.

NOTES

1. As Núria Triana-Toribio has noted, Mr Belvedere was, and still is, a fictional character 'named after Gwen Davenport's homonymous novel of 1946, which appeared in film version as *Sitting Pretty* (Walter Lang), and was released in Spain as *Niñera moderna*'

(2014: 469). Mr Belvedere wrote articles and watched over the letters section where he 'offered his opinion on contemporary releases and classics, and satisfied the curiosity of cinephiles' (2014: 469). This piece was the final part of a four-part series framed under the title 'El cine ¿en busca de una nueva moral?' ('Cinema: the quest for new moral values?'), in which Mr Belvedere provided the readers of *Nuevo Fotogramas* with a view of the ways in which changing sexual mores were reflected in European and world cinema traditions. Part I appeared in issue 1078 (13 June), Part II, about Scandinavian cinema, in issue 1079 (20 June) and Part III in issue 1080 (27 June).
2. The official decree was approved by the Ministry of Information and Tourism on 20 September 1962.
3. Other European film industries had similar sex-comedy traditions, such as the German *sexklamotte* or the Italian sex comedies produced by Dania Films.
4. *La corrupción de Chris Miller* was the most commercially successful of these three films, attracting 1.2 million spectators and making 377,102 euros. *Una vela para el diablo* was also fairly profitable with almost 100,000 euros and over 400,000 spectators. And *El asesino de muñecas* was viewed by 244,972 with takings of 72,587 euros at the box office. All figures consulted at the Instituto de la Cinematografía y de las Artes Audiovisuales (ICAA) website.
5. Women's weekly magazine *Ama*, for example, turned its attention to a possible romance ('Romance with David Rocha?' (*Ama* 1973)).
6. According to the ICAA, there were six horror films produced in 1971, 13 in 1972, 14 in 1973, 8 in 1974 and 12 in 1975.
7. Here Vanaclocha brought together National Catholic manuals, contemporary academic writings on eroticism, and the censorship norms of 1963 and 1975 to explain the cultural, ideological, political and psychoanalytical factors that affected Spanish 'erotic' cinema.
8. The lasting legacy of their work for subsequent readings of Spanish popular genres has been analysed in detail by Beck and Rodríguez-Ortega (2008: 5–8) and Lázaro-Reboll (2012: 27–30).
9. Historians of Spanish horror film have resorted to similar language to define the film. Aguilar describes it as a 'deranged misogynist/homosexual manifesto' (1999: 40), whereas Sala writes that it is 'a pop-gay-perverse delirium' (2010: 151).
10. The physical, emotional and psychological closeness to his sister is further emphasised through the casting of David Rocha's real-life sister playing the role of the fictional sister.
11. Helga Liné had participated, among other films, in *El espanto surge de la tumba/Horror Rises From the Tomb* (dir. Carlos Aured, 1973), José Lifante in *No profanar el sueño de los muertos/The Living Dead at Manchester Morgue* (dir. Jorge Grau, 1974). Cinematographer Pablo Ripoll had worked in *La noche del terror ciego*, whereas Luis Puigvert had been the editor of the Spanish giallo *Jack el destripador de Londres/Seven Murders for Scotland Yard* (dir. José Luis Madrid, 1971).
12. The Spanish physique magazine *Deporte y Salud* published an article on David Rocha with photos in which he is posing as a young striking model practically naked in swimwear (Lizondo Martínez 1974).

REFERENCES

ABC "Blanco y Negro" (1973), 'Nueva pareja del cine español', 8 September 1973, 76.
ABC "Blanco y Negro" (1975), 'Guerra a la pornografía', 22 November 1975, 7.

Aguilar, Carlos (ed.) (1999), *Cine fantástico y de terror español: 1900–1983*, San Sebastián: Donostia Kultura.
Ama (1973), 'Catorce años, quince películas. Inma de Santis, ¿Romance con David Rocha?', October 1973, 333, 59–60.
Aranguren, José (1972), *Erotismo y liberación de la mujer*, Barcelona: Ariel.
Babuscio, Jack (1993 [1977]), 'Camp and the Gay Sensibility', in D. Bergman (ed.), *Camp Grounds, Style and Homosexuality*, Amherst: University of Massachusetts Press, pp. 19–38.
Beck, Jay and Vicente Rodríguez-Ortega (2008), 'Introduction', in J. Beck and V. Rodríguez-Ortega, *Contemporary Spanish Cinema and Genre*, Manchester: Manchester University Press, pp. 1–23.
Belvedere, Mr (1969), 'España 69: La lenta escalada del erotismo', *Nuevo Fotogramas*, 1081, 4 July 1969, 6–9.
Benshoff, Harry (1997), *Monsters in the Closet: Homosexuality and the Horror Film*, Manchester: Manchester University Press.
Bergman, David (ed.) (1993), *Camp Grounds, Style and Homosexuality*, Amherst: University of Massachusetts Press.
Castilla del Pino, Carlos (1971), *Sexualidad y represión*, Madrid: Ayuso.
Cebollada, Pascual (1973), 'La campana del infierno', *Ya*, 4 October 1973.
Equipo 'Cartelera Turia' (1974), *Cine español, cine de subgéneros*, Valencia: Fernando Torres Editor.
Gubern, Román (1974), 'Prólogo', in *Cine español, cine de subgéneros*, Equipo 'Cartelera Turia' (eds), Valencia: Fernando Torres Editor, pp. 9–16.
Johnson, Randal (1993), 'Editor's Introduction. Pierre Bourdieu on Art, Literature and Culture', in P. Bourdieu, *The Field of Cultural Production*, Cambridge: Polity Press, pp. 1–25.
Larsson, Mariah (2010), 'Practice Makes Perfect? The Production of the Swedish Sex Film in the 1970s', *Film International*, 8:6, 40–9.
LaValley, Al (1995), 'The Great Escape', in C. K. Creekmur and A. Doty (eds), *Culture, Gay, Lesbian and Queer Essays on Popular Culture*, Durham, NC: Duke University Press, pp. 60–70.
La vanguardia española (1970), 'Apertura de la XIII Asamblea Plenaria del Episcopado', 1 December, 7.
Lázaro-Reboll, Antonio (2012), *Spanish Horror Film*, Edinburgh: Edinburgh University Press.
Lizondo Martínez, Miguel (1974), 'David Rocha: Un salvaje genial', *Deporte y Salud* 24, 4–13.
López Sancho, Lorenzo (1975), 'Surrealismo y barullo en "El asesino de muñecas"', *ABC*, 17 July 1975.
Martialay, Félix (1972), 'La noche del terror ciego', *El Álcazar*, 15 April 1972.
Martínez Tomás, A. (1975), 'El asesino de muñecas', *La vanguardia española*, 6 February 1975, 55.
Maso, Ángeles (1972), 'La noche del terror ciego', *La vanguardia española*, 20 September 1972, 46.
Medhurst, Andy (1997), 'Camp', in A. Medhurst and S. R. Munt (eds), *Lesbian and Gay Studies. A Critical Introduction*, London: Cassell, pp. 274–93.
Mira, Alberto (2004), *De Sodoma a Chueca. Una historia cultural de la homosexualidad en España en el siglo XX*, Barcelona: Editorial Egales.
Pueblo (1972), 'Sangre, terror y sexo', 2 May 1972.
Sala, Carlos (2010), *La historia jamás contada del cine fantástico español. Profanando el sueño de los muertos*, Villagarcía de Arousa: Scifiworld.

Schaefer, Eric (1999), *'Bold! Daring! Shocking! True!' A History of the American Exploitation Film*, Durham, NC and London: Duke University Press.
Schaefer, Eric (ed.) (2014), *Sex Scenes. Media and the Sexual Revolution*, Durham, NC and London: Duke University Press.
Smith, Paul Julian (1992), *Laws of Desire. Questions of Homosexuality in Spanish Writing and Film 1960–1990*, Oxford: Clarendon Press.
Sontag, Susan (1966 [1964]), 'Notes on Camp', *Against Interpretation and Other Essays*, New York: Dell, pp. 277–93.
Terror Fantastic (1973a), '¿Cine español de exportación?', 19: 7.
Terror Fantastic (1973b), 'Erotismo en el terror' 20: 7.
Triana-Toribio, Núria (2014), 'Film Cultures in Spain's Transition: the "Other" transition in the film magazine *Nuevo Fotogramas* (1968–1978)', *Journal of Spanish Cultural Studies*, 15:4, 455-74.
Triunfo (1970), 'El erotismo en España', *Triunfo* 434, 26 September 1970, 24.
Vanaclocha, José (1974), 'El cine sexy celtibérico', in *Cine español, cine de subgéneros*, Equipo 'Cartelera Turia' (eds), Valencia: Fernando Torres Editor, pp. 193–284.
Vanaclocha, José (1975), 'Entre la represión y el destape. Cine "erótico" en España', *Triunfo* 673, 23 August 1975, 22–5.

FILMOGRAPHY

Alfred Hitchcock Presents, TV series, directed by Alfred Hitchcock. USA: CBS, 1955–65.
Algo amargo en la boca/Something Bitter in the Mouth, film, directed by Eloy de la Iglesia. Spain: Acción Films, 1969.
Bahía de Palma/Bay of Palma, film, directed by Juan Bosch. Spain: Este Films, 1962.
Belle de jour, film, directed by Luis Buñuel. France/Italy: Paris Film Production and Five Film, 1967.
Bésame monstruo/Kiss Me Monster, film, directed by Jesús Franco. Spain/West Germany: Films Montana and Águila Films, 1969.
Calle Mayor/Main Street, film, directed by Juan Antonio Bardem. Spain/France: Cesareo González Producciones Cinematográficas, Play Art, Iberia Films, 1956.
Diferente/Different, film, directed by Luis María Delgado. Spain: Águila Films, 1962.
El asesino de muñecas/Killing of the Dolls, film, directed by Miguel Madrid (*aka* Michael Skaife). Spain: Huracán Films S.A., 1975.
El caso de las dos bellezas/Rotte Lippen, Sadiserotica, film, directed by Jesús Franco. Spain: Films Montana, Águila Films, 1969.
El espanto surge de la tumba/Horror Rises from the Tomb, film, directed by Carlos Aured. Spain: Profilmes, 1973.
El techo de cristal/The Glass Ceiling, film, directed by Eloy de la Iglesia. Spain: Fono España, 1971.
Emmanuelle, film, directed by Just Jaeckin. France: Tinacra Films, Orphée Films, 1974.
Gilda, film, directed by Charles Vidor. USA: Columbia Pictures, 1946.
Helga Vom Werden des menschlichen lebens/Helga, the Intimate Life of a Young Woman, film, directed by Eric F. Bender. West Germany: Rinco Films, 1967.
Historias para no dormir/Stories to Keep You Awake, TV series, directed by Narciso Ibáñez Serrador, Spain: TVE, 1966–8.

Jack el destripador de Londres/Seven Murders for Scotland Yard, film, directed by José Luis Madrid. Italy/Spain: International Apollo Films, Cinefilms, 1971.

La campana del infierno/Bell of Hell, film, directed by Claudio Guerín Hill. Spain/France: Hesperia Films S.A., Les Films La Boétie, 1973.

La corrupción de Chris Miller/The Corruption of Chris Miller, film, directed by Juan Antonio Bardem. Spain: Xavier Armet Producciones Cinematográficas, 1973.

La noche del terror ciego/Tombs of the Blind Dead, film, directed by Amando de Ossorio. Spain/Portugal: Plate Films S.A., Interfilm, 1972.

La noche de Walpurgis/Werewolf's Shadow, film, directed by León Klimovsky. Spain/West Germany: Plata Films S.A., Hi-Fi Stereo 70, 1970.

La novia ensangrentada/The Blood Spattered Bride, film, directed by Vicente Aranda. Spain: Morgana Films, 1972.

La orgía de los muertos/Terror of the Living Dead, film, directed by José Luis Merino. Spain/Italy: Petruka Films S.A., Prodimex Films, 1974.

La orgía nocturna de los vampiros/The Vampires Night Orgy, film, directed by León Klimovsky. Spain: José Fradé Producciones Cinematográficas, 1973.

La residencia/The House that Screamed, film, directed by Narciso Ibáñez Serrador. Spain: Annabel Films S.A., 1969.

La semana del asesino/Cannibal Man, film, directed by Eloy de la Iglesia. Spain: José Truchado Producciones Cinematográficas, 1972.

La tía Tula/Aunt Tula, film, directed by Miguel Picazo. Spain: Eco Films S.A., Surco Films S.A., 1964.

Las vampiras/Vampyros Lesbos, film, directed by Jesús Franco. Spain/West Germany: Cooperativa Cinematográfica Fénix, Telecine Film, CCC Film, 1971.

Los ojos azules de la muñeca rota/Blue Eyes of the Broken Doll, film, directed by Carlos Aured. Spain: Profilmes, 1973.

Muerte de un ciclista/Death of a Cyclist, film, directed by Juan Antonio Bardem. Spain/Italy: Suevia Films, Trionfalcine, 1955.

Nadie oyó gritar/No One Heard the Scream, film, directed by Eloy de la Iglesia. Spain: PICASA/Benito Perojo S.A., 1972.

No profanar el sueño de los muertos/The Living Dead at Manchester Morgue, film, directed by Jorge Grau. Italy/Spain: Flaminia Prodizioni Cinematografiche, Star Films S.A., 1974.

Peppermint frappé, film, directed by Carlos Saura. Spain: Elías Querejeta Producciones Cinematográficas, 1967.

¿Por qué te engaña tu marido?/Why Does Your Husband Deceive You?, film, directed by Manuel Summers. Spain: Impala, Kalender Films International, 1969.

Psycho, film, directed by Alfred Hitchcock. USA: Shamley Productions, 1960.

Una gota de sangre para morir amando/Murder in a Blue World, film, directed by Eloy de la Iglesia. Spain/France: José Fradé Producciones Cinematográficas, Intercontinental Productions, 1973.

Una vela para el diablo/A Candle for the Devil, film, directed by Eugenio Martín. Spain: Vega Films S.A., Mercofilms, 1974.

What Ever Happened to Baby Jane?, film, directed by Robert Aldrich. USA: Associate and Aldrich Company, Seven Arts Pictures, Warner Bros, 1962.

CHAPTER 5

Undressing Opus Dei: Reframing the Political Currency of *Destape* Films

Jorge Pérez

Two-thirds of the way into Pedro Almodóvar's *Los amantes pasajeros* (2013), the three campy stewards played by Carlos Areces, Raúl Arévalo and Javier Cámara beg Norma (Cecilia Roth), a celebrity passenger in the business class section of the aircraft in which they work, to tell them the story of her professional success. Flattered by the request, Norma elucidates that she began as a *destape* film star back in the early 1980s, although her fame came when she appeared naked on the cover of the magazine *Interviú*.[1] Aware of her limited aptitude as an actress, Norma realised that she had a talent for bondage and, thus, became a top-notch dominatrix of Spain's most powerful men. Among her many sex slaves, Norma claims, were members of Opus Dei and the armed forces. Viewers who are familiar with present-day Spain may read this scene as a play on notorious sex scandals of public figures.[2] Those who are also conversant with the history of Spanish cinema may additionally evoke a recurrent pattern in the filmic representations of the religious organisation Opus Dei that appeared in the first years of the transition to democracy. Films such as *La trastienda/The Backroom* (dir. Jorge Grau, 1976), *Cara al sol que más calienta/Facing the Warmest Sun* (dir. Jesús Yagüe, 1977) and *La escopeta nacional/The National Shotgun* (dir. Luis García Berlanga, 1978) featured Opus Dei characters who belonged to the economic and political elites and who became involved in a sexual scandal depicted with large doses of eroticism.

The purpose of this essay is to examine these pioneering representations of Opus Dei to which Almodóvar pays homage. To do so, I need to situate them within the *destape* subgenre popular in that period and, thereby, within the polarised debate about its political implications (whether *destape* was liberating or conservative). The *destape* phenomenon is intrinsic to the history of Spanish cinema and is characterised by the over-provision of sexual images without any apparent narrative intention. Some have seen the *destape* boom as 'a strong indication that the *Franquista* moral order was breaking down' (Kowalsky 2004: 190), so the shift from the sexual repression of Francoism to the sexual obsession of the *destape* era was expected and healthy (Umbral 1976: 56), as it provided a much-needed sexual catharsis for Spanish society (Ponce 2004: 11; Freixas and Bassa 2005: 177). However, other film scholars see the *destape* in negative terms as a marketing strategy and an escapist channel to divert audiences from political concerns while simultaneously helping to reinforce retrograde gender stereotypes (Besas 1985: 93; Hopewell 1986: 79; Jordan and Morgan-Tamosunas 1998: 113; Stone 2002: 184).

Although the contours of that debate provide a backdrop for my discussion, my argument is that it is time to reframe it. The polarising nature of this conversation has reached a point of critical fatigue and needs to be reframed beyond the disjunctive choice between a celebratory and a condemnatory approach. Otherwise, the discussion is limited to asking a question that merely requires an either/or response, and which distributes contributors into pro and con camps. Also, by assuming an all-embracing position on either side of the binary, scholars of Spanish cinema are precluding the kind of contextualised examination that could lead to a better understanding of the politics of sexual representations in the cinema of the Transition, by which I mean the relations of power enacted by those very representations. As my analyses will suggest, there is nothing inherently reactionary or progressive about the commercial exploitation of the eroticised body. As Jorge Marí (2003, 2007) has aptly noted, the *destape* became a politicised phenomenon, since the eroticised body turned into an ideological battleground tinged with discursive ambiguities that replicated the contradictions underlying the broader process of transition to democracy in Spain (Marí 2003: 257). In this sense, detailed examination of films reveals that the politics of eroticism was not one-way traffic.

NARRATIVES OF SUSPICION

Before I embark in my analyses, it is worth pointing out that, even though Opus Dei had an influential role in the public sphere of the late Franco years, including the film industry, it flew under the radar when it came to representations within the actual cultural products. The tentacles of what its critics call 'Octopus Dei' (Hutchinson 2006: 163; Orbaneja 2007: 12) also worked their way into the film industry in venues such as the production company Procusa, the distribution company Dipenfa-Filmayer, the Cine Club Monterols and the journal *Documentos Cinematográficos*, which were somewhat linked to Opus Dei. These connections proved that Opus Dei was savvy in using the channels of media, including those of the film industry, to influence public opinion, while simultaneously keeping its own public exposure to a minimum. It will not take us long to make an inventory of films that addressed the Opus Dei organisation during the Francoist regime. Only a few films come to my mind, although a more extensive search may find other examples: a brief appearance of a secondary character who belongs to the religious organisation in *El buen amor/The Good Love* (dir. Francisco Regueiro, 1963); a succinct reference in Basilio Martín Patino's *Canciones para después de una guerra/Songs for the Post-War* (1971); and an indirect, coded depiction in *La casa sin fronteras/The House Without Frontiers* (dir. Pedro Olea, 1972), which centres on an international sect that operates with dubious ends.

The main explanation for this representational scarcity is Opus Dei's infamous secrecy. The organisation's constitution remained sealed until 1982, and its members were instructed not to reveal their status or the names of other members (Walsh 1992: 120). Opus Dei's justification for this secrecy, which they prefer to call 'strategy of discretion' (Hutchinson 2006: 105), is the apostolate. Discretion ensures maximum efficiency in their aggressive recruiting practices, 'fishing' in the Opus internal lingo (Walsh 1992: 162). Of course, the success of the strategy of discretion/secrecy has not come without a price, for it has triggered a suspicious attitude about the true colours of Opus Dei and about its connections with platforms of power. Accordingly, this suspicion loomed large in the cinematic representations that I identified above. *El buen amor* and *Canciones* briefly suggested those connections, while *La casa sin fronteras* vicariously attacked them. It is therefore almost ironic that the three films I analyse here chose to depict an organisation that is (in)famous for its secrecy (Estruch 1995; Hutchinson 2006; Walsh 1992), for its lack of transparency, through the lens of eroticism and sex, which in its hard-core versions is guided by the principle of maximum visibility (Williams 1999: 48). *La trastienda*, *Cara al sol que más calienta* and *La escopeta nacional* 'undress' (both literally and metaphorically) Opus Dei to seemingly disclose the dark side of its manoeuvring during the late Franco years. Close reading will reveal, however, discordant outcomes behind these exercises of stripping.

THIRTY-SEVEN FRAMES OF FREEDOM

The more relaxed censorship code in the last months of the regime allowed Jorge Grau to make *La trastienda*, which comprises a frontal cinematic representation of Opus Dei. The film focuses on the inner conflicts of Jaime (Frederick Stafford), a doctor and a devoted supernumerary member of Opus Dei whose religious morals are shaken by his sexual attraction to one of his nurses, Juana (María José Cantudo). Meanwhile, Jaime's wife, Lourdes (Rosanna Schiafinno), is having an affair with Fernando (Ignacio de Paúl), one of the couple's closest friends. As if propelled by the atmosphere of debauchery at the festival of Sanfermines in Pamplona, Jaime consummates the adultery and causes a scandal. The hypocritical wife rejects Jaime in his attempt to make amends, and the film closes with Jaime departing to start a life on his own.

Producer José Frade orchestrated a promotion that promised spectators that *La trastienda* 'is not the film of the *apertura* but the film of freedom' (*Cartelera Turia* 1976). This catchy slogan paid off, and the film became an instant hit with almost three million tickets sold, according to the database of the Spanish *Ministerio de Cultura*. Juana's brief nude scene ten minutes into the film seemed to encapsulate that promise of freedom. In this famous scene, Juana comes home and takes her clothes off. As she walks to her bedroom, she plucks an apple from a fruit bowl. Once in her room, she can be seen in a medium close-up contemplating her own face in a mirror while she bites into the apple. Immediately thereafter, the reverse long shot shows her entire naked body as reflected in the mirror. Interestingly enough, this is not a point-of-view reverse shot but a detached view of Juana while she is staring at her naked reflection in the mirror (see Figure 5.1). It is significant that this shot is taken from outside the room and in low angle, as if the camera were taking the position of an uninvited voyeur and forcing viewers to become accomplices in the voyeuristic spectacle. The symbolic apple adds a biblical connotation, since it renders Juana as an Eve-like figure in relation to a post-biblical Western tradition of visualisation of Eve as a seductress embodying sin which, in this case, will be the catalyst of the dramatic conflict of the film.

It is hard to think of another second and a half – a total of thirty-seven frames – in the history of Spanish cinema that had a more crucial impact on the commercial run of a film. *La trastienda* benefited from a frequent filmic proposition during the *destape* years that equated the craving for sex with the craving for political freedom. Producers exploited what Brian McNair (2002: 11–12)

Figure 5.1 María José Cantudo in *La trastienda / The Backroom*, directed by Jorge Grau. Spain: José Frade Producciones Cinematográficas, S.A., 1975.

calls the power of 'striptease culture' to democratise desire: popular access to the erotic images in this film was presented as a metaphor of the increasing democratisation of the public sphere in Spain. This is why Alejandro Melero (2010) mentions *La trastienda* as an example of 'the dance of the seven veils' that Spanish cinema played during the Transition to progressively uncover layers of sexuality hitherto concealed (14). This was the first time that the censorship board had approved a scene with full frontal nudity in a Spanish feature film, and audiences rushed to movie theatres to witness the occurrence first-hand. In the last years of the regime and in the transition to democracy, screening politics and sex sold tickets, especially – as I argue in this essay – if religion was thrown into the equation.[3]

The defining factor of *La trastienda*'s commercial success – female nudity punctuating a 'religious crisis' plot – simultaneously became its main impediment in terms of critical reception. Some critics discarded the film as an attempt to cash in on the surplus value of female nudity during these years (Martí 1976: 34) and for its 'non-existent politicisation' (*Cartelera Turia* 1976). Critics did not forgive Grau, a director who began as a bridge figure between the *Nuevo Cine Español* and the School of Barcelona, for his move towards a middle-brow type of filmmaking that, while trying to offer a quality product, also sought a niche market and commercial viability. Like its female lead, *La trastienda* lost all its layers and garments over time, and historians of Spanish cinema barely remember the film as the first to legally show a nude female on the screen. Other than that, as Peter Besas (1985: 136) boldly put it, *La trastienda* 'had nothing special'.

While Jorge Grau was comfortable with the fact that his film had become 'a symbol of the *destape*' (2014: 176, 184), María José Cantudo always resented becoming an erotic symbol. In fact, she continues to deny that she was ever a *destape* film star (Aguilar 2012: 36). Cantudo has indefatigably refuted that she built her acting career around her physique and justifies her nudity in *La trastienda* as an artistic scene that provided the symbolic context – Juana as the Eve-like embodiment of sexual temptation – necessary to understand the religious conflict of the male lead (Aguilar 2012: 36). Considering how much her star image depended on her erotic appeal, it is hard to give much credibility to her claim. All the media texts that served to construct Cantudo's star image – the films, the promotional material, her interviews in film magazines and tabloids – emphasised the sexual aspect of her performances. One only has to bear in mind how much flesh she showed in both her previous and later film roles, such as in *El secreto inconfesable de un chico bien / Posh Kid's Shameful Secret* (dir. Jorge Grau, 1975), as well as in her interviews for magazines. In the film magazine *Fotogramas* alone, María José Cantudo appeared semi-nude on the covers of five issues between May 1975 and December 1978. The covers teased potential readers with the promise of more nudity to be found in the interviews inside. For example, issue 1386 (May 1975) features a story that is essentially a photographic report of Cantudo posing in a ski resort and wearing only a bikini. The interview in issue 1442 (June 1976) includes abundant pictures of Cantudo wearing only a thong and posing erotically on top of the roulette table in a casino. The first interview was published prior to the shooting of *La trastienda*; the second one appeared a few months after the release of the film. This confirms that, however much Cantudo demands critical attention for her acting merits, her star image before and after *La trastienda* was carved out through her erotic appeal.

Yet Cantudo had a point when she claimed that there is more to *La trastienda* than her famous nudity. With this film Grau offers the most comprehensive cinematographic picture of Opus Dei's controversial idiosyncrasies and, what is more unique, of the ethos that it instils in its members. On the surface, it seems as if Grau's goal was to attack Opus Dei as a reactionary organisation with a coercive impact on personal freedoms. Both the filmmaker and the female star have recently expressed it in those terms (Grau 2014: 176; Aguilar 2012: 36). However, Grau appropriates the dual logic of revelation and concealment that guides erotic cinema to reveal a benevolent side of Opus Dei – 'undressed' for the public eye – while the rest of the provincial society of Pamplona, and Spain at the twilight of Francoism, hypocritically 'conceals' their depravities. Disguised in erotic scandal and democratic promise, Grau's film encompassed a defence of the Opus Dei ethic and its role in the modernisation of Spain during late Francoism.

Jaime Navarro is introduced as a model Opus Dei supernumerary, who commit themselves to live according to the core message of Opus Dei: they strive to purify the secular world through the performance of their everyday tasks, both in their professional work and in their family life. The first scenes of the film show how Jaime Navarro painstakingly carries out all these activities. He complies with his professional, marital and family obligations. Also, Jaime seeks to sanctify his ordinary life by performing a number of spiritual tasks that the Opus Dei training assigns to its members in their 'plan of life', an individual plan to find 'pathways to holiness' (Allen 2005: 30). We see Jaime attending Mass every morning, praying a daily rosary, visiting with his spiritual confessor, Don Pablo (José Suárez), doing spiritual readings – Escrivá de Balaguer's *Camino* – at night, and practising corporal mortification, a common practice among Opus Dei laymen. What we actually see is the outcome of these mortifications in the wounds on the palms of his hands (see Figure 5.2). Opus Dei regards this self-inflicted pain not as an end in itself, but as a channel to achieve spiritual goals. Mortification is a symbolic way to link believers with the passion and suffering of Christ (Allen 2005: 170). Following a time-honoured tradition within Catholicism, corporal mortification is also a means of taming the temptations of the body. In Jaime's case, mortification is a way

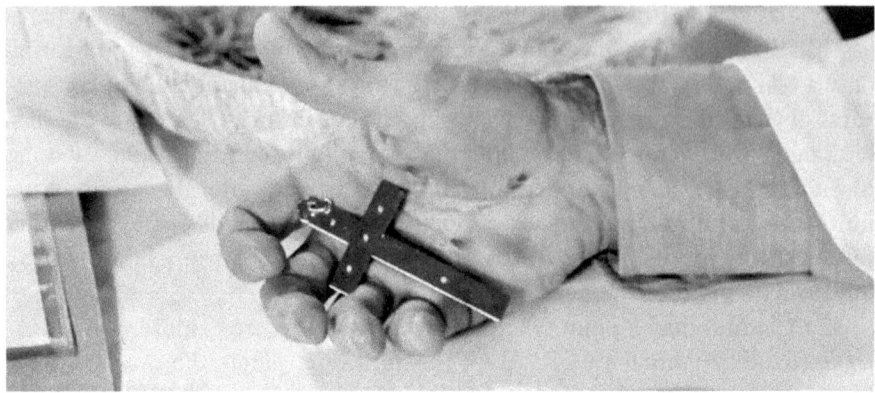

Figure 5.2 Frederick Stafford (hand) in *La trastienda/The Backroom*, directed by Jorge Grau. Spain: José Frade Producciones Cinematográficas, S.A., 1975.

of repenting for having carnal desires for Juana. Jaime methodically plans his daily activities, which we see him writing down in his diary at night. He acts following the staple tenet of the Opus Dei organisation: members must strive to meet the highest standards in the secular world. Jaime embodies Opus Dei members' apostolic mission as defined by Escrivá de Balaguer. Being holy consists of a three-fold task: 'to sanctify work itself, to sanctify oneself in work and to sanctify others with work' (1968: 25). In following this directive, Opus Dei members developed a work ethic not only as a way of achieving personal sanctification but also as the means to carry out the duties of the apostolate.

Given that *La trastienda* delivers an apology for the Opus Dei ethic, it cannot be taken as 'the film of freedom'. *La trastienda* was made when Opus Dei's political influence was fading. In my view, the film is an elegy for the participation of the Opus Dei elites in the modernisation process of the technocratic phase of the regime and for the impulse towards rationalised planning that Opus Dei technocrats instilled in the Spanish economic and political sphere. After the assassination of Carrero Blanco in December 1973, Carlos Arias Navarro was appointed as president and instantly surprised everyone by sweeping all Opus Dei technocrats out of his government. Arias Navarro had a tough time during the two years of his Opus Dei-free administration, which are known as the 'empty administration, without ideas, permanently adrift' (Mateos and Soto 1997: 88), because his administration seemed to function by reacting to events rather than following a credible strategic plan. This lack of political vision combined with other problems Arias Navarro faced, such as the hostility of the Church, the increasing opposition of civil society in favour of democratic plurality, and the economic crisis that put an end to the economic miracle of the *desarrollismo*.

La trastienda should be framed within this socio-historical junction, as a tribute to the role Opus Dei members played in late Francoism and as a critical pun on their dismissal from the frontline of politics. Jaime stands out in the resolution of the film as the moral victor over his hypocritical wife and the two-faced society of Pamplona that condemns his actions. As Lourdes explains, his biggest error was not cheating on her but doing it openly. The upshot of her rationale is that a hidden affair would have been fine. Also, the film narrative sets up the justification for Jaime's behaviour from the start. The main plot alternates with footage of the Sanfermines,[4] shot in documentary fashion with a hand-held camera. The climate of debauchery creates a carnivalesque atmosphere conducive to a temporary subversion of norms. As in the medieval carnival theorised by Bakhtin (1994: 198–200), this collective feast in which everyone from the community participates celebrates a transitory liberation from the established order, including a provisional suspension of rules and prohibitions. Grau has Jaime conveniently give a speech early in the film about the symbolic relevance of Sanfermines as a time to temporarily subvert the social order and release anxieties. It is almost as if Jaime were forced into his sin by the collective atmosphere.

The film differentiates between the two adulteries: Jaime's almost involuntary act versus Lourdes' prolonged affair. Raimundo (Ángel del Pozo), a colleague of Jaime's, justifies the scandal that Jaime's affair generates as a reprisal against the Opus Dei. Also, the film dwells on finding a way to forgive Jaime. Don Pablo, Jaime's priest and confessor, deems Jaime's sin an opportunity for redemption and convinces him to stop seeing Juana and to continue performing his duties as promised in his vows to Opus Dei. Interestingly, the camerawork corroborates the moral hierarchy the film narrative establishes. The conversations between Don Pablo and Jaime, and between Jaime and Raimundo, are carefully shot in shot/reverse shot sequences that situate the camera at shoulder level and do not privilege anybody's point of view. By contrast, in Jaime's final conversations with both Juana and his wife, the shot/reverse shot structure shows an asymmetrical ordering of the camera angles. Jaime's gaze appears from a high-angle perspective, while the reverse, from the female perspective, is consistently shot from low angles that aggrandise Jaime's figure. In tune with Opus Dei's notorious gender asymmetries (Armas 2002: 68; Carandell 1975: 196), it is as if the camera wants to endorse the moral hierarchy by placing Jaime in a superior position.

Just as Jaime in *La trastienda* gets no mercy from the hypocritical social milieu of Pamplona, the Opus Dei technocrats could not endure the retaliation of his political enemies within the Francoist regime who eliminated them from the political vanguard in 1974. However, the new government failed on all fronts, especially in stopping the economic recession. The Opus Dei members of the regime administration were rewarded for their religiously infused economic ethos. Similarly, Grau undressed his male lead but to expose his virtues and, thereby, to render him as the moral champion of the narrative. The undressing is not only metaphorical but also quite literal. After Jaime consummates the adultery and the scandal is made public, Don Pablo pays him a visit at Juana's apartment to convince him to amend his sin. Juana's roommate goes to the bedroom to announce the priest's visit, and a panning camera move displays a long shot of Jaime lying in bed almost naked. Only a pair of stylish black briefs covers Stafford's slim, toned body.

The casting of Frederick Stafford was criticised, as Jorge Grau admitted, for lacking ethnic verisimilitude (Gregori 2009: 504). The Czech-born actor was an international star known for a number of high-profile European spy movies, including Alfred Hitchcock's *Topaz* (1969). Evidently, his height (six feet three inches), his toned body and his chic underwear made him radically different from the male leads Spanish audiences were used to seeing in erotic comedies in those years. Most notably, Alfredo Landa, the star of the cycle of comedies known as 'landismo' (Fouz-Hernández and Martínez-Expósito 2007: 11; Pavlović 2003: 81–6) was short, chubby and usually wore ill-fitting white boxers. Instead of being a flaw, Stafford's 'non-Spanish' sex appeal works well to reinforce the reading I am proposing here. He incarnates the Opus Dei-affiliated professionals that penetrated the top spheres of influence from the late 1950s onwards. Although Grau does not afford Jaime's character an explicit political dimension, any average Spanish viewer could read him as a fictional embodiment of the elites who modernised the economy and crafted a new image of the regime by co-opting narratives of development that were typically associated with modern European democracies. To the average Spanish viewer, Opus Dei epitomised transnational elites of highly educated members like Jaime who began to colonise the pinnacles of power in Spain and elsewhere. Seen in this light, Stafford's European looks appear as an asset rather than a shortcoming.

Given this favourable depiction of Opus Dei, some reviewers accused Grau of being a covert member of the organisation. The magazine *Fotogramas* (1976) introduced an interview with the director by emphasising Grau's connections with Opus Dei. Domènec Font mentioned the director derogatively as 'el opusdeísta Jorge Grau' (1976: 260). My goal here has not been to engage in this guessing game and confirm or deny Grau's belonging to Opus Dei. I am not interested in an exercise of 'religious outing', so to speak, of the filmmaker.[5] Instead, my concern has been to analyse the representational apparatus of the film. In this sense, although many reviewers lambasted the film for sidestepping the public projection of Opus Dei and its association with the political elites (*Cartelera Turia* 1976; Martí 1976: 34), and scholars of Spanish cinema pigeonholed it as a *destape* hit (Besas 1985: 136; Torres 1996: 462), I have shown a different *trastienda* (backroom) of this film. Grau uses eroticism not to distract the spectator from political issues but to offer a political criticism of the two-faced society of Pamplona, and allegorically of Spain as a whole, at the twilight of the Franco regime. Instead of the publicised endorsement of pro-democratic values via the liberation of erotic impulses, the film stands out as a requiem for the technocratic phase of the regime and, most specifically, for the role played by Opus Dei.

MOCKING OPUS DEI

Unlike María José Cantudo, Bárbara Rey never disavowed being a *destape* muse. To be more precise, she has always embraced it by claiming that it had a social function – a means of letting off steam that was repressed during Francoism – while simultaneously providing a form of entertainment that large audiences longed for (Aguilar 2012: 266). Bárbara Rey worked in many erotically charged films during the Transition, and was so at ease with her status of sex symbol that she even parodied herself on the screen. In Luis García Berlanga's *La escopeta nacional*, Rey plays the role of Vera del Bosque, a starlet who becomes sexually involved with the ruling elites of late Francoism to try to reach celebrity status. She arrives at the hunting party that brings together the entourage of characters of the film in spectacular fashion, posing for photojournalists on top of a Land Rover with exaggerated erotic postures. The viewer soon finds out that Vera is the mistress of a Falangist minister of the Franco administration, and then appears comfortable when a kinky marquis played by José Luis López Vázquez kidnaps her. Furthermore, she asks the aristocrat to indulge in sadomasochistic sexual practices with her. In retrospect, any viewer who is familiar with Bárbara Rey's career might interpret her role in this film as a mocking framing story of her trajectory. Apart from parodying herself as a *destape* diva and the star of many photo-reportages that Rey gave during her career for high-profile magazines such as *Interviú* and *Fotogramas*, the role mimics her real-life sexual affairs with the economic and political elite – some confirmed, some denied by Rey in the tabloids.

As a matter of fact, *La escopeta nacional* compels audiences to view it with a retrospective perspective in mind. Drawing on the *esperpento* tradition, Berlanga convenes an ensemble cast to offer a grotesque view of political corruption in the late Franco period. Aristocrats, members of the Francoist administration and entrepreneurs swarm around a country house where the shooting party is an excuse for making illicit political decisions and arranging commercial agreements. Berlanga depicts the unethical dealings of the high-flying spheres of political influence as a bacchanal in which the aristocracy and the Falangists are portrayed as sexual perverts (signifying their declining political influence as the regime advanced) and the Opus Dei technocrats as sexual prudes who distribute copies of Escrivá de Balaguer's *Camino* and try to convince other hunters to refrain from immoral conduct.

The commercial run of the film benefited from the strong demand for the three-piece combo (politics, eroticism, religion) in the late 1970s, as attested by the over two million tickets sold. Viewers responded well to Berlanga's ability to embroider comical situations and to the mockery of the ruling classes soon to be deprived of their power in the embryonic democracy. Or were they heading in that direction? Berlanga's point seems to be less to ridicule the ruling classes of Francoism than to make a poignant commentary on the perennial tentacles of power. As some factions of those ruling elites rose to the top – such as the Opus Dei technocrats – and others seemed to fall, what Berlanga might be suggesting is that the power dynamics and the social order remained unaltered even during the Transition. There were other hunts in which the same and new participants continued to negotiate political concessions and orchestrate matters of national interest to their advantage.[6] The satirised Francoist cadres continued to play a central public role in the first years of the democracy, most of them camouflaged as lifelong democrats (for example, Manuel Fraga) for the sake of defending their interests. The opening credit sequence gives us the clue for this interpretative angle. The credits appear over a panoramic shot of the country house and the surrounding landscape, while we hear the diegetic sound of sheep bleating. As the camera begins panning to a vehicle arriving at the country house, the sound of the sheep turns rowdy and disruptive. We are about to meet Jaume Canivell (José Sazatornil), the entrepreneur who is paying for the hunt and, therefore, the facilitator of this banquet of power transactions. *La escopeta nacional* ultimately invokes viewers as a nation of sheep, conformist citizens who laugh at the elite's eccentricities and sexual perversions while simultaneously allowing those same elites to herd them.

A similar message lies behind Jesús Yagüe's *Cara al sol que más calienta*, a Spanish-Mexican co-production. In this film, Luciano Guerrero (José Luis López Vázquez), a humble worker for an Opus Dei-controlled company, is used as the scapegoat to cover up a scandal of corruption. Luciano is chosen to become the head of a fraudulent business that redirects funds to be used in a luxurious brothel for Opus Dei businessmen. The brothel is led by Nati (Isela Vega), the mistress of Andrés (Mauricio Garcés), the Opus Dei executive who orchestrates the scapegoating scenario, which is a cover for the financial and sexual deals of the Opus Dei elites. Set in the early 1970s, the film echoes a number of shameful scandals that tainted Opus Dei platforms of power in the late 1960s and early 1970s. Most notably, it brings to mind the Matesa scandal of political corruption. Run by prominent Opus Dei members, Matesa was a business enterprise that exported loom machinery. The political enemies of Opus Dei revealed in 1969 that the machinery was a cover for the diversion of capital, including some government loans, to fiscal paradises abroad

(Hermet 1985: 466–7; Hutchinson 2006: 131–3; Walsh 1992: 147–9). Despite this scandal, Franco surprised everyone by reinforcing the Opus Dei-friendly composition of his cabinet in October 1969.

As in *La escopeta*, *Cara al sol* couples political corruption with sexual debauchery, and a country house that is not what it seems also brings together the political and economic elites for illicit affairs, whether political, financial or sexual. The film was originally titled '*Casa de citas*', alluding to the house that symbolises late-Franco Spain. In this symbolic setting, the high-flying businessmen exploit common people – Luciano and Nati – just like the Opus Dei elites manipulated Spaniards in their handling of public affairs. In a scene that makes this exploitation apparent, Andrés gives a speech to Luciano and Nati to motivate them to work harder despite the hardships they endure: 'Work, work, that is the way to let steam off. Working is the best consolation. Franklin already said so, if you hate, work; if you love, work; if you are sad, work.' Meanwhile, Luciano and Nati are bundling up the books illegally sold in Latin America. Disturbing music punctuates the scene, as if reinforcing the distressing reversal of Opus Dei's doctrine of sanctification of work as a spiritual end, since the Opus Dei member is exploiting others instead of preaching with example.

Nati, along with the other girls who work in the brothel, are sexually exploited. From her very first appearance in the film, Nati is depicted as nothing more than a sexual object. She is wearing a transparent negligee revealing her voluminous breasts, which Andrés profusely licks. In exchange for her sexual services, Andrés agrees to open the bordello. What she does not know is that she is further exploited through this business, for it is used to launder money that comes from illegal transactions. In addition, it serves as the site where the Opus Dei members celebrate their bacchanals. The kitschy decor of the house highlights this double standard, as it combines paintings of the Virgin Mary and crucifixes along with erotic paintings. A dream sequence of a former minister of Franco's administration (José Lifante), who is also a devout Opus Dei member, insinuates the abusive nature of the relations taking place in the house. He daydreams while he is kneeling to pray. In his dream, he intervenes in an orgy as a moral saviour, as he tries to prick the gigantic, bubble-like breasts of a prostitute with a sword. The phallic sword gets bent, and the prostitute bursts into loud laughter. This scene fades into another in which he is guiding a singing chorus of children. The whole dream sequence hints at a number of issues regarding this character's sexual insecurities. It points to a castration anxiety and also suggests that he is a sexual pervert who uses violence against women as a defensive mechanism to sublimate his repressed paedophilic desires.

Once the fraudulent business is uncovered, Luciano is made responsible and sent to jail in exchange for a compensatory stipend. As a car takes Luciano to be sentenced, the Opus Dei entourage walks away freely. The musical score changes to a paso doble, which accentuates the broad scope of the message of this film. *Cara al sol* implies that, like the paso doble, political corruption and sexual depravity are cultural markers of traditional Spanishness. A sign in bright red letters – the red of the Spanish flag, the red of 'Spanish' passion – reads 'Continuará' (To be continued). Although it seemingly announces the second instalment of a film saga that never materialised, what it really announces is the impunity with which the economic and political elites, particularly the Opus Dei cadres, will continue to operate in democratic Spain. As in *La escopeta nacional*, the film enacts a representational revenge against the ruling elites of Francoism whose modus operandi is caricatured. The spectators of these two films could rejoice with these celluloid vendettas, but the underlying point is more pessimistic: those with power, irrespective of their political stripe, will always subjugate those without it. Both filmmakers seem to predict that democratic Spain will continue to be a bordello, perhaps of a different nature, in which the ruling elites will keep exploiting, sexually and otherwise, average Spaniards like Luciano and Nati, while a true rupture from power relations seems unlikely.

CONCLUSION

The three films I have focused on reflect upon the role of the Opus Dei elites in the late Francoist period, seemingly from a comparable condemnatory position that uncovers the true colours of the institution while giving filmic expression to anxieties about the regulatory powers of religion in Spanish society during the transition to democracy. The three films 'undress' Opus Dei, both literally (by removing the clothing of its celluloid representatives) and metaphorically (by exposing its dealings with the country's elites and, in some cases, the illicit scheming of some of its members to achieve the higher spheres of economic and political power). These three films illustrate that the visual representation of eroticism, whether on cinema or other media channels, definitely became a politicised phenomenon. However, it is important to summon up that this representation resembled the very contradictions and ambiguous spaces of the transition taking place in Spain. In this sense, my three analyses have illustrated the need to reframe discussions of the *destape* films away from preconceived judgements and categorical parallels between sexual transgressions and right- or left-wing politics. These contradictory politics converged in the three films that have been the object of my inquiry.

La trastienda is a deceptive *destape* hit that packages eroticism in democratic promises but turns out to be laudatory of the Opus Dei ethos. While the film was a commercial hit because of the frontal nude of its female lead, I have shown that the stripping of the male lead is perhaps more significant in political terms. It lays bare a tall and muscular body that differs from the short and chubby masculine figure of the customary *destape* film. The physical appeal of this masculine body goes hand-in-hand with the sympathetic depiction of his character, which the visual style of the film renders morally superior to non-Opus Dei-affiliated characters through framing devices and camerawork. By undressing Opus Dei, Jorge Grau strains some of the negative perceptions about this religious organisation, depicting it through the figure of a professionally accomplished character (one of the assumptions about Opus Dei and its links to the elites) who is nonetheless seen in his humane side – literally stripped to the bones. In a different way, in *La escopeta nacional* and *Cara al sol* the Opus Dei elites are depicted as a lobby that does not hesitate in using its political influence to profit from illegal commercial practices. In both films, the Opus Dei members display equal doses of political aspirations and sexual repression – sublimated through private perversions. While the target is well defined and tackled without leniency, the pessimistic ending of both films suggests that the Opus Dei elites, whether sexually repressed or depraved, will keep a strong hold of the indissoluble branches of power. Seen together, these three films illustrate that eroticism was not a strategy to distract audiences from the political front. To the contrary, eroticism was a cogent lens, almost a framing motif, through which Spanish audiences saw the persistent links between politics and religion within the Spanish socio-political milieu, even if those links were no longer visualised as unilaterally as during the Franco regime.

NOTES

1. *Interviú* is a weekly magazine published in Madrid since May 1976. It is known for publishing nude or semi-nude photographs of celebrities along with articles on political and economic scandals. It became an iconic magazine of the transition to democracy in Spain, reaching a readership of three million by 1979.
2. Given that Norma insinuates that the King of Spain is one of her top clients, the scene echoes the scandal that emerged in April 2012, when the domestic and international tabloids revealed the alleged extramarital relationship between (now retired king) Juan Carlos I and the German businesswoman Corinne zu Sayn-Wittgenstein (Colacello 2013).
3. During the Transition, Spanish cinema frequently conceptualised religious crisis and its broader socio-political impact in sexual terms. The most renowned cases were *El sacerdote / The Priest* (dir. Eloy de la Iglesia, 1978), *Cartas de amor de una monja / Love Letters of a Nun* (dir. Jorge Grau, 1978) and *La portentosa vida del padre Vicente / The Prodigious Life of Father Vincent* (dir. Carles Mira, 1978).
4. The Festival of San Fermín (popularly known as *Sanfermines*), is a week-long celebration (6–14 July) in the Spanish town of Pamplona in honour of San Fermín, the co-patron of the Navarra region. Although the celebration includes many traditional cultural events, it is internationally known for its *encierros* (running of the bulls).

5. Jorge Grau has never hidden his connections with Opus Dei during his early career, but he has denied that he was ever a member of the religious organisation. See his recently published memoirs for an explanation of the extent of his ties with Opus Dei (Grau 2014: 62).
6. In light of the recent scandal of political corruption known as 'Operación Púnica', Berlanga's film indeed appears visionary. The corruption scheme included a series of hunts that the contractors of the Grupo Dico organised between 2002 and 2006 to bribe politicians who, in return, offered them highly profitable public contracts (Gil 2014).

REFERENCES

Aguilar, José (2012), *Las estrellas del destape y la transición: El cine español se desnuda*, Madrid: T&B Editores.
Allen, John (2005), *Opus Dei. An Objective Look behind the Myths and Reality of the Most Controversial Force in the Catholic Church*, New York: Doubleday.
Armas, Isabel de (2002), *Ser mujer en el Opus Dei*, Madrid: Ediciones Foca.
Bakhtin, Mikhail (1994), 'Folk Humour and Carnival Laughter', in Pam Morris (ed.), *The Bakhtin Reader*, London: Arnold, pp. 194–206.
Besas, Peter (1985), *Behind the Spanish Lens: Spanish Cinema under Fascism and Democracy*, Denver, CO: Arden Press.
Carandell, Luis (1975), *Vida y milagros de monseñor Escrivá de Balaguer, fundador del Opus Dei*, Barcelona: Laia.
Cartelera Turia (1976), 'La trastienda', *Cartelera Turia* 642.
Colacello, Bob (2013), 'King and Controversy', *Vanity Fair*: http://www.vanityfair.com/society/2013/10/crisis-spain-royalty-abdication (last accessed 30 July 2016).
Escrivá de Balaguer, José María (1968), *Conversaciones con Mons. Escrivá de Balaguer*, Madrid: Ediciones Rialp.
Escrivá de Balaguer, José María (1979), *The Way*, New York: Scepter.
Estruch, Joan (1995), *Saints and Schemers: Opus Dei and Its Paradoxes*, Oxford: Oxford University Press.
Font, Domènec (1976), *Del azul al verde: El cine español durante el franquismo*, Barcelona: Avance.
Fotogramas (1976), 'El último opus de Jorge Grau', *Fotogramas* 1440.
Fouz-Hernández, Santiago and Alfredo Martínez-Expósito (2007), *Live Flesh: The Male Body in Contemporary Spanish Cinema*, London: I. B. Tauris.
Freixas, Ramón and Joan Bassa (2005), *Cine, erotismo y espectáculo. El discreto encanto del sexo en la pantalla*, Barcelona: Paidós.
Gil, Joaquín (2014), 'El jugoso negocio de las cacerías "púnicas",' *El País* 19 November 2014: http://politica.elpais.com/politica/2014/11/15/actualidad/1416056413_966026.html (last accessed 30 July 2016).
Grau, Jordi (2014), *Confidencias de un director de cine descatalogado*, Madrid: Calamar Ediciones.
Gregori, Antoni (2009), *El cine español según sus directores*, Madrid: Cátedra.
Hermet, Guy (1985), *Los católicos en la España franquista II. Crónica de una dictadura*, Madrid: Siglo XXI.
Hopewell, John (1986), *Out of the Past: Spanish Cinema after Franco*, London: BFI.
Hutchinson, Robert (2006), *Their Kingdom to Come. Inside the Secret World of Opus Dei*, New York: Thomas Dunne Books.

Jordan, Barry and Rikki Morgan-Tamosunas (1998), *Contemporary Spanish Cinema*, Manchester: Manchester University Press.
Kowalsky, Daniel (2004), 'Rated S: Softcore Pornography and the Spanish Transition to Democracy, 1977–1982', in Antonio Lázaro-Reboll and Andrew Willis (eds), *Spanish Popular Cinema*, Manchester: Manchester University Press, pp. 188–208.
Marí, Jorge (2007), 'Desnudos, vivos y muertos: La transición erótico-política y/en la crítica cultural de Vázquez Montalbán', in José Colmeiro (ed.), *Manuel Vázquez Montalbán: El compromiso de la memoria*, London: Tamesis, pp. 129–41.
Marí, Jorge (2003), 'El umbral del destape', in Jorge Marí (ed.), *Valoración de Francisco Umbral (Ensayos críticos en torno a su obra)*, Gijón: Llibros del Pexe, pp. 242–58.
Martí, Octavi (1976), 'La trastienda', *Dirigido por ...* 32, pp. 34–5.
Mateos, Abdón and Alvaro Soto (1997), *El final del franquismo, 1959–1975. La transformación de la sociedad española*, Madrid: Termas de Hoy.
McNair, Brian (2002), *Striptease Culture. Sex, Media and the Democratisation of Desire*, London: Routledge.
Melero Salvador, Alejandro (2010), *Placeres ocultos: Gays y lebianas en el cine español de la Transición*, Madrid: Notorius Ediciones.
Orbaneja Aragón, Fernando de (2007), *Opus Dei: La Santa coacción*, Barcelona: Ediciones B.
Pavlović, Tatjana (2003), *Despotic Bodies and Transgressive Bodies: Spanish Culture from Francisco Franco to Jesús Franco*, Albany: State University of New York Press.
Ponce, José María (2004), *El destape nacional: Crónica del desnudo en la transición*, Barcelona: Ediciones Glenat.
Stone, Rob (2002), *Spanish Cinema*, Harlow: Longman.
Torres, Augusto (1996), *Diccionario Cine Español*, Madrid: Espasa Calpe.
Umbral, Francisco (1976), *Crónicas post-franquistas*, Madrid: A. Q. Ediciones.
Walsh, Michael (1992), *Opus Dei: An Investigation into the Secret Society Struggling for Power Within the Roman Catholic Church*, New York: HarperCollins.
Williams, Linda (1999), *Hard Core: Power, Pleasure, and the 'Frenzy of the Visible'*, Berkeley: University of California Press.

FILMOGRAPHY

Canciones para después de una guerra/Songs for the Post-War, film, directed by Basilio Martín Patino. Spain: Julio Antonio Pérez, 1976.
Cara al sol que más calienta/Facing the Warmest Sun, film, directed by Jesús Yagüe. Spain/Mexico: Lotus Film Internacional/Películas Mexicanas, 1977.
Cartas de amor de una monja/Love Letters of a Nun, film, directed by Jorge Grau. Spain: Constan Films, S.A., 1978.
El buen amor/The Good Love, film, directed by Francisco Regueiro. Spain: Jet Films, S.A., 1963.
El sacerdote/The Priest, film, directed by Eloy de la Iglesia. Spain: Óscar Guarido Tizón/Carlos Goyanes, 1978.
El secreto inconfesable de un chico bien/Posh Kid's Shameful Secret, film, directed by Jorge Grau. Spain: José Frade Producciones Cinematográficas, S.A., 1976.
La casa sin fronteras/The House Without Frontiers, film, directed by Pedro Olea. Spain: Amboto P.C., S.L., 1972.
La escopeta nacional/The National Shotgun, film, directed by Luis García Berlanga. Spain: In-Cine Compañía Industrial Cinematográfica, S.A., 1978.

La portentosa vida del padre Vicente/The Prodigious Life of Father Vincent, film, directed by Carles Mira. Spain: Carlos Mira, 1978.
La trastienda/The Backroom, film, directed by Jorge Grau. Spain: José Frade Producciones Cinematográficas, S.A., 1975.
Los amantes pasajeros/I'm So Excited, film, directed by Pedro Almodóvar. Spain: El Deseo, S.L., 2013.
Topaz, film, directed by Alfred Hitchcock. USA: Universal Pictures, 1969.

CHAPTER 6

Middlebrow Erotic: Didactic Cinema in the Transition to Democracy

Sally Faulkner

As a number of chapters in this volume show, erotic cinema was fundamental to filmmaking in the period of the transition to democracy in Spain (1973–86),[1] with examples ranging from the *'destape'* tendency, which crossed between genres like comedy and melodrama, to the urban youth crime thriller, or *'quinqui'* film (see Faulkner 2016).[2] This chapter stakes a claim for the discussion of this area in middlebrow cinema also. The 'middlebrow', a mobile adjective that may attach to text, institution and audience alike, has been frequently understood – and dismissed – as an unadventurous area of mainstream filmmaking. When describing a film text, middlebrow may refer to serious or educational – but not too challenging – content, and to accessible – but not simplistic – form. When describing an institution it may refer to the ways a certain exhibition space, like an art cinema, may confer value. A middlebrow audience, on the other hand, is one that is culturally aspirant and often – but not always – middle class.

At first sight this may not appear propitious terrain for the appearance of the erotic, commonly associated with highbrow art film, like Pedro Almodóvar's stylised erotic thrillers, or lowbrow genre film, including, but not limited to, hard- and soft-core pornography. The purpose of this essay is not to insist that critics working on these attractive extremes of high and low have overlooked the erotic pleasures of the middle, though this may emerge as a corollary. In making a claim for a distinctive 'middlebrow erotic', it argues, rather, that in the especially overwrought social and political contexts of the Transition, this area of Spanish cinema performed a particular cultural labour: that of educating audiences in new democratic values and freedoms. In the early to mid-1970s, when censorship was still in place and Franco still alive, a timid – and often rancidly misogynist and homophobic – erotic cinema may be located in the sleazy content of *'destape'* films. For example, in subgenres such as *'cine con curas'* (films with a priest), new freedoms were tentatively tested by exploring taboo subjects like the (hetero-)sexual affairs of members of the clergy.³ However, by the late 1970s, the dictator was dead, and censorship breathing its last. Building on the tentative freedoms tested in the early part of the decade, the last Norms of Film Censorship of February 1975 allowed a little more freedom – Item 9 permitted the nude body on screen – a last gasp before full abolition in December 1977. This chapter argues that in this changing context, eroticism in late-1970s Spanish cinema extended beyond subject matter and became the very grammar by which a new film language was constructed, and in this new language, new freedoms could be spoken and understood.

My case study to test this thesis forms part of a 'didactic' cinema that flourished in the late 1970s. In Spanish Television Studies, the pedagogical role of the medium has been a key term since Manuel Palacio established its importance in the Transition in his *Historia de la Televisión* in 2001. In Spanish Film Studies, however, its uptake has been slower, owing to its association with the middlebrow, which, as discussed, has tended to be overlooked. If the erotic and the middlebrow may at first appear – pardon the pun – odd bedfellows, this chapter aims to show that an alliance between the two with the didactic aim of educating the audience arose from the particular circumstances of the Transition. In the political arena, these circumstances included the dictator's death (1975), the forging of a new democracy and the fight for new rights, with its major milestones of the Moncloa Pacts (1977) and the new constitution (1978); in the cultural, as we have seen, the abolition of censorship (1977) and the finite period of relaxation in distribution which allowed the mainstream, soft-core 'S' film category to flourish (1977–82).⁴

My case study for this discussion will be *El diputado/Confessions of a Congressman* (dir. de la Iglesia, 1978), which I will explore through the characterisation of the protagonist, the deployment of editing and the use of space. Released on 20 October 1978 and rated 'S', with an audience of 841,600 in film theatres at the time of its release,⁵ then a stunning fifteen million on its subsequent TVE screening in 1985 (De Stefano 1986: 60), *El diputado* received little serious critical attention until the 1990s, but is today frequently discussed for its representation of homosexuality (the late 1970s predates the use of the term 'gay' in Spain) and its engagement with popular culture. My aim is to reframe our understanding of this film by viewing it through the alternative lens of the middlebrow. This will lead me to ask, in my conclusion, if a focus on questions of sexuality in Spanish film scholarship has tended to obscure other questions such as didacticism and, by extension, the middlebrow. It will also allow me to propose an alternative version of film history in the late Transition, whereby the widely dismissed State-funded cinema of the 'ley Miró' era (1983–94) in fact shared the didactic aims of late-1970s commercial films like *El diputado*.⁶ Rather than the appealing thesis that Spanish cinema of the new democracy simply turned its back on earlier achievements, the chapter thus suggests that continuities in the area of middlebrow cinema have been overlooked.

MIDDLEBROW

Scholars within Spain and without have frequently noted that Basque director Eloy de la Iglesia's work, which numbers twenty-two features in a career which – if interrupted by drug addiction – nonetheless stretched from 1966 to 2003, was originally overlooked as 'mere' popular, genre cinema. *El diputado*, in particular, his thirteenth film, was dismissed owing to its apparent failure to meet highbrow criteria such as a sophisticated plot and an innovative deployment of film form (Hopewell 1989: 233–42; Smith 1992: 144–51; Tropiano 1997; Melero Salvador 2004, 2011; Prout 2005; Marsh 2013). It would be fair to describe *El diputado*'s flashback plot as uncomplicated, though it is worth noting that while the multiple references to contemporary political events, like the Atocha killings, the legalisation of the Spanish Communist Party and the Moncloa Pacts (January, April and October 1977), would have made the film highly topical and thus easier to understand for contemporary audiences, from today's perspective this same topicality now complicates the film, which may appear dense in its references to dated events. After an initial explanatory monologue, *El diputado* tracks the adult life story of the newly elected titular congressman Roberto Orbea, played by José Sacristán, for the fictional amalgam of the contemporary Communist and Socialist parties, 'Partido Radical Socialista'. On one level, then, the film meets an understandable need for audiences to explore, in an accessible narrative format, the extraordinary shift from clandestine political activity under the still-punitive dictatorship (punishment is portrayed through two police interrogations in the past and Roberto's imprisonment in Carabanchel in the near present) to political legitimacy in the fledgling new democracy. A similar narrative area had also been covered by a near-contemporary film released the year before, *Asignatura pendiente/Unfinished Business* (dir. Garci, 1977), in which José Luis Garci also cast Sacristán to explore the shift from illegality to legality, here from the perspective of a left-wing lawyer.

Both the *Asignatura pendiente* and the *El diputado* roles take full advantage of Sacristán's politicised star persona, which was linked to the recently legalised Spanish Communist Party, a fact that *El diputado* echoes in fiction in Sacristán's role as the rising star of the 'Partido Radical Socialista'. Sacristán had also embodied change in the area of sexuality when he played the doomed 1920s transvestite Lluís de Serracant in *Un hombre llamado flor de otoño/A Man Called Autumn Flower* (dir. Olea, 1978), released seven months before *El diputado* to an audience of over a million. In a less challenging role, which was nonetheless enormously popular at the box office, it was Sacristán, again, who provided a vehicle for audiences to test and understand other new freedoms in *Solos en la madrugada/Alone in the Dark* (dir. Garci, 1978). In this film he plays a radio presenter who loquaciously shares his experiences of marital breakdown (divorce would be legalised in Spain in 1981) and a relationship with a '*progre*', or liberated new woman (Emma Cohen's Maite) with both radio listeners within the fiction, and film viewers without it. Weaving together the sexual and political dimensions of these plural Sacristán roles in the late 1970s, Eloy de la Iglesia's innovation in *El diputado*, along with his co-scriptwriter Gonzalo Goicoechea, was to couple Robert's political journey from illegality to legality, from the cells of Carabanchel to the election as Secretary General of the 'Partido Radical Socialista', with the character's homosexuality. De la Iglesia and Goicoechea's message is not just to condemn the homophobic crimes of the past, especially Francoism's infamous introduction of the 'Ley de peligrosidad y rehabilitación social' (Rehabilitation and Social Danger Law) in 1970, which made homosexuality illegal, and which remained in place until January 1979, a full three months after *El diputado*'s release – homophobia that is crudely represented in the film by the portrayal of the group of die-hard fascist thugs. Furthermore, and somewhat more subtly, the film also critiques the failure of the new democracy immediately to include alternative sexualities among the freedoms to be defended by the new order.

To match a script that straightforwardly contrasts positive change (the acquisition of legitimacy in the political sphere) with negative stasis (the continued illegality of homosexuality), de la Iglesia adopts a formal style that renders *mise en scène*, cinematography, editing and soundtrack purely 'functional' (a description made by Paul Julian Smith (1992: 142, 149)). For example, to stress Juanito (José Luis Alonso) and Roberto's class differences, performance style, soundtrack and *mise en scène* act in concert. Alonso's performance style of sulky adolescence meets Sacristán's of middle-aged restraint; jeans and leather jacket meet suits and mackintoshes; pop meets classical music; and Madrid's streets and orgies contrast with tastefully furnished apartments and political rallies. The female characters connected to the lovers are reduced to being further props in *mise en scène*. Queta Claver's worn nightclub cigarette-seller is Juanito's mother, while María Luisa San José's hair, make-up and dress as Roberto's wife Carmen reduce her to being another tasteful object with which to decorate the family apartment. One showy exception here is the film's deployment of racking shots to portray one of the lovers' embraces (cross-cut point of view shots between the men in which the camera shifts from side to side, with eyeline matches to the movement of their heads), though this experimental interruption serves to underscore an otherwise conventional deployment of cinematography and editing. Thus lacking in the rich nuance that critics have admired in the aesthetics of the work of contemporary directors such as Manuel Gutiérrez Aragón and Carlos Saura, this approach was variously dismissed at the time of the film's release as 'pamphleteering', 'thesis cinema' and 'like a newspaper' – though this last description is one that de la Iglesia used positively to describe his films (see Smith 1992: 130). The film was also described negatively as 'didactic', though, again, de la Iglesia and Goicoechea have positively appropriated the term (see Melero Salvador 2004: 99, 2013: 28).[7] As I will go on to argue, the time is ripe positively to re-evaluate this description by relocating it within the framework of studies of the middlebrow.

From the 1990s, film historians have been rightly eager to rescue *El diputado* from the detractors that condemned it on its release,[8] and from the oblivion to which it was consigned by film historians who were uniquely concerned with highbrow film. Paul Julian Smith explores the representation of homosexuality in the director's work, noting that the censors' banning of de la Iglesia's earlier *Los placeres ocultos/ Hidden Pleasures* (1977) led, in Barcelona, to the first *Orgullo* (Pride) demonstration in Spain that year (1992: 3). He concludes that, notwithstanding some areas of schematicism, which are present in *El diputado*, the director deserves to be rescued from those who 'revile' him according to 'art-house criteria', and be celebrated for his own brand of '*auteurisme*' and deployment of popular genres (1992: 161).[9] Subsequent criticism has picked up both these aspects – the representation of homosexuality and the director's distinctive auteurism.

Writing later in the 1990s, Stephen Tropiano stresses, first, de la Iglesia's exclusion from what he terms the '"artistic" work' (1997: 158) of the canon of contemporary Spanish directors, and explores, second, the 'pedagogical aspect' of Roberto and Juanito's relationship according to the Ancient Greek erastes/eromenos model (1997: 173–5). In the 2000s, meanwhile, Ryan Prout reframes *El diputado* in the context of the continuing homophobia he pinpoints in Spanish society (2005: 163–4). Closer to my own argument is Alejandro Melero Salvador's emphasis, in 2004, on the didactic nature of *El diputado*'s representation of homosexuality. Melero Salvador notes that de la Iglesia's films more widely 'tend to lecture' and 'pose [...] questions [...] and provide [...] answers' (2004: 99, 100). Rejecting the understanding of didacticism as 'pamphleteering or as cheap propaganda for gay liberation', Melero Salvador goes on to salute *El diputado* as a film that 'teaches Spaniards that homosexuals do exist, and they exist at all levels of society' (2004: 100). Most recently, Steven Marsh has reprised Smith's suggestion of de la Iglesia's distinctive auteurism that is in tune with popular genres sharply to describe the director's auteurist 'signature' as 'his fascination with the disturbance produced by the meeting of the marginal and the mainstream' (2013: 157).

Departing from the same starting point of defending a film that fails to meet art-house criteria of value, this chapter takes the argument in an alternative direction. In particular, it picks up on the unusual coincidence of 'didacticism' (Melero Salvador) and 'disturbance' (Marsh) in previous studies. I suggest that placing this film within the framework of Spain's wider contemporary audiovisual culture of middlebrow film and TV allows us to mediate between these two positions. In his defence of the pedagogical role TV played in the Transition, Manuel Palacio discusses, perhaps unsurprisingly, news programmes, such as the still-running and well-respected *Informe semanal*, which began broadcasting on 31 March 1973. But the author stresses that the same role is played by fictional series in the period, like *Fortunata y Jacinta* (dir. Camus 1980), which looked to Spain's nineteenth-century history to allow contemporary audiences to reflect on the parallels with the country's contemporary process of reconciliation, a process Palacio terms 'historical pedagogy' (2001: 94, 154). Rather than erect boundaries between film and TV, a consideration of audiovisual culture reveals similar pedagogical aims across both sectors. I have argued elsewhere that class changes from the 1960s in Spain suggest the rise of a newly numerous and newly middle-class audience that was socially mobile and culturally aspirant: in other words, a middlebrow audience (Faulkner 2013, 2016). I suggest that this new middlebrow sector was also the likely audience for *El diputado*'s mainstream theatrical and TV releases. In an interview in 2006, de la Iglesia's co-scriptwriter also stresses that the audience of *El diputado* was not limited to the young: 'it wasn't just a kids' thing. It was a thing for middle-class cinema-goers' (Melero 2013: 27; my translation). However, in this chapter I will explore the term not as a descriptor of audience, but rather as a series of formal characteristics that describe the film text itself. I propose that *El diputado*, in a manner broadly comparable to contemporary TV, is middlebrow for its serious and informative subject matter, accessible form and aspirant deployment of high-cultural references in a popular format.

Thus I reprise Melero Salvador's defence of *El diputado* as didactic cinema that deserves our attention for the particular task it performed in the late 1970s of instructing Spanish audiences. However, I extend this argument to suggest that the film instructs its audience both in questions of homosexuality and questions of politics, whereas Melero Salvador confined his observations to the first area.[10] I will argue that the film explores both sets of questions through a process of fusion, such that politics may only be understood through the erotic portrayal of homosexuality.

CENSORSHIP AND EROTIC CINEMA

As this volume as a whole shows, it is simplistic to take eroticism and nudity as synonymous. One might only turn to the work of Luis Buñuel for evidence that the erotic may emerge from its repression, in this case the repression exerted by the Catholic Church. It therefore may perversely follow that Francoist censorship created an erotic cinema that was not dependent on actual nudity. The audience's over-investment in Rita Hayworth's removal of one glove in the dubbed and cut version of *Gilda* (dir. Vidor, 1946), screened in Spain in 1947, is often cited as evidence of this argument, and is the subject of an early audience study carried out by Esther Gómez-Sierra, in which her interviewee, Matilde Sierra Fernández, recalls, 'Everyone assumed that the censors had cut that scene because [Hayworth] went on stripping' (2004: 94). However, in the context of the 1970s, an alignment between eroticism and nudity is tenable, as this was the decade of the rise of pornography, from which Spain, even before Franco's death and the abolition of censorship, was not immune. If it is tenable that in pornography the sole purpose of eroticism is sexual arousal, this chapter is interested in the didactic purposes to which eroticism may be put in a middlebrow film. Indeed, it hopes to show that in this perhaps unexpected deployment of eroticism lies a further and previously overlooked dimension of de la Iglesia's achievement.

Previous criticism has rightly located, and celebrated, the originality of de la Iglesia's late-1970s cinema in his ground-breaking portrayal of homosexuality in Sacristán's bourgeois politician Roberto – the 'Good Homosexual' in Smith's summary (1992: 144) – and in his explicit focus on male nudity, including a shot of possibly the first erect penis of mainstream Spanish cinema, as Melero Salvador muses (2011: 137). This chapter argues that we may also locate his originality in his location of same-sex eroticism in a didactic, middlebrow film, where he fuses the erotic with the political. Consider the ways this breaks with the previous deployment of erotic images in mainstream Spanish cinema of the decade. Illicit love affairs in films of the early 1970s starring Ana Belén, like *Españolas en París/Spanish Women in Paris* (dir. Bodegas, 1971), which includes pre-marital sex, and *Tormento/Torment* (dir. Olea, 1974), which includes a love affair with a priest, are conveyed through incongruous shifts in tone, from melodrama in the first case and period drama in the second, to soft-focus, semi-clad bedroom scenes. It is as if directors Roberto Bodegas and Pedro Olea are adding in unnecessary soft-porn '*destape*' sequences in order to make up for the ways such scenes had been – also unnecessarily, in their view – cut by the censors in the past. If the removal of scenes in censored cinema led to a jump in tone that was detectable by viewers, as in the previously mentioned case of *Gilda*, the addition of these scenes in early '*destape*' cinema also leads to a jump in tone that is detectable by viewers, not only for the incongruous shift in formal presentation, but also for the distracting detour from the otherwise forceful narratives of the films of female suffering and forbearance. Even after the death of Franco, this incongruous addition of nudity – to compensate, I insist, for its previous incongruous removal – continues, and in this context of gratuity *El diputado*'s fusion of eroticism and politics, with a didactic, middlebrow aim, acquires more force.

FUSION

As we have seen, Marsh has argued of de la Iglesia's work more widely that it brings together disparate elements of marginal and mainstream in order to effect 'disturbance'. In *El diputado* it would be possible to isolate this effect, for example, in the cut from housewife Carmen's simpering 'I've made a lovely dinner for you, Congressman Sir' to the male orgy, or in the introduction of working-class petty crook and rent boy Juanito into Roberto's manifestly middle-class home and otherwise orthodox marriage (*mise en scène* and performance style are, we recall, strictly functional in the film) to disturb the reproductive family (Juanito passes for Roberto and his wife Carmen's son) with a ménage à trois (when Carmen's sexuality is finally introduced in the film, then, it can only be understood within the framework of male homosexual desire). However, in the film as a whole I argue that the bringing together of disparate elements like still-illegal homosexuality and newly legal left-wing politics is a process of fusion, in which one is understood in terms of the other, rather than of disturbance.

The fusion of sex and politics in *El diputado*, or its language of the middlebrow erotic, draws on José Luis Garci's previously discussed *Asignatura pendiente* (1977) and *Solos en la madrugada* (1978). In these films José Sacristán's character's heterosexual relationships with the characters played by Fiorella Faltoyano (named Elena in both films) and the character played by Emma Cohen in the second (Maite) are used as a vehicle to explore contemporary issues like the legalisation of left-wing political parties and social change like divorce and feminism. In both films, the bedroom scenes between the lovers deliver only timid nudity and no explicit sexual activity, but instead, and in these very same scenes, the viewer is afforded references to politics: the looming poster of Lenin in the first case and an explanation of women's rights in the second. The settings are erotic in both cases, yet the didactic introduction of current affairs makes them middlebrow. If sex and current affairs lessons look an odd combination on the page, they are not juxtaposed to incongruous or disturbing effect on screen. These are examples of middlebrow fusion as one becomes the language through which to speak the other.

El diputado likewise fuses eroticism and politics, with a didactic, middlebrow aim. The erotic is not therefore an added extra for a sensation-seeking audience, as in the case of the early 1970s '*destape*', but rather provides the very grammar by which the filmmaker speaks to audiences about new freedoms. Montage is a key component of this grammar, as is announced by the film's credits. The images cross-cut between an icon of homosexual desire, Michelangelo's David – first in long shot, and then in close-ups of isolated body parts – and classic Marxist images of speech-making and revolution. This juxtaposition is not played to disturb through incongruous juxtaposition, but rather to teach us how to view the film that follows. In it, we are invited to view homosexuality and left-wing politics as two forms of dissent – one of which, by 1978 in Spain, was legal, the other of which still was not – and that one helps us understand the other and vice versa.[11] I aim further to track this didactic procedure through characterisation, space and cross-cutting.

Roberto's characterisation and Sacristán's performance style are crucial for the film's didacticism. In order for his character to carry *El diputado*'s dual purposes of exploring with audiences the areas of previously banned left-wing politics, and still illegal homosexuality, Sacristán plays a rather vacant Roberto. Smith summarises the performance somewhat witheringly as one of 'curious anaemia', which in fact, and for this very reason, confers on the character 'value as an emblem' (1992: 148). The emptiness of the performance thus allows it to be filled with competing ideologies: anti-Franco politics and alternative sexualities intertwined. In this way Sacristán's Roberto is able to deliver lines like: 'After so many years of clandestine activity, persecutions, I wonder what my police file is like?' (my translation), in a tone that is so neutral that it is straightforward for the audience to read its double references. Similarly, in a celebrated scene that is a fiction within a fiction, Roberto's memory of his time as a barrister defending ETA terrorists before the Francoist state in a military court segues to a fabricated memory where he imagines himself in the dock and wonders if he would be capable of defending his own homosexuality?

The spatial metaphor of being in the dock, which conveys *El diputado*'s intertwining of sexuality and politics, is repeated in de la Iglesia's portrayal of the Carabanchel prison, where prisoners are detained side by side for both homosexual and political activities (this is where Roberto, who is imprisoned for the latter, meets pimp Nes [Ángel Pardo], who is imprisoned for the former). This use of space to intertwine sexuality and politics is further developed in the portrayal of Roberto's secret apartment. De la Iglesia's didactic aim to teach his audience about clandestine activities under Franco could scarcely be clearer here. While we watch in the present Roberto and Juanito's still-illegal erotic activities in the apartment we are constantly reminded – an unsympathetic reading might say that this reminding is somewhat heavy-handed – that this very same space was used for clandestine political activity during Francoism. Since all elements of film form are functional, further elements of *mise en scène* and soundtrack are deployed to underscore the message: first 'The Internationale' on the cassette player and second the Marxist propaganda posters on the wall (see Figure 6.1).

As in the opening credits, it is through the technique of didactic cross-cutting

Figure 6.1 José Sacristán and José Luis Alonso in *El diputado/Confessions of a Congressman*, directed by Eloy de la Iglesia. Spain: Figaro Films, Ufesa, Prozesa, 1978.

that de la Iglesia stresses this point. During Roberto and Juanito's first encounter in the flat, de la Iglesia includes a 30-second sequence in which he crosscuts between Juanito and Roberto in close-up with images of the leading figures of international Marxism also in close-up, all of which are posters that the viewer has previously glimpsed on the walls: Marx; Lenin (a nod to the bedroom scene of *Asignatura pendiente*); Che Guevara. The viewer is thus encouraged first to understand and sympathise with Roberto's homosexuality – his love for Juanito is stressed and is, we gradually learn, reciprocated, but, in a context in which homosexuality is still illegal despite Franco's death and the transition to democracy, the affair ends in the actual brutal murder of Juanito by the fascist thugs and the assumed future ruin of Roberto's political career as a consequence. The fiction closes as he is simultaneously about to be elected Secretary General of his party and as his affair and Juanito's death are about to be exposed. Furthermore, the cross-cutting between the lovers and the Marxist figures also encourages the audience to understand that left-wing political activism under Franco was subject to similar persecution.

I suggest that it is therefore in this repeated fusion of sex and politics that we may pinpoint the middlebrow erotic. For example, in de la Iglesia's hands, the erotic potential of the men's camping trip becomes instead an opportunity for expository inclusion of Marxist politics. Juanito's question about Roberto's political position prompts the older man to read communist theory later in the evening in the tent. The audience accesses the text's reflections on the 'dictadura del proletariado' (dictatorship of the proletariat) and the role of the

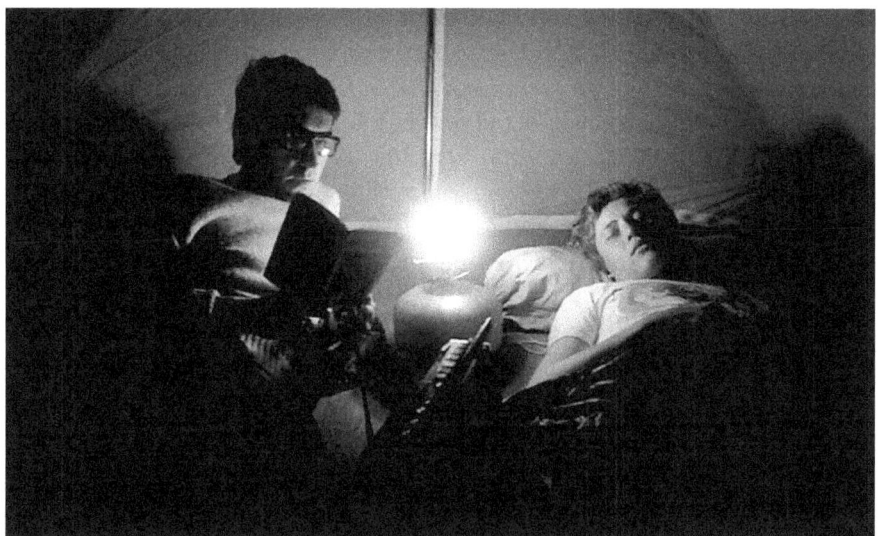

Figure 6.2 José Sacristán and José Luis Alonso in *El diputado/Confessions of a Congressman*, directed by Eloy de la Iglesia. Spain: Figaro Films, Ufesa, Prozesa, 1978.

'revolución del 1848' (1848 revolution) in voiceover as Roberto reads, between gazing at and caressing Juanito's angelic golden curls and listening to Vivaldi, part of a range of Baroque musical motifs that accompany the intimate scenes between the lovers throughout the film (see Figure 6.2). Likewise, the libidinous and the political are intertwined in the portrayal of Juanito's political awakening. When the rent-boy-who-falls-in-love raises his fist and gazes at Roberto in response to his speech at the political rally, is this a look of love, or a response to the politician's rousing rhetoric? The point is that it is both, with the didactic aim of encouraging the audience to consider both the left-wing politics and the homosexual practices that Francoism repressed.

As Paul Julian Smith rightly stresses (1992: 150), such an approach to plotting is highly schematic, reducing, in these examples, Marxist politics to 'The Internationale', a few posters, the odd fragment of theory and one or two speeches. The portrayal of Francoism, too, is reduced to the activities of the die-hard fascists who are simplistically caricatured as 'baddies'. Forty years on, the three 'simplistic narrative devices' that Smith observed in 1992 are perhaps even more obvious: 'schematic simplification, sentimentality, and crude topicality' (150). Reframing the analysis of *El diputado* from the perspective of the middlebrow, while not excusing a film's weaknesses, does however allow for a critical approach that may positively valorise didacticism within the very particular contexts of the Transition. An earnest desire to educate is typical of the middlebrow film, and is a tendency within Spanish cinema that continues today through humanist dramas on topics ranging from the re-evaluation of

Francoism via literary adaptations in the 1980s (for example, *La colmena / The Hive* [dir. Camus, 1982]), through to exploration of urban deprivation in the *cine social* of the 1990s (for example, *Solas / Alone* [dir. Zambrano, 1999]), to the heritage trend that reworks the past in the 2000s (for example, *Alatriste / Captain Alatriste: The Spanish Musketeer* [dir. Díaz Yanes, 2006]).[12] Reaching a mass audience on its theatrical and, especially, its TV screenings, *El diputado* is simultaneously a film that teaches Spaniards about the liberations and limits of their new political freedoms. Its innovation is to read political and sexual freedoms through one another, so that, at this particular moment in Spanish film history, when the 'S' category allowed the mainstream distribution of soft porn, eroticism was the very grammar in which film could speak to audiences of new freedoms.

CONCLUSION

Writing of the recovery of the middlebrow in literary studies, Janet Galligani Casey has noted that efforts to recuperate the middlebrow often have common cause with those of scholars seeking to recover other texts excluded from the canon for gender, ethnic or racial reasons. However, she rightly cautions that while this overlap is potentially productive it has often, in fact, been to the detriment of recovering the middlebrow. 'Texts have typically been recuperated through the efforts of feminist scholars, or scholars of race/ethnicity,' she suggests, 'while the middlebrow as a concept unto itself remains largely an uninvestigated "other"' (2012: 26). This appears to be the case with *El diputado*: it has attracted the attention of scholars for its treatment of its homosexual characters, but this foregrounding of questions of sexuality has moved its other, middlebrow, achievements into the background. Relocated in a middlebrow framework, S-rated *El diputado* may be read as a film that deploys eroticism didactically to explore sexuality and politics intertwined.

Writing of contemporary transnational film, Rosalind Galt and Karl Schoonover note that films that explore queer sexuality and the middlebrow may in fact be especially linked. Whereas Paul Julian Smith wrote in 1992 of de la Iglesia's Transition cinema that 'the very choice of a homosexual hero in these films must pose a challenge to [...] codes of representation and structures of identification inherent in dominant cinema practice' (134), Galt and Schoonover suggest in 2016 that while 'earlier models of art cinema include gay auteurs [...] as central figures, in contemporary world cinema queerness can operate as a middlebrowing factor, indicating a certain identitarian or social problem status that disbars films from truly highbrow taste', or, even, that 'Queerness Makes Films Middlebrow' (2016: 198). While the authors are careful to limit their remarks to the contemporary period, and use the post-

1980s term 'queer' advisedly, it is rewarding to reconsider the case of 1978's *El diputado* in the light of their argument. Forty years on, de la Iglesia's especial stress on contemporary political references and events both dates and localises the film significantly. Nonetheless, his didactic approach, 'teaching Spaniards about homosexuality' in Melero Salvador's words, resonates, surprisingly perhaps, with the contemporary queer middlebrow trend identified by Galt and Schoonover, which includes films like Lucía Puenzo's *Contracorriente/Undertow* (2009), and which, like *El diputado*, 'address bourgeois audiences concerned with the status of the family' (2016: 199).

Finally, reframing *El diputado* as a middlebrow film also brings into view surprising continuities in Spanish film history. Rated 'S' for its relatively explicit portrayal of eroticism, it has become a critical commonplace to contrast these films with those produced following Pilar Miró's reform of film production, exhibition and distribution when Director General of Cinema (1983–5). Even though the 'S' rating allowed the development of a 'domestic softcore film industry in Spain, predominantly produced for local consumption', which, between 1977 and 1982, numbered some 130 features, as Daniel Kowalsky has shown (2004: 189), Miró's reforms banned this exhibition category, replacing it with the hard-core 'X' rating. This extinguished the soft-core industry, and Miró's system of subsidies encouraged instead a type of film that was less tied to local context – period settings rather than the thick layers of contemporary references of *El diputado* – and a type of transnational film that was thought to be more appropriate for foreign film festivals, like heritage cinema. Spanish film historians have heaped scorn on this instance of government meddling, noting the perversity of banning the genuinely popular 'S' category, the naivety of a top-down attempt to impose 'quality' values on the national cinema, and the irony that many of the 'Miró' films failed at the box office, and that the first and still fundamental Spanish triumph at foreign film festivals is the work of Pedro Almodóvar, which itself drew on some of the eroticism of the 'S' category (though he in fact received Miró support too). What has been lost in all of this stress on change is that the middlebrow, didactic aims of the cinema of the Miró period in fact share those of a film like *El diputado*. While the transition to democracy in the 1970s and 1980s in Spain was clearly a time of change, a nuanced history of its culture also acknowledges continuities, continuities that are especially evident in the middlebrow culture of the period.

NOTES

1. While I use the standard dates here of 1973, when ETA assassinated Franco's successor Carrero Blanco, and 1986, the year of Spain's entry to the European Community, in the social, cultural and economic – if not political – arenas it is possible to argue for an earlier beginning, even as early as the 1960s, which has the advantage of decoupling the origins

of contemporary Spanish democracy from terrorism. It is also becoming increasingly accepted in all arenas that the Transition remains an open-ended process that is still not fully complete.
2. Literally 'uncovering', '*destape*' films refer mainly to partial nudity, and only occasionally to the 'uncovering' of new freedoms in other areas besides sex.
3. In their introduction to *Contemporary Spanish Cinema and Genre*, Jay Beck and Vicente Rodríguez Ortega explain that while the Spanish term '*subgéneros*' was first used to indicate that Spanish genres were 'subpar to American and European genres' (2008: 5), this problematic erection of a hierarchy between 'good' and 'bad' cinemas (2008: 8) betrays a bias against popular culture in Spain, well documented in the field of cinema by Núria Triana-Toribio (2003) and Antonio Lázaro-Reboll and Andy Willis (2004), among others. I use 'subgenre' in the neutral sense of an internal subdivision in a genre, in this case melodrama.
4. It is unclear whether 'S' is for 'sex' or for 'sensibility', as the films carried the (enticing) warning 'puede herir la sensibilidad del espectador' (may injure the sensitivity of the spectator) and both are blurred in the popular memory of the films, a memory into which *Los años desnudos (Clasificada S) / The Naked Years (Rated S)* (dirs. Ayaso and Sabroso, 2008) attempted to tap, with only partial success.
5. This and all following information on audience figures is taken from the 'Base de datos de películas calificadas' of the *Ministerio de Educación, Cultura y Deporte* website: http://www.mecd.gob.es (last accessed 20 April 2016).
6. Leading film director Pilar Miró served as Director General of Cinema in the first PSOE (Partido Socialista Obrero Español) government of democracy from 1982 to 1985. Her successor, Jorge Semprún, continued the controversial legislation she introduced in 1983, which provided subsidies to Spanish film as well as altering the ratings system and thereby abolishing the 'S' category. The Ley Miró was replaced by the Ley Semprún in 1989; under another Socialist minister, Carmen Alborch, it was dismantled in 1994.
7. When reflecting on being criticised for didacticism in Melero Salvador's interview of 2006, Guicoechea notes that the term has become more accepted (2013: 28); the same might be said of 'middlebrow'.
8. See Smith 1992: 129–32, for a detailed appraisal of press reviews on the film's release.
9. Smith's argument differs from my own in his suggestion that critics who insist on arthouse criteria themselves betray a 'middle-brow respect for art', thus attaching the descriptor to this culturally aspirant sector of the audience. Conversely, I deploy 'middlebrow' in this chapter to describe the didactic characteristics of the film text *El diputado* itself.
10. Melero Salvador has developed this in subsequent publications on the film's representation of homosexuality (for example, 2011).
11. I am grateful to Santi Fouz-Hernández for pointing out that this approach is reprised in *Another Country* (play by Julian Mitchell [first performed 1981] and film directed by Marek Kanievska [1984]).
12. For a full discussion of these continuities, see Faulkner 2013.

REFERENCES

Beck, Jay and Vicente Rodríguez Ortega (2008), 'Introduction', in Jay Beck and Vicente Rodríguez Ortega (eds), *Contemporary Spanish Cinema and Genre*, Manchester: Manchester University Press, pp. 1–23.

De Stefano, George (1986), 'Post-Franco Frankness', *Film Comment* 22:3, June, 58–60.
Faulkner, Sally (2013), *A History of Spanish Film: Cinema and Society 1910–2010*, New York: Bloomsbury Academic.
Faulkner, Sally (2016), 'Rehearsing for Democracy in Dictatorship Spain: Middlebrow Period Drama 1970–77', in Sally Faulkner (ed.), *Middlebrow Cinema*, London: Routledge, pp. 88–106.
Galligani Casey, Janet (2012), 'Middlebrow Reading and Undergraduate Teaching: the Place of the Middlebrow in the Academy', in Erica Brown and Mary Grover (eds), *Middlebrow Literary Cultures: The Battle of the Brows, 1920–1960*, Basingstoke: Palgrave Macmillan, pp. 25–36.
Galt, Rosalind and Karl Schoonover (2016), 'Hypotheses on the Middlebrow Queer', in Sally Faulkner (ed.), *Middlebrow Cinema*, London: Routledge, pp. 196–211.
Gómez-Sierra, Esther (2004), '"Palaces of Seeds": From an Experience of Local Cinemas in Post-War Madrid to a Suggested Approach to Film Audiences', in Antonio Lázaro-Reboll and Andrew Willis (eds), *Spanish Popular Cinema*, Manchester: Manchester University Press, pp. 92–112.
Hopewell, John (1989), *El cine español después de Franco*, Madrid: El Arquero.
Kowalsky, Daniel (2004), 'Rated S: Softcore Pornography and the Spanish Transition to Democracy', in Antonio Lázaro-Reboll and Andrew Willis (eds), *Spanish Popular Cinema*, Manchester: Manchester University Press, pp. 188–208.
Lázaro-Reboll, Antonio and Andy Willis (2004), 'Introduction: Film Studies, Spanish Cinema and Questions of the Popular', in Antonio Lázaro-Reboll and Andrew Willis (eds), *Spanish Popular Cinema*, Manchester: Manchester University Press, pp. 1–23.
Marsh, Steven (2013), 'Neville, Berlanga, and de la Iglesia: A Strategically Disruptive Auteurism', in Jo Labanyi and Tatjana Pavlović (eds), *A Companion to Spanish Cinema*, Malden: Wiley-Blackwell, pp. 153–60.
Melero Salvador, Alejandro (2004), 'New Sexual Politics in the Cinema of the Transition to Democracy: de la Iglesia's *El diputado* (1978)', in Steve Marsh and Parvati Nair (eds), *Gender and Spanish Cinema*, Oxford: Berg, pp. 87–102.
Melero Salvador, Alejandro (2011), 'Armas para una narrativa del sexo. Transgresión y cine "S"', in Manuel Palacio (ed.), *El cine y la transición política en España (1975–1982)*, Madrid: Biblioteca Nueva, pp. 127–44.
Melero, Alejandro (2013), *La noche inmensa: La palabra de Gonzalo Goicochea* (Cuadernos Tecmerin, Volumen 3), Madrid: Universidad Carlos III.
Palacio, Manuel (2001), *Historia de la televisión en España*, Barcelona: Gedisa.
Prout, Ryan (2005), '*El diputado / Confessions of a Congressman*', in Alberto Mira (ed.), *The Cinema of Spain and Portugal*, London: Wallflower Press, pp. 159–67.
Smith, Paul Julian (1992), *Laws of Desire: Questions of Homosexuality in Spanish Writing and Film 1960–1990*, Oxford: Oxford University Press.
Triana-Toribio, Núria (2003), *Spanish National Cinema*, London: Routledge.
Tropiano, Stephen (1997), 'Out of the Cinematic Closet: Homosexuality in the Films of Eloy de la Iglesia', in Marsha Kinder (ed.), *Refiguring Spain: Cinema / Media / Representation*, Durham, NC: Duke University Press, pp. 157–77.

FILMOGRAPHY

Alatriste/Captain Alatriste: The Spanish Musketeer, film, directed by Agustín Díaz Yanes. Spain: Estudios Picasso, Origen Producciones Cinematográficas, NBC Global Networks, 2006.

Another Country, film, directed by Marek Kanievska. UK: Goldcrest Films International, National Film Finance Corporation, 1984.

Asignatura pendiente/Unfinished Business, film, directed by José Luis Garci. Spain: José Luis Tafur, 1977.

Contracorriente/Undertow, film, directed by Lucía Puenzo. Peru: Elcalvo Films, Dynamo Producciones, La Cinéfacture, Neue Cameo Film, 2009.

El diputado/Confessions of a Congressman, film, directed by Eloy de la Iglesia. Spain: Figaro Films, Ufesa, Prozesa, 1978.

Españolas en París/Spanish Women in Paris, film, directed by Roberto Bodegas. Spain: Ágata Films, 1971.

Fortunata y Jacinta, TV series, directed by Mario Camus. Spain: Radio Televisión Española, Telvétia, Téléfrance, 1980.

Gilda, film, directed by Charles Vidor. USA: Columbia Pictures Corporation, 1946.

La colmena/The Hive, film, directed by Mario Camus. Spain: Televisión Española, Ágata Films, 1982.

Los años desnudos (Clasificada S)/The Naked Years (Rated S), film, directed by Dunia Ayaso and Félix Sabroso. Spain: Antena 3 Films, Little Giraffe Producciones, 2008.

Los placeres ocultos/Hidden Pleasures, film, directed by Eloy de la Iglesia. Spain: Alborada, 1977.

Solas/Alone, film, directed by Benito Zambrano. Spain: Maestranza Films; Canal Sur Televisión, Canwest Entertainment, Fireworks Pictures, Vía Digital, 1999.

Solos en la madrugada/Alone in the Dark, film, directed by José Luis Garci. Spain: José Luis Tafur, 1978.

Tormento/Torment, film, directed by Pedro Olea. Spain: José Frade Producciones Cinematográficas, 1974.

Un hombre llamado flor de otoño/A Man Called Autumn Flower, film, directed by Pedro Olea. Spain: José Frade Producciones Cinematográficas, Panoramica, 1978.

CHAPTER 7

Revisiting Bigas Luna's *Bilbao*: The Female Body-Object

Carolina Sanabria

BIGAS LUNA'S *BILBAO* AND EROTIC CINEMA IN POST-FRANCO SPAIN

The production of sex-themed cinema in Spain is inevitably linked to the political climate. There are other factors to take into account such as the crisis in the wider film industry – caused by a lack of international investment and poor box office takings in domestic markets. As John Hopewell notes, sex narratives became increasingly popular on Spanish screens from 1977. As he explains, this was partly due to the liberties allowed to filmmakers after the end of the dictatorship and the abolition of censorship, but also as a direct result of the crisis in the sector, which led to the exploration of new possibilities (1989: 287). In this period, films became more sexually explicit. New film classifications were introduced: the 'S' category was used for films that contained scenes that could offend the still-unadjusted sensitivity of conservative spectators; while the 'X' category was used for pornographic films. As Monterde has argued, the first post-Franco years saw 'the emergence of sexual polymorphism, that is, of the variety of forms of relationships which Francoist censorship had repressed [...]: homosexuality, transsexuality, incest, fetishism and various other "perversions"' (1993: 165).

The political transition in Spain brought about a new democratic pluralism that encouraged new forms of artistic expression. Pepón Coromina, an exceptional producer in Figaro Films, was a decisive figure at that time. He pushed through a number of transgressive projects that set the tone for a vibrant new climate that energised the Spanish film industry of the Transition. It is thanks to Coromina that now-iconic projects including Bigas Luna's *Bilbao* (1978) or Almodóvar's *Pepi, Luci, Bom y otras chicas del montón/Pepi, Lucy, Bom and Other Girls Like Mom* (1980) came to fruition in Barcelona and Madrid almost simultaneously.[1]

Bigas Luna's *Bilbao* (1978) stands out as a fundamental film of post-Franco Spanish cinema. It could be argued that the very stark depiction of the female body somehow deprives the film of its erotic content. This might explain why Vicente Benet writes that, unlike the films of Berlanga or even Almodóvar, the unsophisticated, commercial images that characterise *cine S* productions make us experience 'an uneasiness that cannot be analysed just in terms of the film's socio-political contexts' (Benet 2012: 386). Prior to *Bilbao*, Bigas Luna had only directed the uneven *Tatuaje/Tattoo* (1978), as well as some kitschy pornographic short films periodically distributed on video, which served as the thematic and aesthetic foundations of *Bilbao*.[2] To some extent, this material would influence the trajectory of a director who made his particular depiction of the female body on the screen part of his personal signature. The point I wish to make here is that even though the importance of *Bilbao* could have resided in having constituted the basis for Spanish erotic film production after the Transition,[3] this film – unlike much of the rest of Bigas Luna's filmography – is not, in fact, particularly erotic. As I am about to show, the female body in this film is presented as anything but sensual.

A DECADENT COLLECTOR

The protagonist of the film reveals a certain pathological condition that the film is not interested in explaining. Rather than attempting to psychoanalyse or rationalise his conduct, the film simply visualises it as his everyday, routine activity. Leo (Ángel Jové) is a member of one of the best-established, bourgeois families of Barcelona. The family is based in an indeterminate town of the Barcelona province which Leo occasionally visits in the company of María (María Martín), the woman with whom he lives in a strange, loveless relationship.[4] This location itself draws attention to the dysfunctional configuration of the family, which is not unusual in the work of Bigas Luna. Indeed, this is a recurring characteristic in his three most personal and career-defining films: *Bilbao*, *Caniche/Poodle* (1979) and *Angustia/Anguish* (1987). As Ramón Espelt argues, the male protagonist in these films is immersed 'within a family structure completely dominated by the maternal figure, with the father being secondary or absent', adding that 'the impulsive, irrational, animal-like, asocial world of the characters seems to be the consequence of this potent, dominant influence of the maternal figure' (1989: 48).

María's relationship with Leo (she is noticeably older than him) often resembles that of a mother with her child. María is the maternal woman-uterus and as such, the one he returns to at the end of the film looking for help. In a climactic scene that takes place in María's bedroom, Leo cries inconsolably on her lap in a clearly foetal position. She listens and attempts to soothe him

– in vain. A similar situation will be recreated by Bigas Luna later in *Angustia*, between the anxious Dr Hoffmann (Michael Lerner) and his mother (Zelda Rubinstein). But in *Bilbao* María is determined to take action and protect Leo: in desperation she drives to the warehouse, picks up and covers Bilbao's body, then sets off for his uncle's home, where she takes care of the disposal of the body while Leo waits passively in the passenger seat.

The family interaction lingers on like an imprecise insinuation of incestuous relationships, and although marriage does not come into the equation, there is an implicit, silent acceptance of the situation in Leo's family circle that further underlines that dynamic of closed relationships. This is further complicated by the fact that María is occasionally Leo's uncle's lover. This family dynamic is reminiscent of the nineteenth-century English bourgeoisie, which encouraged marriage between relatives in order to keep their fortunes in the family (Kuper 2009), but also consistent with what Marsha Kinder calls the 'Oedipal narratives' of Spanish films during the democratic transition:

> Oedipal conflicts within the family were used to speak about political issues and historical events that were repressed from filmic representation during the Francoist era and [...] continue to be used with even greater flamboyance in the post-Franco period after censorship and repression had been abolished. (1993: 197–8)

This idea was made even more explicit by Bigas Luna in his next film, *Caniche*.[5] In most of his filmography, relationships in wealthy family environments tend to degrade considerably as a result of tacitly accepted perversions. In *Bilbao* this decadence is found in the intimate, everyday portrait of Leo, a solitary, distant character, as well as a fetishist and voyeur. The diegesis is a paradoxical mix of intimate, secretive moments and a sense of distancing and refusal to engage with his complex psyche. The characterisation of Leo can be regarded as part of the twentieth-century renewed interest in vanguards and experimentation (especially in literature – Kafka, Camus, Robbe-Grillet), expressed in certain character types that are eventually revealed as urban anti-heroes.[6] In turn, this characterisation prevents the traditional identification of the viewer with the protagonist (inherited from nineteenth-century novels) by virtue of his psychological impenetrability, visually reinforced through his perpetual dark glasses. The film does not narrate what he feels or believes, but just what he sees or does, although his routine is not perceived as repetitive, nor redundant. The film imagines every detail of his daily life, to the point that it becomes a sort of visual(ised) diary.[7]

Perhaps Leo can be better understood in relation to Frederic Clegg, another similarly introspective, abstract character, who is also an orphan and an avid collector in John Fowles' homonymous novel, first published in 1963.[8] The two characters illustrate Laura Mulvey's assertion that film satisfies a primordial desire of experiencing pleasure in looking (scopophilia) (1992), that is, the same disposition of a certain male gaze that projects and organises its fantasies around the female figure. This is clear in Leo, who locks himself in rooms to watch porn (a kind of *mise en abyme* because those films are Bigas Luna's own kitschy short porn films). Leo's gaze drives the main plot, which follows the stalking and kidnapping of the woman with whom he is obsessed. This is not objective narration; rather it is presented as Leo's inner experience in his obsessive interior quest. Thus we have a tempered, almost emotionless, first-person narration reminiscent to that of Fowles' novel, especially in the moment when he realises that his precious prisoner is dead. 'I suddenly knew she was dead and dead means gone for ever, for ever and ever' (Fowles 2004: 165), Clegg says, coldly, with a hint of resigned acceptance that is echoed in Leo's voiceover when he realises the fate of his own captive victim: 'She's not breathing. She's dead. My entire world has been destroyed.' This event throws him back into the unbearable reality of his life, that he was trying to avoid through his obsessive quest.

Leo is thus the filmic equivalent of an emotionally wounded literary character. He is motivated by a perverted perception of the object, of the transgression of his domineering social value, a deviation from the norm (Vilches 1978: 26). This is expressed in traits such as his agoraphobia, clearly reminiscent of the aforementioned uterine subjection. Hence his declared preference for enclosed – not necessarily private – places: the interior of the house, buses, stores, shopping centres, the nightclub, and so on. In contrast, he relates to exterior spaces through filters, be it glass windows or screens (Espelt 1989: 52). As a member of the declining bourgeoisie, Leo is infantilised (like Bernardo in *Caniche*, or John Hoffmann in *Angustia*). He is also jobless, dedicated full time to his obsessive fixation with Bilbao, a woman radically opposed to her counterpart María. She is dark-skinned, young and streetwise, but also submissive. These are necessary traits for her job as a prostitute, a factor that makes her even more of an object in his view.

JUST ANOTHER POSSESSION

Leo's trajectory is fuelled by his obsession for the objectified woman. This objectification is manifested as the product of the protagonist's desire for the female body. In turn, his desire seems to be fuelled by a perceived 'to-be-looked-at-ness' quality of the female figure. As Mulvey posits in her much-commented article from 1975: '[i]n their traditional exhibitionist role women are simultaneously looked at and displayed, with their appearance coded for strong visual and erotic impact' (1992: 27). As an object to be looked at and exhibited (in the seedy club where she dances – as seen on the cover image of this volume), Bilbao uses her desirability to present herself as a threat. In this sense, she is juxtaposed with María, who, in contrast, seems constrained by the space of the home and therefore implicitly controlled by Leo.[9] But while María becomes a twisted version of the stay-at-home mom, to paraphrase Gubern (1997: 792), Bilbao is silent, she's an object: not only does she accept what is done to her, no questions asked, but she doesn't create problems. Unlike Miranda, Fowles' female protagonist, she does not question her captor's motivations. The only time we hear her voice is when Leo hires her services and insists that she must remain quiet. As a female object she is not even in a position to realise that she is being kidnapped.

Bilbao activates the scopophilic urge in Leo in ways that, once again, illustrate Mulvey's argument. He fetishises her as a female-object. He channels his fetishist obsession through the meticulous collection of everyday objects that he associates with her: pieces of the type of underwear that she uses, the famous song by Lotte Lenya entitled *Bilbao*, a train ticket to the Basque city of the same name, the intimate photos that he takes of her as she fellates him, and so on. This list of significant items is articulated along a convoluted route interpreted in Lacanian psychoanalysis as mobilisation of desire. The accumulation of objects, which ultimately function as substitutes, works as a metonymic strategy with the purpose of transforming Bilbao into a provisionally tranquilling figure, into an object. Nevertheless, this path, that may *appear* to be unlimited, will eventually reach a point of exhaustion and thus fail to satisfy Leo. The act of ownership will unavoidably lead to her death. Simultaneously, Leo also tries to mitigate the threat of castration that Bilbao represents.[10] In a logic of sadistic appropriation, she imposes her dominance in her complicity with the kidnapping. This transgression will inevitably be punished (with death).

Like the film itself, the female protagonist Bilbao has an instrumental, object-like quality.[11] She is 'a thing', as Leo says, comparable to the other things that he has been obsessively collecting for his personal album.[12] 'In my car she's like rubber, she reminds me of my *things* but she's different' [emphasis mine], murmurs Leo. As I have argued in my previous analysis of this film, this is why Leo administers drugs to Bilbao, 'not only so that she puts up no resistance, but also to complete her objectification' (Sanabria 2010: 25). Bilbao's very profession reinforces this perception. To paraphrase Bataille, in mobilising her desire, the prostitute contributes to making herself the object of men's own aggressive desire (1985: 137). She may be degraded to the level of an object, but not just *any* object. Rather, she is an object of distinct *artistic* worth, because Leo seems devoted to her – only as long as she does not speak. At the time of the film release, Bigas Luna tried to pre-empt any possible feminist criticisms (which never actually materialised then) by stating that

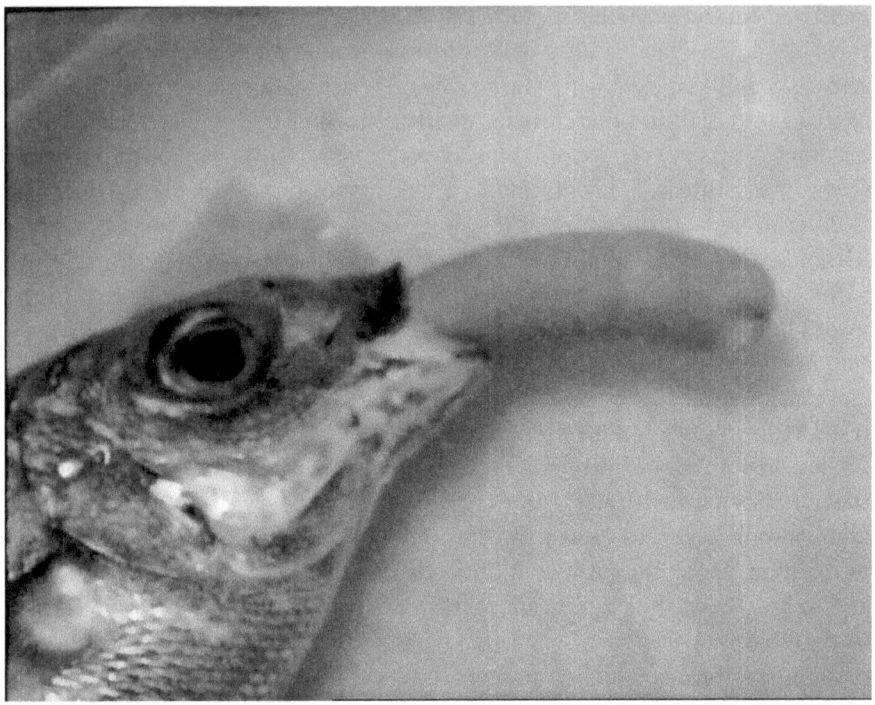

Figure 7.1 *Bilbao*, directed by Josep Joan Bigas Luna. Spain: Figaro-Ona Films, Ona Films.

the film was an artistic 'tribute to the woman as an object of desire' (cited in Xavier-Daniel 1978: 28). In other words, the film proposes a metaphorical representation of woman-as-art.

Through Leo, *Bilbao* allows Bigas Luna to pay tribute to his own surrealist beginnings – a sort of personal signature that is also indebted to his background in graphic design.[13] Bilbao becomes a sort of still-life (in the encounter between organic and processed 'food'), but one that is full of sexual connotations and that responds to the obsessive, hermetic world of the protagonist. The famous scene of the fish with a frankfurter in its mouth (see Figure 7.1) functions as a further graphic metonymy for fellatio, a sex act that becomes an obsession for Leo, as suggested by his dental hygiene rituals. However, this image evokes a certain ambivalence because Leo is clearly disgusted when he touches 'the object'. Gubern sees this as reminiscent of infantile sexuality and other internal associations: the fish being wet and thus evocative of oral sex, but also cold and passive (1997: 793), just like Leo. This image also evokes the kind of associations that Georges Bataille (1995) establishes in his novel *Story of the Eye* (*Histoire de l'oeil* – originally published in 1928), specifically in the chain enunciation of signifiers plate-egg-eye, here ending in an orifice: fish-frankfurter-mouth. The castration imagery does not end here. The frank-

Figure 7.2 Isabel Pisano in *Bilbao*, directed by Josep Joan Bigas Luna. Spain: Figaro-Ona Films, Ona Films.

furter is associated with desire, with the symbolic (Bilbao) and is later eaten, by María, in another highly metaphoric scene.

The vision of the floating uterus in the maternal body is recreated in the arrangement of the hanging body (see Figure 7.2). This responds to Leo's explicit desire to 'raise' the body of the prostitute to the level of an artwork. Before becoming a film director, Bigas Luna was famous for his performance art pieces with inanimate objects (including broken chairs and tables) in surrealist exhibitions like the celebrated *Taules* (1973) in the Vinçon Gallery in Barcelona. Aside from the director's artistic background, classic art also offers a source of inspiration for the hanging body in terms of the central character of the disquieting Baroque painting by José de Ribera, *El martirio de San Felipe/ Martyrdom of Saint Philip* (1639). In both images there is a shared obsession 'with the waste, with the corpse, [a] wish to leave the body intact and whole, that is, dead' (Sollers 1978: 49). Despite the obvious differences – the painting is religious – both images depict naked, hanging bodies. Bigas Luna thus recontextualises the act of Bilbao's immolation and makes it sacred. This is further emphasised in the animal sacrifices represented by the pigs hanging in the family warehouse. Above all, it is a parodic resignification because Bilbao is not a martyr, nor a saint. She isn't even what Girard would call a ritualistic victim (2005: 21); there is no cause to defend in her case. At the end of the day, she is 'just' an anonymous prostitute, who does not have anyone to turn to – not even the pimp she lives with, as he is just as insignificant as she is. Nobody is likely to miss her or look for her. Thus, the chosen woman is ultimately regarded as *a thing* to be sought, undressed, arranged, hung and suppressed, *but not* assassinated. As previously stated, as an object, Bilbao cannot die: 'in the end, well, she does not die. She simply breaks and nothing has happened here', as Delclós wrote in his review (1978). The camera itself reinforces this point: the objectification of the woman is displaced by the man's desire. She is part of the collection of objects and symbolises an act of fetishism. Leo's metonymic search ends with the annihilation of Bilbao. It had started by following her, observing her, hiring her services, slowly intensifying the harassment, and finally making her disappear. In the end Leo – deprived of his toy – becomes the real – and only – victim.[14]

CONCLUSION: THE DE-EROTICISED BODY

This chapter argues that, unlike in so many films by Bigas Luna, the female body in *Bilbao* is not represented as sensual or erotic.[15] Instead, we find a more cold-hearted depiction of Bilbao's body as a mere instrument of (sadistic) pleasure for a pathological male subject.[16]

Stylistically *Bilbao* has a certain affinity to pornography insofar as it works with the same kind of goods, resources and rhetoric. More broadly, one might argue that the beginnings of the erotic discourse in post-Franco Spanish cinema required that the object be depicted as explicitly as possible. This is consistent with the conception of the project. Pepón Coromina saw in the twenty-eight-page script written by Bigas Luna a 'suggestively pornographic story' (cited in Font, Garay and Batlle 1978b: 28). John Hopewell wrote that *Bilbao* illustrates the frustration of pornography (1989: 290), and for Marsha Kinder the film 'could easily be called soft core and even includes an excerpt from hard core pornography' (1993: 262). Domènec Font adds that the film utilises expressive strategies characteristic of porn insofar as the story is constructed as an abstraction of sex (1978: 21–2). This argument is echoed by Pérez Perucha (1979: 34–5).

The first-person point-of-view perspective is underscored with the use of medium and close-up shots, at one point focusing on Bilbao's shaved pubis. Leo's gaze breaks up the body into its iconic parts in ways that are more characteristic of porn than of mainstream erotic cinema. Thus, the visual emphasis is on the female face (which focalises desire), as well as on her breasts and legs (Gubern 2005: 30). The resulting effect is rather unpleasant. More precisely, it is not so much that the film is not constructed around the erotic object, but rather that it revolves around a particular relationship of the protagonist with the objects that surround him. As Vilches states: 'the objects in the film (Bilbao included) exist for Leo at the same level of reality as the film exists for the spectator. The hallucinogenic connections that he establishes between himself and the objects are represented in the real acts of cutting, assembling, tying up, binding, cleaning, drying, and so on' (1978: 26).

This particular kind of relationship between the subject and the objects is filtered into the conventional narration, only occasionally materialising in fragments that acquire a certain schizophrenic tone, and which can be confused with the subjectivity of the character. For example, the psychotic nature of the moments leading up to Bilbao's kidnapping initially creates some confusion between fantasy and reality (a strategy that will be used more intensively in *Angustia*). However, the sequence that follows suggests that those moments were just a product of Leo's imagination (Sanabria 2010: 39). As Pérez Perucha has argued, this could not be any other way, as 'in order to have a conversation on the effects of pornography through a fictional character, the spectator has to experience those effects first-hand' (1979: 34). Thus, the film encourages some complicity between the spectator and the film's male protagonist. His journey is one marked by a compulsive attraction towards objects connected with his obsession. His position is thus restricted to passive scopophilia. Only exceptionally will he make a move to put his visual fantasies into practice, as when he spills milk over María's behind (see Figure 7.3) and then over Bilbao's body. These milk-spilling scenes are another, clear example of the film's hard-core aesthetics.[17] It is in one of these rare instances in which Leo seems to abandon his passive attitude in favour of action that he will end up paying the price by losing his most precious object.

I am not proposing that *Bilbao* is a pornographic film, but it is certainly not a conventionally erotic film, at least not in the same category as Bigas Luna's other films of this period. The connection that *Bilbao* establishes with reality is similar to the one that porn 'forces the spectator to have with the usual referents for this type of film and the representation of sex that it proposes/imposes' (Pérez Perucha 1979: 34). The very format of the film adds to this effect: it was shot in 16mm and later blown up to 35mm, giving it a 'dirty feel' (Bigas Luna in Font, Batlle and Garay 1978a: 23). This is further intensified in the fragmented representation of objects. These effects create a morbid and intimate complicity (if not necessarily identification) between the character and the spectator.

This chapter, then, has argued that *Bilbao* can be regarded as a foundational text of Spanish sex-themed cinema; one which suggests a sense of disillusionment with the female body, presented in its purest expression, totally degraded, stripped of any accessories that would make it desirable – and therefore distant from one of the main traits of eroticism. The female body is carefully dissected, but not presented for any kind of elaborate pleasurable

Figure 7.3 María Martín in *Bilbao*, directed by Josep Joan Bigas Luna. Spain: Figaro-Ona Films, Ona Films.

viewing. The objectification of the female body culminates in the absence of life. Unlike in other Bigas Luna films, in *Bilbao* there is no place for seduction. Sex here is closest to what Baudrillard conceived as the staging of disillusion with the body and with the world (1989: 46). The woman who appeared desirable throughout the film ends up becoming an object in Leo's collection: completely serene, detached, and whose nakedness suggests that her annihilation was the ultimate resolution of desire.

The culmination of what had been presented as the metonymic journey of the film's protagonist comes when Bilbao, drugged and naked, is hung in the family warehouse, her pubis shaved. This is a scene coded as pornographic, even for the unsubtle and explicit standards of sexual representation in Spanish cinema of the Transition. The female genitals had to be shaved to allow a clear view, clean and whole for the spectator.[18] As Font put it, 'stripped now of all ornamentation, of all fetishist emphasis, the object of desire is revealed, in its naked reality: Bilbao's sex, carefully shaved by Leo, is not only the most shocking shot of the film but also its symbolic depiction' (1978: 22). The sight of Bilbao's shaved sex becomes a focus of anxiety, a threatening vacuum that opens up to nothingness. Leo's quest to satisfy a desire that is slowly achieved and culminated in the fateful final sequence turns *Bilbao* into a film about the disillusionment with the body, rather than the erotic film that it is often perceived to be. Importantly, *Bilbao* is also a turning point in Bigas Luna's trajectory, as it marks the start of what I would call 'the black period', after which his work would take a new direction and make his name essential in any discussion about erotic cinema in Spain.[19]

NOTES

1. Both films, in effect, responded to the personal aesthetics of their directors (sordid in Bigas Luna's case, and 'ugly' in Almodóvar's), who were also the scriptwriters at the time. These were groundbreaking storylines for the period. Sexual explicitness in both cases was related to fluids: milk in *Bilbao*, urine in *Pepi, Luci, Bom y otras chicas del montón*. It is also worth noting that both films had very small budgets: *Bilbao* was made with just 11 million pesetas (see Font, Garay and Batlle 1978b: 28–9; Gubern 2014: 15–27).
2. At two points during the film, the protagonist locks himself in the bedroom to watch *The Millionaire*, one of the eleven kitschy porn shorts made by Bigas Luna in 16mm. Leo will watch them again with Bilbao, before realising that she is dead.
3. John Hopewell sees *Bilbao* as *the* most important Spanish film (1989: 290).
4. The visits clearly allude to the oppressive environment that characterises bourgeoisie families – metaphorically represented in their geographical isolation. They appear in the films of Jaime Chávarri or Carlos Saura. Weinrichter emphasises that while it is not a matter of righting wrongs from the past, Bigas Luna uses them as a reminder of the Francoist regime (1992: 29).
5. In *Caniche* the male protagonist, played by the same actor, lives in an all-but-ruined house – a symbol for the decadent bourgeoisie – and seems doomed as a result of the attraction he feels for his sister Eloísa (Consol Tura).
6. The parallelism of Leo with Mathias, the imperturbable protagonist of Robbe-Grillet's objectivist novel *Le voyeur* (first published in 1955) is particularly interesting. Like Leo, Mathias is constantly looking around and describing the context that he wishes to alter; but is neither punished for his crimes, nor psychoanalysed. Above all, this punctilious story revolves around the character and has almost no plot, a characteristic of the *Nouveau Roman*. Bigas Luna's film partakes in this experimentalism that has its origins in literature (*chosisme*). This literary phenomenon had taken off around a decade earlier, but is here adapted by Bigas Luna to cinematic language.
7. There are few of these scenes, but they are all significant. One of these focuses on Leo's visit to the club where Bilbao dances. The scene starts with a close-up of Leo's face, followed by a point-of-view shot of Bilbao's head. Slowly, the camera tilts down Bilbao's body, reaching her abdomen. As if interrupted by sound, the tilt stops just before reaching her pubis. This is cross-cut with a close-up shot of Leo's razor, while he is shaving the following morning back home. As I argue elsewhere, this editing technique links 'not only two different places and moments, but also two body parts of the characters (her pubis and his mind)' (Sanabria 2010: 25). The editing also anticipates the consummation of Leo's desire.
8. He also shares the propensity for collecting with another disturbed character from Bigas

Luna's filmography, John Hoffmann, the psychopathic ophthalmologist's assistant who steals and stores the eyes of his victims in *Angustia*.

9. This becomes very clear when he serves her a glass of milk – a reference to Hitchcock – or when she is shown waiting for him in the bed that they do not share.
10. Inasmuch as the search for the object is motivated by an internal quest, an inner experience, as Bataille argued (1985: 33).
11. The very name of the prostitute is part of the same (extra-diegetic) objectification. She is named after Euskadi's capital, but this is a false signifier. There is no topographical connection here; Bilbao was chosen as a name because it sounded good, like Berlin – as acknowledged by the director himself (see Tele/eXprés 1978: 26).
12. As I mentioned earlier, as protagonist, Leo organises and articulates a discourse reminiscent of the *chosisme* of the *Nouveau Roman*. Marsha Kinder proposes that '[t]he film has nothing to do with real women but is merely the fantasy projection of men' (Kinder 1993: 275). That is to say, the woman is once more a clear narrative pretext, in the sense expressed by director Bud Boetticher, cited by Mulvey (1992: 27): 'What counts is what the heroine provokes, or rather what she represents. She is the one, or rather the love or fear she inspires in the hero, or else the concern he feels for her, who makes him act the way he does. In herself the woman has not the slightest importance.'
13. The Catalan film movement arose in part as a reaction against Francoist repression. Following the emergence in the previous decade of the School of Barcelona or the *gauche divine*, surrealist influences gave way to a more plastic kind of cinema, as Bigas Luna himself suggested in an interview in *La mirada* (see Font, Batlle and Garay 1978a: 24).
14. With the loss of Bilbao comes the loss of control of the *fort/da* dynamic, as Kinder asserts: 'When her body is ground up in the factory, she literally becomes a sausage, the missing phallus that speaks *his* castration, not *hers*' (1993: 274 – original emphasis).
15. Twenty years later the film *La camarera del Titanic* (1997) re-examines the idea of the woman as object, but in the later film desire is sublimated by the male protagonist in the context of an amorous (and yet, still addictive) discourse.
16. It could be argued that, in Leo, Bigas Luna revisits Bataille's idea of the avidity 'for everything that transgresses order [and] is linked to profound sexuality, for example: blood, sudden terror, crime' (1995: 30).
17. The image of the milk running down María's legs is an allusion to the initial passage of Bataille's (1995) aforementioned novel. Like María in the film, Simona in the novel also wears black tights. This produces a dramatic contrast with the white milk running down the characters' legs in both instances.
18. Some extra-filmic anecdotes corroborate this perception of *Bilbao* as a pornographic film. On one occasion Román Gubern took a group of film studies students from the University of Southern California to a screening of *Bilbao* at the Maryland Cinema in Barcelona. As I mentioned elsewhere, 'they walked out frustrated and bothered, confused as to why they had been taken to watch a "pornographic film"' (Sanabria 2010: 13). When the film was originally released, a journalist witnessed a group of young people at the box office of that same film theatre in Barcelona attempting to buy tickets well after the film had started. When they were warned that the film had started more than half an hour ago, they said that it did not matter, as the scenes that they were interested in were yet to come (Catalunya Exprés 1978).
19. The 'black triptych' includes *Angustia*, which shares much of the form and content strategies of the two other films. Originally, however, the project was composed of *Caniche* and *El niño del estanque/The Child of the Pond*, which was never filmed, presumably due to its controversial paedophilic content.

REFERENCES

Bataille, Georges (1985), *El erotismo*, Barcelona: Tusquets.
Bataille, Georges (1995 [1928]), *Historia del ojo*, Mexico City: Ediciones Coyoacán.
Baudrillard, Jean (1989), *De la seducción*, Madrid: Cátedra.
Benet, Vicente (2012), *El cine español: Una historia cultural*, Barcelona: Paidós.
Catalunya Exprés (1978), 'Los estrenos, todos a una', *Catalunya Express*, 20 September 1978.
Delclós, Tomàs (1978), 'Bilbao', *Tele/eXprés*, 8 June 1978.
Espelt, Ramon (1989), *Mirada al món de Bigas Luna*, Barcelona: Laertes.
Font, Domènec, Jesús Garay and Joan Batlle (1978a), 'Entrevista con Bigas Luna', *La mirada* 4, 23–4.
Font, Domènec, Jesús Garay and Joan Batlle (1978b), 'Entrevista con Pepón Coromina', *La mirada* 4, 28–9.
Font, Domènec (1978), 'Saturación de la mirada', *La mirada* 4, 21–2.
Fowles, John (2004 [1963]), *El coleccionista*, trans. Susana Onega, Madrid: Cátedra.
Girard, René (2005 [1972]), *La violencia y lo sagrado*, Barcelona: Anagrama.
Gubern, Román (1997), 'Bilbao', in Julio Pérez Perucha (ed.), *Antología crítica del cine español 1906–1995*, Madrid: Cátedra, pp. 791–3.
Gubern, Román (2005), *La imagen pornográfica y otras perversiones ópticas*, Barcelona: Anagrama.
Gubern, Román (2014), 'Movida y transgresión en el primer Almodóvar', in Pedro Poyato Sánchez (ed.), *El cine de Almodóvar: una poética de lo 'trans'*, Sevilla: Universidad Internacional de Andalucía, pp. 15–27.
Hopewell, John (1989), *El cine español después de Franco (1973–1988)*, Madrid: El Arquero.
Kinder, Marsha (1993), *Blood Cinema: The Reconstruction of National Identity in Spain*, Berkeley: University of California Press.
Kuper, Adam (2009), *Incest and Influence: The Private Life of Bourgeois England*, Cambridge, MA: Harvard University Press.
Monterde, José Enrique (1993), *Veinte años de cine español (1973–1992): Un cine bajo la paradoja*, Barcelona: Paidós.
Mulvey, Laura (1992 [1975]), 'Visual Pleasure and Narrative Cinema', in Screen (eds), *The Sexual Subject: A Screen Reader in Sexuality*, London and New York: Routledge, pp. 22–34.
Pérez Perucha, Julio (1979), 'Bilbao', *Contracampo. Revista de cine* 5, 34–5.
Robbe-Grillet, Alain (1987 [1955]), *El mirón*, Madrid: Cátedra.
Sanabria, Carolina (2010), *Bigas Luna, el ojo voraz*, Barcelona: Laertes.
Sollers, Philippe (1978), 'Porno año cero', *La mirada* 1, 48–9.
Tele/eXprés (1978), 'Charla morbosa en torno a *Bilbao*', *Tele/eXprés*, 29 June 1978, 26.
Vilches, Lorenzo (1978), '*Bilbao*: un objeto alucinante', *La mirada* 4, 25–7.
Xavier-Daniel (1978), 'Pre-estreno de *Bilbao* de Bigas Luna', *Mundo Diario*, 30 June 1978, 28.
Weinrichter, Antonio (1992), *La línea del vientre: El cine de Bigas Luna*, Gijón (Festival de cine): La Versal.

FILMOGRAPHY

Angustia/Anguish, film, directed by Josep Joan Bigas Luna. Spain: Luna Films, Pepón Coromina, Samba P.C., 1987.

Bilbao, film, directed by Josep Joan Bigas Luna. Spain: Figaro-Ona Films, Ona Films, 1978.
Caniche/Poodle, film, directed by Josep Joan Bigas Luna. Spain: Figaro Films, 1979.
La camarera del Titanic, film, directed by Josep Joan Bigas Luna. France/Italy/Germany/Spain: UGC YM, La Sept Cinéma, France 2 Cinéma, 1997.
Pepi, Luci, Bom y otras chicas del montón/Pepi, Lucy, Bom and Other Girls Like Mom, film, directed by Pedro Almodóvar. Spain: Figaro Films, 1980.
Tatuaje/Tattoo, film, directed by Josep Joan Bigas Luna. Spain: Profilmar P. C., 1978.

CHAPTER 8

The Male Body in the Spanish Erotic Films of the 1980s

Alejandro Melero

Spanish films have been known historically for their nudity and sex. Particularly during the 1990s, the international success of Pedro Almodóvar, Julio Medem, Vicente Aranda and many others contributed to this kind of notoriety, but perhaps this was not sufficient to make critics and academics appreciate the relevance of screening sex in Spanish film history. Unfortunately, the contemporary impact of Erotica and Porn Studies in Anglophone academia has not yet reached studies of Spanish cinema (especially not in Spain), and a thorough study of the complexities of performing sex onscreen is yet to be produced. As a result, there are still some areas of Spanish Porn and Erotica Studies that need intense exploration, such as the portrayal of male sexuality and bodies. This chapter analyses the representation of the eroticised male body in Spanish films of the transition to democracy, a crucial time for the understanding of visual representations of sex in Spain. I will analyse representations of the male body in erotic cinema, a genre that has not been traditionally examined from this perspective. My case of study will be the actor Tony Fuentes, who worked as a main character in six sexploitation films between 1976 and 1982. My analysis focuses on *Deseo carnal/Desire of the Flesh* aka *Carnal Desire* (dir. Manuel Iglesias, 1978) to examine the representation of the male body as a site of vulnerability, and *Jóvenes viciosas/Dirty Young Ladies* (dir. Manuel Iglesias, 1980) to study the homosexual body.

After 1976, as democratic values took over Spain and the country started to move from a dictatorship to a parliamentary system, there was a proliferation of erotic films, fostered by a new legislation. The *Real Decreto* law of 1977, which eliminated censorship, proposed the so-called 'S' rating for films 'whose content or theme could damage the spectator's sensibility' (B.O.E. 1977). The majority of films were classified 'S' on the basis of their sexual content. Very soon, producers learnt that they needed to find a new generation of actors and actresses willing to perform the demands of these erotic films. One of the best ways to understand the relevance of 'S' films is by looking at the vast presence that they had in the film magazines of the time. Film critics were inclined to analyse the popularity of 'S' films, rather than the films themselves (as they generally did with non-'S' films). This resulted in a wealth of materials for film scholars that provide very little film analysis but plenty of detailed information about the history and impact of 'S' films. For instance, in October 1979, film critic A. F. complained: 'the number of "S" films is increasing. In 1978, 59 films were classified "S", but in the first five months of 1979 there are almost 51 films worthy of this distinction.' He goes on to say that producers are keen, even anxious, to commission 'S' films, which are 'a life raft for the box office, because they guarantee a hoard of spectators hungry for sex', adding, '"S" stands for salvation of the box office and the distributor jumps with joy because his business is safe' (A. F. 1979: 6).

It is no coincidence that the first academic studies of *Cine S* focused on the representation of the female body. An example of this is Daniel Kowalsky's (2004) analysis of films including *Las eróticas vacaciones de Stella/Intimate Confessions of Stella* (dir. Zacarías Urbiola, 1978), concluding that many of the 'S' films 'give expression to female sexual empowerment, while also celebrating the subversiveness of the protagonist's sexual imagination' (Kowalsky 2004: 194). Kowalsky also remarks on the proliferation of lesbian scenes, which he notes 'would soon become *de rigeur* in most S films' (194). Similarly, María Donapetry, after exploring the legacy of the work of *destape* stars such as Nadiuska, claims that 'the female nude has been employed in Spanish film of the noughties as an unproblematic symbol of liberalism' (Donapetry 2012: 12). Donapetry values the work of the actresses of the transition to democracy and their pioneering effort in the representation of the body and argues that, without their work, images of sex in contemporary Spanish cinema could not be understood. Approaches such as Kowalsky's and Donapetry's have been invaluable for appreciating the importance of *Cine S*. It is true, as Palacio and Vernon have noticed, that 'the so-called *cine de destape* (nudity cinema) [had a] fondness for peppering its narratives with images of naked bodies, *mostly* female' (Palacio and Vernon 2012: 480, my emphasis). However, *mostly* does nothing but confirm that there was also room for male naked bodies, and this deserves critical attention, too. The stress on the relevance of the female star-system and the insistence on the popularity of lesbianism fail to recognise the corresponding important presence of male characters in the erotic films of the time. This is reminiscent of Peter Lehman's ideas on the role of academic studies and their approach to the study of the human body in cinema. According to him, film theory has

> perpetuated the dominant cultural paradigm wherein women's bodies are displayed and men's bodies are hidden and protected. Countless

pages have been devoted to analyzing how women's bodies are fetishised and controlled via the star system, fashion, lighting, camera position and cutting patterns, narrative structure, and so forth. Thus, academics have replicated as well as deconstructed the very sexual ideology they are analyzing. Women's bodies have occupied the critical spotlight in a way analogous to which they have been center stage as a spectacle in the culture in which we live. (Lehman 2007: 5)

Lehman's criticism is particularly revealing when it comes to understanding many of the Spanish erotic films of the Transition, for, in several cases, the narratives of these films were more concerned with male bodies rather than those of their female counterparts. The films starring Tony Fuentes are clear examples of this. Before analysing them, however, I would like to look at the work of two other popular actors who were very prominent in erotic films: Jorge Rivero and Pedro Mari Sánchez. Their very different physiques, and the use that they made of these, help us to understand the variety of male bodies in Spanish erotic films.

The case of Jorge Rivero (1938) is particularly interesting, and demonstrates how erotic cinema welcomed a varied typology of male bodies. Rivero was already a star in Mexico, his country of origin, when he arrived in Spain to participate in several erotic films, including his starring role in *La playa vacía / The Deserted Beach* (dir. Roberto Gavaldón, 1977), in which he played the object of attraction of a mature lady, played by Amparo Rivelles. A few years later, Rivero starred in *Profesor Eroticus / Professor Eroticus* (dir. Luis María Delgado, 1981). In this erotic comedy, Rivero's character is the centre of attention and has more nude scenes than his female counterparts. The plot revolves around situations that favour the display of Rivero's body, and it could be argued that there is even a progression that leads to the revelation of his full nudity. First, we see him wearing swimming briefs while he is on the beach, and then in underwear escaping through a balcony. There is even a scene in which Rivero performs a strip-tease. This is done in a medium shot and the camera is static while Rivero takes his shirt off. Then, when his girlfriend comes into this shot, Rivero gets rid off his underwear (which we do not see, as the shot cuts his body from the waist up) and stretches his arms as if to offer his naked body to the lady. Interestingly enough, this image was used in the publicity posters of the film. And, in the final scene, his completely naked body (shown from behind) covers his female lover's nakedness, as if to confirm that female nudity is of less relevance in this film. The climactic sex scene that closes the film is not about the lady, whose nudity spectators do not see, but about him. Rivero's looks come closer to the muscled men of Tom of Finland than the more effete bodies that will be analysed later, and he easily fits into the category of 'rock', as described by Susan Bordo (1999). According to her,

Figure 8.1 Jorge Rivero in *Profesor Eroticus/Professor Eroticus*, directed by Luis María Delgado. Spain: Producciones Esme S.A., Ízaro Films, 1981.

'rocks' are big, muscled men, active in terms of physical activity, whose looks and poses aim to suggest power and dominance. In his Spanish films, Rivero has many chances to be shirtless and, therefore, to show off his six-pack abs and intimidating biceps. Indeed, his looks are not unlike the Marlboro Man, who is Bordo's example of the quintessential 'rock': square-jawed, intense gaze, broad shoulders. Nothing in him denotes weakness.[1] Rivero did not play the role of the Marlboro cowboy, but in *La playa vacía* he rides a horse on a beach, shirtless, and the lighting invites the spectator to compare his silhouette to that of a centaur. Meanwhile, the female characters observe him from inside a house, as if they are waiting for him. His hard and phallic body (he had been a professional water polo player as well as a body builder) is presented as both an object of desire and a subject full of power, for it is he who decides when to have sex, and with whom.

Pedro Mari Sánchez's persona in erotic films has completely different connotations. Sixteen years younger than Rivero, Sánchez is a clear example of what Bordo categorises as a 'leaner': feminised, inviting to be looked at but rarely holding the gaze. In his films, Sánchez is beardless, with long blond hair, and a lean, not overly muscular body. In *La siesta/The siesta* (dir. Jorge Grau, 1976), he plays Rodri, a character who, to use Bordo's description of the 'leaner', has 'the freedom to indulge in some of the more receptive pleasures traditionally reserved for women' (Bordo 1999: 190). Indeed, what Rodri likes is to be looked at. His body is presented as an object for contemplation, with no other agency than his willingness to be contemplated. In one scene, spectators observe Rodri looking at himself in the mirror while flexing his arms to check the size of his biceps. The shot is wide enough to reveal his body from his waist up, so that when he later flexes other muscles (his back, his shoulders, his triceps), spectators won't miss any detail. Tony Fuentes, who was the same age as Sánchez, had a similar body: lean, hairless, with long hair ... and a tendency to be shirtless in most films. Although Fuentes too could be also categorised as a 'leaner' type, the presence of his body in erotic cinema was more than an invitation to be looked at. In the next two sections I analyse the use of Fuentes' body as representations of vulnerability and homosexuality.

THE VULNERABLE BODY

Manuel Iglesias directed Tony Fuentes in two erotic films. A comparison between these two films enables us to understand the representation of Fuentes' eroticised body as an object of desire from different perspectives. While in *Jóvenes viciosas* Fuentes played the role of a hurt and unstable homosexual man, in *Deseo carnal* his character is presented as a young heterosexual man who is the object of desire of many women. In the latter film, his young body is a place for abuse and vulnerability, an instrument appropriated by other characters and by the technical devices of the film.

Deseo carnal tells the story of Luis (Fuentes), a teenager who leaves the orphanage where he has spent all his life after his mother, Ana (Marujita Díaz), a prostitute, abandoned him as a baby. Luis goes to Amsterdam to look for her. He starts working in a nightclub owned by Margot (played by *destape* star Ágata Lys). One night, Margot drugs him and discovers that he is very talented when it comes to pleasing women sexually. Under Margot's guidance, Luis becomes a gigolo for mature women. Eventually, Luis goes to live in his mother's house as a housekeeper, without her knowing that he is her son. Ana falls in love with Luis and when he tells her that he is her son, she runs away.

The sexualised presence of Tony Fuentes' body in *Deseo carnal* challenges Laura Mulvey's famous and much-discussed hypothesis of 1975. According to her, 'the male figure cannot bare the burden of sexual objectification. Man is reluctant to gaze at his exhibitionist like' (Mulvey 2000: 36). It is worth noting that *Deseo carnal* was released around the time of Mulvey's original publication and, in many ways, this film was contesting Mulvey's ideas before future film theory and practice demonstrated the possibility of the objectification of the male body. The reluctance towards male exhibitionism is tested by Manuel Iglesias' script and *mise en scène*, as they both work to present Fuentes' body as a place for sexual pleasure, no matter the character's willingness or otherwise.

In the film Luis has no agency over his sexualised body. On the contrary, the other characters decide what to do and how to use Luis' often-naked body. The first sex scene is a good example of how far this is true, since he is drugged and unable to control his body. Spectators see how Margot and her assistant, Frank (an older homosexual played by José Riesgo), drug Luis until he is unconscious. Luis asks 'where are you taking me?' and, although he is told that they are putting him to bed, in the next scene we see Margot asking her assistant to undress Luis. Margot shows no concern when Frank tells her that she has given Luis too many drugs: 'it's ok, he seems strong'. Then we see Frank undressing Luis, who is completely unconscious by this point. The camera is static and the long shot reveals Fuentes' full body, first his underwear, then fully naked. The shot frames Fuentes' naked body in full, as if to reinforce the idea that he cannot escape the sexual abuse he is about to suffer. Frank stares at Luis' body and then, when it seems that he is going to caress him, Frank slaps Luis on his genitals (which we do not see, for they are hidden behind Luis' leg), to wake him up. Frank informs Margot that Luis is available for her ('there you have him') and leaves. We then see Luis lying on the bed and Margot sitting on top of him. Although he is semi-unconscious now, Margot is being penetrated and, as her moaning suggests, enjoying the experience. But Iglesias' camera is not interested in Margot. What we see is a close-up of Luis' face. He is biting his lips and moaning with pleasure. His acting clearly shows that he is about to reach an orgasm and, when this happens, the editing immediately cuts to a close-up of Margot, who is obviously climaxing too. These two shots are long and uninterrupted, as if to show the full length of the orgasm, and then the scene is apparently over, as the next shot is an establishing shot outdoors.

In this sense, this scene follows that traditional pattern of the representation

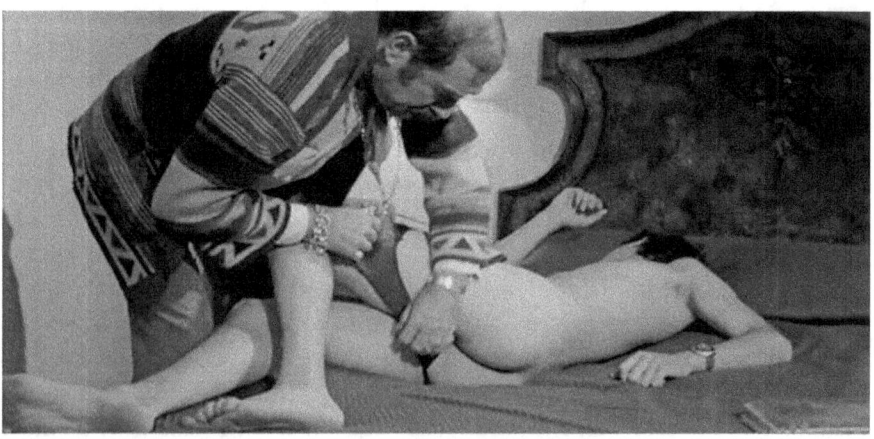

Figure 8.2 Tony Fuentes in *Deseo carnal/Desire of the Flesh* aka *Carnal Desire*, directed by Manuel Iglesias. Spain: Alba Films, 1978.

of sex acts in erotic cinema, as noted by Linda Williams, who distinguishes the more traditional 'finite, masculine concept of sexual pleasure as climax and crescendo' versus the 'feminist sexological revisions of female sexual pleasure as potentially infinite' (Williams 2008: 168), the former being the norm in sexploitation cinemas. However, Iglesias finds a way to complicate this scene in ways that separate it from Williams' division. For, although the sex scene seems to be over after Margot's orgasm, it actually continues. We see Luis waking up and suffering the effects of a hangover. He is completely naked and shown from behind. This gives Iglesias one more chance to display his butt and make him strike different poses as he stretches his arms to wake himself up. The narrative justification for his nudity is that his clothes are missing ('where are my clothes?'). He then goes into the shower. This coda to the traditional sex scene subverts one of the most emblematic locations of Spanish sexploitation films: the shower. As film critic José Luis Guarner noted: 'if Spaniards got a coin every time we saw a naked girl in the shower, we would be millionaires' (Guarner 1977: 14). The shower scene became a routine for many actresses of the *destape*, and a symbol of the gratuitous nudity of erotic films such as *La muerte ronda a Mónica/Death Haunts Monica* (dir. Ramón Fernández, 1976). In *Jóvenes viciosas*, Iglesias appropriates this female space so that the traditional orgasm-led sex scene is prolonged until the female character, Margot, actively looks for Luis' naked body. When she finds him in the shower, she lathers his back, caressing it, then rinses him off, and finally kisses him. Luis simply lets Margot actively use his body for her sexual pleasure. In other words, the sex scene does not end with the orgasm, as spectators are first meant to believe; it continues when the woman decides to join the naked man in the shower. This scene is therefore an example that challenges erotic cinema's disinterest in what Williams called the 'revisions of female sexual pleasure as potentially infinite' (2008: 168).

In the shower scene, while Margot is caressing and kissing Luis, she is completely dressed while he is completely naked. This is not the only scene in which this happens. When we see Luis in bed with one of his clients, 'La Ejecutiva' ('The Executive'), he is wearing tight underwear while she is dressed in a long nightgown. Moreover, Luis is in the foreground while she is in the background of the shot, revealing that Luis' body is the main focus of interest. Again, what we see here is a mature woman who looks to obtain pleasure from Luis' body. Not only is she paying to have sex with him, throwing cash at him, she is also paying him with alcohol, and Luis is visibly drunk. Later, we learn that what she actually wants is for Luis to beat her up ('Come on, hit me, what are you waiting for? I like it'), a task Luis finds repulsive (he calls her 'filthy pig') and difficult to perform. This scene adds little information to the plot, but reinforces the film's premise: the more powerful women are, the more vulnerable the male body becomes. The scene is interrupted but spectators are meant to understand that Luis will have to fulfil La Ejecutiva's wishes. By presenting Fuentes' naked body together with the covered bodies of his female partners, the film is, firstly, relocating the objectification of desire from the female to the male body; at the same time, it reinforces the vulnerability of the male character in opposition with the active and powerful presence of the female characters. Margot's elegant dress in the shower scene covers most of her body: long sleeves, long skirt down to her knees, and even a hat. These clothes conceal her body as much as they reveal her power. Margot's and La Ejecutiva's attire denote their power status, something they are not willing to renounce, even when having sex, or, precisely, because they are having sex. For it is Fuentes' nudity that makes his character vulnerable and, subsequently, unable to refuse what women ask of him (Margot wants him to become a gigolo, and La Ejecutiva wants to be hit). This use of Tony Fuentes' body in *Deseo carnal* complicates Bordo's famous historicisation of the display of the male body and the construction of women as passive and objectified bodies versus men as active agents and powerful viewers (Bordo 1999: 168–201). As we have seen, his naked body is manipulated by women to such an extent that his character has no choice but to let them use his body as they (the women) please. His nudity marks his weakness and limits his character's agency. Moreover, the question of whether he obtains pleasure (as he does when he has sex with Margot) or does not (as when he has to hit La Ejecutiva) is irrelevant.

Despite the many scenes in which Fuentes' body is completely naked, his genitals are seen only in one scene. Iglesias' camera finds ways to either hide them behind other bodies (as when he has sex with Margot) or to just leave them out of shot. For instance, when we see Luis in the shower, the long shots reveal his backside; however, the frontal shots in this scene are medium shots, so that we can only see as far as his pubic hair. The *mise en scène* is more complex in the scene when he stretches his muscles; Fuentes looks towards the camera while he is in the foreground, closer to it, so that we can see only the upper half of his body. However, when he turns his back, he walks away from the camera, which now reveals his body down to his knees. The only time that we see a full frontal of Fuentes is in the scene when he tries to save Loli, his girlfriend, from drowning in a lake. Luis' flaccid penis is seen as a symbol of his incapacity to save her. His nakedness is not gratuitous sexploitation, as a superficial viewing might suggest, but a contribution to the presentation of his character. Nudity here is not contemplative (as when he is taking a shower or stretching his muscles in long shots); on the contrary, it is an essential part of the narrative elements of this scene. He is not the hero of the traditional narrative who saves the princess from doom – he is weak, exhausted (he has to dive and swim, then drag Loli out of the water). The display of his penis is not related to sexual pleasure. Its purpose, as it were, is to reveal that in action his body no longer functions as a sight of desire but of impotency. In Bordo's terms, the 'leaner' stops being passive to become the agent. In this sense, Iglesias follows the tradition of pictorial art studied by Jacqueline Murray, for whom, ever since the Middle Ages, the representation of 'men's genitals [is] a sign of their vulnerability and weakness' (Murray 2006: 266). The scene also conforms to a pattern identified by Peter Lehman, what he calls the 'melodramatic penis', the result of 'the dominant ideological drive to retain the awe and mystique surrounding the penis' (Lehman 2000: 39). He argues that 'the melodrama surrounding the representation of the penis paradoxically cries out to reaffirm the spectacular importance of the penis even as the very assault on the taboo seeks to dislodge that importance' (2000: 39). This is the same paradox that we find in *Deseo carnal*. The nudity in the first sex scenes, as I have shown, is presented in such a way that the actor's penis is cleverly concealed (by the size of the shot, the disposition of other parts of the body that cover the genitals, the very movements of the actor). In these penis-less scenes, his body is a site of pleasure. When unseen, Fuentes' penis is the confirmation of his character's ability to sexually satisfy women; all Margot has to do is to use him. However, when the penis is finally (and melodramatically) revealed, his weakness is exposed too. Luis' passive body can be used for pleasure only when it is carefully captured, both by the women in the film and by the camera.

THE HOMOSEXUAL BODY

Tony Fuentes belongs to the generation of actors who started working when eroticism was the leading trend in Spanish cinema. As such, he was perceived by the audience and the press as part of an emerging star-system of erotic cinema. For instance, in 1977 the magazine *Party*, aimed at male gay readers, included one report about his success in this genre with an interview. The journalist introduced Fuentes as an important actor in erotic cinema with the following words: 'Tony is well positioned in the wave of juvenile nudity that is flooding Spanish cinema.' The headline quoted Fuentes as saying, 'Miguel Bosé is the best-looking', anticipating that the purpose of the feature was to appreciate Fuentes' body. Indeed, Fuentes discusses his looks and compares himself to Bosé, who was then one of the most famous singers and a teenage idol: 'I think that I am good-looking, but Miguel Bosé is much better-looking.' This interview was illustrated with five pictures in which Fuentes is naked save a well-positioned towel that covers his body. His skin and hair are wet, as if to indicate that he has just left the shower. Interestingly, the only nude photograph is purposefully cropped by another, superimposed, picture framing Fuentes' body image and strategically concealing his genitals. As in the films analysed in this chapter, the frame and size of the shots are manipulated to both conceal and reveal certain parts of Fuentes' body.

Fuentes' first important role had been in Eloy de la Iglesia's *Los placeres ocultos/Hidden Pleasures* (1977), where he played Miguel, a teenager with whom Eduardo (Simón Andreu), a mature man, falls in love. *Los placeres ocultos* was the last film banned by Franco's censorship and has received critical attention from academics, particularly for its pioneering treatment of homosexuality (Smith 1992; Ballesteros 2001; Melero 2010). Looking at Fuentes' career four decades after it started, it is quite meaningful that his first important role, which introduced him to Spanish audiences, was as a character whose body is desired by a mature homosexual man. This role is repeated four years later in *Jóvenes viciosas*, in which Fuentes plays the main character, Toni. The synopsis on the cover of the VHS edition of *Jóvenes viciosas* reveals many of the aspects that will be discussed later:

> Two young girls and an effeminate man share a flat [...] when their relationship becomes tense and they must separate, they decide that they will meet again in the same place one year later [...] Their lives go on in different directions. One of the girls works as a prostitute and the other as an illegal dealer. He becomes the protégé of a mature man.

The fact that both actor and character share the same name (Tony/Toni) does nothing but reinforce the short distance between the performer and the role he played. Perhaps part of the audience still remembered Fuentes' participation in Eloy de la Iglesia's scandaling *Los placeres ocultos*.[2] The similarities between both characters, particularly in the scenes that show how mature men desire Fuentes' naked young body, allow spectators to establish an interesting dialogue between both films. The action is the same in both films: a mature man, fully clothed, looks at Fuentes' naked body, without him (Miguel/Toni) knowing. Then, the camera pans over the naked body, in a POV shot, as if to suggest that it is the mature man's gaze staring at the perfectly lit skin of the teenager. In their study of the representation of homosexual bodies in Spanish cinema Fouz-Hernández and Martínez-Expósito noted that 'the gap between the subject and the object affects the representation of the gay body in so far as the elder subject tends to remain clothed and act as the vehicle of the audience's desire for the object' (2007: 133). There is, however, a very relevant difference between Fuentes' characters in *Los placeres ocultos* and *Jóvenes viciosas*: while in the former, Miguel never reciprocates the homosexual desire of his admirer, in *Jóvenes viciosas*, Toni goes through a process of transformation from internalised homophobia to accepting his desires. This process involves, above all, transformations of his body.

Jóvenes viciosas presents many of the narrative conventions of the erotic cinema of the time, such as the idea that women can 'turn' a gay man straight.[3] Thus, the film presents the body of the homosexual man as a place of instability and open to change. There are several moments in the film when this can be seen. After one of the girls unsuccessfully tries to seduce Toni, she explains that she is only trying to help: 'I'm just trying to stop you from becoming effeminate and soft, I mean, queer.' Later, when Silvia receives a massage from Toni, she gets naked and, seeing that he is not aroused, complains that he 'is not very manly'. The effeminacy of Toni's body is confirmed, interestingly, because Silvia is bisexual. Silvia does not cope well with Toni's constant rejection of her sexual approaches. Once she urges him to make up his mind: 'get out and learn to be a man, or a queer'. Later, when Silvia recognises Toni's effeminate mannerisms (the way he holds a cup and wears a foulard) she confesses that if she wasn't having an affair with Loli, she would have sex with him, 'because he is like a woman'. Later, when the three main characters are living together, Toni does not work and all his expenses are paid by his two female friends. This reverses the traditional pattern of the male providing for the female, who stays at home.[4] Toni's homosexual body is maintained (the food he eats, the clothes he wears, the place where he lives) thanks to the help of his female friends, and later with the money that he receives from mature men. Although he is visibly fit and, if not muscled, indeed athletic and in shape, Toni's body is perceived by other characters – in their own words – as '*suave*' [soft]. His sexual orientation determines the perception that other characters have about his body as much as his body seems to determine how he feels about his sexual orientation. In the universe of *Jóvenes viciosas*, homosexuality is something that can be 'learnt' (as the characters say) as much as heterosexuality. And the learning of homosexuality seems to depend exclusively on the use of one's body. Toni's friends urge him to learn how to move, drink, dress and how to have sex depending on whether he is gay or straight. And Toni follows his friends' advice. He wants to be sure about his sexuality ('I have to learn to be a man ... or whatever') and, in order to do so, he manipulates his body. The first thing he does is to pierce his ears to wear earrings, which he perceives as a sign of effeminacy. Later, he starts to work for a mature gay man who introduces him to other gay characters but, when Toni refuses to kiss him, an assistant to the boss (another mature gay man played by actor Fabián Conde, famous at the time for playing gay roles) pays two men to beat Toni up. This is the ultimate punishment and the result of Toni's body's metamorphosis from straight to gay: bloody, with a broken lip and a swollen eye, and with no clothes to cover his nakedness, Toni has found that, as long as he does not accept himself, his homosexual body is not a site for pleasure, but for pain. After that, he meets his female friends again and delivers a message of liberation, urging them to accept that they are lesbians: 'we have to liberate ourselves'.

Homosexual characters were not rare in the erotic films of the early years of the democracy. As early as 1976, Octavi Martí, a film critic in *Fotogramas*, wrote: 'the essential typology of Spanish porn includes numerous homosexual characters, always treated disrespectfully' (Martí 1976: 9). In *Jóvenes viciosas* there are several gay characters, but to think that they are treated disrespectfully would not do justice to the complexity of the film's approach to the construction of the homosexual body. Toni's body is desired by (mature) men and (young) women alike. He alone is incapable of recognising his body as a place for pleasure and, despite many transformations, only after punishing his body can he fully accept it.

CONCLUSION

It may not come as a surprise to discover that, in between working in *Deseo carnal* and *Jóvenes viciosas*, Tony Fuentes played the role of Críspulo in the non-erotic comedy *La familia, bien, gracias/The Family, Fine, Thanks* (dir. Pedro Masó, 1979). Críspulo had been played by Pedro Mari Sánchez in the two previous films of the popular saga created by Pedro Masó: *La gran familia/The Big Family* (dir. Fernando Palacios, 1962) and *La familia y... uno más/The Family Plus One* (dir. Fernando Palacios, 1965). These films became an instant hit and are now seen as landmark comedies of the cinema of '*desarrollismo*'. Sally Faulkner has analysed 'the persuasiveness of the conservative message of *La gran familia*' to conclude that it 'is due in large part to its excellent cast' (2006: 35), which consisted of mature popular actors such as José Isbert and José Luis López Vázquez, and a new generation of actors and actresses which became very famous, such as María José Alfonso, Jaime Blanch, and Pedro Mari Sánchez, who was a child at the time. By replacing Pedro Mari Sánchez with Tony Fuentes, *La familia, bien, gracias* provided an interesting intertextual opportunity to create a space for relocating the bodies of the children and teenagers of Francoist cinema, who were becoming adults during the transition to democracy. Críspulo, the child who had become immensely popular in the Spain of the 1960s, had grown into an attractive young man. Pedro Mari Sánchez, the 'leaner' who strikes poses in front of a mirror in *La siesta*, had been everyone's favourite child just a few years before. This intertextual game evidenced that the children of *desarrollismo* had developed into the men and women of the *destape*. Furthermore, Pedro Mari Sánchez was responsible for dubbing Tony Fuentes' voice in *Los placeres ocultos*. Fuentes' naked body was then new to the cinema of Spain, but his voice was familiar to the spectators, as if to suggest that the representations of male nudity might be a new, democratic practice, but not completely free from the cinema of the dictatorship. A few years later, when Tony Fuentes inherited Sanchez's most famous role,

Fuentes was regaining his own voice both literally (for he was not dubbed) and figuratively, for he was telling the audience that Críspulo was not a child anymore, but a man whose body could be looked at.

ACKNOWLEDGEMENT

This work has been written as a part of the research project I+D+i 'El cine y la televisión en la España de la post-Transición (1979–1992)', financed by the Spanish Ministry of Economy and Competitiveness. Ref.: CSO2011-15708-E.

NOTES

1. Indeed, Bordo problematised the iconicity of the 'rock' type, particularly after the demise of some of the men who embodied this character, such as actor Tom McBride. However, Jorge Rivero was working before the AIDS epidemic and before these new readings of the Marlboro type. By 1981, when *Profesor Eroticus* was released, his body type and looks were quintessentially 'rock'.
2. The poster of *Los placeres ocultos* includes the line 'Introducing Tony Fuentes'.
3. I have studied this narrative convention elsewhere (see Melero 2010).
4. Spaniards had seen this pattern in hundreds of popular films during Francoism and the transition to democracy. Perhaps one of the clearest examples is *La gran familia/ The Big Family* (dir. Fernando Palacios, 1962) and its sequels *La familia y ... uno más/ The Family Plus One* (dir. Fernando Palacios, 1965) or *La familia, bien, gracias/ The Family, Fine, Thanks* (dir. Pedro Masó, 1979), about a man played by Alberto Closas who provides for his family of fifteen children, and his wife.

REFERENCES

A. F. (1979), 'Las "S" crecen como la esmupa', *Cineinforme*, 1a Quincena, October 1979, p. 6.
Ballesteros, Isolina (2001), *Cine (ins)urgente. Textos fílmicos y contextos culturales de la España post-franquista*, Caracas: Editorial Fundamentos.
B. O. E. (1977), Decreto Ley 3071, B.O.E., 11 November 1977.
Bordo, Susan (1999), *The Male Body. A New Look at Men in Public and Private*, New York: Farrar, Straus and Giroux.
Donapetry, María (2012), 'The "Noughty Nude": Naked Women in Spanish Cinema of the Noughties', in Kathy Bacon and Niamh Thornton (eds), *The Noughties in the Hispanic and Lusophone World*, Cambridge: Cambridge Scholars Publishing, pp. 12–24.
Kowalsky, Daniel (2004), 'Rated "S": Softcore Pornography and the Spanish Transition to Democracy, 1977–1982', in Antonio Lázaro-Reboll and Andrew Willis (eds), *Spanish Popular Cinema*, Manchester: Manchester University Press, pp.188–208.
Faulkner, Sally (2006), *A Cinema of Contradiction: Spanish Film in the 1960s*, Oxford: Oxford University Press.

Fouz-Hernández, Santiago and Alfredo Martínez-Expósito (2007), *Live Flesh: The Male Body in Contemporary Spanish Cinema*, London and New York: I. B. Tauris.
Guarner, José Luis (1977), 'Cara a cara al desnudo', *Fotogramas* 1481, March 1977, 14.
Jóvenes viciosas, VHS cover, Madrid: Metromedia Video, 1984.
Lehman, Peter (2007), *Running Scared. Masculinity and the Representation of the Male Body*, Detroit: Wayne State University Press.
Lehman, Peter (2000), 'Crying Over the Melodramatic Penis: Melodrama and Male Nudity in the Films of the 90s', in Peter Lehman (ed.), *Masculinity: Bodies; Movies and Culture*, London and New York: Routledge, pp. 25–41.
Los placeres ocultos, Film poster, Madrid: Alborada P.C., 1976.
Martí, Octavi (1976), 'El cine español a pelo descubierto', *Fotogramas* 1422, January 1976, 7–9.
Melero Salvador, Alejandro (2010), *Placeres ocultos. Gays y lesbianas en el cine español de la Transición*, Madrid: Notorious Eds.
Mulvey, Laura (2000 [1975]), 'Visual Pleasure and Narrative Cinema', in E. Ann Kaplan (ed.), *Feminism and Film*, Oxford: Oxford University Press, pp. 34–47.
Murray, Jaqueline (2006), 'Sexual Mutilation and Castration Anxiety: A Medieval Perspective', in Matthew Kuefler (ed.), *The Boswell Thesis: Essays on Christianity, Social Tolerance, and Homosexuality*, Chicago: University of Chicago Press, pp. 254–72.
Palacio, Manuel and Kathleen Vernon (2013), 'Audiences', in Jo Labanyi and Tatjana Pavlović (eds), *A Companion to Spanish Cinema*, Oxford: Wiley-Blackwell, pp. 464–85.
Party (Hispania Press) (1997), 'Tony Fuentes: El más guapo es Miguel Bosé', *Party*, Year 1, No. 14, July 1977, 22.
Smith, Paul Julian (1992), *Laws of Desire. Questions of Homosexuality in Spanish Writing and Film 1960–1990*, Oxford: Oxford University Press.
Williams, Linda (2008), *Screening Sex*, Durham, NC: Duke University Press.

FILMOGRAPHY

Deseo carnal / Desire of the Flesh aka *Carnal Desire*, film, directed by Manuel Iglesias. Spain: Alba Films, 1978.
Jóvenes viciosas / Dirty Young Ladies, film, directed by Manuel Iglesias. Spain: Jacintos Santos Parra PC, 1980.
La familia, bien, gracias / The Family, Fine, Thanks, film, directed by Pedro Masó. Spain: Impala, Pedro Masó Producciones Cinematográficas, 1979.
La familia y uno más / The Family Plus One, film, directed by Fernando Palacios. Spain: Impala, Pedro Masó Producciones Cinematográficas, 1965.
La gran familia / The Big Family, film, directed by Fernando Palacios. Spain: Pedro Masó Producciones Cinematográficas, 1962.
La muerte ronda a Mónica / Death Haunts Monica, film, directed by Ramón Fernández. Spain: Arturo González PC, 1976.
La playa vacía / The Deserted Beach, film, directed by Roberto Gavaldón. Spain: Conacite Uno, Lotus Films, 1977.
La siesta / The siesta, film, directed by Jorge Grau. Spain: José Frade Producciones Cinematográficas S.A., 1976.
Las eróticas vacaciones de Stella / Intimate Confessions of Stella, film, directed by Zacarías Urbiola. Spain/France: Góndola, Gondole, International Thanos Films, 1978.

Los placeres ocultos/Hidden Pleasures, film, directed by Eloy de la Iglesia. Spain: Alborada PC, 1977.

Profesor Eroticus/Professor Eroticus, film, directed by Luis María Delgado. Spain: Producciones Esme S.A., Ízaro Films, 1981.

CHAPTER 9

Sonorous Flesh: The Visual and Aural Erotics of Skin in Eloy de la Iglesia's *Quinqui* Films

Tom Whittaker

Like several of his contemporaries in the early 1980s, the director Eloy de la Iglesia turned his attention to the theme of juvenile delinquency. Set on the outskirts of the city, his films *Navajeros/Knifers* (1980), *Colegas/Pals* (1982), *El pico/Overdose* (1983), *El pico II/Overdose II* (1984) and *La estanquera de Vallecas/Hostages in the Barrio* (1987) pivot on themes of drug taking and urban alienation, through a particular emphasis on the naked male body. Indeed, Eloy de la Iglesia's particular evocation of the delinquency film – or *cine quinqui*, as these delinquent films have come to be known – was most characterised by his erotic fascination with the fragile beauty of male teenagers.[1] This was most significantly played out in the depiction of José Luis Manzano, a non-professional actor who was cast as protagonist in all five films, and who also allegedly became the lover of the director. While long derided by critics, *cine quinqui* has acquired something of a cult status in recent years, and de la Iglesia's films are no exception. Younger audiences have nostalgically resurrected the films for their subcultural kudos and retro-aesthetics, while recent cultural production in Spain – as attested most notably by the television programme *Ochéntame otra vez* ('Take me back to the 1980s') produced by RTVE, a recent exhibition entitled '*Quinquis de los 80. Cine, prensa, calle*' ('Quinquis in the 1980s: Cinema, Press, Street'), and Javier Cercas' recent novel *Las leyes de la frontera/Outlaws* (2012) – has sought to revindicate the *quinqui* subculture as a long-forgotten but integral narrative of the transition to democracy.

With his chiselled features and distinctive curly locks, José Luis Manzano was the most striking cover boy for the *quinqui* subculture, frequently appearing in the pages of weekly magazines such as *Fotogramas* and *Interviú*, and even once on the cover of *Party*, Spain's first gay magazine (see *Party* 1984). While de la Iglesia's films similarly displayed a visual fascination with Manzano, it is not so much the image as the texture of his body that I wish to explore in this chapter. Youthful and smooth, taut yet fragile – the surface of Manzano's skin emerges as a crucial motif in his *quinqui* films, one that brings into play a more tactile and sensory engagement with cinema. As a skin that is frequently damaged, distressed and, in the case of *El pico*, punctured, its troubled surface also provides an eloquent example of how, in the words of Bryan Turner, 'dominant concerns and anxieties of society tend to be translated into disrupted, disjointed and disturbed images of the body' (2003: 1). In alerting us to the visual erotics of touch and skin, however, Eloy de la Iglesia's films also crucially possessed a powerful affective charge – one that, to borrow the words of Steven Shaviro, was able to 'confront the viewer directly, without mediation' (1993: 26). This finds a particularly vivid expression in two of his most commercially successful films, *Colegas* and *El Pico*, whose visceral immediacy and unmediated directness I would like to explore further in this chapter. In tilting the emphasis away from the gaze and towards the senses of touch and sound, this chapter aims to show how Eloy de la Iglesia's *quinqui* films established an embodied response in their audiences. Through the writing of Linda Williams, Laura Marks and Jennifer Barker – critics who each advance non-ocular approaches to understanding film – the chapter offers a new reading of de la Iglesia's films, one in which texture and noise alert us to the sensuousness of our own bodies.

ELOY DE LA IGLESIA AND *CINE QUINQUI*

The sensationalism of Eloy de la Iglesia's *quinqu*i films echoed much of the Spanish media's coverage on delinquency in the 1970s and early 1980s, whose affective structure all too often contributed towards the moral panics around the figure of the delinquent. De la Iglesia reportedly called for a cinema that would be 'like a newspaper' (Bayón 1992: 177) – an aspect which is literalised in the opening title sequence of *Navajeros*, whose words appear in a typewriter font across a white page. The prurient fascination with delinquency was most strikingly found in the pages of *El Caso*, a weekly magazine of the so-called morbid Spanish *prensa negra*,[2] which frequently ran extended stories on Spain's most famous *quinqui* delinquents, most notably with 'El Lute' (Eleuterio Sánchez Rodríguez) and later on 'El Jaro' (José Joaquín Sánchez Frutos). Indeed, 'El Jaro's' descent into crime and untimely death in 1979 provided the narrative for *Navajeros* (1980), which, like de la Iglesia's other *quinqui* films, featured Manzano as the protagonist, El Jaro. More sympathetic exposés on delinquency, which attempted to explore the causes of the phenomenon rather than its mere effects, could regularly be found in the dailies *Diario 16* and *El País*, and the monthly *Cuadernos para el diálogo*, as well as the weekly magazines *Interviú, Cambio 16* and, most pertinently, *Triunfo*. In the latter, several reports on drugs, criminality, *chabolismo* (shanty towns) and Spain's crumbling penal system at the time were written by the left-wing journalist Gonzalo Goicoechea, who was also the co-screenwriter of several of de la Iglesia's films in this period.[3] Like the other *quinqui* films at the time, then, in particular the *Perros callejeros/Street Warriors* (1977) cycle directed by José Antonio de la Loma (including *Perros callejeros II: Busca y captura/Street Warriors 2* (1979); *Los últimos golpes del Torete/Torete's Last Blows* (1980) and *Yo, El vaquilla* (1985)) and *Deprisa, deprisa/Fast, Fast* (Carlos Saura, 1980), de la Iglesia's films were examples of what André Bazin has famously termed an 'impure cinema', in which filmmaking interbreeds freely with other arts, cultural forms and media (1967).

The immediacy of the *quinqui* film owes much of its commercial success to its impure form, which, in explicitly drawing on newspaper and media coverage of delinquency at the time, also famously blurred the boundaries between reality and fiction. In common with other *quinqui* films, de la Iglesia mostly cast non-professional teenagers for the roles of the delinquents, and José Luis Manzano would become something of a celebrity in his own right.[4] Contemporaneous articles reported that Manzano was discovered by the director when he was just seventeen, when he replied to a casting call placed in *Fotogramas* which was looking for teenagers for a film on juvenile delinquency (Gurruchaga 1983: 31). This version of events, however, is inconsistent with later accounts. For instance, in an interview shortly before his death, Manzano reported that he met de la Iglesia when he was just fourteen (Sherry 1992a: 82), while Goicoechea more recently commented that they met many of their teenage actors because they were rent boys they visited at the time, who also dealt in drugs on the side (cited in Melero 2013: 49). De la Iglesia and Goicoechea therefore maintained a more intimate relationship with their actors than the directors of other *quinqui* films, such as Saura and de la Loma. Indeed, Manzano would end up living with de la Iglesia for two years, commenting some years later that 'he was like a father to me' (Sherry 1992a: 83). If, for many commentators at the time, their sequences of male nudity were gratuitous to the demands of the narrative, Goicochea has argued that they were in fact largely observational, inspired by the sites they saw on their regular visits to the *barrios*. The scene in which Antonio Flores appears topless playing the guitar in *Colegas*, for instance, was a recreation of something that they saw in the area (cited in Melero 2013: 66–7).

Like many of the delinquents who featured in the press and cinema at the time, Manzano grew up in the outskirts of Madrid in Vallecas, an area which provided overly cramped housing for many of the migrants who flocked to the city to seek employment during Spain's miracle years (1969–73). According to Juan Carlos Usó, the sudden rise of juvenile delinquency in the late 1970s developed in tandem with the unprecedented appearance of heroin abuse in Spain, which became a serious epidemic between the years 1979 and 1982

(1996: 330). While the two phenomena were not always interconnected, Usó shows how delinquency and heroin abuse were nevertheless both influenced by the deep recession (following the World Oil Crisis of 1973) and subsequent high rates of youth unemployment, as well as the increased levels of consumerism during the transition to democracy (1996: 316). As with many of the *quinqui* films, life would end up mirroring art: Manzano and the director would themselves end up succumbing to heroin addiction, just a few years after the production of *El pico* and *El pico II*, two of de la Iglesia's films which most explicitly represented the reality of heroin abuse. Soon after spending eighteen months in Carabanchel jail, Manzano tragically died of a heroin overdose in 1992, while de la Iglesia lived destitute and penniless for several years. Despite famously declaring 'my addiction to drugs is little compared to my addiction to cinema' (cited in Melero, 2013: 77), he was unable to make another film until 2001.[5] In living alongside the delinquents and taking drugs together (or, at least in the case of de la Iglesia and Manzano), the filmmakers had an unusually close connection with their subjects, a proximity which, according to Alejandro Melero (2013), distinguished them from the likes of Carlos Saura.

A CINEMA OF SENSATIONS

While de la Iglesia's films frequently enjoyed commercial success, they nonetheless drew a less than favourable treatment from critics. Like many of the other films associated with the *quinqui* genre, de la Iglesia's filmmaking was primarily one of shock and confrontation. His trademark raw, visual style and often startling images sat uncomfortably with the critical establishment, who frequently dismissed his cinematic language as crude and excessive – criticism levelled against him both during censorship and the years that followed it. Yet in an interview in *Triunfo* in 1979, de la Iglesia not only defended his cinematic excesses – described here by the journalist as sensationalist, 'melodramatic' and '*panfletaria*' (demagogic), terms that are frequently associated with his work in the Spanish media – but commented that he actively sought to encourage them in his filmmaking (Galán 1979). The hallmarks of his 'obvious' cinematic language are well known: Manichean structures of morality in which the marginalised victims are dialectically pitted against their exploiters; a rapid, shock cutting which underscores contrasts and correspondences between images and themes; a hyperbolic *mise en scène*, whose décor and props serve as heavy-handed indexes for characterisation. But most of all, his filmmaking is marked by its fascination with the fragile glamour of male youth, an aspect which is most strikingly borne out in his *quinqui* films. Indeed, several of his scenes feature the naked or semi-naked flesh of José Luis Manzano and other teenage boys, creating a visual surface that Manuel Hidalgo at the time dubbed as an '*estética de calzoncillo*' (aesthetic of the underpants) (1983: 38). The male erotic imagery of his films has subsequently drawn comparisons with Pier Paolo Pasolini and Rainer Werner Fassbinder, gay directors who similarly held a fascination for the vulnerability of youth and masculinity. Yet de la Iglesia's 'crude' aesthetics also crucially distinguished him from the formal rigour and auteurist credentials of these directors, whose filmmaking frequently erected an aesthetic distance between spectator and work. If Pasolini's filmmaking offers a poetic meditation on lumpen youth, and Fassbinder diffuses the erotics of the male body through Brechtian distanciation, then de la Iglesia provides a far closer and – most crucially for this chapter – a more sensorial engagement with its subject matter.

De la Iglesia has argued that this directness is crucial to his particular invocation of what he terms '*cine popular*', allowing the films to reach as broad an audience as possible. In an interview that coincided with the release of *Navajeros*, the director commented that 'this direct contact with the public in many of my films is the true basis of their commercial appeal' (*Contracampo* 1981: 30). In their unmediated ability to shock and awe, de la Iglesia's films are vivid examples of what Linda Williams has famously termed 'body genres', a cinema that elicits 'a sense of over-involvement in sensation and emotion' (2009: 604). Williams shows how body genres, which she attributes in particular to pornography, horror and melodrama, have in turn 'functioned traditionally as the primary embodiments of pleasure, fear and pain' (2009: 605). In watching these films, she writes that the body is '"beside itself" with sexual pleasure, fear or terror' (Williams 2009: 605) and 'caught in the grip of intense uncontrollable emotions' (Williams 2009: 604). The cinematic excesses of de la Iglesia's filmmaking similarly provoke a body that is 'beside itself'. For instance, during a screening of his schlock horror film *La semana del asesino/The Cannibal Man* (1973), which took place in Berlin, the German distributors reportedly gave out sick bags into which the audience could vomit (*Contracampo* 1981: 31). Not only, then, is de la Iglesia's filmmaking one in which the bodies are frequently on display, but one that elicits an embodied response in the audience. In their power to arouse and touch the viewer, his filmmaking demanded a palpable, visceral response from the public. As a cinema primarily of immediacy rather than reflection, sensation as opposed to mind, de la Iglesia's films speak not only of the body but through the body. If his films have received a low cultural status (a status which, as Williams (2009) has shown, has frequently been attributed to body genres), it is arguably because of their lack of aesthetic distance between film and audience. In losing ourselves in their gratuitous display of flesh and bodily fluids, their veins and their viscera, both the cinematic body and the body of the audience momentarily dissolve into each other, creating the 'direct contact' that the director has said is crucial to his commercial success.

Eloy de la Iglesia's films, then, vividly alert us to the slippage of meaning between sensationalism and the sensorial. In doing so, their direct visual language elicits a particularly tactile structure of spectatorship, one that appears to encourage an erotic fascination with surface and skin. Their distinctively embodied mode of address can be illuminated usefully through the writing of Jennifer Barker and Laura Marks, who each explore the potential for cinematic touch. According to Barker, the encounter between film and spectator 'occurs not only at the skin or the screen, but traverses all the organs of the spectator's body and the film's body' (Barker 2013: 151). Our relationship with film is thus considerably more far-reaching than merely visual and aural: its images and sounds not only touch the skin but move beneath it, vibrating through the viscera and bones of our bodies. For Marks, this kind of cinema elicits what she has referred to as 'haptic visuality'. The haptic connection between cinema and audience, by virtue of its very closeness, also constitutes an erotic encounter. Marks writes:

> Haptic images are erotic regardless of their content, because they construct an intersubjective relationship between beholder and image. The viewer is called upon to fill in the gaps in the image, engage with the traces the images leaves. By interacting up close with an image, close enough that figure and ground commingle, the viewer *gives up her own sense of separateness from the image*. (1998: 341 – emphasis original)

Crucially, in encouraging the viewer to lose oneself in the image, haptic visuality differs markedly from the eroticism of pornography. If, for Marks, in pornography the viewer establishes their visual mastery over the image through a secure relationship of distance, a more haptic response obscures these spatial boundaries, thereby complicating the separation between viewer and image, subject and object. Haptic visuality therefore brings to bear an altogether different invocation of the erotic, one that Marks refers to as 'visual erotics'. Visual erotics does not bring into question the gaze as much as the sensuous operation of the whole body, calling forth a way of looking – and, crucially, feeling – in which the spectator finds themselves viscerally implicated.[6] *El pico* and *Colegas*, as this chapter will now show, similarly present us with a mutual imbrication of skin and self, in which the cinematic body and the body of the audience rub up against each other.

VISUAL EROTICS OF SKIN AND FILM

The motif of skin is strongly evoked in the title of *El Pico*, which is derived from a play on words: '*picoleto*' is slang for a *guardia civil* (Civil Guard), while 'pico' is a colloquial word for syringe, from the verb '*picar*', to shoot up. In a schematic way wholly typical of de la Iglesia and Goicoechea, the title gestures towards the dialectical forces at play in the film, where authority and order are clumsily pitted against marginal drug taking – a tension further spelled out in its iconoclastic promotional poster, in which a bloody needle sits alongside a *tricornio* (a three-pointed hat worn by the Civil Guards). Significantly, the title serves to conflate the materiality of the skin with the social: the violation of the skin is, by extension, a violent and visceral transgression of the law. As Barker writes, 'in general, humans experience the skin as limit and a container: it is the thing that brings us into contact with the world, but also that which separates us from everyone and everything else' (2009: 49). A similar opposition is played out in the opening sequence of *Colegas*, but here the motif of skin is invoked through the display of tattoos. The protagonists José (José Luis Manzano) and Antonio (Antonio Flores, the son of the *folklórica* singer, Lola Flores) sit with their group of friends on a piece of wasteland next to the M-30 ring road, an iconographic setting of several *quinqui* films.[7] One boy (simply referred to in the script as the '*Tatuado*') strips off his shirt and trousers to show off his new tattoo to the others. Noticing an approaching police vehicle, another friend tells the rest of the group to disperse – '*¡abrirse!*' ('scram!') – whereupon the '*Tatuado*' puts his clothes back on hastily. Like the pierced skin of the junky, the tattoo is introduced here as an image of subcultural defiance: its scarred surface marks out the border between the delinquents and the rest of society, a transgressive display of flesh which should be covered up and contained.

As well as demarcating both limit and border, the depiction of skin at the beginning of *Colegas* also establishes a haptic mode of apprehending the film. A brief succession of shots captures the individual faces of friends, each with a curious expression on their face. The scene then cuts to an eyeline-match, a close-up shot that lingers on the boy's tattooed abdominals. If the shot-reverse-shot sequence alerts us to the eroticism of looking, the dialogue which ensues tilts our attention towards the significance of texture, as one friend exclaims: 'I bet that must really hurt to get that done!' He uses the word '*pinchar*', which here refers specifically to tattooing, although it also more generally denotes the puncturing or piercing of skin. From the outset of the film, then, the erotic fascination of youthful flesh – presented here as taut and toned but also tattooed and deviant – is inextricably bound up with pain and, by extension, the significance of touch.

As Paco (again played by José Luis Manzano) in *El pico* becomes increasingly

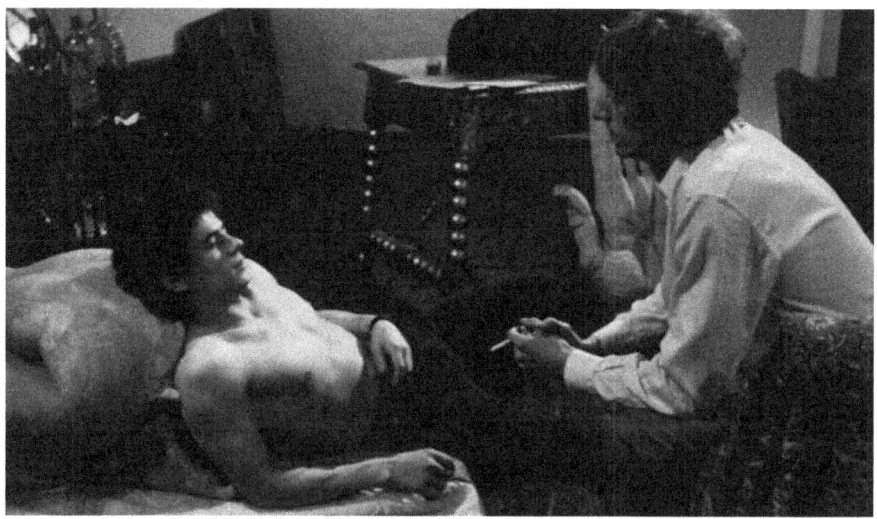

Figures 9.1 and 9.2 José Luis Manzano and Enrique San Francisco in *El pico/ Overdose*, directed by Eloy de la Iglesia. Spain: Ópalo Films, 1983.

hooked on heroin, he starts to suffer from dry and excessively itchy skin, one of the first visible signs of heroin addiction. In an early scene that takes place after Paco has sex with the sculptor Mikel (played by Enrique San Francisco, one of de la Iglesia's regular actors) for money, high-contrast *noirish* lighting cross-illuminates Manzano's body, throwing into relief the contours of his chest and stomach (see Figure 9.1). Pacing around Mikel's studio, Manzano repeatedly scratches his pectoral and abdominal muscles; after observing that Mikel looks concerned, he says: 'Listen, I don't have lice alright? It's just that smack makes you itchy ... But it's a great feeling, scratching yourself feels really nice.' His performance here serves to conflate the visual with the textural: his hands draw our eyes to the shape of his sculptural body, while his fingers and nails alert us to the itchy, flaky texture of his skin. The *mise en scène* of Mikel's studio, filled with sculptures of somewhat dubious quality, further underscores the importance of touch in the film (see Figure 9.2). After Paco has run away from home, Mikel offers Paco refuge in his studio, but on the condition that he abandons heroin for good. Some hours later, Mikel returns to his building to find Paco in the throes of withdrawal symptoms. Manzano lies feverishly on his front, dragging himself across the floor, and attempts to tear apart a mound of wet clay with his hands. Mikel tries to lift Manzano's body up from the ground, as he writhes around in agony. His body smothered in blood and saliva, Manzano suddenly ejects a stream of vomit into Mikel's face – a vivid illustration of Williams' 'body genres', which confront us directly with the presence of bodily fluids. Relayed in a series of dissolves and slow-motion shots, the distended temporality emphasises the materiality and texture of the image.

Elsewhere in *Colegas*, tactile visuality alerts us to what is hidden deep beneath the skin, viscerally engaging us at the level of our entrails – or, as Barker evocatively puts it, the 'murky recesses of the body' (Barker 2013: 151). When Antonio and José arrive in Morocco to collect the drugs they must traffic to Spain, they discover to their dismay that they must each secrete five large balls of hashish in their anuses. When José, in discomfort, asks the drug dealer, 'But how are they all going to fit up the ass?', he responds, 'They go up, into the guts', and advises them to use lots of lubricating cream. Associated with excrement and bodily excess, the anus – and that which lies beyond it – is also vividly here dramatised as the kind of 'cinematic excess' that Linda Williams encounters in body genres. As they attempt, legs suspended mid-air, to insert the drugs into their anuses, we are impelled to partake in their pain. Conveyed through their contorted facial expressions, their physical discomfort also provides a mirror to our own distress – our faces become, in the words of Williams, 'caught up in an almost involuntary mimicry of the emotion or sensation on screen' (Williams 2009: 616).

Yet the most physically discomfiting scenes occur in *El Pico*, where a number of shots depict the insertion of syringes into Paco's and Urko's veins. Their graphic physicality is compounded further through the striking contrast of colours: as the needle punctures the surface of their pale skin, the syringe is filled with a sudden pulse of dark red blood. The play of red and white provides a vivid counterpoint to the otherwise muted palette of the film, whose hues of grey and brown atmospherically evoke the rain-drenched, post-industrial Bilbao of the early 1980s. Registered in extreme close-up (and therefore disconnected from the rest of the body), these shots that linger on the surface of the skin compellingly illustrate haptic visuality. As Marks writes, 'haptic looking tends to rest on the surface of its object rather than to plunge into depth not to distinguish form so much as to discern texture' (Marks 2002: 8). Yet here, the surface of damaged skin also brings to mind Roland Barthes' famous definition of punctum, a category of photographic images which punctures, injures, bruises and pricks the body of the viewer. As Barthes writes, the punctum 'shoots out [of the photograph] and pierces me' (1982: 51). Although Barthes refers here to aspects of the photographic image that are unintentional (and therefore rather different from, say, the 'obvious' visual style of de la Iglesia), his writing is nonetheless productive here. For Barthes, the punctum 'escapes language' and resists being pinned down and known, for what can be named cannot truly prick (Barthes 1982: 51). In prompting us to react instinctively with our bodies, the evasiveness of punctum has something in common with the viscerally 'direct' images of de la Iglesia: they both appear to suggest an excess that prefigures or exceeds representation, an immediacy of sensation rather than mere reflection. For Weimar, who explores the visual imagery of heroin abuse in American culture, the 'hypodermic needle violates the boundary between the self and the outside world' (2003: 260–81). The eponymous needle in *El pico* enacts a similar violation: in wounding both the skin of the viewer and the film, it pierces the boundary between inside and outside, subject and object. Its red-on-white incisions – a startling image which echoes around the mind long after the film has ended – would therefore appear to literally bear out Laura Marks' assertion that in the intersubjective relationship in visual erotics, 'the viewer is called upon to [...] engage with the traces the image leaves' (2000: 183).

AURAL EROTICS OF SENSATION

If in Eloy de la Iglesia's *quinqui* films, the image leaves a palpable mark on the viewer, then so too does their sound design. The sensuousness of sound is felt through the voice of the delinquents, and in particular the voice – or, rather, voices – of José Luis Manzano. In his debut, *Navajeros*, his voice was allegedly dubbed by Ángel Pardo and in *El Pico II* by Pedro María Sánchez, while in *El Pico* he dubs his own voice. Post-synch sound, a practice where actors effectively dubbed themselves and ambient sounds were created entirely in post-production, was still a relatively standard practice in Spanish film in the early 1980s, and de la Iglesia's films were no exception.[8] In speaking directly into the microphone in the dub, Manzano's vocal performance always appears to sound as if in an auditory close-up, regardless of his spatial distance from the camera. This effect is particularly significant in the scenes which feature sex and masturbation. In an early scene in *Colegas*, a number of long shots depict

Manzano and Lolita Flores making out in an abandoned building, yet we hear the sounds of their kissing and their gasps as if they were in a close-up shot. A similar effect is created when Manzano's younger teenage brothers (including the real-life delinquent José Luis Fernández Eguia, 'El Pirri') are seen masturbating in the bedroom they share together. The sound design clearly alerts us to their heavy breathing and moans of pleasure, which are punctuated by the sound effects of the rhythmic creaking of their beds. Jacob Smith draws on the writing of Linda Williams to show how 'post-sync "sounds of pleasure" have a certain clarity that makes them seem to come from very close up' (2012: 46). Following Williams, he shows that this not only lends 'a certain ambiguity as to the performer's position in space (a sense of 'spacelessness') but porno-performativity also provides an index of intimacy' (2012: 47).

Vocal performance is crucial also to *El Pico* not only in its explicitly erotic moments, but to vividly convey the visceral and embodied effects of drug taking. For instance, we hear in auditory close-up the sharp intake of breath as Paco and Urko shoot up, the gut-wrenching noise of Paco vomiting, and, most alarmingly, the rapid, suffocating sounds of chest movement after Urko overdoses on heroin. Although she only mentions the significance of the soundtrack briefly in body genres, Linda Williams writes that 'aurally, excess is marked by recourse not to coded articulations of language but to inarticulate cries of pleasure in porn, screams of fear in horror, sobs of anguish in melodrama' (2009: 605). Significantly, it is during their moments of excess – scenes which, as I have shown, confront the corporeality of the viewer most directly – that verbal language similarly breaks down in the films. Heard primarily as sonority rather than signification, their vocal performance affords us intimate access to the sounds of their bodies. The films' inarticulate sounds of gasping and vomiting nevertheless crucially heighten our affective and sensory involvement with the film.

Partly as a result of their low production values, the soundtracks of the film were crudely and hastily put together; sound, as such, often appears to be registered in one overwhelmingly loud volume. On *Navajeros*, for instance, a critic from *El Periódico* called it 'a dynamic, noisy and violent antiauthoritarian ballad' (*El Periódico* 1980). Yet in spite of their lack of sonic nuance, their noisiness eloquently captured the social location of youth culture during these years. Like the *quinquis*, noise creates both disturbance and disarray – a sound which is marked as an excess to what is held socially respectable. This is brilliantly conveyed in the opening sequence of *Colegas*, in which we hear the loud, jarring sound effects of a Space Invaders arcade game. Its synthesised gunfire sounds foreshadow the film's narrative to come, in which the drug traffickers and the teenagers become violently ensnared in a predator–prey relationship. Most significantly, the disproportionate levels of loudness lend the films' soundtracks a particularly affective charge, one which in common with the plastic quality of their images would contribute towards their unmediated closeness to the viewer.

A significant example is the scene in *El Pico* in which Paco and Urko visit the drug trafficker 'El cojo' (played by Ovidi Montllor) and his wife. The soundtrack is dominated by the dissonant sounds of their young baby crying who, because his mother took heroin during the pregnancy, is now also addicted to the drug. Writing on *El Pico*, a critic complained that it was the most excruciating film he had ever seen, noting: 'the sequences in which the boys inject themselves in the vein with their syringes, the withdrawal symptoms of José Luis Manzano and everything related to the couple of drug traffickers and their baby – with the help of a *wounding sound* in close-up – are brutal moments which are hard to bear' (Hidalgo 1983: 38 – emphasis mine). In registering the sound of the baby at close mike (an effect which was most likely also enhanced during the sound mix), its sounds have a 'wounding' effect on the body of the viewer/auditor. As Michel Serres and Lawrence Schehr have observed: '[n]oise and nausea, noise and nautical, noise and navy have the same etymology' (1983: 4). In alerting us to the connection between the two words, Serre and Schehr point to the ways in which our experience of sound is, above all, an embodied experience: like nausea, noise is felt through the body. In traversing and vibrating through us, sound can thus similarly possess the haptic quality which is pivotal to Marks' discussion of 'visual erotics', insofar that it implicates the viewer and demands their response. Like the images that evoke texture and surface, the soundtrack serves to enhance the visceral encounter between the film and the viewer, thereby contributing to the 'direct contact' that was so crucial to Eloy de la Iglesia's popular style of filmmaking.

CONCLUSION

As this chapter has sought to show, Eloy de la Iglesia's filmmaking speaks through texture and sound as much as it does through image. Through their emphasis on the delicate pallor and fleshy materiality of adolescent skin, *Colegas* and *El Pico* reveal a cinema which is at once both sensationalist and sensorial, of the body and embodied. While unabashedly erotic in places, the crucial immediacy and directness of the films can be more productively explored through Laura Marks' 'visual erotics', a cinema of touch and texture. This chapter has also sought to understand the distinctive tactility of the *quinqui* film through its sound design, whose noisy resonance and affective charge vibrate through the body of the viewer. Like José Luis Manzano's skin, as well as the veins and viscera that lie just beneath it, their soundtracks prick, puncture and wound the viewer into being. In exploring the erotics of de la Iglesia's films as operating through texture and acoustics, rather than just through the image, this chapter ultimately seeks to broaden our understanding of the erotic in Spanish film.

NOTES

1. The term *cine quinqui* has been applied retrospectively to the cycle of films which centred on juvenile delinquency in the late 1970s and early 1980s. As well as de la Iglesia's five films, the most significant *quinqui* films were directed by José Antonio de la Loma and Carlos Saura.
2. The genre of news known as *prensa negra* (literally 'black press' in English) was particularly popular during the development years of the 1960s and 1970s, during which time Spain became increasingly urbanised. Magazines such as *El Caso* tapped into the increasing anxieties and fears of the population in the face of a rapidly modernising country.
3. Goicoechea's first screenplay for de la Iglesia was *Los placeres ocultos* (1977). They collaborated together until de la Iglesia's last *quinqui* film, *La estanquera de vallecas*. For an excellent extended interview with Goicoechea, see Melero (2013), which also contains reproductions of articles he wrote for *Triunfo*.
4. 'El Torete' similarly became famous in José Antonio de la Loma's films, and to a lesser degree 'El Mini' in Saura's *Deprisa, deprisa*.
5. In a 1992 article in *Interviú* (Sherry 1992b), the journalist notes that the director is living penniless without water and electricity, and is addicted to heroin.
6. As Marks notes elsewhere, 'Visual erotics allows the object of vision to remain inscrutable. But it is not voyeurism, for in visual erotics the looker is also implicated' (2000: 184).
7. Antonio González Flores would also tragically die of a heroin overdose in May 1995, just two weeks after the death of his mother.
8. For an introduction to the history of post-synch sound and vocal performance in Spanish film, see Whittaker (2013) and Whittaker (2016).

REFERENCES

Barker, Jennifer (2009), *The Tactile Eye: Touch and the Cinematic Experience*, Berkeley, Los Angeles and London: University of California Press.
Barker, Jennifer (2013), 'Touch and the Cinematic Experience', in Francesca Bacci and David Melcher (eds), *Art and the Senses*, London and New York: Oxford University Press, pp. 149–60.
Barthes, Roland (1982), *Camera Lucida: Reflections on Photography*, London: Hill and Wang.
Bayón, Miguel (1983), 'No cerrar el pico', *Cambio 16*, 116–17.
Bazin, André (1967), 'In Defense of Mixed Cinema', in *What is Cinema*, vol.1, edited and translated by Hugh Gray, Berkeley, Los Angeles and London: University of California Press, pp. 53–75.
Cercas, Javier (2012), *Las leyes de la frontera*, Barcelona: Mondadori.
Contracampo (1981), 'El primer plano y el aceite de colza', *Contracampo*, 25–26 December 1981, 27–36.
El Periódico (1980), 'Navajero' (sic), *El Periódico*, 17 October 1980.
Galán, Diego (1979), 'Eloy de la Iglesia: la ambición de un cine popular', *Triunfo*, 24 April 1979.

Gurruchaga, Carmen (1983), 'José Luis Manzano: "Vivimos en una sociedad drogada"', *Diario 16*, 19 September 1983, 31.
Hidalgo, Manuel (1983), 'Arrojarse a los pies del "caballo"', *Diario 16*, 18 September 1983, 38.
Marks, Laura (1998), 'Video Haptics and Erotics', *Screen*, 39:4, 331–48.
Marks, Laura (2000), *The Skin of the Film: Intercultural Cinema, Embodiment and the Senses*, Durham, NC: Duke University Press.
Marks, Laura (2002), *Touch: Sensuous Theory and Multisensory Media*, Minneapolis: University of Minnesota Press.
Melero, Alejandro (2013), *La noche inmensa: La palabra de Gonzalo Goicochea* (Cuadernos Tecmerin, Volumen 3), Madrid: Universidad Carlos III.
Party (1984), *Party* 247, September 1984.
Serres, Michel and Lawrence R. Schehr (1983), 'Noise', *SubStance* 12:3, 48–60.
Shaviro, Steven (1993), *The Cinematic Body*, Minneapolis: University of Minnesota Press.
Sherry, J. J. (1992a), '"Me arrepiento de haber conocido el mundo de las drogas"', *Interviú* 819, January 1992, 80–3.
Sherry, J. J. (1992b), '"Arruinado, Enfermo y Solo"', *Interviú* 828, 16 March 1992, pp. 55–7.
Smith, Jacob (2012), 'Sound and Performance in *Night Dreams* and *Café Flesh*', in Xavier Mendik (ed.), *Peep Shows: Cult Films and the Cine-Erotic*, London: Wallflower Press, pp. 41–56.
Turner, Brian (2003), 'Social Fluids: Metaphors and Meanings in Society', *Body and Society* 9, 1–10.
Usó, Juan Carlos (1996), *Drogas y Cultura de Masas: España 1855–1995*, Madrid: Taurus.
Weimer, Daniel (2003), 'Drugs-as-a-Disease: Heroin, Metaphors, and Identity in Nixon's Drug War', *Janus Head*, 6:2, 260–81.
Whittaker, Tom (2013), 'Locating "la voz": The Sound and Space of Spanish Dubbing', *Journal of Spanish Cultural Studies* 13:3, 292–305.
Whittaker, Tom (2016), 'The Sounds of José Luis López Vázquez: Vocal Performance, Gesture and Technology', in Dean Allbritton, Alejandro Melero and Tom Whittaker (eds), *Performance and Spanish Film*, Manchester: Manchester University Press, pp. 96–109.
Williams, Linda (2009 [1991]), 'Film Bodies: Gender, Genre and Excess', in Leo Braudy and Marshall Cohen (eds), *Film Theory and Criticism*, 7th edn, London: Oxford University Press, pp. 602–16.

FILMOGRAPHY

Colegas/Pals, film, directed by Eloy de la Iglesia. Spain: Ópalo Films, 1982.
Deprisa, deprisa/Fast, Fast, film, directed by Carlos Saura. Spain, France: Elías Querejeta Producciones Cinematográficas, Les Film Molière, 1981.
El Pico/Overdose, film, directed by Eloy de la Iglesia. Spain: Ópalo Films, 1983.
El Pico II/Overdose II, film, directed by Eloy de la Iglesia. Spain: Ópalo Films, 1984.
La estanquera de Vallecas/Hostages in the Barrio, film, directed by Eloy de la Iglesia. Spain: Compañía Iberoamericana, Ega Medios Audiovisuales, Televisión Española, 1987.
La semana del asesino/The Cannibal Man, film, directed by Eloy de la Iglesia. Spain: Atlas International Film, 1973.
Los últimos golpes del Torete/Torete's Last Blows, film, directed by José Antonio de la Loma. Spain: Films Zodiaco Prozesa, Sadilsa, 1980.

Navajeros/Knifers, film, directed by Eloy de la Iglesia. Spain: Acuarius Films, Figaro Films, Producciones Fenix, 1980.
Perros callejeros/Street Warriors, film, directed by José Antonio de la Loma. Spain: Films Zodiaco, Profilmes, 1977.
Perros callejeros II: Busca y captura/Street Warriors II, film, directed by José Antonio de la Loma. Spain: Films Zodiaco Prozesa, 1979.
Yo, El Vaquilla, film, directed by José Antonio de la Loma. Spain: Golden Sun, Jet Sun, In-Cine Companía Industrial Cinematográfica, 1985.

CHAPTER 10

Masochistic Nationalism and the Basque Imaginary

Rob Stone

There is a coldness to Basque cinema that separates it, perhaps deliberately, from the rich vein of eroticism in Spanish cinema that is mined in this volume and others (Jordan and Morgan-Tamosunas 1998; Perriam 2003; Fouz-Hernández and Martínez-Expósito 2007; Sánchez-Conejero 2015). Whereas 'Spanish cinema is known for producing more explicit images (of both sex and violence) than most other contemporary European cinemas' (Jordan and Morgan-Tamosunas 1998: 112), the emphasis on violence in Basque cinema is more exclusive. Apart from the films directed by Julio Medem, whose cinematic exploration of imaginative passions is the exception that proves the rule of a comparatively sexless Basque cinema, there are very few attempts at eroticism in relation to the Basque Country. The reasons for this paucity of sexual content centre upon the impact and legacy of the cultural oppression visited on the Basque Country during the Francoist dictatorship, which delayed the emergence of modern Basque cinema until *Ama Lur/ Motherland* (dirs. Nestor Basterretxea and Fernando Larruquert) in 1968; but blame is also due to the Basques themselves. The denial of sexual content and eroticism in Basque cinema extends so far into democracy that neither Spain's national censorship, which ended with the Transition, nor the prudery prompted by strict Catholicism, which has greatly loosened its hold, can be held wholly accountable for this lack. Something else is restricting erotic content in Basque cinema. In seeking to understand the sexlessness of Basque cinema, this chapter fixates on rare instances of eroticism in relation to torture and identifies a resultant tendency towards masochistic imagery and description that acquires complex symbolism in a context of political conflict and even violent armed struggle. Analysis suggests that, until recently, the abnegation of the sexual impulse in Basque cinema was indicative of the postponement of individualistic desire until the primary collective objective of independence or at least a degree of self-government and self-determination could be achieved.

That is to say, the Basque body in Basque cinema appears to be yoked to a higher purpose, with gratification and release deliberately withheld pending the resolution of conflict over the status of the Basque Country. Consequently, the puritanical Basque body, which is sexualised by being subject to rape-like tortures, represents both suffering on the part of the Basques and the masochistic pleasures of their self-sacrifice when this results in the embodiment of martyrdom. Paradoxical in even the briefest of instances, eroticism in Basque cinema is both subject to, and a product of, masochist tendencies that eroticise what is meant to be desexualised, rendering the brutalised Basque body a potently perverse symbol of nationalist pride. By considering the place and function of this spiralling paradox and references to martyrdom through torture in the collective imagination of the imagined community, this chapter diagnoses the possibly traumatic effect on Basque cinema, which has otherwise shunned eroticism in deference to a more exclusively politicised role for the Basque body instead. The chapter also examines the discrepancies between the depiction of torture on males and females and, with particular reference to Gilles Deleuze's writing on *Masochism: Coldness and Cruelty* (1989), it considers the spiralling paradox of desexualisation and resexualisation that resulted in the temporary displacement of eroticism. Finally, it posits a future on film for revitalised Basque bodies.

Sexualised torture is not uncommon as allegory or example of oppression in Spanish period films such as *El crimen de Cuenca/The Cuenca Crime* (dir. Pilar Miró, 1980) and *Las 13 rosas/The 13 Roses* (dir. Emilio Martínez Lázaro, 2007). Whereas many Spanish films speak of violence in the past that haunts and threatens contemporary Spain, however, Basque films containing images of torture, even when explicitly allegorical, have until recently tended to imply that such violence occurs in the present. Depictions of torture in fiction films and testimonies of the same in documentaries are tantamount to a trope in Basque cinema that contributes to the cultural process of creating a representational tradition around the theme of martyrdom. This tradition depends upon the resources and sympathies of the filmmakers as well as the political and cultural context and the willingness of the martyr's supporters to make up the film's audience. In Basque cinema an emphasis on the sexual elements of tortures inflicted on Basque bodies appears at first sight to prompt an immediate and consequent rejection or abnegation of the sexual impulse. The sexualised torture of a young woman in *Akelarre/Witches' Sabbath* (dir. Pedro Olea, 1984) and the sodomisation of a young man in *Estado de excepción/State of Emergency* (dir. Iñaki Núñez, 1977), for example, result in traumatised individuals that symbolise the suffering of the Basque Country at the hands of its Spanish oppressors. These representations of torture should lack value because of their fabrication, but these artificial martyrdoms were also metaphors of an otherwise undocumented history of ETA. Their erotic content therefore challenged the idea that guided radical thinking on the function of film in the late 1970s and early 1980s. As Santiago De Pablo recounts, the post-dictatorship National Cinematic Seminar held in Galicia in 1976, which was attended by filmmakers from several Spanish regions that were soon to be designated autonomous communities, including the Basque Country, declared its support for those 'that saw cinematic creations as an instrument of struggle on behalf of the exploited classes of the various nationalities of the Spanish state' (2012: 64). The Basque producer Antxon Eceiza would subsequently instigate and oversee the radical *Ikuska* (Inspection) documentary series as part of 'the violent struggle in which we are now engaged to recover our culture' (De Pablo 2012: 65), in which ethnographic documentary realism included the advocacy of a pre-eminent role for the Basque language of Euskara. This revolutionary intent set a challenge for Basque cinema to effectively unsex itself in order to present a meaningful contrast with the contemporary erotic frivolities of the Barcelona School and the soft-core films of the post-Transition *destape* that was associated with Madrid. These aforementioned depictions of torture and martyrdom thus set in motion a cycle of desexualisation and resexualisation that occurs in relation to the Basque imaginary.

In an attempt to theorise martyrdom, Jolyon Mitchell makes the point that although we have 'prison diaries, smuggled notes and last words from the scaffold, there are, for obvious reasons, no complete first-hand accounts of martyrdom written by the martyrs themselves' (Mitchell 2012: 110). The apparently insurmountable problem that 'we can only imagine what it might have felt like' (Mitchell 2012: 110) is partly and problematically rectified by films that re-enact or imagine these scenes, and documentaries that deliver first-hand testimony of those who survived and claim to have experienced torture as well as second-hand testimonies of those who claim to represent those who did not survive. The violent yet noble death of the protagonist is occasionally the focal point of films and documentaries about terrorism, although this may also be subverted as in the 'honour killing' of the Basque activist Mikel by his own mother in *La muerte de Mikel/Mikel's Death* (dir. Imanol Uribe, 1984) and the rogue suicide of the bomber Antonio (Carmelo Gómez) at the climax of *Días contados/Running out of Time* (dir. Imanol Uribe, 1994). In general, however, an emphasis on non-lethal torture as process and traumatised victims as product displaces the dead-end symbolism of executions, because there is, in effect, a distinction to be made between ongoing and concluded martyrdoms. Both the tortured and the dead add to the historical narrative that justifies activism but traumatised survivors must be accommodated within the future. Thus, those who represent or testify to torture also express or evoke a suspension of closure that is pending the recognition of their suffering that, it is suggested, could only ever be realised in a utopian Euskadi. This postponement of reparations carries with it the displacement of the sexual identity of the tortured and those who might support or even seek to avenge them. This is partly a result of their trauma and the profound empathy of the others, but also partly a consequence of the realisation that identity itself, when understood as self-determining Basqueness, must also be postponed until that utopia can be realised via political, cultural or even violent means.

Paul Middleton notes that 'the claim to martyrdom is often a claim of legitimacy' (2011: 191). Moreover, 'the way these death stories are recounted – positively or negatively – reflects a wider conflict in which the narrator and his community find themselves' (Middleton 2011: 17). Testimony in documentaries, whether first- or second-hand, is usually intimate, self-searching and arguably free from considerations of performativity, whereas acting the experience of torture in fiction films foregrounds that performativity. In the documentary *La pelota vasca: la piel contra la piedra/The Basque Ball. Skin Against Stone* (dir. Julio Medem, 2003), for example, Anika Gil, who was detained by the Civil Guard in May 2002 on suspicion of collaboration with ETA and released without charge five days later, delivers her testimony in Euskara partly in shadow and in a ritualised manner that seems flattened by repetition:

> They told me 'take off your clothes'. I said that I wouldn't. A man started to take off my sweater from behind, then my blouse and my bra, and they carried on like that. The next time, they made me strip off completely. They touched me on my breasts and on my backside. They made me do squats up and down until I fell over. The sessions on the first day were like that. I was naked and on the second and third day too. They threatened to rape me with a vibrator. I had an anxiety attack. I couldn't breathe.

By way of contrast, in *La fuga de Segovia/Escape from Segovia* (dir. Imanol Uribe, 1981), which stages a re-enactment of the breakout from Segovia prison by members of ETA, a virginal bride who marries her jailed sweetheart in prison is separated from him after the ceremony and subjected to a strip-search and an invasive physical examination before being allowed to consummate the marriage. As her virginity is symbolically taken by the Spanish State as if it were a medieval tyrant, so the plaintive score and soft focus enhance her symbolic representation of the abused Basque Country. Whether in fiction or documentary, testimonies and depictions of sexual abuse and torture illustrate Carlin Barton's assertion that in the ancient world 'to be violated was to be […] extinguished' (2002: 25). As Carole Straw maintains, however, 'death was only of the body (and even that was temporary), never of the soul' (2002: 39). What matters most in relation to testimony, performance, representation and especially reception is 'a martyr's feelings of control over death and torture –

the voluntary, even eager acceptance of condemnation [that] transformed the sordid ordeals one suffered into a most honourable vindication' (Straw 2002: 40). Indeed, it is the sexualisation of torture that complicates its representation in relation to what might be described as masochistic nationalism: that is, the desire of a nation to represent itself, and see itself represented, as subject to violence.

Several Basque documentaries including *El proceso de Burgos/ The Burgos Trial* (dir. Imanol Uribe, 1979), *La pelota vasca: la piel contra la piedra* and *Barrura Begiratzeko Liehoak/Windows Looking Inward* (dirs. Josu Martínez, Txaber Larreategi, Mireia Gabilondo, Enara Goikoetxea and Eneko Olsagasti, 2012) tend to tell the history of ETA in archive images that give way to interviewees and their testimonies of torture that include descriptions of sexual violence. This abuse is only ever recounted by females, however. Any sexual violence visited on male prisoners is absent from these films, perhaps because admission is taboo and perhaps because it would confuse the simplistic gendered demarcation of victimhood and, indeed, the heteronormative gender roles associated with the iconography of Basque nationalism. Female members of ETA who are brutalised perform a dual function in this discourse. Firstly, they illustrate claims of oppression. Female interviewees come to the fore when their testimony underlines the brutality of opponents, who allegedly utilise rape as a shocking signifier of oppression. At the same time, the exclusivity of female interviewees both illustrates and serves the rigid delineation of gender roles in relation to the more traditional, nationalist tendencies of Basque culture. That is to say, because female terrorists are themselves transgressive, taking on the traditional soldier-role of the male, their descriptions of rape push them back into a submissive female role that is, if not condoned by hard-line Basque nationalist attitudes to gender, at least more suitable for integration within a simplistic schema of ETA as defenders of Basque tradition. These documentaries tend to frame their female interviewees against Basque flags, maps and evocative landscapes that connect this emphasis on martyrdom with that of the Basque Country as a whole and posit the tortured female as symbol of a suffering nation. The way they describe their experiences of humiliation, abuse and torture exemplifies a cultural process of creating representational traditions. Moreover, fiction films that also illustrate torture corroborate this claim of violence via its representation, which then enters the national imaginary. This foments a strategy or mood of masochistic nationalism in which the imagined community takes pleasure in seeing representations or hearing declarations of its suffering that justify campaigns for its self-determination. The complexity of this arrangement, which identifies pleasure in or as a result of the representation of torture, requires careful examination.

The imaginary, according to Jacques Lacan, is based on the formation of the ego in the mirror stage via its identification with the specular image.

When transposed to the study of film, it explains why audiences can identify with onscreen representations of their individual and collective identity. Fundamentally narcissistic, this process can also inform the depiction of suffering and how these might reflect and thereby justify an audience's view of itself as oppressed. The mirror image causes concerns over a fragmented body's ability to cohere albeit in a manner that becomes subject to a symbolic order. In relation to Basque cinema, for example, the audience of *Ama Lur* could be said to have sought and found in this documentary film, and in other ethnographic documentaries that focused on Basqueness, images of itself as a coherent whole – as what Benedict Anderson (2006) theorises as an imagined community but which the film insists was not at all imaginary – thereby alleviating fear of erasure under Franco and during the Transition. Films that showed the Basque Country as whole enabled the Basque audience to make a connection between its internal self and an external image. Seeing itself onscreen as whole also fuelled the idea of itself as Other, however, and so the understanding of Basque difference could be grasped in a way that fed into nationalist campaigns for Basque independence. According to Lacan, the movement from semiology to ideology both unfolds and is connected to – even hinges upon – the joint of the imaginary and the symbolic, where, as Kelly Oliver explains, 'the imaginary provides a momentary spatial unity which gives rise to a temporal unity within the symbolic which, in turn, supports it' (1998: 97). Whereas the imaginary becomes the internalised image of this coherent ideal and may be understood without mediation or meditation, the symbolic involves the construction of signifiers, associations and language. The tortured Basque body is one such signifier, which possesses great complexity. The Basque body should be whole, but its torture threatens the image with fragmentation, both psychologically in the descriptions of rape by traumatised interviewees in documentaries and literally so in the forced spreading of the victim's legs in *Estado de excepción* and in *Akelarre*, where the Basque body is about to be torn apart by racks (see Figure 10.2). Yet, having no Other with which to identify, because all Others in these scenes are the torturers and so clearly non-Basque, the Basque audience identifies with the symbolic Basque body that is enduring torture and so the fear of a fragmented Basque Country returns. The function of eroticism in this process is to alert the senses to the cycle or, as we shall see, the spiralling paradox of desexualisation and resexualisation.

The representation, testimony, evidence and experience of tortured Basques not only illustrate the cause of Basque independence but also have the potential to turn those who perform, or testify to suffering into martyrs. Valérie Rosoux states:

> Studying the politics of martyrdom brings us closer to some of the most teleological and ambivalent uses of death – teleological as individuals

turn into gods, become myths and legitimise whoever may claim them; ambivalent since politically speaking, martyrdom is always open to appropriation, competition, and contestation, even though some political leaders regard martyrs as unambiguous signs of virtue and truth. (2004: 83)

The issue of masochism in relation to nationalism is undoubtedly complex and multilayered, but can be condensed to Hugh Barlow's statement that 'martyrs find pleasure in their self-sacrifice' (2007: 183). In a chapter entitled 'The Martyr's Smile', Barlow explains that 'martyrs may be smiling because the wait, at once uncertain, guarded, and thrilling, is finally over' (2007: 192). This postponement of sexual congress pending the self-immolation of suicidal terrorist acts carries a powerful erotic charge. Barlow recounts that any young man recruited for such missions in Palestine is told that 'from the moment his first drop of blood spills, he feels no pain, and he is absolved of all his sins; he sees his seat in heaven [and] is married to black-eyed virgins' (2007: 196). Whereas the Western press has mostly sought political reasons for terrorist activities, Barlow advises that 'the heavenly virgins are firmly on young men's minds' (2007: 197). Leaving aside the possibility of an afterlife, the eroticisation of the terrorist act is clearly defined by the paradox of deliverance or transcendence – the veritable climax of the action – being withheld till after death. Faith plays a part in recruitment, but so too does the eroticisation of the body of the terrorist, because young men offered a way to see themselves as desirable are probably more susceptible to the call of martyrdom. As Raz Yosef (2001; 2005) has examined, the depiction of masochism, the construction of heterosexual masculinity, homoeroticism and both the marginalisation and normalisation of queerness in Israeli cinema is a potent vehicle for uncovering paradox in relation to the Israeli–Palestinian conflict. Yosef demonstrates, for example, that Israeli heterosexual masculinity assumes exclusive superiority but cannot conceive of itself without comparison to homosexual Others. Paradox is also foremost in Basque cinema, where the body of the activist/ soldier/terrorist is both eroticised in provoking a specifically sexual kind of torture and at the same time potentially desexualised by the torture that harms and even destroys the flesh. In other words, just as torture is also an erotic practice in BDSM (Bondage and Discipline, Dominance and Submission, Sadism and Masochism), the supposedly purposeful dehumanisation of the Basque body in these films cannot escape the paradox of actually accentuating the eroticisation of its flesh. Crucially, the informed consent of the tortured is, of course, absent from the events onscreen. Neither the man in *Estado de excepción* nor the woman in *Akelarre* self-identify as deriving pleasure from the suffering, while the Basque audience, which has consented to witness the specular image and might therefore be accused of sadistic impulses, has the possibilities of its identification with the onscreen figures in this imaginary limited to that of the tortured Basque.

Both *Estado de excepción* and *Akelarre* counter the more usual unsexing of the Basque imaginary, which results in a Basque cinema that is desexualised in order to emphasise its own revolutionary function. Like abstinence before a fight, such voluntary desexualisation might prepare the combatant and nullify to some extent the threat of rape as part of torture, meaning that this masochistic self-effacement is also weaponised in its preparation for conflict. Deleuze declares this spiralling paradox suitably remarkable because the process of desexualisation 'is accompanied by a resexualisation which does not in any way cancel out the desexualisation, since it operates in a new dimension which is equally remote from functional disturbances and from sublimations' (1989: 117). The tortured Basque body is therefore moving in two directions at the same time or, better said, its meaning is spiralling. For Deleuze, 'it is as if the desexualised element were resexualised but nevertheless retained, in a different form, the original desexualisation' (1989: 117). As shall be seen in *Estado de excepción* and *Akelarre*, the torturers' attempts to desexualise the Basque body result in its eroticisation and their consequent arousal because, as Deleuze concludes, 'the desexualised has become in itself the object of sexualisation' (1989: 117). At the same time, this attempt to impose desexualisation resonates in, and is ironically mirrored by, the unsexing of the Basque nationalist imaginary that is constituted by its deliberately unerotic films, which express difference from the erotic charge of Spanish cinema. And yet, the spiralling paradox that results in the resexualisation of Basque bodies that are depicted or described as undergoing torture also pulls in the films that include them, resulting in the eroticisation of Basque cinema. This spiralling paradox means that the self-abnegation that initiates the masochistic tendency, which powers the desexualisation of the Basque protagonist, ultimately results in the fetishisation of the body, which is then debased by the sexualised torture that is provoked by this fetishisation and aims to annul it. This spiralling process not only confirms the eroticism of the Basque body onscreen but also vindicates its owner, whose martyrdom fulfils the commission to represent Basque suffering to an imagined Basque audience, one that finds pleasure in seeing representations of its victimisation because they play to a nationalist discourse that justifies resistance. Indeed, this pleasure is only heightened when the tortured is a female, because the symbolism may therefore be incorporated within rigid notions of gender roles that are concomitant with traditional, nationalist beliefs.

Previously in Basque cinema, the gendered iconography associated with a nationalist view of the Basque Country was illustrated in terms of binary oppositions that idealised the active, visible male and the passive, invisible female. The men in the aforementioned *Ama Lur*, for example, are virile sportsmen, burly farmers or noble soldiers, whereas the females are rarely shown except in servile roles (Stone and Rodríguez 2015: 98–111). Subsequently, an emphasis on the collective effort of the Basque community was imagined in the many ethnographic documentaries that engaged in stocktaking and extrapolating what remained of Basqueness following the end of the dictatorship (Anderson 2006). The aforementioned *Ikuska* series, for example, tended to show that all energies were being subsumed into the task of nation-building, thereby suggesting that an unsexed citizenry was the somewhat paradoxical base of the modern Basque nation. This is also evident in the short film *Estado de excepción*, which illustrates this process of desexualisation for a higher purpose as well as the emergent masochistic tendency, the resultant fetishisation of the Basque body, and its ultimate resexualisation. As Santiago De Pablo recounts, *Estado de excepción* was 'removed from circulation by Spanish government authorities, and Núñez as well as others who had been involved in the making of the film were briefly imprisoned [because] it was filmed at a time when an idealised representation of ETA was still unacceptable – as was the kind of forthright denunciation of the repression in Spain in a rather provocative documentary' (De Pablo 2012: 186). The film is not a documentary, however; rather it unfolds in an avant-garde 'underground' mode composed primarily of a succession of still images in the manner of *La jetée/The Pier* (dir. Chris Marker, 1962) that at first resembles a simplistic exposition of causality in the matter of Basque nationalism. The first photographs to appear have basic ethnographic value but they are gradually replaced by staged photographs whose deployment is indicative of an intertextual discourse. Early images of a Basque rural idyll, for example, resemble Jean-François Millet's *The Gleaners* (1857) and *The Angelus* (1857–9), thereby elevating the condition of Basque peasantry to the archetypical religiosity of Millet's monumental French equivalents. The film continues in this vein as archive images of the destruction of Guernica during the Civil War give way to staged photographs of a classroom in which a pupil is punished for speaking the Basque language and made to stand facing the wall beneath a framed photograph of General Franco. From here the film emphasises causation, cutting to images of the grown man training to fire arms, and his arrest, imprisonment and torture. Although theatrical in their poses, these black-and-white images are still shocking. The captive is shown being beaten, stripped and hung over the edge of a table in a back-breaking position as the plaintive wailing of Mikel Laboa on the soundtrack accompanies slow zooms into the photographs. Then his three torturers with lascivious expressions turn him over and force his legs apart before anally penetrating him with what appears to be a wooden or metal rod. An alternate angle of his sodomisation depicts the force with which the rod is inserted until a close-up of the anal penetration is amplified by an inward zoom.

To claim eroticism for this scene means asserting a degree of masochism on the part of the intended audience; yet the sequence acts directly on the senses, rendering objective criteria at least temporarily redundant. Eroticism is also present because the sequence broaches a taboo by depicting an act that has proven inadmissible on both sides, with neither male Basque prisoners nor their alleged torturers admitting to the kind of sexual abuse that is common to testimony by females. The sequence is therefore exceptional because, in its accordance with Deleuze, it illustrates how the language that is used to describe torture is paradoxical. Deleuze states that 'only the victim can describe torture; the torturer necessarily uses the hypocritical language of established order and power' (1989: 17); yet the stark aesthetics of *Estado de excepción* cannot avoid resembling pornography, which Deleuze describes as 'a few imperatives followed by obscene descriptions [where] violence and eroticism do meet, but in a rudimentary fashion' (17). Consequently, the film asks what is obscene: the act that is depicted or the depiction of the act? It also complicates the question and any response by appearing to resist eroticising the torture by the zooming in on its brutal details, while simultaneously fetishising the tortured figure. This sequence effectively culminates in, and reduces the victim to, what amounts to an ironic, even oppositional mirror image of the realistic, graphic eroticism of Gustave Courbet's *L'Origine du monde* (1866). Instead of the pliant, receptive female lying on her back, the film delivers a forcefully restrained male lying on his front and being penetrated from behind. Both images offer the erotic sight of flesh that is only partly revealed and both images could be said to bully the spectator into arousal, via erotic incitement to political awakening, moving from body to art and from art to idea. The inversion – or perversion – of the painting by the film is suggested by the title too, for instead of the origin of the world, the shot represents the end of the Basque one. Linda Nochlin writes of *L'Origine du monde* that 'the ultimate-meaning-to-be-penetrated might be considered the "reality" of woman herself, the truth of the ultimate Other' (Nochlin 1986: 76). In response, might we consider whether the meaning of the Basque body in *Estado de excepción* is 'to-be-penetrated' because this represents the Basque nationalist view of the political situation that holds Spanish political and military forces as incursive in the Basque territory that the body symbolises and is therefore the 'reality' of the Basque Country itself, the truth of the Basque Country as 'the ultimate Other'?

Yvonne Tasker (1993) and Gaylyn Studlar (1988) have deconstructed the habitual binary relation between the Others of the active/sadistic/masculine/male and the passive/masochistic/feminine/female in relation to visual pleasure, with Studlar positing 'the creation of a masochistic aesthetic as a specific film style offering certain narrative and visual strategies as well as textual pleasures' (1988: 12). The minimalism of *Estado de excepción* both limits and summarises these strategies. However repulsed the audience might be by the violence, zooms into each photograph direct the gaze in such an irresistible manner that they embroil the spectator in the anal penetration, igniting spontaneous erotic contemplation of the image as it approaches abstraction until the curtailment of the zoom leaves a lack, which is essential to the fetishisation of the image. The wider image clearly expresses the oppression of the Basque Country by Francoist forces. Yet the close-up eradicates context and leaves an image that dismisses distinctions between passive and active participation and, therefore, between sadism and masochism, which 'are twin ways in which the monstrous exhibits itself in reflection' (Deleuze 1989: 23). The zoom-in also erases any differentiation between female and male body parts (as the buttocks and anus are common to both sexes) and, therefore, between the feminine and the masculine gaze in relation to visual pleasure. Because 'there can be no masochism without fetishism' (Deleuze 1989: 32), so there can be no masochistic gaze without the fetishisation of what is onscreen or suggested by what is onscreen. The question of what is being fetishised in *Estado de excepción* is answered by the symbolism that the film, among others, attributes to the Basque body throughout: the martyr's body is that of the Basque Country under Francoism. Masochistic nationalism is found in the Basque body that binds itself to the noble task of representing the plight of the Basque Country via its torture. This masochistic endeavour also empties of meaning the apparent sadism of the torturer, rendering Francoism hollow, bereft of ideology and only 'interested in something quite different, namely to demonstrate that reasoning itself is a form of violence, and that he [the torturer] is on the side of violence' (Deleuze 1989: 18–19). In this regard, Deleuze concludes, 'the sadistic "instructor" stands in contrast to the masochistic "educator"' (1989: 19). Torture, martyrdom, the fetishisation of the Basque body and masochism therefore combine in *Estado de excepción* to depict the monstrous even though 'the process of death and destruction that it represents is only a partial process' (Deleuze 1989: 27). What completes this process is the unseen martyr's smile.

Masochistic nationalism and the unsexing of the Basque imaginary also feature in *Akelarre*, only here the eroticism is more suitable for contextualisation within conventional narrative strategies of visual pleasure because the Basque body is the lithe naked one of a beautiful female, which Deleuze asserts 'can only be contemplated in a mystical frame of mind' (1989: 21). *Akelarre* recounts the battle of insurgent Basques in the seventeenth century against their invasive Spanish overlords, who use rumours of witchcraft as an excuse to imprison, interrogate and torture the radicalised Basques. Blatantly allegorical for its allusions to the torture allegedly carried out on members of ETA by Spanish security forces at the time of the film's making, *Akelarre* centres on the doe-eyed and beauteous Garazi, played by the actress and dancer Silvia Munt. Her sensual and seductive skipping around a bonfire that culminates in her promiscuity during the annual *akelarre* is used as an excuse by a jealous Spanish nobleman to arrest her on charges of being a witch. Brought to trial by a visiting inquisitor (José Luis López Vázquez), Garazi denies the accusations of orgiastic blasphemy and is subject to increasingly sexualised torture as her abusers struggle to hide their excitement. Still denying the accusations of witchcraft and the demand to name collaborators, she is first strapped on a rack and has water poured into her mouth in a grotesque parody of fellatio (see Figure 10.1). The inquisitor quivers at the sight of her and orders worse. She is then stripped and tied to four racks that stretch her limbs and suspend her at the waist-height of the inquisitor (see Figure 10.2). The film notably alters its *mise en scène* to accompany the sexualisation of the martyr. At first the drab hues of the dungeon appear to deny the sexual and erotic aspect of the torture until the shot of Garazi spitting up water excites the torturers. Then the *mise en scène* changes to warmer hues, the dungeon is lit by flames and her naked body acquires a warm, golden tone. The stretching of her limbs recalls the opened legs of *Estado de excepción* and *L'Origine du monde*, while the milieu recalls the Italian director Mario Bava's painterly horror films such as *La maschera del demonio/Black Sunday* (1960) as well as the more exploitationist European horror genre. Although the frame retains the painterly tableaux, the change of *mise en scène* emphasises the increasing eroticism of the encounter. As the racks are tightened, the film cuts to a close-up of Garazi's head hanging down and her long dark hair frames her upside-down face as she gasps 'no' and then surrenders a 'yes' in seemingly orgasmic abandon.

The eroticism of the masochistic element that is latent in *Estado de excepción* is manifest in *Akelarre*, while the fact that the tortured body is that of a young female plays to the conventions of visual and narrative pleasure by exploiting the complicity of the spectator, who is imagined as male, with the characters (also male) who inflict the torture. The female victim is even glamorised as the erotic potential of the scene is realised, thereby sexualising the martyr to an extreme degree. However, the scene also confuses spectatorship by situating the spectator, as theorised by Laura Mulvey (1975), Tasker (1993) and Studlar (1985), among others, as desirous of seeing and deriving visual pleasure from the torture inflicted on the female because 'spectatorial pleasure has also been linked to the representation of the female as a masochistic object for the male's scopophilia/voyeurism' (Studlar, 1985: 5). The complex and paradoxical nature of this spectatorship, which wants to witness what it also wants to prevent, enables the fetishisation of the tortured body in scenes of eroticised torture and declarations of sexualised abuse that fulfil a complex exchange of pain and pleasure. This is because, as Deleuze explains:

> At the same time as pain fulfils what is expected, it becomes possible for pleasure to fulfil what is awaited. The masochist awaits for pleasure as something that is bound to be late, and expects pain as the condition that will finally ensure (both physically and morally) the advent of pleasure. He therefore postpones pleasure in expectation of the pain which will

MASOCHISTIC NATIONALISM AND THE BASQUE IMAGINARY 181

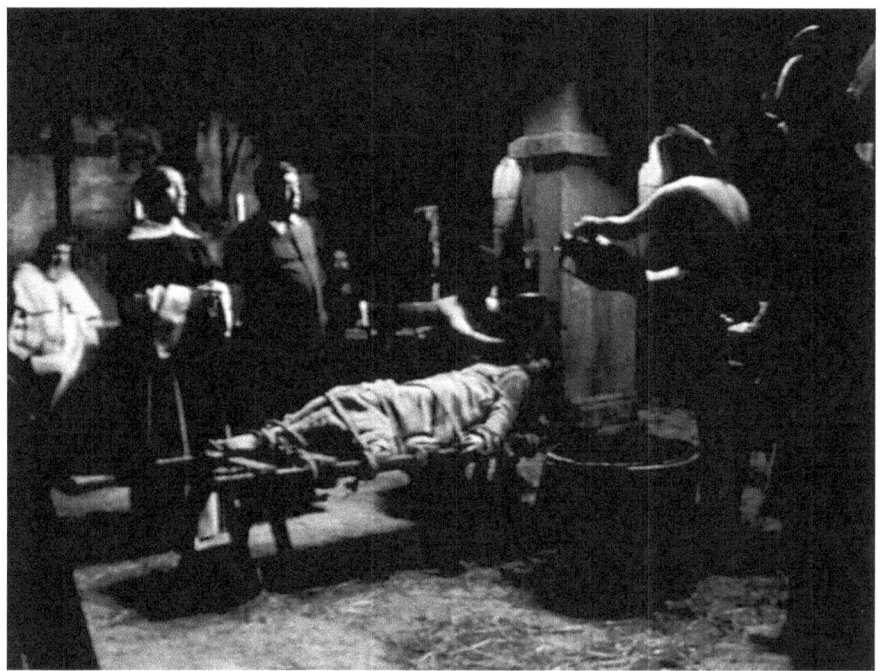

Figures 10.1 and 10.2 Silvia Munt and José Luis López Vázquez in *Akelarre/Witches' Sabbath*, directed by Pedro Olea. Spain: Amboto Producciones Cinematográficas, 1984.

make gratification possible. The anxiety of the masochist divides therefore into an indefinite awaiting of pleasure and an intense expectation of pain. (1989: 71)

Postponement wins out because of the nature of masochistic nationalism, which desires to witness the martyrdom of the Basque body because this corroborates Basque nationalist sympathies for its own suffering. Meanwhile, no empathy or doubt is allowed to divert the increasingly lascivious zeal of the torturers either here or in *Estado de excepción*. Just as rape is less about sex than about power, so the aim of the sadistic torturers, it seems, is not to eradicate the sensuality of the bodies before them but to disavow their Basqueness until they no longer exist in their own right but as subject to Spanish rule. The aim is thwarted, however, because of the radicalism aroused by the conjunction of the intrinsic and extrinsic masochistic nationalism, which suggests that deep down Garazi, whose suffering inspires the peasantry to rise up and rescue her from execution, will endure in order to become an icon of the incipient Basque resistance. Thus, too, those who respond to her torture or see it as emblematic of a seventeenth-century cause that continues in the present are keen that she be tortured because, as Deleuze concludes, 'all resistances spring from repression' (1989: 57).

Whereas most cinemas, such as the Spanish, might be expected to respond to the end of a period of oppression such as the Francoist dictatorship and the subsequent repeal of censorship by liberating, exploring and even exploiting the sexual content of their films, Basque cinema stymied its own erotic potential. It therefore sustained a simulacra of oppression in films that suggested, as many radical Basque nationalists maintained, that the conditions for Basque independence had not been met by the transition to democracy. The high percentage of abstentions in the 1978 referendum on the Statute of Autonomy were a protest at the terms of this remapping, which excluded Navarre from the three regions that became the Autonomous Basque Community. The deliberate denial of most sexual content in Basque cinema unless it was associated with trauma and violence therefore continued alongside (and arguably in representation of) the prolongation of militancy and terrorist violence into democracy. As Basque cinema progressed into the 1980s and 1990s, it rarely, apart from the aforementioned films of Julio Medem, explored the potential of erotic content and style. Popular Basque films of the 1990s tended to exhibit a Freudian degree of abhorrence at sexual matters. Sexual trauma was essayed in *Alas de mariposa/Butterfly Wings* (dir. Juanma Bajo Ulloa, 1991) and *La madre muerta/The Dead Mother* (dir. Juanma Bajo Ulloa, 1993), while the erotic impulse was diverted into violence in *Salto al vacío/Jump into the Void* (dir. Daniel Calparsoro, 1995) and *Todo por la pasta/Everything for the Bread* (dir. Enrique Urbizu, 1991). The slow movement towards a complete ceasefire by ETA that would be formalised in 2011 led to films that responded to the prolongation of the potential for violent conflict so far into democracy with sexual frustration. *Pagafantas/Friend Zone* (dir. Borja Cobeaga, 2009) depicts the bumbling of a young man from Bilbao played by Gorka Otxoa whose best efforts at ingratiating himself with a vivacious Argentinian woman result in him being sexually sidelined as her friend. The withholding of sex was indeed a favoured theme: *Bypass* (dirs. Patxo Telleria and Aitor Mazo, 2012) found its hapless male (played by Otxoa again) obliged to feign the gentlest of romantic feelings for a terminally ill young woman out of fear that anything else would occasion her relapse, while *Ocho apellidos vascos/Spanish Affair* (dir. Emilio Martínez Lázaro, 2014) saw a lustful Andalusian frustrated in his attempts to bed a belligerent Basque called Amaia (Clara Lago). In one comic scene, Amaia describes the protocol of prolonged courtship and sustained celibacy in the Basque Country to her horrified pretender, explaining that many months will likely go by before they even get to the stage of unaccompanied dating.

The cinemas of other nations and regions that revel in nationalism or seek independence (or at least some degree of self-determination) tend to eroticise the bodies of their protagonists as carriers of nationalist symbolism and so render desirable their political, historical and cultural identities. Susan Sontag described the 'utopian aesthetics' of the Nazi propaganda film *Olympia 2. Teil – Fest der Schönheit/Olympia Part Two: Festival of Beauty* (dir. Leni Riefenstahl, 1938) as 'an ideal eroticism (sexuality converted into the magnetism of leaders and the joy of followers) [in which] one straining scantily clad figure after another seeks the ecstasy of victory' (1975), while the patriotic poetry of the eponymous Welsh poet-soldier in *Hedd Wynn* (dir. Paul Turner, 1992) stems from his nationalist-minded muse being fuelled by the female passions he arouses with his womanising. In contrast, as has been shown, the desexualisation of the national Basque imaginary was prey to resexualisation in perverse ways, most notably in the descriptions and depictions of sexual abuse as part of the torture inflicted upon Basque bodies. These instances of the resexualisation of a few real and representative individuals did not eradicate the desexualisation of the collective but they did transcend it. This was because the masochistic element that informs the cinematic representation of those subject to torture in Basque cinema, whose suffering embodies the oppression of the Basque Country and for some justified its defence, resulted in the fetishisation of the Basque body that was martyred and commemorated as symbolic. In effect, therefore, the desexualised Basque body/Country/cinema became, as Deleuze maintains, 'in itself the object of sexualisation' (1989: 117). Recently, however, this spiralling paradox has stalled. If, as Deleuze maintains, 'the deeper the coldness of the desexualisation, the more powerful and extensive the process of perverse resexualisation' (1989: 118), then following the ceasefire, the disbanding of ETA and the progressive liberalisation of the more hard-line aspects of Basque politics, the opportunity exists for Basque cinema to overcome the need to save the Basque body for a higher purpose. Indeed, if the Basque body can now be de-politicised, then this rebound might even augur erotic films that uphold the tradition of Basque cinema always seeking to express how different it is, not only from other cinemas but from its own history too.

REFERENCES

Anderson, Benedict (2006), *Imagined Communities*, London and New York: Verso Books.
Barlow, Hugh (2007), *Dead for Good: Martyrdom and the Rise of the Suicide Bomber*, Boulder, CO: Paradigm Publishers.
Barton, Carlin (2002), 'Honor and Sacredness in the Roman and Christian Worlds', in Margaret Cormack (ed.), *Sacrificing the Self: Perspectives on Martyrdom and Religion*, New York: Oxford University Press, pp. 23–38.
Deleuze, Gilles (1989), *Masochism: Coldness and Cruelty*, New York: Zone Books.
De Pablo, Santiago (2012), *The Basque Nation On-Screen: Cinema, Nationalism, and Political Violence*, Reno: Center for Basque Studies, University of Nevada at Reno.
Fouz-Hernández, Santiago and Alfredo Martínez-Expósito (2007), *Live Flesh: The Male Body in Contemporary Spanish Cinema*, London and New York: I. B. Tauris.
Jordan, Barry and Rikki Morgan-Tamosunas (1998), *Contemporary Spanish Cinema*, Manchester: Manchester University Press.
Middleton, Paul (2011), *Martyrdom: A Guide for the Perplexed*, London and New York: Continuum.
Mitchell, Jolyon (2012), *Martyrdom: A Very Short Introduction*, Oxford University Press.
Mulvey, Laura (1975), 'Visual Pleasure and Narrative Cinema', *Screen* 16:3, 6–18.
Nochlin, Linda (1986), 'Courbet's "L'origine du monde": The Origin without an Original', *October* 37, 76–86.
Oliver, Kelly (1998), 'Tracing the Signifier Behind the Scenes of Desire: Kristeva's Challenge to Lacan's Analysis', in Hugh J. Silverman (ed.), *Cultural Semiosis: Tracing the Signifier*, New York: Routledge, pp. 83–104.
Perriam, Chris (2003), *Stars and Masculinities in Spanish Cinema: From Banderas to Bardem*, Oxford and New York: Oxford University Press.
Rosoux, Valérie (2004), 'The Politics of Martyrdom', in Rona M. Fields (ed.), *Martyrdom: The Psychology, Theology, and Politics of Self-Sacrifice*, Westport, CT: Praeger, pp. 83–116.
Sánchez-Conejero, Cristina (2015), *Sex and Ethics in Spanish Cinema*, New York: Palgrave Macmillan.
Sontag, Susan (1975), 'Fascinating Fascism', *The New York Review of Books*, 6 February: http://www.nybooks.com/articles/1975/02/06/fascinating-fascism/ (last accessed 26 December 2015).
Stone, Rob and María Pilar Rodríguez (2015), *Cine Vasco: Una historia política y cultural*, Salamanca: Comunicación Social.
Straw, Carole (2002), '"A Very Special Death": Christian Martyrdom in its Classical Context', in Margaret Cormack (ed.), *Sacrificing the Self: Perspectives on Martyrdom and Religion*, New York: Oxford University Press, pp. 39–57.
Studlar, Gaylyn (1985), 'Sexual Difference', *Journal of Film and Video* 37:2, 5–26.

Studlar Gaylyn (1988), *In The Realm of Pleasure: Von Sternberg, Dietrich and the Masochistic Aesthetic*, Chicago: University of Illinois Press.
Tasker, Yvonne (1993), *Spectacular Bodies: Gender, Genre and the Action Cinema*, London and New York: Routledge.
Yosef, Raz (2001), 'The Military Body: Male Masochism and Homoerotic Relations in Israeli Cinema', *Theory and Criticism* 18, 11–46.
Yosef, Raz (2005), 'Spectacles of Pain: War, Masculinity and the Masochistic Fantasy in Amos Gitai's "Kippur"', *Shofar: An Interdisciplinary Journal of Jewish Studies* 24:1, 49–66.

FILMOGRAPHY

Akelarre/Witches' Sabbath, film, directed by Pedro Olea. Spain: Amboto Producciones Cinematográficas, 1984.
Alas de mariposa/Butterfly Wings, film, directed by Juanma Bajo Ulloa. Spain: Gasteizko Zinema S.L., Iberoamericana Films Producción, 1991.
Ama Lur/Motherland, film, directed by Fernando Larruquert and Nestor Basterretxea. Spain: Distribuciones Cinematográficas Ama Lur, Frontera Films S.A., 1968.
Barrura Begiratzeko Liehoak/Windows Looking Inward, film, directed by Josu Martínez, Txaber Larreategi, Mireia Gabilondo, Enara Goikoetxea and Eneko Olsagasti. Spain: Zinez, 2012.
Bypass, film, directed by Patxo Telleria and Aitor Mazo. Spain: Abra Producciones, 2012.
Días contados/Running out of Time, film, directed by Imanol Uribe. Spain: Aiete Films S.A., Ariane Films, Sogepaq, Instituto de la Cinematografía y de las Artes Audiovisuales (ICAA), 1994.
El crimen de Cuenca/The Cuenca Crime, film, directed by Pilar Miró. Spain: In-Cine Compañía Industrial Cinematográfica, Jet Films, 1980.
El proceso de Burgos/The Burgos Trial, film, directed by Imanol Uribe. Spain: Cobra Films, Irriutzi Zinema, 1979.
Estado de excepción/State of Emergency, film, directed by Iñaki Núñez. Spain: 1977.
Hedd Wynn, film, directed by Paul Turner. United Kingdom: Pendefig Ty Cefn, Sianel 4 Cymru (S4C), 1992.
La fuga de Segovia/Escape from Segovia, film, directed by Imanol Uribe. Spain: Frontera Films, S.A., 1981.
La jetée/The Pier, film, directed by Chris Marker. France: Argos Films, 1962.
La madre muerta/The Dead Mother, film, directed by Juanma Bajo Ulloa. Spain: Gasteizko Zinema S.L., 1993.
La maschera del demonio/Black Sunday, film, directed by Mario Bava. Italy: Galatea Film, Jolly Film, Alta Vista Productions, 1960.
La muerte de Mikel/Mikel's Death, film, directed by Imanol Uribe. Spain: Aiete Films S.A., Cobra Films, José Esteban Alenda, 1984.
La pelota vasca: la piel contra la piedra/The Basque Ball. Skin Against Stone, film, directed by Julio Medem. Spain: Alicia Produce, 2003.
Las 13 rosas/The 13 Roses, film, directed by Emilio Martínez Lázaro. Spain/Italy: Enrique Cerezo Producciones Cinematográficas S.A., Pedro Costa Producciones Cinematográficas S.A., 2007.
Ocho apellidos vascos/Spanish Affair, film, directed by Emilio Martínez Lázaro. Spain: Lazonafilms, Kowalski Films, Snow Films, Telecinco Cinema, 2014.

Olympia 2. Teil – Fest der Schönheit/ Olympia Part Two: Festival of Beauty, film, directed by Leni Riefenstahl. Germany: Olympia Film GmbH, International Olympic Committee, Tobis Filmkunst, 1938.

Pagafantas/ Friend Zone, film, directed by Borja Cobeaga. Spain: Antena 3 Films, Canal+ España, Euskal Irrati Telebista (EiTB), Sayaka Producciones Audiovisuales, Telespan 2000, Vertice 360, 2009.

Salto al vacío/ Jump into the Void, film, directed by Daniel Calparsoro. Spain: Canal+ España, Fernando Colomo Producciones Cinematográficas S.L., Filmanía S.L., Siurell Producciones Cinematográficas y de Televisión S.L., Televisión Española (TVE), Yumping Film Production, 1995.

Todo por la pasta/ Everything for the Bread, film, directed by Enrique Urbizu. Spain: Creativideo, Departamento de Cultura del Gobierno Vasco, Ministerio de Cultura, 1991.

CHAPTER 11

Erotohistoriography, Temporal Drag and the Interstitial Spaces of Childhood in Spanish Cinema

Sarah Wright

In a series of films from the final years of the political regime of General Francisco Franco to the recent past, a child figure is seen to be the conduit for the exploration of the trauma and loss of the Spanish Civil War and its aftermath of dictatorship in Spain. In films such as *El espíritu de la colmena/ The Spirit of the Beehive* (dir. Víctor Erice, 1973), *Cría cuervos/Raise Ravens* (dir. Carlos Saura, 1976), *Secretos del corazón/Secrets of the Heart* (dir. Montxo Armendáriz, 1997) and *Pa negre/Black Bread* (dir. Agustí Villalonga, 2010), children are figures of loss linking trauma, war and memory. As I noted in my book *The Child in Spanish Cinema* (2013), the returns through time to the motifs of child, trauma and memory are so marked that 'it may make sense to speak of a new *cine con niño*, a genre in itself' (Wright 2013: 101), a reference to the well-known cycle of child-centred films from the 1950s and '60s.[1] In an article of 2016, Erin Hogan coined the term *nuevo cine con niño* to refer to this more recent cycle of child-centred films (Hogan 2016: 1).

Repeatedly, these films feature a scene where a child views adult erotic acts in a rendition of Freud's 'primal scene' (Freud 1992: 364).[2] In *Cría cuervos*, for example, a little girl (Ana Torrent) witnesses her father's adulterous lovemaking and plots revenge on behalf of her terminally ill mother (Geraldine Chaplin). The scenario recalls the primal scene, but where for Freud the primal scene (whether real or imagined) involved love for the parent of the opposite sex and a death wish against the parent of the same sex, here the situation is reversed. Furthermore, with its striking central image where Ana refuses to look into the coffin of her dead father (Héctor Alterio), who is dressed in military uniform, the scene has been interpreted (by, for example, Smith 2011) as capturing a death wish against the dictator, General Franco, who was on his deathbed as filming took place. In addition, through the presence of Ana's mother as an apparition from the past, the film has been seen to highlight the context of intergenerational memory which connects in interesting ways to recent attempts to recuperate Spain's traumatic past as well as to national debates over 'memory wars' (Kim 2005: 69–84).[3] Presenting another variation on the theme, in *Secretos del corazón*, Javi (Andoni Erburu) hears the sounds of his mother's lovemaking with his uncle but this comes to signify the moans of the civil war dead. For Freud, the primal scene is a trauma barely understood by the child and repressed: it returns only later when trauma is experienced once more by the subject. Whether the motif of the primal scene emerged intuitively or was plotted deliberately, it has served as a useful way for filmmakers to introduce the theme of the trauma of the war in Spain and its repression in an oblique way, even against the background of film censorship. The primal scene ushers in the temporal matrix of trauma, with its repetitions, hauntings and delays, and its central motif of a scene returned to after the fact. The films, with varying degrees of obviousness, refer to the central trauma of the Spanish Civil War and its aftermath, and the inability of that trauma to be openly expressed for many years after the war.[4] These are films whose structures of feeling are melancholic, expressing a sense of loss over the traumas of the past. It has been important to tell the stories of losers, the side repressed under Francoism.[5]

But further to these motifs, the obsessive return of the child as a witness to the primal scene may also represent a return to the 'Oedipal knot', and to a desire to unpick what Lee Edelman has termed 'reproductive futurism' (Edelman 2004: 2). For Edelman, politics, 'however radical the means by which specific constituencies attempt to produce a more desirable social order [politics] remains, at its core, conservative insofar as it works to affirm a structure, to authenticate social order, which it then intends to transmit to the future in the form of its inner Child' (Edelman 2004: 2–3). The anxiety of the primal scene, meanwhile, lays the foundation for the Oedipus Complex, which is a heteronormative theory of development. As I have written elsewhere, Francoism was based on reproductive futurism according to Edelman's definitions: it was a project for the future centred on the child and which had the heterosexual family as its prime political unit (Wright 2013: 31). The primal scene might be seen as the scenario which sets into motion the familial pattern which is the bedrock of reproductive futurism. Francoism might be seen as a conservative version of this schemata, wherein Franco is the head of the supreme family of the State.

Recent work on the child figure in the *nuevo cine con niño* has been informed by the temporal turn in queer studies. Building on writing by queer theorists such as Halberstam (2011) and Stockton (2009), Hogan (2016) and Allbritton (2014) have made the case for the child in *Pa negre* to be seen as a queer child. Fiona Noble, meanwhile, has observed how the temporalities ushered in by the child can disrupt Francoism's repro-futurism. I wish to draw on the work of these scholars to rethink the obsessive return to the primal scene in these films.[6]

Applications of Derridean hauntology to the films of the *nuevo cine con niño* have brought with them new understandings of forms of historical justice as well as the potential for new combinations of the social order.[7] But structures of melancholia run the risk of offering endless repetition. What would it take, then, to move on or beyond this repetition? Queer temporalities may offer a way to reconfigure melancholic structures. In *Time Binds: Queer Temporalities, Queer Histories* (2010), Elizabeth Freeman challenges queer theory's emphasis on loss and trauma, preferring to foreground bodily pleasure in the experience and representation of time and history. As O'Rourke and Mulhall put it, Freeman asks, what would an 'attention to a hauntology that focused on erotic pleasure, on bliss, unfold in the oscillating warp and weft of queer temporalities and the subjects that such queer times traverse, bind and undo?' (O'Rourke and Mulhall 2012). Freeman's powerful concoction of embodiment, pleasure and alternative beats of time interests me as I try to plot alternatives to the traumatic time put forward by the *nuevo cine con niño*. Perhaps there is no better example of the 'braided time' nor the 'visceral pull of the past on the present' than the Frankenstein's monster of *El espíritu de la colmena*.[8] This is the past texturing the present, a lumbering, embodied past which refuses to be laid to rest. But as the relationship of Ana with the monster in the film illustrates so well, the child of the *nuevo cine con niño* also provides an embodied relationship to history; its wide-eyed gaze often returning the spectator to what Emma Wilson has termed 'a state of helplessness (motor, emotional or political)' (Wilson 2005: 330). Moreover, the spectator as 'adult-child-seer' engendered in these films can be overwhelmed by a lack of mastery through the child's gaze and yet also aware of the child's historical circumstances, even if the child character is not (Martin-Jones 2011: 81). This resonates with Freeman's description of the taking on of the past as a bodily experience, of 'using the body as a tool to effect, figure or perform an encounter with history in the present' in which the present becomes rather a hybrid between the past and the present (Freeman 2010: 95).[9]

The child in these films displays, as Eric Thau has remarked of Ana Torrent, the 'historicising gaze', which also marks it as a victim (2011: 131). To view these children differently would mean, in some sense, to 'queer' the child. In addressing the queer temporalities engendered by these films, my aim is not to contend that all childhood should here be read as queer.[10] Childhood is, however, cited in the same breath as eroticism, a position that can be controversial: our dominant fantasies about children demand that innocence mean innocent of sexuality. As Steven Bruhm and Natasha Hurley have written, 'there is currently a dominant narrative about children: children are (and should stay) innocent of sexual desires and intentions', but, as they continue, there is a correlative: 'at the same time, children are also officially, tacitly, assumed to be heterosexual' (Bruhm and Hurley 2004: ix). To acknowledge children as sexual beings therefore might open the way for those children who experience same-sex desire. Furthermore, to acknowledge pleasure in these films seemed to be a way, not to deny the trauma present, but to open up new avenues from which to conceive of alternative realities to the heteronormative reproductive futurism seen as the dominant order in these films. Edelman wrote that '*queerness* names the side of those "not fighting for the children"' (Edelman 2004: 3). As McGuire asks, 'what happens to this symbolic and political opposition when the ultimate figure of futurism comes to embody the death drive?' (McGuire 2016: 65). McGuire's solution is to see the ways that children can 'destabilise the binaries between life and death', reminding us that the child represents *a* future, rather than *the* future: 'children represent more than a nebulous concept of a forward-reaching temporality; instead they are the embodiment of *a* specific future, that of compulsory heteronormative reproduction' (65 – emphasis original). Given the association of these characters with death, it might be attractive to explore McGuire's queer child as one who blurs the 'already porous boundaries between life and death' in these films, with a view to finding, as he does, that the child who refutes 'both social death and normative life' can offer an escape to the 'ceaseless drive of resistance and dissent' that he finds in, for example, Edelman's queer politics (McGuire 2015: 75). But I find that I am more attracted to Freeman's erotohistoriography, a 'deeply embodied pleasure' which can 'operate outside of our usual sense of developmental time' and 'counter the logic of development' (Freeman 2010: 59). The pleasures in these films, as we shall see, are not always about same-sex desire, but they may offer alternatives to modes of chrononormativity and, by implication, to the reproductive futurism provided by Francoist politics as the background to these films.[11] In this chapter, I shall focus on three films: *Cría cuervos* (1976), the less well-known *Dulces horas/Sweet Hours* (dir. Carlos Saura, 1981), and the most recent in the cycle, *Pa negre* of 2010.

THE EROTICS OF MATERNAL LOVE IN *CRÍA CUERVOS*

Cría cuervos, set in the 'present' Spain of the 1970s, is bathed in melancholy: Ana's summoning of the ghost of her dead mother is the guiding structure of the film. These segments of the film are juxtaposed with the fantasies that Ana entertains that she has poisoned her father (in fact she has administered bicarbonate of soda) in sequences in which she casts herself as the lead in a crime melodrama. But the scenes with Ana's mother perform what Elizabeth Freeman might refer to as a 'visceral sense' of the hauntological, or of hauntology as bliss (2010: 14): Ana's mother returns in Ana's fantasies as the loving embodiment of maternal eroticism.[12]

In Martha Nussbaum's *Upheavals of Thought*, a book in which the author describes her emotional reaction to the death of her own mother, Nussbaum cites a passage from Proust's *Remembrance of Things Past*, where the narrator, on waking up in the night, feels a 'primitive longing for comfort that derives from his early childhood' (Nussbaum 2001: 176). She goes on, 'in an attempt to mother himself, he presses his cheeks "tenderly" against the "comfortable cheeks" of his pillow' (175), and dreams of a woman: 'he feels the warmth of his body mingle with hers; he feels the warmth of her kiss on his cheek, he feels his body pressed down by her weight. As he attempts to "become one with her", he awakens' (176). The erotic attachment the narrator feels to this woman is notable but also the way he attempts to 'mother himself' through the memory of an embodied holding. In *Cría cuervos*, Ana's hauntological mother is equally embodied: she presses her cheek against Ana's when she kisses her goodnight; she sits on her bed to hug her to tuck her in. We know that this is Ana's fantasy because of the mother's exclusivity: in the selfishness of childhood (and, probably, of most grief), Ana's mother appears only to her. She plays a game of fort/da, endlessly making her mother appear and disappear, or plays the pop song 'Por qué te vas?' (Why Are You Leaving?) by Jeanette on her turntable – the foreign singer reminiscent of her mother's foreign accent speaking Spanish as she sits cocooned in the armchair in an intimate composition.[13] Thus, although we sense Ana's pain and deep loss of her mother, we also experience the moments of bliss, rapture and sensuousness of an embodied memory as self-comforting. This is maternal love as a form of erotic, visceral, sentient attachment through time.

In addition to the deeply felt relationship between mother and child, *Cría cuervos* also observes the intimate contact between sisters. Ana's sisters do not appear to share Ana's deep grief over their mother but nevertheless the sisters are allied and complicit, particularly in their games. The children occupy queerly interstitial times and spaces. The long and languorous summer holidays stretch out infinitely, just as hours stretch into days in the twilight of the grandmother's fading memories. Ana's powerful reveries allow her to draw a time apart from chrononormative time.[14] Memories, daydreams, reveries, photographs and intimate sequences such as the children's bath-time create an alternative time which is juxtaposed to the 'historical' or 'official' time (and memory) of Francoism suggested by the posed photographs of Ana's father in military uniform, or even his military-style funeral: a queer time to be found 'in the interstices of national-political life' (Freeman 2010: x).

In one famous sequence of the film, the girls dress up as adults (presumably modelled on their mother and father) and play out a scene from domestic life. The scene might be seen as a rendition of what Freeman terms 'temporal drag': but where she suggests an 'outdated' as well as cross-gendered performance, featuring 'retrogression, delay and the pull of the past on the present', here there is a different sort of temporal lag involved (Freeman 2010: xxi). Ana

Figure 11.1 Conchi Pérez in *Cría cuervos/Raise Ravens*, directed by Carlos Saura. Spain: Elías Querejeta, 1976.

Figure 11.2 Ana Torrent and Conchi Pérez in *Cría cuervos/Raise Ravens*, directed by Carlos Saura. Spain: Elías Querejeta, 1976.

dresses up as her mother, in black wig, necklace and a dress that is too large for her. The scene questions the social and sexual roles available to young women, particularly as Ana, playing her mother, scolds her sister, playing her father, for arriving home late. When Elizabeth Freeman dresses in her mother's outdated clothes, she writes that the embodiment of 'Mom circa 1969' 'writes onto my body crucially at least two distinct forms and meanings of womanhood' (2010: 70). But more than simple parody, this is, rather, 'an earnest montage of publicly intelligible subject-positions lost and gained' (70). Arguably, we have a similar situation here, as Ana manages to reject the roles available to her mother through the dressing up, to look forward to something new. Cadwallader has written of Freeman's scenario, that 'the illusion of a singular, ahistorical essence of "womanhood" is undermined here, because (at least) two essences are performed and enacted' (Cadwallader 2014). The scene may also remind us of the sequence of 'temporal drag' when Ana smears mud on her face in such a way that resembles a beard after she buries her pet guineapig. I agree with Fiona Noble (2012) here that the scene may serve to 'queer' Ana, referring to a nascent same-sex desire. After all, the narrator (Ana as an adult) dwells on the shots of her father with his lover, musing of her that it was not surprising that he should have fallen for her as she was so beautiful (Noble – in preparation).[15]

In the final scenes of the film, the adult Ana speaks directly to the camera. The adult Ana is played by Geraldine Chaplin but dubbed with a Castilian accent which in itself appears as a form of 'temporal drag', particularly in the light of the earlier scene of dressing up. The time of the sequence is projected forward into the future, a hybrid time in which Ana is able to reflect on her past ('changing tempos, by remixing memory and desire, by recapturing excess' – Freeman 2010: 173) and to choose an identification with her mother in which, as we sense, she also differentiates herself in an act of self-determination.

DULCES HORAS AND THE OEDIPAL STUTTER

Dulces horas (1981) represents something of an anomaly in Carlos Saura's *oeuvre*. It was not generally well received by either critics or public. In the film, Juan (Iñaki Aierra) writes a play called '*dulces horas*' (a line from the famous song from the 1930s by Imperio Argentina, 'Remember, the sweet hours of yesterday'), and employs actors to act out scenes from his childhood in the apartment his family occupied in his youth. Unlike other child-centred films, the Spanish Civil War is not a source of trauma for the protagonist: rather it is the source of pleasure. Thus, although there are scenes featuring the young Juanico in bed listening to the bombs going overhead,[16] nevertheless, the sequences of the 1937 aerial bombing of Madrid, a blend of black-and-white found footage interspersed with fictional scenes, come across like excerpts from neorealist child-centred films with Juanico as the protagonist. Furthermore, they are pleasurable to the boy Juanico because he remembers them as a time when he was together exclusively with his mother. The film cross-cuts between Juan the adult and his childhood self (Juanico): there are even scenes where the adult Juan witnesses scenes with the child Juanico. As we come to realise, Juanico (the child) is caught in an 'Oedipal phase' in which he experiences erotic love for his mother and rivalry against his father. This is played out graphically in scenes where Juanico spies on his mother and father embracing in a park and wrenches his parents apart before substituting himself in the embrace. In the film, we see how as a child Juanico was taken by his father to a brothel to be initiated by an older woman. We also learn that Juanico's father went abroad to Argentina, leaving the family to take up an adulterous relationship with another woman, an act that Juanico believes led to his mother's suicide. Juan's trauma and the guilt he has lived with all of his adult life is that as a child he bought the pills (on his mother's instructions) that would lead to his mother's suicide. The film indulges Juanico's fantasies: in one scene his mother undresses for/before him until she is naked. Meanwhile, the actress the adult Juan contracts to play his mother is the identical image to his mother (both are played by Assumpta Serna). The eroticism Juanico felt for his mother crosses over into his adult sexual relationship.

The film stages scenes where we (with Juan) watch Juanico's erotic pleasure gained from watching adult eroticism. Some critics such as Caparrós Lera saw the film as Saura's playing out of autobiographical tics in which 'Carlos Saura rebels against the Spanish past and indulges in clearly Freudian schematas until he reaches the most absolute amorality – or immorality – with regards to a surrealist incest, falling into obscenities which might be reflected in the Penal Code (corruption of minors)' (Caparrós Lera 1992: 212).

But for others, such as José Colmeiro, the film has to do with the 'fetishisation of the past'. It is, then, a 'parody of the compulsive fetishisation of the past, of the cultivation of the idealing nostalgia of a romanticised past' (Colmeiro 2001: 293). Marvin D'Lugo relates this nostalgia specifically to a trend in the 1980s towards idealing the civil war and the early years of dictatorship (1991: 173). Certainly there are scenes in which characters retell stories of war bravery which verge on camp excess. But most camp of all are the scenes featuring Berta, the actress who plays Juan's mother in the play of his life. Juan's sister Marta succeeds in her mission to readjust Juan's rose-tinted view of his mother. When he visits her at her rural home, she shows Juan a series of letters between their mother and father which show that, far from being a victim, Juan's mother was a domineering matriarch who drove his father from the home. Marta is heavily pregnant, but the theme of 'false' motherhood is introduced by her two little girls, who put pillows under their dresses to fake pregnancy in a form of temporal drag. After reading the letters, Juan realises that his mother was as domineering as Marta maintains and that, furthermore, she deliberately engineered to commit suicide in such a way as to leave Juan with a guilt complex and adoration of her (in an extended Oedipal complex) after her death. Juan, freed from the ghosts of the past, can now look forward to a future with his new wife, Berta. For Nancy Berthier, 'the final sequence shows him liberated from his family demons, open to a promising future represented by the baby that he is expecting with his partner who happily sings 'Remember''' (Berthier 2011: 217). But this reading does not take full account of the temporal drag present in the scene. This is, rather, a continuation of an 'Oedipal stutter', a delay in the heteronormative social fabric, which sees Juan in a relationship with a woman who resembles his mother and who is, in the final scene, sponging him in the bath as she calls him 'Juanico'. She mouths the words to Imperio Argentina's song in a clear 'temporal drag': she is playing the role of Juan's mother in his idealised version of the past.[17] Nevertheless, the ending of the film parodies the trauma of the primal scene even as it celebrates Juan's ability to carve out an alternative ending for himself (in this sense it loosens the Oedipal knot), at the same time it parodies the fetishisation of a nostalgic view of the past. In this sense, it performs the function of what Freeman refers to as jamming 'whatever looks like the inevitable' (2010: 173).

PA NEGRE: INTERSTITIAL SPACES OF QUEER

Pa negre, set in 1940s Catalonia, is a coming of age drama centred on Andreu (Francesc Colomer), who finds his friend Culet (Miquel Borrás) dying in the wood and, after hearing his dying word, 'Pitorliua', a name the children had given to a ghost who lives in the forest, sets out to discover the truth – in fact, he will discover a series of unpleasant truths about his family; in particular, his father whom he idolises. When Andreu witnesses his mother and father making love in *Pa negre*, this is not a traumatic event for Andreu. When, later, he spies his mother offering sexual favours to the Captain of the local Civil Guard this signals the start of his journey towards a loss of innocence. But it is the (possibly imagined) scene of the castration of Pitorliua in a cave which is when he realises that his adored father was in fact a member of a violent lynch-party of a local man guilty of nothing other than homosexuality.

Erin Hogan is right when she suggests that the intertextual reference points of this film offer a 'queering of the *bildungsfilm*' (Hogan 2016: 3). In what may turn out to be the last in the series of films which centre on a child to discuss questions of historical memory, the child here is 'queered', in that the protagonist refuses the advances of his female friend, Núria, in favour of thwarted sexual desire for a young tubercular adolescent. Here, Pitorliua, as

Hogan notes, presents a form of 'homo-spectrality' which 'hints at Andreu's sexual stirrings and warn the boy to escape a similar fate' (Hogan 2016: 6). Pitorliua is the monstrous other, a time-lagged intertextual reflection of the Frankenstein's monster in *El espíritu de la colmena*: thus *Pa negre* offers a queering of the relationship between child and monster engendered in that earlier film.[18] Andreu is thus a figure of textual accretion; one that points to the changes in queer viewing attachments, political and social changes and revised readings of historical and personal justice that have emerged belatedly through the years since the release of *El espíritu de la colmena*. But if monstrosity is linked in *Pa negre* to homosexuality through references to the abject (tuberculosis, death) (Hogan 2016), the child protagonist is also able to explore nascent same-sex desire as also linked to pleasure and eroticism. Pleasure associated with same-sex desire is expressed through imagery of birds and angels. Through reverse angles of longing looks and naked skin as Tisic, the tubercular adolescent bathes by the river, the film builds up a storehouse of images of pleasurable homoeroticism which exist alongside the imagery of abjection which is also expressly linked with homosexuality.

The notion that the burgeoning love between Andreu and Tisic cannot be fulfilled is expressed through imagery of flight, but conversely this is also associated with death: Tisic says that he cannot escape with Andreu towards the end of the film as he must take flight (the intimation is that he is going to die). As we later learn, instead of escaping alone, Andreu goes to the Francoist school selected for him by his adoptive right-wing family. The reconstruction of the Francoist classroom (with resonances of other filmic classrooms of the genre such as, for example, in the film *Secretos del corazón*), the starchy uniform and scowl appear to bring to life the static Francoist posed school photographs that are featured earlier in the film: they come across like a temporal drag.

In terms of Freeman's erotohistoriography, then, the film does describe homosexual love as a 'deeply embodied pleasure' which can 'operate outside of our usual sense of developmental time' and can 'counter the logic of development' in an interstitial mode. The film performs an erotohistoriography; there is an anachronism about the scenes of nascent same-sex desire which create a sense of knowingness. Thus, not only does the film perform affective attachments across time but it also 'queers' notions of historiography. Citing Hamlet's line 'the time is out of joint', Elizabeth Freeman suggests that time can be 'felt in the bones, as a kind of skeletal dislocation'. She suggests that asynchrony, or time lags, can be viewed as a queer phenomenon, 'something felt on, with, or as a body, something experienced as a mode of erotic difference or even as a means to express or enact ways of being and connecting that have not yet arrived or never will' (Freeman 2007: 159). *Pa negre* constructs queer love spectrally but also gives it bodily form: if these would-be lovers lived in a different time their love would not be thwarted. Thus, there is an anachronism or belatedness about the scenes of thwarted same-sex love in this film, which is matched by the almost 'hyper-real' aesthetic afforded by the brilliantly colourful materiality of the digital in this film, which allows the spectator to appreciate the 'temporal lag' involved in these scenes. What is simultaneously clear, however, is that this alternative history, this nascent phantom 'other' erotic life, is written under erasure. This, then, is a central theme of the film: that neither the history of the '*rojos*' under Francoism nor that of queers can ever really be fully realised.[19]

Can anything positive come out of the crushing of this nascent homoeroticism into the strictures of Francoism that we have at the end of the film? Dean Allbritton gives a powerful argument of the need to acknowledge the damage wrought on the child: he shows how the imagery of birds bears 'the symbolic weight of freedom and its loss, happiness and sadness, crisis and its resolution' to build up a powerful argument for the way that the film asks us to understand how darkness can be refashioned into something generative, 'not a *No Future*, but a new future' (2014: 635). In his reading, the child is an image of damaged futurity: 'recast as the damaged child of the Spanish Civil War, insisting that we understand him', while he also maintains that damaging futurity is also 'a necessary move, one that helps to release the grip of health and heteronormativity as impossible, sweeping standards for humanity' (635). Ultimately, this seems like the most reparative possibility for Andreu. Erotic pleasure, however crushed, signals new possibilities for understanding the Spanish past with a view to moving into the future.

NO FUTURE?

The constant returns over time to the figure of the wide-eyed child as witness to Spanish history create a kaleidoscoping of time which positions us as witness to the ongoing process of self-reflection with regards to both history and social politics. *Pa negre* appears to have signalled the end of the image of the wide-eyed child as witness to history, if not entirely of the theme.[20] Erotohistoriography allows us to reflect on that process of self-reflection, as well as to celebrate the affective attachments created across time. Indeed, the opportunities these films afford for a focus on children's desires, for their erotic attachments across time, what Freeman terms 'remixing memory and desire' (Freeman 2010: 172), not only creates the potential for alternative configurations of the places where time and sexuality meet but also posits these children as agents of their own pasts as well as their futures.

NOTES

1. The original *cine con niño* was a hybrid collection of films from the 1960s which centred on child figures. Examples might include the films of Joselito, known as the 'singing nightingale', and those of Marisol (Pepa Flores).
2. Freud introduced the term in his case study of 'The Wolf Man', whose real name was Sergei Pankeiev, in 1914. The child's parents' sexual activity was fantasised by the child to be an attack by the father on the mother.
3. On the polemic over how to represent the past, see Labanyi (2006) and Ferrán (2007).
4. Spain's 'memory boom' is a response to the sense that a 'Pact of Silence' may have been tacitly agreed upon following Franco's death for the sake of moving peacefully towards democracy. The Law of Historical Memory in 2007 went some way towards acknowledging the need to recognise the unacknowledged trauma of the past. See Labanyi (2008).
5. The figure of the child in these films has had other ramifications, too, chiming with the emergence of recent news items about children disappeared, repatriated or given to new families under Francoism. See Tremlett (2011) and Vinyes, Armengou and Belis (2003).
6. I am grateful to Erin Hogan, Fiona Noble and Emma Wilson for sending me their work prior to publication.
7. Labanyi (2000) was responsible for the sea change which introduced Derridean hauntology to Spanish cultural products of this period.
8. See Chris Perriam's (2008) article on the changes effected by scholarship over time in approaches to the monster and to the film in general. For Freeman (2007), Frankenstein's monster embodies an erotic relationship to history. Part of the erotic relationship to history that Ana's relationship to the monster engenders in *El espíritu de la colmena* is the suggestion, through the ellipses in the film just after Ana meets the monster by the lake, that she has been sexually assaulted by the monster. Perriam points out the importance of a girl entering puberty and the resonances from the horror genre that carry over to the film (2008).
9. Allowing for Ana's erotic relationship to history permits a reading which sees the Frankenstein's monster as a product of her fantasies which have to do with her growing awareness of sexuality at the onset of puberty.
10. See Stockton (2009: 11), whose concept of 'growing sideways' also opens up the field to allow 'queering' to signify other 'ways of growing that are not growing up'.
11. For Freeman, chrononormativity is the 'use of time to organise individual human bodies toward maximum productivity', where 'flesh is bound into socially meaningful embodiment through temporal regulation' (2010: 3). In other words, 'people are bound to one another, engrouped, made to feel coherently collective, through particularly orchestrations of time' (3).
12. On the maternal erotic, see for example Taniguchi (2012).
13. This may remind us of Mary Cassatt's paintings, for example, of the child Mary in an armchair. Cassatt's paintings recreate the intimacy of the mother/child relationship through everyday objects. See, for example, Griselda Pollock's work on this painting (Pollock 1988: 92–3).
14. Noble (in preparation) draws on the work of Halberstam. As she notes, for Halberstam, children 'inhabit different understandings of time, and experience the passing of time differently' (2012: xxiii); they are 'always already anarchic and rebellious, out of order and out of time' (2011: 27).

15. See also Emma Wilson's paper (2016) (in a reading which has influenced my own), where she argues for the relationships between sisters, female friendship and same-sex desire as part of a possible continuum. If read in this way, *Cría cuervos* might present a (belated) dynamic reminiscent of Freud's realisation of Ida Bauer's homosexuality in the case of 'Dora'.
16. See Berthier (2011) on the childhood fear onscreen in this film.
17. See two articles on this view: D'Lugo (2012) and Bloch-Robin (2011). Also of interest is Stephen Farrier's article on the ways that the lip-synching of drag queens can engage with the past and with questions of history (Farrier 2016).
18. Cadwallader, glossing Freeman, writes of Frankenstein's monster (as written by Mary Shelley) that it engenders 'befores, afters, and monstrous patchworks of temporality' (Cadwallader 2014).
19. See, for example, Amago (2013: 99), who writes that rather than recovering historical memory 'through a responsible and reflexive historiography, *Pa negre* approaches memory and history in a very different way, ultimately proposing a critical form of forgetting conceived as a psychic and emotional strategy that would allow Catalan viewers to deconstruct historical failure "as a category levied by the winners against the losers"' (here Amago is quoting Halberstam 2011: 174).
20. The recent film *La isla mínima / Marshland* (dir. Alberto Rodríguez, 2014), which engages with the Spanish transition to democracy, can be read, as I have done elsewhere, as representing a shift: here Pedro (Raúl Arévalo), the adult cop, takes on the role of witness to history, thereby forcing him to face up to personal responsibility for his silence about historical events (something which the child, with its partial view of events, can often sidestep). See Wright (2016).

REFERENCES

Allbritton, Dean (2014), 'Recovering Childhood: Virulence, Ghosts and *Black Bread*', *Bulletin of Hispanic Studies* 91:6, 620–36.
Amago, Samuel (2013), *Spanish Cinema in the Global Context: Film On Film*, London: Routledge.
Berthier, Nancy (2011), 'Ficcionalización del miedo en en cine: La mirada retrospective de Carlos Saura', in Nancy Berthier and Vicente Sánchez Biosca (eds), *Retóricas del miedo: Imágenes de la Guerra Civil española*, Madrid: Colección de la Casa de Velázquez, pp. 209–21.
Bloch-Robin, Marianne (2011), 'Música y narración en *Dulces horas*: de la inmersión nostálgica en la vorágine del pasado a la distancia irónica de la instancia narrative superior', in Robin Lefere (ed.), *Carlos Saura: Una trayectoria ejemplar*, Madrid: Biblioteca filológica hispana, pp. 47–66.
Bruhm, Steven and Natasha Hurley (2004), *Curiouser: On the Queerness of Children*, Minneapolis: University of Minnesota Press.
Cadwallader, Jessica Robyn (2014), 'Trans Forming Time', *Social Text*: http://socialtextjournal.org/periscope_article/trans-forming-time/ (last accessed 8 May 2016).
Caparrós Lera, José María (1992), *El cine español de la democracia: de la muerte de Franco al 'cambio' socialista (1975–1989)*, Barcelona: Anthropos.
Colmeiro, José F. (2001), 'Metateatralidad y psicodrama: los escenarios de la memoria en el cine de Carlos Saura', *Anales de la literatura española contemporánea* 26:1, 277–98.

D'Lugo, Marvin (1991), *The Films of Carlos Saura: The Practice of Seeing*, Princeton, NJ: Princeton University Press.
D'Lugo, Marvin (2012), 'Auteurism and the Construction of the Canon: Carlos Saura', in Jo Labanyi and Tatjana Pavlović (eds), *A Companion to Spanish Cinema*, Oxford: Wiley-Blackwell, pp. 124–30.
Edelman, Lee (2004), *No Future: Queer Theory and the Death Drive*, Durham, NC and London: Duke University Press.
Farrier, Stephen (2016), 'That Lip-Synching Feeling: Drag Performance as Digging the Past', in Alyson Campbell and Stephen Farrier (eds), *Queer Dramaturgies: International Perspectives on Where Performance Leads Queer*, London: Palgrave, pp. 192–209.
Ferrán, Ofelia (2007), *Working Through Memory in Contemporary Spanish Narrative*, Bucknell, PA: Bucknell University Press.
Freeman, Elizabeth (2007), 'Introduction to Queer Temporalities', *GLQ* 13:2–3, 159–76.
Freeman, Elizabeth (2010), *Time Binds: Queer Temporalities, Queer Histories*, Durham, NC and London: Duke University Press.
Freud, Sigmund (1992 [1900]), *The Interpretation of Dreams*, Penguin Freud Library, edited by James Strachey, Alan Tyson and Angela Richards, vol. 4, London: Penguin.
Halberstam, J. (2011), *The Queer Art of Failure*, Durham, NC and London: Duke University Press.
Halberstam, J. (2012), *Gaga Feminism: Sex, Gender, and the End of Normal*, Boston, MA: Beacon Press.
Hogan, Erin K. (2016), 'Queering Post-War Childhood: *Pa negre* (Agustí Villaronga, Spain 2010)', *Hispanic Research Journal* 17:1, February, 1–18.
Kim, Yeon-Soo (2005), *The Family Album: Histories, Subjectivities, and Immigration in Contemporary Spanish Culture*, Lewisburg, PA: Bucknell University Press.
Labanyi, Jo (2000), 'History and Hauntology, or What Does One Do With the Ghosts of the Past?', in Joan Ramón Resina (ed.), *Disremembering the Dictatorship: The Politics of Memory in the Spanish Transition to Democracy*, Amsterdam: Rodopi, pp. 65–82.
Labanyi, Jo (2006), 'Historias de víctimas: la memoria histórica y el testimonio en la España contemporánea', *Iberoamericana* 6:24, 87–98.
Labanyi, Jo (2008), 'The Politics of Memory in Contemporary Spain', *Journal of Spanish Cultural Studies* 9:2, 119–25.
Martin-Jones, David (2011), *Deleuze and World Cinemas*, London: Continuum.
McGuire, Riley (2015), 'Queer Children, Queer Futures: Navigating *lifedeath* in *The Hunger Games*', *Mosaic* 48:2, June, 63–76.
Noble, Fiona (in preparation), '"Once Upon A Time": Childhood Temporalities in Post-Franco Spanish Cinema'.
Noble, Fiona (2012), 'You Won't Fool the Children of the Transition: A Deconstruction and Queering of Ana Torrent', unpublished paper presented at the Modern Languages Research Forum, University of Aberdeen, 10 May 2012.
Nussbaum, Martha (2001), *Upheavals of Thought: The Intelligence of Emotions*, Cambridge: Cambridge University Press.
O'Rourke, Michael and Ann Mulhall (2012), 'In a Queer Time and Space: Slowly, Closely, Over Reading in Elizabeth Freeman's *Time Binds*', *Social Text*: http://socialtextjournal.org/periscope_article/in-a-queer-time-and-space-slowly-closely-over-reading-elizabeth-freemans-time-binds/ (last accessed 8 May 2016).
Perriam, Chris (2008), '*El espíritu de la colmena*: Memory, Nostalgia, Trauma (Víctor Erice, 1973)', in Joan Ramón Resina (ed.), *Burning Darkness: A Half Century of Spanish Cinema*, Albany, NY: State University of New York Press, pp. 61–81.

Pollock, Griselda (1988), *Vision and Difference: Feminism, Femininity and the Histories of Art*, London: Routledge.
Smith, Paul Julian (2011), 'Spanish Spring: Cinema After Franco', BFI: http://old.bfi.org.uk/sightandsound/feature/49738 (last accessed 20 June 2016).
Stockton, Kathryn Bond (2009), *The Queer Child, Or Growing Sideways in the Twentieth Century*, Durham, NC and London: Duke University Press.
Taniguchi, Kyoko (2012), 'The Eroticism of the Maternal: So What If Everything is About the Mother?', *Studies in Gender and Sexuality* 13:2, 123–38.
Thau, Eric (2011), 'The Eyes of Ana Torrent', *Studies in Hispanic Cinemas* 8:2, 131–43.
Tremlett, Giles (2011), 'Hundreds of Spanish Babies "Stolen from Clinics and Sold for Adoption"', *The Guardian*, 27 January 2011: https://www.theguardian.com/world/2011/jan/27/spanish-babies-stolen-clinic (last accessed 12 June 2016).
Vinyes, Ricardo, Maria Armengou and Ricardo Belis (2003), *Los niños perdidos del franquismo* Barcelona: Plaza y Janés.
Wilson, Emma (2005), 'Children, Emotion and Viewing in Contemporary European Film', *Screen* 46:3, pp. 329–40.
Wilson, Emma (2016), 'Céline Sciamma's Sisters', paper presented at *Childhood and Nation in World Cinemas* conference, Royal Holloway, University of London, 19 April.
Wright, Sarah (2013), *The Child in Spanish Cinema*, Manchester: Manchester University Press.
Wright, Sarah (2016), 'The Female Adolescent Body as Trope for the Spanish Nation in *La isla minima* (2013)', paper presented at *Childhood and Nation in World Cinemas* conference, Royal Holloway, University of London, 19 April.

FILMOGRAPHY

Cría cuervos/Raise Ravens, film, directed by Carlos Saura. Spain: Elías Querejeta, 1976.
Dulces horas/Sweet Hours, film, directed by Carlos Saura. Spain: Elías Querejeta, Jacques Roitfeld, 1981.
El espíritu de la colmena/The Spirit of the Beehive, film, directed by Víctor Erice. Spain: Elías Querejeta, 1973.
La isla mínima/Marshland, film, directed by Alberto Rodríguez. Spain: AXN, Atresmedia Cine, Atresmedia, Atípica Films, Audiovisual Avai SGR, Canal Sur Televisión, Canal + España, ICO, ICAA, Junta de Andalucía, Sacromonte Films, 2014.
Pa negre/Black Bread, film, directed by Agustí Villalonga. Spain: Isona Pasola, 2010.
Secretos del corazón/Secrets of the Heart, film, directed by Montxo Armendáriz. Spain: Imanol Uribe and Andrés Santana, 1997.

CHAPTER 12

Sex After Fifty: The 'Invisible' Female Ageing Body in Spanish Women-authored Cinema

Barbara Zecchi

During the Goya Awards Ceremony of 2010, Pilar Bardem, who was nominated for her role in *La vida empieza hoy/Life Begins Today* (dir. Laura Mañá, 2009), pretended to be surprised when host José Corbacho kept his distance from her, having kissed on the lips all the other *younger* women that he had just introduced. Pilar Bardem's reaction appeared to be no less than an astute remark on the patriarchal logic described by the Spanish proverb 'El que besa a una vieja, no besa' ('He who kisses an old woman does not kiss') that led Corbacho to ignore completely an older female actor: because of her age, Bardem was invisible to him.

In a context of obsession with physical perfection and eternal youth, the cinematic representation of the older body, especially the older *woman*'s body, implies a thematic and aesthetic challenge. As film critic Mimi Swartz has pointed out, 'Hollywood has been notoriously merciless to women of a certain vintage or else dismissive of them' (2004). How are middle-aged women – their body and sexuality – depicted in films directed by women filmmakers in Spain? How does 'gynocine' tackle female eroticism after 50?[1] Unlike mainstream cinema, where glamorous girls are in the spotlight and ageing female actors are virtually invisible, a considerable number of female-authored films feature powerful (and often erotic) mature women centre-stage.

With no claim to be exhaustive, in these pages I will indicate some recurring patterns of how several Spanish women filmmakers approach 'unseen' eroticism. I will argue that their goal is to give visibility to the invisible, to reinscribe in public discourses what tends to be left out, and to grant depth and meaning to the female body: a signifier with no signified in Hollywood cinema, as Ruby Rich (1986) has described it.

In the following pages I will identify three groups of films. The first group attempts to eroticise and 'spectacularise' the uncommon view of the aroused mature woman. Despite its age, the older female actor's body is represented as the glamorous and erotically charged object of heterosexual desire, usually of a younger man. In order to eroticise the mature woman, these films intentionally adopt the strategies used by commercial cinema to represent and fetishise the younger female's body. The gorgeous leading character undresses for her male partner's visual pleasure. She is aroused exclusively through vaginal penetration and shows no interest in any other sort of stimulation. Furthermore, the couple reaches a perfectly timed simultaneous orgasm. The only apparent subversive element, that is, the only striking difference between commercial cinema and women's filmic imaginary, is the age of the female protagonist. By making use of mainstream discourses, these films suggest that nothing changes in a woman's sex life after she has turned fifty, sixty or even older.[2]

A second group of films intentionally represents the mature woman's body as unglamorous, as a means of denouncing the very stereotypes that have condemned it to scorn. In all these films, the woman is not the object of a traditional male protagonist's scopophilia. The gaze of the camera neither embellishes nor conceals the older body; rather, it reveals and exhibits it the way it is, often using a style of representation that is graphically and intentionally over-realistic (for example, with techniques of *cinéma vérité* or neorealism). In spite of our anti-ageing culture, by rejecting what Margaret Gullette has called the 'master narrative of decline' (2004: 138), these texts argue that there is nothing wrong with becoming older.[3] Sex can be enjoyed even when the body loses firmness and the skin wrinkles; and menopause becomes the beginning of a new freedom.[4]

Finally, by challenging 'androgynisation', that is, by confronting the claim of a 'same experience of material conditions for both genders' (de Lauretis 1987: 11), and by defying heteronormativity, a third group of films presents women's sexual pleasure in a different fashion to that which Hollywood cinema has taught us to expect. By representing a mature female eroticism that can be called, in the words of Carla Lonzi (1974), 'clitoral sexuality', these films suggest that women's sexual desire does not have to rely on the erect penis or on vaginal penetration, thus also defying the Freudian conception that clitoral pleasure is a sign of immaturity. From a formal point of view, these films present (homo)erotically charged haptic images as alternatives to traditional scopophilia. Tactile pleasure (the pleasure of touching and of being touched) replaces visual pleasure.

As I will show in the following pages, these women filmmakers question the norms adopted in mainstream cinema, norms that affect the way we think about gender and the way we internalise the concept of women's sexuality after fifty: they deconstruct the two myths that, according to Simone de Beauvoir (1970), are responsible for the construction of women and old people as Others: the myth of femininity and the myth of old age.[5]

EROTICISM AND SCOPOPHILIA: THE GLAMOROUS MIDDLE-AGED BODY

A group of films that belongs to diverse historical moments and to different genres – such as *El paseíllo/The Bullfighters' Parade* (dir. Ana Mariscal, 1968), *¡Vámonos, Bárbara!/Let's Go, Barbara!* (dir. Cecilia Bartolomé, 1978), *Lo más natural/The Most Natural Thing* (dir. Josefina Molina, 1990), *Sexo por compasión/Compassionate Sex* (dir. Laura Mañá, 1999) or *A mi madre le gustan las mujeres/My Mother Likes Women* (dirs. Inés París and Daniela Fejerman, 2002), among others – reflects upon the situation of middle-aged women after a break-up with their male partners (generally a sexist husband), their struggle with loneliness and their new relationship with sex. In all instances, the female body is portrayed intentionally as a glamorous object for the male gaze, that is, like the traditional spectacle of commercial cinema, in an attempt to present age (or, rather, to hide it) as an irrelevant element that is not addressed by the plot. The twofold intent of these films is to give visibility to, and to glamorise, those older women who are made invisible and unglamorous by mainstream cinema. In this section I will focus on two of these examples: Cecilia Bartolomé's *¡Vámonos, Bárbara!* and Laura Mañá's *Sexo por compasión*.

The so-called second-wave feminism implied, among other key goals, the appearance of a new ontology and politics of the female body. However, this emerging awareness was almost strictly confined to the young woman's body. For historian Lois W. Banner, the relative lack of interest of feminism, until lately, in issues relating to ageing was caused by the fact that 'we were in rebellion against older generations perceived as antifeminist' (1992: 6). Similarly, Roberta Rubenstein argues that 'the changes that feminism catalysed in the public sphere, notably in matters of economic and social equity, bypassed more intimate personal matters, notably aging, sexuality, and what might be termed *erotic equity*, particularly in the years of midlife and beyond' (2000: 1 – emphasis in the original). Furthermore, as Kathleen Woodward (1991) points out, feminist theory sprang mainly from the college student population, that is, from an ever-young group with little interest in issues concerning women of another generation. It is only recently that feminist theory has shown a preoccupation with ageing matters.

Given this context, *¡Vámonos, Bárbara!* is a groundbreaking and pioneering work that focuses on a middle-aged woman's experience after her matrimonial separation, only one year after the abolition of Francisco Franco's censorship by the decree of 1977, and three years before the introduction of the 1981 Divorce Law.[6]

By eroticising the older female body and presenting it as 'spectacle', Cecilia Bartolomé subverts traditional modes of representation that conventionally keep the mature woman out of sight. The film begins provokingly with a sex scene. In front of a large fish tank, we glimpse Ana's naked body (played by 45-year-old Amparo Soler Leal) making love to a man. Against the luminous background of the water tank, the silhouettes of the two lovers are almost indistinguishable. The backlight gives the impression that they are inside, immersed in the blue liquid.[7] However, in the following sequence, a new camera angle – this time without screens – reveals and displays the same woman's naked body after intercourse. She is no longer invisible and she is no longer entrapped.

After thanking her much younger partner for the moments of pleasure, still half-undressed, Ana telephones her husband and informs him that she wants a separation. Despite her revengeful spouse's threats and actions (he immediately freezes her bank account) and against her conservative parents' wishes, Ana begins her new life with a road trip along the coasts of Catalonia and Valencia, in the company of Bárbara (Cristina Álvarez), her supportive daughter. The journey becomes not only an opportunity for Ana to strengthen her bond with her child, but also a pivotal moment to explore her own eroticism and to learn to become completely independent, in an empowering rite of passage towards liberation.

As in traditional road trip films, a genre that features, according to Jorge Pérez, 'a prominent surplus of testosterone and that is not particularly hospitable to women' (2011: 129), the protagonist embarks on a journey that will have a transformative effect on her. Throughout her trip, Ana encounters several men, accidental partners whose presence has no other relevance than that of satisfying her sexual pleasure. Bartolomé reverses the traditional parameters of commercial cinema (that is, the male character leads the story, while the woman's presence corresponds to a halt in the narrative, Laura Mulvey (2009) *dixit*) by using Ana's lovers as a pause in the action. These men fail as travelling companions, let alone as life partners. Eventually mother and daughter decide that they do not want to 'return to the same' and that they 'prefer to be alone'.

Ana's rite of passage, from oppression and invisibility to independence and visibility, implies full awareness that her age does not prevent her from enjoying sex. Her naked body is exposed in the film several times,[8] and in particular it is shown as a spectacle when Ana, thinking she is alone, wrapped in a shawl after a shower, sings and dances on her friend's store balcony. The balcony thus becomes a sort of runway, or a porno set: when Ana loses grip of her shawl, her naked, wet body is revealed to a crowd of customers who stare at her in bewilderment from below. Realising that she is not alone, Ana looks for her shawl in amusement (see Figure 12.1).

Such an exhibition has at least two functions: it exposes the body of a mature woman as an object of voyeurism (an intradiegetic and extradiegetic spectacle for the customers in the store and for the audience in the cinema theatre alike) and, from Ana's subjective perspective, it offers a comment on the pleasure of

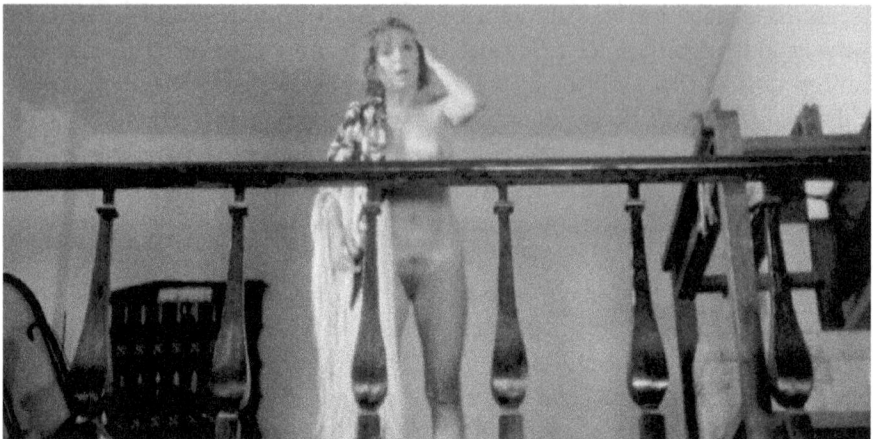

Figure 12.1 Amparo Soler Leal in ¡Vámonos, Bárbara!/Let's Go, Barbara!, directed by Cecilia Bartolomé. Spain: In-Cine Compañía Industrial Cinematográfica, Jet Films, 1978.

such a display – the middle-aged body as the site of *jouissance* and narcissism. This spectacle corresponds only in appearance to the parameters of commercial cinema denounced by Laura Mulvey (2009), since its objective is precisely that of giving visibility to the traditionally invisible woman. Active scopophilia – male voyeurism – is displaced into passive scopophilia – feminine narcissism, a pleasure of being-looked-at that could empower women's spectatorial gaze.

While Ana's slender body, despite her age, is not too far from the canons of beauty imposed by Hollywood, the protagonist of *Sexo por compasión* represents the ultimate challenge to the status quo of film aesthetics. Dolores, played by 54-year-old French actor Elisabeth Margoni, is a short, overweight woman with a chubby round face, who nonetheless represents the embodiment of sexual attraction. Her beauty is never questioned and her age is never addressed.

In a remote village in an unknown location, Dolores is abandoned by her husband because she is too much of a '*santa*' (saint). To win him back, Dolores finds no better solution than to embrace the lifestyle of a 'sinner', by having sex with all men who need any form of compassion. Villagers line up outside her door, waiting for their turn to receive their share of love, empathy and sex from Dolores, who has changed her name to Lolita.

The 'saint' has thus turned into a 'whore', or rather into a 'holy whore', that is, a prostitute who performs miracles. Thanks to her agency, a mute child gains the ability to speak, a paralysed old lady leaves her bed and walks, and all the men in the village regain their vital energy and sexual desire, thus making their wives happy. Even the village improves: it is brightened up with a fresh coat of paint and with flowers while, extradiegetically, the film switches from black and white to colour.

The film ends with Lolita's announcement of her pregnancy. Since no child has been born in the village for the last ten years, this baby is the symbol of the village's rebirth. Moreover, given that no one knows who the biological father is, not even the mother-to-be, all the men decide they will share paternity. The representation of a 'consecrated femininity', in Kristeva's words (1983), does not correspond to the 'virginal maternal' of the biblical tradition, but rather to a collective parenthood that is the result of an exercise of prostitution. Dolores/Lolita simultaneously embodies the three roles traditionally attributed to women by patriarchal society: paradoxically she is a saint, a whore and a mother, all at the same time. Her body symbolises multiple subversions: it defies the scientific status quo, through Dolores'/Lolita's pregnancy late in life; it challenges the social status quo, because although the biological father is unknown, her pregnancy is celebrated by the entire village, including the priest; and it challenges the status quo of the cinema industry, because even with her old, overweight body, she is presented as the embodiment of eroticism and beauty.

DENOUNCING THE STEREOTYPE: THE UNGLAMOROUS MATURE BODY

While the strategy of estrangement in the corpus analysed above was that of sexualising the mature woman's body as 'spectacle' by ignoring her age, films such as *Función de noche/Night Function* (dir. Josefina Molina, 1981), *La Lola se va a los puertos/Lola is Going to the Ports* (dir. Josefina Molina, 1993), *Nosotras/Women* (dir. Judith Colell, 2000), *53 días de invierno/53 Days in Winter* (Judith Colell, 2006), *La vida empieza hoy/Life Begins Today* (dir. Laura Mañá, 2009), *Elegy* (dir. Isabel Coixet, 2008) and *Learning to drive* (dir. Isabel Coixet, 2015), among others, use an opposite technique: that of denouncing without eroticising. In this section I will focus on the *cinéma vérité*-style film *Función de noche* and on the comedy *La vida empieza hoy*, two examples of a common intent to represent the older female body graphically, with all its 'defects' and without concealing its age. Contrary to its treatment in commercial cinema, such an imperfect body is not the object of scorn, but rather the instrument used to denounce the view that 'male and female ageing are culturally marked in highly asymmetrical ways. [...] Men are usually credited with a longer plateau at their prime, whereas women climb the slope of social desirability more swiftly and are more rapidly thrown from its peak' (Gardiner 2001: 98).

In *Función de noche*, Molina laments that for women, middle age means the loss of sex appeal and regrets that, according to patriarchal scientific discourse, menopause is the 'beginning of the end'. The protagonist (Lola Herrera, playing herself) consults a cosmetic physician on breast reduction surgery; however, drawing on his 'unquestionable' scientific authority, the doctor discourages her from going ahead with the procedure. He reminds her of the inevitability of her situation as a menopausal woman, when 'everything collapses', and reiterates that breast reduction would not delay her ageing process, let alone cure her depression. In the sequence at the doctor's practice, Molina's camera lingers on close-ups on Herrera's bare breasts, examined by the surgeon, who touches and fondles them to highlight their sagginess and flaccidity in a humiliating manner. In this way the camera's intrusive gaze is evocative of the scientific gaze that, as Foucault remarks (1975), observes not only the exterior, but 'penetrates' and demystifies the interior. The doctor embodies the patriarchal scientific discourse that has despised the ageing female body since antiquity. While the male body represents health and perfection at any age, the female body epitomises pathology and imperfection, especially when it becomes old (that is, sterile). Menstruation, breastfeeding, pregnancy and even female orgasm have been treated at some point in the history of medicine as female diseases, and menopause has been inscribed in scientific discourse as the end of women's meaning and value, as the termination of their sexual pleasure, as a symbolic death. However, as Anna Freixas has put it, 'if menopause used to signal "the beginning of the end", now we can be certain that it is the beginning of "there's more to come"' (2007: 34).

Lola Herrera plays herself and builds her 'real' character as an ambivalent and contradictory figure. On the one hand, she continues to be romantically anchored to the memory of a relationship that ended fourteen years before. For instance, she wants to find out more about how her former husband felt during their engagement, and asks him questions that reinforce traditional gender roles (the man as the agent of courtship, the woman as its object), in what appears to be a need for reassurance about her fairy tale, even if it is over. Furthermore, she seems incapable of imagining happiness without being in a relationship.

On the other hand, Herrera is able to confess feelings to which a woman educated in sacrifice and abnegation would rarely admit. First, she recognises that motherhood was not a fulfilling experience for her, and that her children were an obstacle to her freedom. Another confession, even more exceptional in its context, is that she had always faked her orgasms. If such a revelation fits the model of female asexuality promoted by the dictatorship, it also subverts the patriarchal order on a different level. On the one hand, it deconstructs Catholic norms that confined sexuality, especially women's sexuality, to the exclusive domain of procreation. Lola's regret at not having enjoyed sex is an assertion of her right to pleasure. On the other hand, in a political context in which faking was a weapon of resistance, its displacement to the field of sexuality and marital intimacy situates Lola Herrera as a victim and establishes the notion of lying both as a survival strategy for women and as empowering in sexual performance (she knows something that he does not). Furthermore, her confession is a direct attack on the man (in this case on her ex-husband) and on his manhood: in a system of power relations that attributes a passive role to women, female orgasm is considered to be the result of male skill and experience. Hence the absence of orgasm is not interpreted as a woman's inadequacy, but as a man's incompetence (Jackson and Scott 2001: 107).

While *Función de noche* dealt with a generation of women who were raised and oppressed under Francoist values and were made to believe that sex was meant only for procreation, thirty years later, in the comedy *La vida empieza hoy* (Laura Mañá, 2009), this same generation of women (now in their seventies) defeats another notion, the assumption that older people do not have a sex life. The film begins with a voiceover by a woman, the instructor of a sex education class for seniors, who states that pleasure lasts one's entire life and does not have to be shared with a partner. Controversial topics in gerontology, namely intercourse and masturbation, are addressed in the very opening scene of a film that gives voice and visibility to 'the very aged among the aged', to borrow Penelope Deutscher's definition (2014: 29). Women over the age of seventy have been notably neglected by Simone de Beauvoir's essay *La Vieillesse*, and still receive little attention in contemporary ageing studies.

The voiceover continues by remarking that, even at an older age, we have to enjoy sexual pleasure by rediscovering our own senses. However, for one of the sex class students in particular, the new widow Juanita (Pilar Bardem), it is not a matter of *re*discovering, but of discovering. Not only has she never experienced an orgasm: she does not even know *what* her clitoris is. After realising that she has been sexually repressed for her entire life by her late husband, she requests a sort of 'divorce post-mortem': she informs the funeral home of her firm determination not to be buried near him in their family grave. Only then will she finally feel free to learn to enjoy her own sexuality.

While Juanita has to overcome her own prejudices, both Herminia (Sonsoles Benedicto) (another student in the sex class) and Rosita (Mariana Cordero) have to deal with the ignorance of younger family members regarding their sexuality. Herminia's daughter misinterprets her mother's sexual sparks as signs of senility and takes her to a nursing home. She will be completely shocked by the revelation that Herminia is in fact dating someone. Similarly, Rosita will first have to rebel against the exploitation of being used as a full-time babysitter and day-care provider for her grandchildren, and second, will have to recapture the attention of her unfaithful husband by forcing him to *see* her. With the help of sexy lingerie and sex toys, Rosita will manage to attract his interest and become visible again, while she will in turn rediscover her own erotic pleasure. As in the previous film, Juanita, Herminia and Rosita are not represented as glamorous objects of desire, but as women whose bodies are shown with all their imperfections.

Just as *Sexo por compasión* ends with a collective pregnancy, *La vida empieza hoy* concludes with a collective orgasm. The movie culminates in a series of parallel scenes: Rosita makes love to her husband; Herminia eats a cake while her partner hides his head between her large breasts; and Juanita caresses her own body with a sex toy, a strawberry-shaped vibrator. The three scenes represent three forms of sexual gratification: Rosita's vaginal penetration through intercourse, Herminia's oral pleasure (that of eating and of being eaten), and Juanita's masturbation. Juanita's orgasm, the first in her life, is echoed, in a sort of an explosion, by the other characters, who also simultaneously reach their climax. Their 'old' age does not prevent them from enjoying their bodies. As Freixas, Luque and Reina have shown, 'Despite the accumulation of factors that seem to prevent female pleasure, numerous studies claim that women's sexuality improves from midlife onwards. In fact, some women experience an increase in their sexual activity' (2012: 119).[9]

Although these films challenge the status quo in forms that are still strictly anchored to a heteronormative imaginary, they envisage a female eroticism that frequently dispenses with men and the erect phallus. Juanita's gigantic strawberry-shaped dildo is an irreverent substitute for a penis. As octogenarian sex educator Betty Dodson once explained in her provocative bestseller *Sex for One* (first published in 1974), masturbation is a safe and liberating tool, a 'primary form of sexual expression' (1996: 8) that overcomes, in Rachel Maines' words, the 'relative inefficiency of penetration as a means of producing female orgasm, [and] conflicts at a visceral level with the androcentric paradigm' (1999: xiii).

The challenge proposed in *La vida empieza hoy* is twofold. The protagonists enjoy sex after menopause and they do it through masturbation, the most extreme manifestation of the separation of sex from procreation. Furthermore, this film attempts to counterbalance the injustice of cultural norms by stressing that biology has in fact favoured women, who do not need an erection for intercourse and whose age is never an impediment to reaching an orgasm, with or without the need for a penis.

TACTILE EROTICISM: THE AGEING FEMALE BODY CHALLENGES HETERONORMATIVITY

In *The Skin of Film* (2000) and in *Touch: Sensuous Theory and Multisensory Media* (2002), Laura Marks analyses the tactile sensory experience in film, distinguishing between 'optic' and 'haptic' visualities. Unlike the traditional film gaze, the sense of touch comes into play when the image produces a palpable impression, and the sense of sight functions as the organ of touch. Tactile sensation is evoked by different strategies, such as the grain of the image, extreme or out of focus close-ups, camera movements that somehow 'caress' the surface of the picture (that is, panning or tracking shots), as well as by a persistent use of images that suggest contact, such as, for instance, shots of people hugging, close-ups on hands or zooms on the skin. While optic visuality penetrates the image, tactile visuality caresses it and interweaves with it.

Unlike Luce Irigaray (1985, 2009), who argued that women's eroticism is infused with tactility, Laura Marks (2000, 2002) believes that resorting to touch is not an inherently feminine tendency, but rather a feminist strategy. In different ways, films such as *El pájaro de la felicidad/The Bird of Happiness* (dir. Pilar Miró, 1993), *Seres queridos/Only Human* (dir. Dominic Harari and Teresa Pelegrí, 2004), *Sevigné* (dir. Marta Balletbò-Coll, 2004), *53 días de invierno/53 Days in Winter* (dir. Judith Colell, 2006), *Mataharis* (dir. Icíar Bollaín, 2007), *Mejor que nunca/Better than Ever* (dir. Dolores Payás, 2008) and *De tu ventana a la mía/From Your Window to Mine* (dir. Paula Ortiz 2011), among others, engage in such a strategy by producing scenes that evoke a tactile eroticism, one that centres on the mature female body as an escape from the prominently heterosexual visual economy of commercial cinema. They dispense with the phallocentric and heteronormative paradigm of pleasure through vaginal penetration, and challenge the myth that identifies sexuality with genitality. These movies represent 'affirmative ageing bodies', that is, they 'aim to acknowledge the material specificities of the ageing body [...] in terms of difference, but without understanding it as a body marked by decline, lack or negation' (Sandberg 2013: 12).

In this section I will focus on two films, Pilar Miró's *El pájaro de la felicidad* and Paula Ortiz's *De tu ventana a la mía*, that represent good examples of this third approach to female eroticism after fifty. Even though they cannot be considered as lesbian films, they have enough of a homoerotic discourse to show that ageing, as Winterich (2003) has demonstrated, does not impact on lesbians in the same way that it affects straight women. For Winterich, homosexuality frees women from the market of men hunting for sex, and from all its repercussions.

El pájaro de la felicidad begins with some dramatic sequences. After a dinner with her son's new family – an encounter full of bitterness and recriminations – Carmen Figueres (played by 46-year-old Mercedes Sanpietro) is attacked by a group of young men. They steal Carmen's car and one of them tries to rape her, but, apparently incapable of penetrating her with his penis, he masturbates against her body, while his friends laugh at him for forcing himself on an older woman (a woman who could be his mother). Carmen is thus a victim not only of robbery and of sexual assault, but also, paradoxically, of the humiliation of being mocked for not being young enough to arouse a rapist.

After this traumatic event – a punishment, according to María Elena Soliño, for having abandoned her son with his father when he was still a child

(1996: 42) – Carmen begins a journey in search of herself. She first stops off at her parents' place and then moves south to the coasts of Almería, where she focuses on the restoration of a Murillo painting depicting the Virgin Mary and Santa Isabel in an affectionate embrace. The painting 'will have an unexpectedly specular effect [...] by linking maternity with a homosocial and sexual relationship' (Villamandos 2012: 1). As if Miró were establishing a dialogue with ageing studies theories, the restoration begins with a scratch on Santa Isabel's face, a sort of a wrinkle around an eye, as if Carmen were trying to rejuvenate the saint's skin. Then she continues with the strokes of her brush on the two women holding hands, a sort of highlighting of the haptic female bonding.

In Almería, Carmen has two erotic encounters: the first one (implicit and cut by an ellipsis) with a male professor who owns the property she is renting; the second with a woman, her daughter-in-law Nani (Aitana Sánchez Gijón). Their sexual exchanges are represented explicitly through long sequences, dense with haptic eroticism. The homoerotic encounter occurs when Carmen treats a burn on Nani's wrist. The scene begins with the shot of a white background (a sort of a canvas) in which Carmen's outstretched hand enters the frame from the left. On the right side of the frame, Nani responds with the same wrist movement. She gently rests her hand on her mother-in-law's, with the exposed wound upwards. Again, from the left, Carmen's right hand enters the frame holding a tube of ointment that she smooths over Nani's burn. The encounter of the women's hands produces a strong sensual impression with haptic tones, creating a tactile sensation for the audience. Slowly, with her fingertips, Carmen applies the cream to Nani's wrist, gliding down her skin in an erotic caress. In this sequence there is no exchange of words, just music for strings that gives a solemn but sweet tone to the images. The overhead light illuminates the clasped hands, leaving them partially in darkness, thus reproducing the effect of the characteristic chiaroscuro of Murillo's paintings. As Soliño (1996: 47) has already noted, the focus on the women's hands, on the pleasure of touch, contrasts with the brutality of the physical encounter of the initial rape scene in which the attackers' hands had another function: that of assaulting, holding their victim and masturbating.

This initial physical contact is followed by an even more intimate one: one evening, while preparing dinner, Nani confesses to Carmen that she often wakes up distraught at night, fearing that her husband is trying to kidnap her. She adds, gently grabbing her mother-in-law's wrist: 'I want you to know that I'm fine here, with you and the child.' Carmen does not reply. Nani moves closer to Carmen and takes her hand. She caresses her face and hair. She touches her lips with her fingertips (as she had done earlier with her wounded wrist) and finally kisses her on the mouth.

At the end of the film, Carmen is redeemed from her original sin through a new chance at motherhood: she will agree to take care of her son's child and raise him, while her daughter-in-law finds happiness with another man. Although it can be argued that the plot of homoerotic desire remains undeveloped, and Carmen's relationship with Nani is diluted and resolved as a mere moment of transition to the child (Nani's son), at the end of the film, Carmen attains her independence and freedom. For Dodson, 'menopause can be our time of power with renewed self-confidence, energy, inner beauty, and sexual abundance' (1996: 160).

A similarly empowering ending can be found in Paula Ortiz's debut movie, *De tu ventana a la mía*. The film interweaves the stories of three women who belong to different historical contexts which correspond, symbolically, to their different ages: the events that surround Violeta (Leticia Dolera) take place in the spring of 1923, when she is in the 'spring' of her life, in her twenties. The story of Inés (Maribel Verdú), a woman in her forties, is set in the summer of 1940. Likewise, Luisa (Luisa Gavasa) is diagnosed with cancer in the winter of 1975, when she is in her seventies, in the winter of her existence. Each woman undergoes an experience that is almost exclusive to the female body. Violeta is raped, Inés gets pregnant and gives birth to her child, and Luisa undergoes a mastectomy.

Through the use of parallel scenes, the three women are portrayed in analogous positions (for example, sucking the blood from a small wound on their finger), or in similar situations (cutting off their beautiful long hair). These references to female bodily experiences and repetitions of incidences point to an ahistorical, atemporal female essence, underlined by a symbolic red thread that connects them, through their windows, throughout the different times.

Violeta, Inés and Luisa could be considered as one woman, a woman born at the beginning of the twentieth century and represented at three different moments of her life; a woman who, through age and experience, becomes stronger and more independent. When she is young (like Violeta), she is delicate and sick, and depends completely on the love of a man. When she is in her forties (like Inés), she is tougher and can endure hunger, persecution and humiliation. However, as patriarchal society has dictated to women, she finds her strength and her sole fulfilment in being a mother. It is only when she reaches a later age (in the guise of Luisa), that she is able to liberate herself from patriarchal rule and to find erotic satisfaction. All her life, Luisa has searched for her prince charming and for a Hollywoodesque love story. However, she finds love and erotic pleasure on her doorstep, with Isabel (Cristina Rota), the woman she has lived with her entire life, when the two of them are already 'wrinkled like two lemons'. In suggestive scenes dense with haptic, tactile tones produced by extreme close-ups, Isabel, who is now nursing Luisa, cleans her body, and caressingly wipes the breast wound with a sponge. Luisa asks her for a kiss, because she does not want to die without experiencing a Hollywood-style love story (see Figure 12.2).

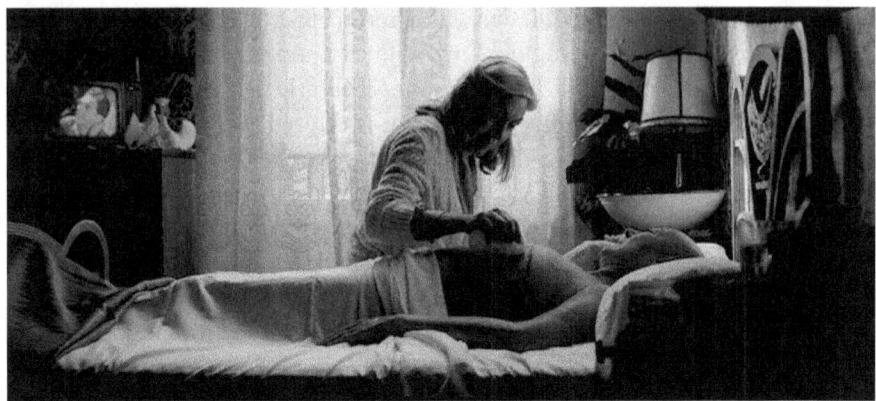

Figure 12.2 Luisa Gavasa and Cristina Rota in *De tu ventana a la mía / From Your Window to Mine*, directed by Paula Ortiz. Spain: Amapola Films, Oria Films, 2011.

If it may be argued that the repetitions and similarities of the three women's experiences naturalise an essence of femininity, it is precisely this continuity that displaces age from the field of the natural and places it in the cultural. Despite the fact that the film marks three different moments in a woman's lifespan, there is no difference in their physical experience and in their sexual drives. Age is much more about culture than about nature. Only in her maturity will Luisa be able to overcome her inhibitions and free herself from patriarchal constraints. The film ends with Luisa at a demonstration, walking against the direction of the crowd. She goes literally against the grain and throws her wig into the air, thus leaving her bald head uncovered. While having the hair cut off was experienced by Violeta and Inés as self-mutilation and castration respectively, for Luisa her bald head becomes a symbol of the beginning of a new freedom.

Linn Sandberg summarises the binaries of decline and success that have dominated contemporary discourse on age and ageing:

> The decline narrative, on the one hand, is highly centred on the decline of the ageing body as frail, leaky and unbounded, and on how old age is characterised by non-productivity, increasing passivity and dependency. Discourses on successful ageing, on the other hand, rely heavily on neoliberal imperatives of activity, autonomy and responsibility. In successful ageing, the specificities of ageing bodies are largely overlooked while the capacity of the old person to retain a youthful body, for example, with the aid of sexuopharmaceuticals, is celebrated. (2013: 11)

While the first group of films I have analysed in this chapter challenged the discourses of 'successful ageing' by showing and celebrating the older body the way it is, the second group of films actively resisted the 'decline narrative' by denouncing how this discriminates against ageing *women* in particular. In the third group, the binary between success and decline is displaced towards a discourse on 'affirmative ageing': the older body is different, but not in a way that depicts it as degraded by decline or loss. In this context the close-up of Luisa, in *De tu ventana a la mía*, is the epitome of difference and affirmation.

By resisting the hegemonic narratives of ageing, despite their different approaches, the majority of women film directors coincide in representing the older female body as the site/sight of sexual pleasure: they reveal that, as Margaret Gullette (2004) has taught us, we age by culture. These narratives also reclaim what Michelle Fine (1988) has called 'the missing discourse of desire'. In essence, women filmmakers give voice to the unspoken and visibility to the invisible, thereby contributing to the fight to free the female ageing body from mainstream cultural impositions.

NOTES

1. To overcome the limitations of the terms 'feminine cinema', 'feminist cinema', 'cinema by women' or 'women's cinema', and to respond to a crisis of naming in feminist film criticism, I named this corpus 'gynocine'. For a more detailed explanation of this concept, see my volume *La Pantalla sexuada* (Zecchi 2014) and my digital humanities project *Gynocine: History of Spanish Women's Cinema* (Zecchi 2011).
2. For Gullette '[t]he "natural" is conventionally constituted as the Other to the "cultural" – while the masters of the natural busily erase culture. Age studies undoes the erasure of the cultural in the sphere of age and ageing. Feminist theory denaturalised female/male difference, and then started on older/younger differences' (2004: 102).
3. According to Margaret Cruikshank, recurrent terms such as 'successful ageing' or 'productive ageing' instil temporality with questions of 'marketing and competition' (2009: 40). The films I study in these pages do not present ageing with the traditional connotation of marketing and competition, but rather aim at denaturalising and deconstructing patriarchal notions of ageing that are conventionally presented as natural.
4. As director Dolores Payás has stated in regard to the protagonist of her movie *Mejor que nunca / Better than Ever* (2008) (another powerful embodiment of women's eroticism after fifty), menopause is the best period in a woman's life: 'We are menopausal. Yes. Don't be shy. [...] We are not "those" abandoned women, abnegated mothers, protagonists of teary scenes, obsessed with looking out for signs of our decline in the mirror. Life bustles at maturity and can be extremely lively, interesting and full of adventure if we have the right attitude' (Payás 2008).
5. Written in 1970, Simone de Beauvoir's *La Vieillesse* (*The Coming of Age*) is considered the first book on the subject. Margaret Gullette refers to de Beauvoir as the 'godmother of age studies' (2004: 101).
6. Even before Bartolomé, Ana Mariscal was a pioneer in the representation of glamorous middle-aged women. In her films she included strong and seductive female characters, often in the form of her own cameo appearances.
7. Bartolomé's leading character is in front of the fish tank, completely in control of her

actions. In contrast, in the establishing sequence of *The Graduate* (dir. Mike Nichols, 1967) the protagonist is behind the aquarium, confused. His alienation will culminate when he is seduced by an 'older' woman, Mrs Robinson, interpreted by 38-year-old (!) Ann Bancroft.

8. Women's exposure is typical of the films of the *destape* genre that corresponds to a new sexual freedom after decades of censorship and repression. However, it is not a narcissistic display: in those films, women undress merely to satisfy male visual pleasure. Conversely, even though *¡Vámonos, Bárbara!* has been inserted in the *destape* genre, in this film the female protagonist undresses for her own pleasure.

9. As Mayor (2004) has illustrated, women's sexual dysfunction is a myth created by the very pharmaceutical industry that tried to launch a new drug, a sort of Viagra for women, but its effectiveness could not even be supported by its own clinical trials.

REFERENCES

Banner, Lois W. (1992), *In Full Flower: Aging, Women, Power, and Sexuality*, New York: Alfred A. Knopf.
Cruikshank, Margaret (2009), *Learning to Be Old: Gender, Culture, and Aging*, Lanham, MD: Rowman & Littlefield Publishers.
de Beauvior, Simone (1970), *La Vieillesse*, Paris: Gallimard.
de Lauretis, Teresa (1987), *Technologies of Gender. Essays on Theory, Film and Fiction*, Bloomington and Indianapolis: Indiana University Press.
Deutscher, Penelope (2014), 'The Sex of Age and the Age of Sex', in Silvia Stoller (ed.), *Simone de Beauvoir's Philosophy of Age: Gender, Ethics, and Time*, Berlin and Boston, MA: Walter de Gruyter, pp. 29–42.
Dodson, Betty (1996 [1974]), *Sex for One: The Joy of Selfloving*, New York: Three Rivers Press.
Fine, Michelle (1988), 'Sexuality, Schoolong, and Adolescent Females: The Missing Discourse of Desire', *Harvard Educational Review* 58:1, 54–63.
Foucault, Michel (1975), *The Birth of the Clinic: An Archaeology of Medical Perception*, New York: Vintage Books.
Freixas, Anna (2007), *Nuestra menopausia: una versión no oficial*, Barcelona: Ediciones Paidós.
Freixas, Anna, Bárbara Luque and Amalia Reina (2012), 'Secretos y silencios en torno a la sexualidad de las mujeres mayores', *Estudios Etarios y relaciones intergeneracionales*, México Distrito Federal: MIC Género, pp. 117–27.
Gardiner, Judith Kegan (2001), 'Theorizing Age with Gender: Bly's Boys, Feminism, and Maturity Masculinity', in Judith Kegan Gardiner (ed.), *Masculinity Studies and Feminist Theory*, New York: Columbia University Press, pp. 90–118.
Gullette, Margaret Morganroth (2004), *Aged by Culture*, Chicago and London: University of Chicago Press.
Irigaray, Luce (1985 [1974]), *Speculum of the Other Woman*, Ithaca: Cornell University Press.
Irigaray, Luce (2009), 'Toward a Divine in the Feminine', in Gillian Howie and J'annine Jobling (eds), *Women and the Divine: Touching Transcendence*, New York: Palgrave Macmillan.
Jackson, Stevi and Sue Scott (2001), 'Embodying Orgasm: Gendered Power Relations and Sexual Pleasure', *Women and Therapy* 24:1–2, 99–110.
Kristeva, Julia (1983 [1977]), *Tales of Love*, New York: Columbia University Press.

Lonzi, Carla (1974), *Sputiamo su Hegel. La donna clitoridea e la donna vaginale e altri scritti*, Milano: Scritti di Rivolta femminile.
Maines, Rachel (1999), *The Technology of Orgasm*, Baltimore: The Johns Hopkins University Press.
Marks, Laura (2000), *The Skin of the Film: Intercultural Cinema, Embodiment and the Senses*, Durham, NC and London: Duke University Press.
Marks, Laura (2002), *Touch: Sensuous Theory*, Minneapolis: University of Minnesota Press.
Mayor, Susan (2004), 'Pfizer will not Apply for a Licence for Sildenafil for Women', *British Medical Journal* 328, 542.
Mulvey, Laura (2009 [1975]), 'Visual Pleasure and Narrative Cinema', in Laura Mulvey, *Visual and Other Pleasures*, Basingstoke: Palgrave Macmillan, pp. 14–27.
Pérez, Jorge (2011), *Cultural Roundabouts: Spanish Film and Novel on the Road*, Lewisburg, PA: Bucknell University Press.
Payás, Dolores (2008), 'Mejor que nunca': http://www.mejorquenunca.es (last accessed 10 December 2009).
Rich, Ruby (1986), 'Anti-Porn: Soft Issue, Hard World', in Charlotte Brunsdon (ed.), *Films for Women*, London: British Film Institute, pp. 31–43.
Rubenstein, Roberta (2000), 'Feminism, Eros, and the Coming of Age', *Frontiers: A Journal of Women Studies* 22:2, December, 1–19.
Sandberg, Linn (2013), 'Affirmative Old Age: the Ageing Body and Feminist Theories on Difference', *International Journal of Ageing and Later Life* 8:1, 11–40.
Soliño, María Elena (1996), 'La restauración de la iconografía de la maternidad en *El Pájaro de la felicidad*', *Foro hispánico: Revista hispánica de Flandes y Holanda* 10, 41–51.
Swartz, Mimi (2004), 'Hollywood Casts an Unexpectedly Realistic Eye on Aging Womanhood', *Slate*: http://www.slate.com/id/2093444 (last accessed 8 March 2015).
Villamandos, Alberto (2012), 'Añorar el futuro que no existe: el desencanto en *El pájaro de la felicidad* (1993) de Pilar Miró': https://www.academia.edu/2108881 (last accessed 2 May 2016).
Winterich, Julie (2003), 'Sex, Menopause, and Culture. Sexual Orientation and the Meaning of Menopause for Women's Sex Lives', *Gender and Society* 17:4, 627–42.
Woodward, Kathleen (1991), *Aging and its Discontents. Freud and Other Fictions*, Bloomington and Indianapolis: Indiana University Press.
Zecchi, Barbara (2014), *La pantalla sexuada*, Madrid, Valencia: Cátedra.
Zecchi, Barbara (2011), *Gynocine: History of Spanish Women's Cinema*: www.umass.edu/gynocine (last accessed 30 July 2016).

FILMOGRAPHY

53 días de invierno / 53 Days in Winter, film, directed by Judith Colell. Spain: Ovideo TV, 2006.
A mi madre le gustan las mujeres / My Mother Likes Women, film, directed by Inés París and Daniela Fejerman. Spain: Fernando Colomo P.C., 2002.
De tu ventana a la mía / From Your Window to Mine, film, directed by Paula Ortiz. Spain: Amapola Films, Oria Films, 2011.
El pájaro de la felicidad / The Bird of Happiness, film, directed by Pilar Miró. Spain: Central de Producciones Audiovisuales S. L., 1993.
El paseíllo / The Bullfighters' Parade, film, directed by Ana Mariscal. Spain: Bosco Films, 1968.
Elegy, film, directed by Isabel Coixet. USA: Lakeshore Entertainment, 2008.

Función de noche/Night Function, film, directed by Josefina Molina. Spain: Sabre Films, 1981.

La Lola se va a los puertos/Lola is Going to the Ports, film, directed by Josefina Molina. Spain: Lotus Films Internacional S.L., Canal Sur, 1993.

La vida empieza hoy/Life Begins Today, film, directed by Laura Mañá. Spain: Ovideo, TVE, Televisió de Catalunya, 2009.

Learning to Drive, film, directed by Isabel Coixet. Spain: Broad Green Pictures, 2015.

Lo más natural/The Most Natural Thing, film, directed by Josefina Molina. Spain: Sabre Televisión, 1990.

Mataharis, film, directed by Icíar Bollaín. Spain: La Iguana, Sogecine, 2007.

Mejor que nunca/Better than Ever, film, directed by Dolores Payás. Spain: JLA Productions, Magic Lantern, Production Group, Tutor Cine, Zahorí Media, 2008.

Nosotras/Women, film, directed by Judith Colell. Argentina: El Calefón Cine, 2000.

Seres queridos/Only Human, film, directed by Dominic Harari and Teresa Pelegrí. Spain/United Kingdom/Portugal/Argentina: Tornasol Films, Greenpoint Productions, Madragoa Produçao des Filmes, Patagonik Film Group, 2004.

Sevigné, film, directed by Marta Balletbò-Coll. Spain: Costabrava Films, 2004.

Sexo por compasión/Compassionate Sex, film, directed by Laura Mañá. Spain/Mexico: Sogedasa, Visual Group, Resonancia Productora, 1999.

The Graduate, film, directed by Mike Nichols. USA: Lawrence Turman, 1967.

¡Vámonos, Bárbara!/Let's Go, Barbara!, film, directed by Cecilia Bartolomé. Spain: In-Cine Compañía Industrial Cinematográfica, Jet Films, 1978.

CHAPTER 13

Boys Interrupted: Sex between Men in Post-Franco Spanish Cinema

Santiago Fouz-Hernández

The history of male same-sex desire in Spanish cinema has been widely documented in a plethora of articles, PhD theses and books published in the last twenty-five years or so, starting with Smith in 1992 and culminating most recently with dedicated monographs by Melero Salvador (2010), Perriam (2013) and Berzosa (2014). As these studies convincingly argue, we have come a long way from what Alfeo Álvarez, writing in 2000, called 'veiled representations' during the Francoist period. Indeed, authors including Llamas (1995) have talked about a certain over-exposure of gay men and especially gay male bodies in Spanish films since the 1990s. This new visibility, however, has not necessarily brought about sexual fulfilment for gay male characters on screen. While male nudity has become commonplace in recent Spanish cinema (although full frontals are still somewhat taboo),[1] actual sex scenes between men are still relatively rare, obliquely represented or extremely short, often interrupted halfway through. Interruptions, of sorts, are by definition part of what differentiates erotic cinema from pornography. As Tanya Krzywinska has argued, films aimed at broad audiences have to find ways 'of suggesting sex without actually showing it' (2006: 29). Some of these 'ways', as she goes on to explain, include ellipses, cutaways or visual barriers (27–31). One of the main points that Linda Williams makes in *Screening Sex* is precisely about the double meaning of the verb 'to screen' 'as both revelation and concealing' (2008: 3), a tension that is productively explored throughout her book. The remit of this book is to study Spanish *erotic* cinema, not pornography. In that sense, it is perhaps to be expected that in the films I am about to discuss, sex between men will not be represented in overtly explicit ways. It is worth noting that when discussing the 'concealment' of sex both Krzywinska and Williams are referring mostly to either family-friendly mainstream films or films produced within certain censorship or commercial boundaries. The films that I will discuss in this chapter were all released after the abolition of censorship in post-Franco Spain and, especially the more recent ones, are aimed at GLBT or GLBT-friendly audiences. It is the persistence of abrupt, awkward and sometimes violent disruptions of erotic scenes involving sex between men that concerns me here, especially when these occur in sharp contrast with heterosexual sex scenes.[2]

Many Spanish films of the last two decades still present sex between men as illicit or in some ways off-limits. As Melero Salvador has noted, while gay sex gained visibility in specialised magazines during the Transition, it was almost invisible in the cinema of the period. His discussion of Manuel Iglesia's *Jóvenes viciosas/Dirty Young Ladies* (1980) perfectly sums it up: 'sex scenes involving the girls were everywhere, while those involving the gay guy were over before even starting' (2011: 133–4). Even openly gay male directors like Eloy de la Iglesia or Ventura Pons have tended to stage gay male sex scenes in contexts associated with prostitution, or based on the traditional Greek Model with considerable age and class differences between the two men involved.[3] These modes of representation reveal a recurring pattern that could lead some audiences to perceive sex between men as criminal and risky, sometimes leading to illness and even death – patterns that were memorably critiqued by Vito Russo (1987) in his groundbreaking study about 'homosexuality in the movies' over three decades ago (the book was first published in 1981). By frequently cutting short erotic scenes between men, these films are not only ironically decreasing the visibility of a social minority characterised precisely for its sexuality, but also frustrating the visual/sensual pleasure for those spectators who may identify with the characters involved in the sex act. This creates a sense of frustration that could be interpreted as 'queer failure' in psychoanalytical and capitalist modes of thinking that read same-sex relationships as unauthentic, unreal, unsuccessful – as Halberstam summarises (2011: 94–6). As Edelman argues, the disassociation of gay sex from reproduction leads to its perception as incompatible with the idea of futurity symbolised in the figure of the child (2004: 11–13), and therefore incomplete within the paradigm of heterofuturity, a concept symbolically contained in the frequent recurrence of unfinished business in the film examples that I am about to discuss.[4]

This chapter will focus in particular on well-known commercial feature films produced in the last two decades, but will also make reference to pioneering examples found in the early work of Eloy de la Iglesia and Pedro Almodóvar – directors whose more recent work will also be considered. To start I will examine technical effects used to curtail erotic scenes between men, either through editing, props, sets or lighting effects, then focus on more literal interruptions by female and male characters that enter the scene, preventing the sex act from culminating onscreen – or, sometimes, from starting altogether. I will then reflect on possible reasons why this happens so frequently, and finally discuss some examples in which queer spectators may be able to reimagine this apparently unrepresentable act as (at least somewhat) satisfying.

BRIEF ENCOUNTERS[5]

Eloy de la Iglesia's *El diputado / Confessions of a Congressman* (1978) is often discussed as one of the earliest films to represent sex between men on the screen – as indeed Faulkner does elsewhere in this collection.[6] Although not explicit by today's standards, the film's portrayal of sex is remarkable for its directness. As Ballesteros (2001: 95–8), Martínez-Expósito (2015: 171), Mira (2004: 504) and Melero Salvador (2004, 2010: 235–50, 2011) have shown, the film uses the clandestine sexual relationship between the congressman (José Sacristán) and the much younger Juanito (José Luis Alonso) – a kid of humble origins – *didactically* as part of its political and gay-activist agenda. The relationship between the congressman and Juanito also illustrates a number of tropes of homosexual relationships on the Spanish screen typical of the Transition, some of which still apply today: age difference, class difference, ambiguous sexuality of at least one of the characters, secrecy and a sense of illicitness that ultimately leads to a tragic ending. Although, as Melero (2011) has convincingly argued, this film will always be remembered as groundbreaking for its focus on homosexuality and its refusal to avoid physical contact between the two men on the screen (including a kiss shown in close-up), the central erotic scene between the congressman and Juanito also encapsulates the kind of filming techniques that preclude the visual pleasure of queer spectators. The two men lie in bed in the moments prior to the sex act that we have to assume will follow off-screen. Remarkably, the soundtrack that dominates these brief moments of coy foreplay is typical of the erotic scenes of the *destape* films discussed in other chapters of this collection. The diegetic laughter mixed with non-diegetic music emphasise the relaxed atmosphere of this moment, suggesting, some might argue, a remarkable matter-of-factness about this unusual episode of intimacy between two men on the screen, but also, as Williams has explained, a musical interlude to make the sexually explicit content more palatable for audiences who were not yet used to the sounds of sex on the screen (2008: 82–4). Yet, this sense of harmony timidly implied by the soundtrack is negated in the wardrobe and camerawork, which seem to suggest the opposite. The congressman remains fully clothed and positioned on top, temporarily reaffirming the power imbalance while assuming the position of the voyeuristic camera, which, in a series of overhead shots, focuses on the half-nude body of the blond adolescent youth. The lighting, overwhelmingly focused on Juanito, emphasises his objectification and also his fair skin, which adds an extra visual layer to the juxtaposition with the older man whose body, as Martínez-Expósito notes with regards to openly gay (usually mature) characters in the films of de la Iglesia, remains 'invisible' (2015: 171). In the build-up to the sex act, the body language further disrupts the power balance. The congressman (and, by extension, the camera – through point-of-view shots) practically worships the young man's body with kisses. Juanito eventually reverts the power balance by literally holding the congressman's head in his hands, moving it from side to side at his will and ultimately directing it to his (unseen) penis. This rebalancing of power is underscored by the POV shots, now switched to Juanito's perspective. A fade to black is used to omit the actual sex act just as the older man is about to perform fellatio on the boy, cutting directly to the congressman opening the curtains the next morning.

Another famous erotic scene between men during the Transition is that almost immediately following the first encounter between Rizza (Imanol Arias) and Sadec (Antonio Banderas) in one of Almodóvar's earliest films, *Laberinto de pasiones/Labyrinths of Passion* (1982). Perhaps surprisingly, sex is similarly absent here. As in *El diputado*, here the scenes leading up to the sex act build up considerable homoerotic tension. The *mise en scène* at Sadec's apartment further sexualises the scene: the room is decorated with posters of naked male pin-ups and a mirror that reflects the men's bodies as they embrace (and, we are led to assume, while they have sex off-screen). Yet the sex act is, once again, omitted. A sudden cut takes us to the bathroom where Rizza washes his (off-screen) genitals, thus confirming that he has just ejaculated.

Sex between men in Almodóvar's later *La ley del deseo/Law of Desire* (1987) is much more explicit and this is one of the reasons why the film is often heralded as groundbreaking for its representation of gay male relationships (see, for example, Fouz-Hernández and Perriam 2000: 97). The oft-commented opening sequence includes a scene of simulated masturbation in a pornographic film-within-the-film followed by a brief scene where Antonio (Antonio Banderas), one of the spectators at the cinema, starts masturbating in the theatre's bathroom. The depiction of solitary pleasure within the first few minutes of the film has been praised for ensuring 'maximal identification between both screen/spectator pleasure and activity', especially at a time when the panic associated with the HIV and AIDS crisis was at a peak in the Western world, leading to an increase of both male masturbation films and the practice itself (Jackson 1995: 175). Yet, the emphasis on the constructedness of the first scene (the presence of a crew member at the end, the shots of the dubbing actors and the cutting room), and the fact that Antonio's masturbation scene is barely initiated on the screen potentially works against both processes of identification and pleasure celebrated by Jackson. Later on in the film, the first sex scene between Pablo (Eusebio Poncela) and Antonio is encouraging in that it not only shows the two men embracing, kissing, naked in bed – and mostly in close-up shots, drawing the spectators closer into the action – but also getting ready for full-on anal intercourse. Interestingly, as Mira has noted, those scenes were enough to make some critics of the conservative Spanish press particularly uncomfortable, suggesting that Almodóvar was seeking to implicate spectators into the homosexual lifestyle depicted on the screen (Mira 2004: 559–60). However, Antonio's inexperience (highlighted by a painful facial expression that Bersani (2010: 75) reads as emphasising the scene's non-pornographic realism), his concerns about venereal diseases and a false start, keep the spectator uncomfortably on edge. The camera gradually zooms out and an invasive overhead shot breaks the sense of intimacy created in the previous close-up shots, literally distancing the spectator from the action. Antonio's outstretched arms also depict him as a martyr as the sex act that we will never see is about to commence.[7] The necessary interruption to reach for the lubricant leads to another fade to black when Antonio turns the light off.

Sex scenes between men in Almodóvar's more recent work are still relatively scarce and, under close inspection, curiously mild. *La mala educación/Bad Education* (2004) stands out in that it contains frequent and explicit examples of sex between men in ways that, as Gutiérrez-Albilla has argued very persuasively, reconceptualise 'the bodily self's participation in the cinematic experience' (2013: 338). As he writes, with reference to the sex scene between Ángel/Juan (Gael García Bernal) and Sr Berenguer (Lluís Homar), the camerawork (which alternates objective and subjective shots from two different points of view) and, in particular, the subjective shots filmed with a 'trembling' Super 8 camera held by the characters during the act itself, produce 'a kind of psychological and emotional disturbance and a physical fragility and disorientation' (2013: 338), not dissimilar to what we saw in *El diputado*. While, as Gutiérrez-Albilla argues, the camerawork situates the subject 'at the centre of the filmic space' (338), and while homoerotic desire impregnates the entire visual narrative of the film, the complex editing and entangled plot lines also add a sense of risk and clandestineness to the sex acts. The sex scene between Ángel/Juan and Sr Berenguer is characterised by a feeling of rush and frustration, as the older man is keen to engage in an intercourse that never materialises onscreen. Indeed, they are interrupted by Ignacio (Francisco Boira), who enters the scene unannounced. In another crucial sex scene between Ángel/Juan and Enrique (Fele Martínez), the camera focuses close-up on the facial expressions of the characters, especially the former, as he is penetrated. The focus on the face during the sex act is common even in hard-core pornography. In porn, ecstatic (or painful) facial expressions can be used as a substitute for those parts of genital sex that cannot be shown for practical (technological) reasons – sustained penetration, for example. As Jagose, among others, has explained (2013: 145–8), this is also usually the case in mainstream cinema even in the most liberal markets: facial expressions and soundtrack are used to convey sexual pleasure while avoiding the display of genitalia. In the scene between

Ángel/Juan and Enrique the sex act arguably symbolises the power imbalance in the relationship: Enrique's facial expressions suggest ecstasy; Ángel/Juan's a mixture of pleasure and excruciating pain. Once again, however, the scene ends midway with just another fade to black.

In *Los amantes pasajeros/I'm So Excited* (2013) gay sex is quite literally kept in the closet. The film's main setting is the cabin of a long-haul flight that is experiencing technical difficulties on its way to Mexico City. In desperation, the cabin crew administers a sedative drink to Economy-class passengers and an explosive combination of alcohol and drugs to those in Business class. In the bacchanal that ensues, heterosexual sex is depicted quite explicitly. In contrast, the plane's pilot Alex (Antonio de la Torre), a married man, hides in the plane's bathroom with his secret male lover Joserra (Javier Cámara), the chief steward, for a quick sexual encounter that happens off-camera and literally behind closed doors. While the bathroom door, relentlessly pushed by the two hurried lovers as they seemingly engage in full-on penetrative anal sex may humorously and brilliantly be interpreted as a metaphor for Alex's closet, the storyline and the visual representation of sex between men is compromised. A similar pattern applies to the two other gay sex scenes in the film between another member of the cabin crew, Ulloa (Raúl Arévalo) and co-pilot Benito (played by heartthrob Hugo Silva), as we will see in the final section of this chapter.

IMAGES IN THE DARK

Editing and literal hiding are not the only forms of concealment of sex between men in Spanish film. Lighting also plays an important part. Darkness – indirectly implied in the frequent fades to black in the examples discussed so far – is also common. In Armendáriz's *Historias del Kronen/Stories from the Kronen* (1995) the brief sexual encounter between the protagonist Carlos (Juan Diego Botto) and his closeted friend Roberto (Jordi Mollà) is also partly veiled. The film's visual narrative builds up an increasingly intense homoerotic tension between the two men, reaching climactic proportions at the party towards the end. Yet the only sexual contact between the two friends is reduced to a rushed scene of masturbation in the dark (shown from the waist up). Carlos gives Roberto a quick hand-job, but immediately dismisses the event as a meaningless drunken one-off experience, and rejects Roberto's kiss with the same aggression that characterised the brutal one-way sex act.[8]

In another well-known example of sex between young men, in Cesc Gay's *Krampack/Nico and Dani* (2000), poor lighting also obscures the already awkward main sex scene between gay teenager Dani (Fernando Ramallo) and his mostly heterosexual friend Nico (Jordi Vilches). After engaging in a series of mutual masturbations and one episode of oral sex (scenes shot from behind and ending with fades to black), Dani persuades Nico to have penetrative sex with him – shortly after interrupting a sexual encounter between Nico and his girlfriend. In the sex scene between the two adolescent boys, not only is Dani offering himself as a consolation prize (and potentially coming across as a manipulative predator), but the sex act, hardly visible in the dark, is once again interrupted because Nico does not even seem aware that he was not actually quite fucking his friend. He climaxes all too soon and then refuses to wait for Dani to reach an orgasm, instead turning around with the excuse that he has a headache. Nico's attitude serves both as a parody of heterosexual sex and a critique of the neglect suffered by some heterosexual women with selfish male partners who put a frustrating end to the sex act once they are done (see Fouz-Hernández and Martínez-Expósito 2007: 55). What concerns me in the context of this chapter is that the scene also aggravates the sense of frustration of spectators seeking to identify with Dani, the gay character, while Nico, the straight one, manages to climax even in these admittedly unfavourable circumstances.

In a more recent example in *Mentiras y gordas/Sex, Party and Lies* (dirs. Albacete and Menkes, 2009), explicit sex between young men is staged in the back room of a nightclub, where, naturally, the poor lighting partly obscures this casual sex encounter. Importantly, the scene symbolises the final blow in the gay protagonist's (Toni – Mario Casas) fast decline in a destructive lifestyle fuelled by addiction that will lead to his imminent death as he leaves the club shortly after; turning him, as Perriam argues, into a classic tragic queer figure that must be killed off (2013: 89). The overwhelming sense of sexual frustration for the gay character is heightened, as noted by Gras-Velázquez (2013: 116–19), by contrast with scenes of heterosexual sex involving Toni's best friend Nico (Yon González) and his girlfriend Carmen (Elena de Frutos) in a well-lit room. The warm ambience of this domestic space also contrasts sharply with the cold and seedy blue lighting of the club's 'dark room'.

Plenty of Spanish films of the last two decades or so depict sex acts between men in plain lighting. The scenes are, however, disrupted in other ways. This is the case of the film *Más que amor frenesí/Not Love, Just Frenzy* (dirs. Albacete, Bardem, Menkes, 1996), which contains one of the most explicit scenes of sex between men in Spanish cinema to date. The sequence starts with atmospheric low lighting while the camera follows the men on medium shots while they undress and kiss, walking together towards the bathroom. In the well-lit scene that follows (in plain daylight), the men kiss and caress each other's naked bodies while preparing for anal intercourse in the shower. This is followed by a succession of close-up shots showing various body parts of both men, clearly signalling their sexual roles. Their lips lock under the shower, Alex (Javier Albalá) lifts Alberto (Gustavo Salmerón) up in the air, opening his legs, gently penetrating him with a finger. The highly erotic scene continues, with the camera now zooming out onto a long shot as Alex uses some shower gel to lubricate Alberto, then proceeds to full penetrative sex – apparently without protection. The sex act, however, is shown only for a few seconds and only as a reflection on the bathroom's mirror – a foreboding effect, since the mysterious stud that is shown vigorously fucking the gay protagonist will once again turn out to be heterosexual and will never have a relationship with the smitten gay character (see Fouz-Hernández and Perriam 2000: 107–8; Fouz-Hernández and Martínez-Expósito 2007: 121).

Ten years later, *Chuecatown/Boystown* (dir. Juan Flahn, 2006) goes as far as showing Rey's (Carlos Fuentes) bare behind, as he gets ready for sexual intercourse with his boyfriend. The couple kiss in close-up, then the camera zooms out to show how, with the help of his boyfriend, Rey removes all his clothes and then turns around, ready for intercourse. Just before the sex starts, however, a travelling takes the spectators away from the scene and into the couple's apartment's dark corridor to focus instead on a murder scene shown through an objective shot from a window in the couple's apartment. A scene that had started with close-up shots of the couple kissing and medium shots of loving foreplay is interrupted by creating – once again – a literal distance between the couple and the spectator, as the camera gradually zooms out and leaves the bedroom, directing our attention instead to a scene of death by strangulation of the couple's beloved elderly neighbour. The connection established between anal sex and death here could hardly be more explicit, even though the murder is part of the master plan of a caricaturesque estate speculator (Pablo Puyol) to obtain properties from elderly ladies and resell them to gay couples at the height of the gentrification period of Madrid's Chueca gay district. At a time when the threat of AIDS seemed to be gradually contained (or at least manageable), the association of gay sex and death persisted. Here, it is not the gay characters who die; however, the death of third, innocent parties could be interpreted as a displaced desire to kill gays – as Watney observed in his study of mass media coverage of the AIDS crisis in the USA (1987: 82).[9]

FAMILY AFFAIRS AND DANGEROUS LIAISONS

Perhaps the most common form of disruption of sex between men in contemporary Spanish films is actual interruption by various characters that walk into the scene. As already seen in *La mala educación*, the most common 'intruders' are usually family members, but especially unsuspecting wives of men who are involved in affairs with other men. *Perdona bonita, pero Lucas me quería a mí/Excuse me, Darling, but Lucas Loved Me* (dirs. Ayaso and Sabroso, 1997) provides some classic examples propitiated by a fairly simple storyline: three gay men share an apartment with an attractive heterosexual man, with whom they separately fantasise to be having a secret affair. Not only are these affairs a figment of their imagination, even in their fantasies they keep interrupting one another as they are about to initiate erotic contact with the heterosexual stud of the title, Lucas (Alonso Caparrós). Interestingly, the various fantasised stories – frustrated in themselves as they are just that, fantasies – insist on the very idea of interruption and sexual frustration, an idea perhaps best contained in the very fact that Lucas, the object of the gay men's desire, ends up dead. The constant interruptions of the various imagined homoerotic scenes between Lucas and each of the gay men is partly unconsciously motivated by the suspicion that he was indeed secretly having sex with one of them. Meanwhile, as we find out later, the person with whom the protagonist Lucas had been having sex all along was one of their female acquaintances.

Examples of sex between men interrupted by wives or girlfriends are abundant. In well-known films including Gerardo Vera's *Segunda Piel/Second Skin* (1999), Bigas Luna's *DiDi Hollywood* (2010) or the more recent *El sexo de los ángeles/Angels of Sex* (dir. Villaverde, 2012), closeted men lead double lives. Their same-sex relationships are defined and punctuated by passionate scenes overshadowed by the underlying fear of getting caught. In *Segunda Piel*, one of the much-anticipated erotic scenes between Diego (Javier Bardem) and Alberto (Jordi Mollà) is eventually interrupted by an insistent mobile phone call that Alberto pretends is from work but that is in fact from his wife Elena (Ariadna Gil).[10] The interruption (see Figure 13.1) transforms a pleasurable experience into a particularly frustrating episode that sets the tone of this doomed same-sex relationship for the rest of the film, ending in tragedy, once again insisting on the equation of gay sex and death seen in *Chuecatown* and *Mentiras y gordas*. In the other two films, the opposite-sex couples will find creative ways of reinventing their relationships, following equally traumatic discoveries in

Figure 13.1 Javier Bardem and Jordi Mollà in *Segunda Piel/Second Skin*, directed by Gerardo Vera. Antena 3 Televisión, Lolafilms, Vía Digital, 1999.

the midst of two otherwise memorable steamy sex scenes between the men – in both cases they are caught with their male lovers in the shower.

In other films, usually comedies, mothers are the ones who enter the scene, disrupting sex between their son and another man. Examples include another scene of the aforementioned *Chuecatown* and also *Reinas/Queens* (dir. Gómez Pereira, 2005). These sexual disruptions are particularly interesting. In the context of these light comedies, the erotic disruption provides comic relief by means of a double Freudian joke at the expense of the homosexual men's overbearing mothers, and also through the queer reversal of the primal scene. Importantly, the comic effect of these interruptions is also politically charged: in presenting mothers apparently at ease with seeing their sons in bed with another man (in both films the mothers stay in the scene, chatting with the lovers as if nothing had happened, even laying in bed with them in the case of *Chuecatown*), the scenes provide casual evidence of familial acceptance of same-sex relationships. In so doing, these potentially awkward situations become symbolic of a new domesticity and GLBT visibility in contemporary Spain. This provides an interesting counterpart to those previous cases where sex acts between men were always undercover. In that sense, while frustrating the erotic potential of the scene, then, these moments also add political currency to the films, especially perhaps in the case of *Chuecatown*, since Concha Velasco, who plays Rey's mother, achieved gay icon status after playing another key role in the important gay-themed film *Kilómetro 0/Kilometre Zero* (dirs. Yolanda García Serrano and Juan Luis Iborra, 2000). Three of the mother figures in *Reinas* are also famous 'Almodóvar's girls'. As noted by Ellis (2010: 73), the film also advertises the capitalist value of same-sex weddings and gay tourism in Spain. In some sense, then, *Reinas* thus offers a problematic counter-argument to the vision of same-sex relationships as failure from a capitalist perspective that Hocquenghem (1993) critiques.

There are instances of much more disturbing interruptions involving attacks (or the threat of one) by male characters. An early example of this is Eloy de la Iglesia's *Los placeres ocultos/Hidden Pleasures* (1977), or his final film *Los novios búlgaros/Bulgarian Lovers* (2003), an adaptation of the homonymous novel by Eduardo Mendicutti, but we could also include the violent murder of Villaronga's *El mar/The Sea* (2000). In *Los placeres ocultos*, as in *El diputado*, the protagonist (also a middle-aged, closeted, powerful professional – in this case a banker, Eduardo, played by Simón Andreu) is infatuated with a younger, lower-class adolescent (Miguel – Tony Fuentes). Eduardo displaces his desire for Miguel (who has a girlfriend and an older female lover on the side) by having casual sexual encounters with (heterosexual) rent boys. As in *El diputado*, the bodies of the younger men, well-toned and often topless, are also at the centre of the homoerotic spectacle of the film. Yet sex with them is all but unachievable for the gay male protagonist. When Eduardo invites rent boy Ness (Ángel Pardo) back to his apartment and starts to touch his torso in erotic anticipation, Ness' friends show up unannounced (it was all part of a plan orchestrated by Ness) and threaten him with a knife, then rob him in his own home. *El mar*, a film that, as Allbritton has pointed out, is characterised by 'the sexualisation, and the intense cinematic gaze placed on the overt physicality of the male body' (2012: 64), turns what some might have expected to be the climactic sex scene between friends Andreu (Roger Casamajor) and Manuel (Bruno Bergonzini) into a scene of violent rape followed by self-defence murder. As Allbritton also notes, 'the eroticisation and fixation on the male body are concepts that are woven into the entire film, and they have very negative consequences' (65) that are tied partly to religion and Villaronga's challenging of and emphasis on 'complacency and heteronormativity' (64). Yet the homoerotic narrative once again culminates in a scene of violent sex, with fatal consequences for the characters. The role of the phallic knife in both *Los placeres ocultos* and *El mar* is an unsubtle reminder of the same pattern that equates anal penetration with death. Bersani (2010: 18–25) sees this pattern as a manifestation of a historical fear of a practice that challenges established conceptions about sex with regard to both gender and power – as Edelman has also discussed at length (1991).

As we will see towards the end of the chapter, Eloy de la Iglesia's *Los novios búlgaros* stands out as perhaps the film with the most explicit and uninterrupted scenes of sex between men. Yet it does not quite buck the trend of the case studies examined so far. While the sex scenes between the gay protagonist (once again, older and upper-middle-class gay protagonist Daniel – Fernando Gillén Cuervo) and a Bulgarian working-class married man Kyril (Dritan Biba) are mostly fulfilling, one of the most explicit sex scenes between Daniel and another Bulgarian rent boy (Emil – Oscar Iniesta) is also violently interrupted midway by two gunmen who break into the house looking for Kyril, due to his involvement in underground criminal activities. The violence of the act is doubly emphasised, visually through the emphasis on the gun pointed at the men while they are having sex, aurally through the diegetic sound of the weapon being loaded – which effectively alerts the men about the break-in, causing them to stop sex abruptly. The gun is then shown in close-up, another reminder of the phallus-in-rectum as a killer in the one scene where Daniel is the one on top, furiously penetrating his male companion.

In other films, the entrance of a third person into the sex scene disturbs it only temporarily, without stopping it altogether. Examples include *Cachorro/ Bear Cub* (dir. Albaladejo, 2004) – where the vigorous morning sex scene that opens the film continues quite naturally when a third man enters the room after using the bathroom – and *20 centímetros/20 Centimetres* (dir. Salazar, 2005) – where a neighbour catches a fairly explicit scene between Marieta (a pre-op transsexual woman played by Mónica Cervera) and the film's stud ('El reponedor', played by Pablo Puyol) from her window. 'El reponedor' enjoys so much being penetrated by Marieta that he refuses to stop. The sense of risk and ridicule, although presented as comedy, overwhelms the erotic spectacle, and then the scene comes to a sudden end when Marieta hurriedly draws the blind on the neighbours. The curious neighbour is a classic voyeur figure that stands in for the spectator, perhaps suggesting that it is also inappropriate for us to snoop on the characters during this intimate moment. Her frenzied reaction, however, also implies that the act is scandalous and undignified, a circus (she excitedly summons others in her house to come and watch). The blind, like the shut toilet door in *Los amantes pasajeros*, is a symbolic reminder both of what we as spectators are deprived of, but also of our very desire to see what apparently cannot be shown – or at least not without interruption.

ANTI-CLIMAX

Perriam's work (2013) has been fundamental in drawing attention to the importance of short films and video art pieces in Spanish queer cinema production. As he argues, the short film has become a key format not only because it allows new filmmakers with basic means to present their products to relatively large audiences through festivals, art galleries and online streaming, but also due to its versatility and aesthetic peculiarities (2013: 15–16, 108–11). In six minutes, the critically acclaimed short film *Fuckbuddies* (dir. Juanma Carrillo, 2011) encapsulates the idea of interruption and sexual frustration discussed throughout this essay. One of the trailers for the short film starts with the following lines written across the screen: 'He wants quick sex. He also wants sex. Many film festivals want sex.' The trailer, like the film, starts with the promise of sex and sets high expectations for it, but the sex is never actually realised, despite a certain verbal and visual explicitness characteristic to the work of video artist and filmmaker Juanma Carrillo.[11] The whole film takes place almost exclusively in the inside of a car where two men (played by Domingo Fernández and Richard García Vázquez) are about to have sex.[12] From the start, the film makes a clear statement about the explicit depiction of sex. The excitement of anonymous, quick sex is what drives the narrative. The film builds up the sexual tension swiftly with a series of close-up and medium close-up shots of one of the men smoking, the other opening a condom with his teeth, the two men removing their clothes, uncomfortably lying in between the two front seats on top of each other, without talking. The lack of dialogue for most of the first two minutes (almost a third of the duration of the film) draws our attention to the diegetic sounds, anticipating, it seems, a steamy sex scene (heavy breathing, bodies getting undressed and rubbing against each other). The scene is another example of sexual awkwardness involving anal sex. It turns out that the man in the receiving position had lied to the 'top' about his sexual preferences (he also prefers to 'top'). The conversation then reveals that both men are in relationships with women. The promising sex scene is thus (once again) interrupted while the dialogue gradually takes over, turning attention to the possibility of having anal sex with their female partners, then to domestic worries of their stable relationships with women: house ownership, mortgages fees, bank accounts. This capitalist narrative, then, explicitly infiltrates and prevents this scene of anal sex. The two are, as Hocquenhem argues, mutually exclusive: pleasure associated with that organ that belongs only in the private sphere, the anus, must be sublimated (1993: 97–103). The film ends with the two men sitting side-by-side in the back of the car, one of them smoking, a parody of the post-coital cigarette cliché but here perhaps more evocative of sexual frustration, since the phallic imagery of the man sucking on the cigarette seems also inescapable in this context.

Comically, during sex, the man in the receiving position and with his legs still up in the air (see Figure 13.2) first asks the other man to rim him, then, keeping a straight face, states that it is not ok to have anal sex with a steady girlfriend, because that is what you do with 'dirty sluts'. In his influential essay 'Is the Rectum a Grave?' (originally published in 1987), Bersani states that 'Women and gay men spread their legs with an unquenchable appetite for destruction' (2010: 18), adding that 'this is an image of extraordinary power'. He goes on to say that the 'image of a grown man, legs high up in the air, unable to refuse the suicidal ecstasy of being a woman' was 'intolerable' for the average citizen (18).[13] Is this powerful image, quite explicitly presented in some of the examples discussed (*La ley del deseo* and, partly, *Chuecatown*), too powerful even for queer audiences to bear? Is this the unbearable prospect, the 'intolerable image', to use Rancière's term (2011: 83–105), that prevents

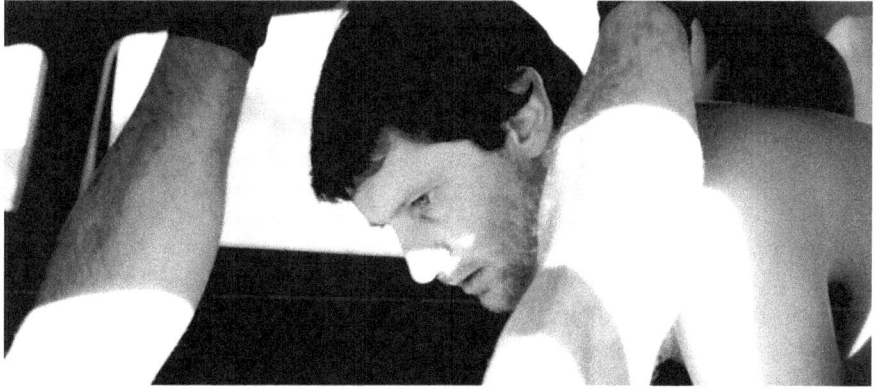

Figure 13.2 Domingo Fernández and Richard García Vázquez in *Fuckbuddies*, directed by Juanma Carrillo. Emociones Produce, 2011.

us from seeing uninterrupted sex acts between men on the screen? The two examples I have saved for the closing section provide some evidence to the contrary, albeit in two very different representational models.

CLIMAX

As mentioned earlier, Eloy de la Iglesia's *Los novios búlgaros* stands out among the examples discussed in this chapter for its explicit and, in one case, *uninterrupted* depiction of sex between men. The film visually constructs the physical bonding between Daniel and his Bulgarian lover Kyril by alternating between medium shots of vigorous penetrative sex and close-up shots of the gay protagonist's face, aided by a diegetic soundtrack that combines Daniel's groaning sounds with those of Kyril's vigorous pounding. Contrary to some of the facial expressions of pain seen in the previous examples, Daniel's ecstatic expression in the climactic moment, his smiling, his sobbing at the end, allows for a sense of erotic relief and satisfaction so often denied to the queer spectator. This sense is undoubtedly magnified by the insistent use of objective close-up shots for the best part of the minute leading up to the climax. As Doane has lucidly argued in her study of the close-up, historically the analytical discourse of this shot type has tended to treat it 'synchronically rather than diachronically, as stasis, as resistance to narrative linearity, as the vertical gateway to an almost irrecoverable depth behind the image' (2003: 97). As she maintains, this discourse suggests 'a desire to stop the film, to grab hold of something that can be taken away' (97). Importantly, the fixation on the close-up can also be understood as 'an attempt to reassert the corporeality of the classically disembodied spectator', since scale 'can only be understood through its reference to the human body' (108). In showing the full sex act uninterrupted and including frequent close-up shots of Daniel's ecstatic face, then, *Los novios búlgaros* succeeds in drawing the queer spectator into the erotic experience of the film. The use of close-ups shortens the distance between the fictional sex act and the spectators, enabling an intense and sensorial identification. Arguably this applies to all the examples of intimate close-ups discussed throughout the chapter, except in this case the narrative and visual experiences are complete. There is no awkwardness here, no false starts, no sudden stops, no darkness, and no interruptions. The camera stays close to the characters until they climax, grabbing the moment. The line is drawn perhaps in the absence of any palpable proof that the orgasm has taken place.

This brings me back to Almodóvar's *Los amantes pasajeros* and the other veiled gay sex scenes that I referred to at the start of this chapter. Both scenes involve steward Ulloa (Raúl Arévalo) and the plane's co-pilot Benito (played by heartthrob Hugo Silva). Like the captain, Alex, Benito won't identify as

Figure 13.3 Raúl Arévalo and Carlos Areces in *Los amantes pasajeros/I'm So Excited*, directed by Pedro Almodóvar. El Deseo, 2013.

gay or acknowledge the sexual tension with Ulloa. The only evidence we have of their sex act, apart from Benito's ecstatic facial expression, is the presence of semen on the side of Ulloa's face. The evidence is further tested (and, importantly, *tasted*) by Fajas (Carlos Areces) (see Figure 13.3), the comical but jealous fellow steward who is left out of the action, and thus stands in for the film's (queer) spectator. Like the spectator, he wants the palpable proof of the sex act that he hasn't been able to see, one that, like the money shot in porn, satisfies the viewer's desire by substituting 'the relation between the actors [with] the more solitary (and literally disconnected) visual pleasure of the male performer and the male viewer' (Williams 1999: 101). As Jagose explains, there is effectively a contradiction of terms between the desire to represent orgasm and the impossibility and resistance to do it (2013: 28–34). This resistance to represent the sexual climax is even stronger in scenes between men, which are repeatedly cut short by ellipsis, fades to black, darkness or interruptions by other characters that walk into the scene. It goes without saying that penetrative (or phallic) sex is not the ultimate goal here. There are many other ways in which sex between men, or any type of sex, can be satisfying and complete. The problem lies in that the majority of the examples discussed make an issue out of penetrative sex, only to then stop the lovers in their tracks, often by surprise and sometimes quite aggressively. These examples are quite different, for example, to those that Williams, citing Bersani, refers to as 'an itch that does not seek to be scratched' (2008: 14). I also take Krzywinska's point that the ellipse has the potential to let the viewer 'project into the gap their own personally tailored fantasy' (2006: 29). As I hope to have shown, however, many of these sex scenes do not exactly encourage identification or personalised fantasies. This is where *Los amantes pasajeros* is quite different. In touching, smelling and tasting the evidence of the orgasm that was hidden from view, Fajas is preparing the spectator for the film's haptic and affective climax, one that will see the queer spectator finally rejoice in a wonderfully excessive amount of white, frothy stuff. While the homoerotic narrative of the film was always visually evident from the very image of the phallic plane – and, as Levy noted (2015: 115), the very name of the airline, *Península* – the foam path sprayed on the runway in preparation for the emergency landing is particularly suggestive. In the final moments of this film, released internationally as *I'm So Excited*, the foam surrounding the phallic plane serves the perhaps contradictory purpose of hiding just another heated sex scene between men while at the same time, at last, giving the queer spectator something to be really excited about.

NOTES

1. See Chapter 8 of Fouz-Hernández and Martínez-Expósito (2007).
2. I would like to thank my colleagues Alfredo Martínez-Expósito (University of Melbourne) and Fiona Noble (Durham) for their constructive comments and suggestions on an earlier version of this chapter.
3. Tropiano (1997) explores the work of de la Iglesia from that perspective. I have studied this and other aspects of the homoerotic gaze in the work of Pons elsewhere (see Fouz-Hernández 2015).
4. I am very aware of the problematic issue of terminology surrounding the 'gay', 'homosexual', 'queer' and 'LGBT' labels and of the importance of not using them interchangeably. In this chapter I will be mostly talk about 'sex between men' to refer literally to sex acts between two male characters on the screen, regardless of whether or not they may identify as 'gay'. Some of these characters may potentially identify (or may be perceived) as queer, gay, bisexual or even heterosexual. While identity politics is not the main concern of this chapter, it does affect the argument about spectatorship and identification. I will make this as clear as possible in the relevant passages.
5. This and the next section's titles are references (and homages) to Bourne's (1996) history of lesbians and gays in British Cinema (1930–71) – itself entitled after David Lean's famous film *Brief Encounter* (1945) – and to the first encyclopedia of gay and lesbian film and video, *Images in the Dark* (Murray 1996) respectively. Much has been written about the gay and camp sensibilities of Lean's heterosexual narrative (see, for example, Dyer (1993)), an argument partly based on the sexuality of the film's writer, Noel Coward. Bourne's book adopts the title to refer precisely to the 'wink-and-you-miss-it' nature of same-sex desire in the history of British cinema (and perhaps also to the format of the book, that deals briefly with key relevant films and names of the period studied). Here the section title refers to the length of sexual encounters between men in some classic examples in Spanish cinema. The section 'Images in the Dark' refers to the fact that in many cases these encounters are obscured by literal darkness – as well as fades to black.
6. Melero Salvador has noted how at the time of its release some critics perceived *El*

diputado as 'pornographic', a perception that, as he also writes, would be possibly unthinkable for present-day audiences (2011: 136).
7. As Paul Julian Smith explains, the power balance is reversed by the end of the film, when Diego will be forced to obey Antonio (1997: 187).
8. In contrast, the visual narrative of this film culminates with explicit home video footage of the death – by enforced alcohol intoxication – of Pedro (Aitor Merino), a character bullied on the basis of his perceived weakness due to illness (he is a diabetic), his effeminacy and (suspected) homosexuality.
9. The sex scene anticipates the murder from the start. As part of the foreplay Rey initiates a sexual role play by pretending to be a Wolverine character 'ready to murder'.
10. Eight years earlier these two successful actors had co-starred in Bigas Luna's *Jamón, jamón* (1992), where their characters were also involved in a love triangle with homoerotic undertones (although in that case they were competing for the attention of a woman, played by Penélope Cruz). Years after the release of *Segunda Piel*, director Gerardo Vera revealed that some television stations and distributors did not buy the film due to the explicit sex scenes between the two men (RTVE 2011). This seems to confirm the main thesis of this chapter, that sex scenes involving two men are still too difficult to 'sell' to the general public, even if they are incomplete.
11. Perriam examines Carrillo's important work in detail (2013: 16–17, 107–11).
12. There are only two brief shots filmed outside the car: an establishing shot showing the car from outside, parked in a vantage point outside the city, and a close-up of the rear-view mirror showing the reflection of the two men having sex.
13. In their provocative essay *Por el culo*, Sáez and Carrasco (2011) discuss at length the cultural taboo surrounding the representation of the anus as a sexual organ.

REFERENCES

Allbritton, Dean (2012), 'On Infirm Ground: Masculinity and Memory in *El Mar*', *Post Script. Essays in Film and the Humanities* 31:3, 58–70.
Álvarez, Alfeo (2000), 'El enigma de la culpa: la homosexualidad y el cine español 1962–2000', *International Journal of Iberian Studies* 13:3, 136–47.
Ballesteros, Isolina (2001), *Cine (ins)urgente: textos filmicos y contextos culturales de la España postfranquista*, Madrid: Fundamentos.
Bersani, Leo (2010), *Is the Rectum a Grave? And Other Essays*, Chicago: University of Chicago Press.
Berzosa, Alberto (2014), *Homoherejías filmicas: Cine homosexual subversivo en España en los años setenta y ochenta*, Madrid: Brumaria.
Bourne, Stephen (1996), *Brief Encounters: Lesbians and Gays in British Cinema 1930–1971*, London and New York: Cassell.
Doane, Mary-Ann (2003), 'The Close-Up: Scale and Detail in the Cinema', *differences: A Journal of Feminist Cultural Studies* 14:3 (Fall), 89–111.
Dyer, Richard (1993), *Brief Encounter*, London: BFI.
Edelman, Lee (1991), 'Seeing Things: Representation, the Scene of Surveillance, and the Spectacle of Gay Male Sex', in Diana Fuss (ed.), *Inside/Out. Lesbian Theories, Gay Theories*, New York and London: Routledge, pp. 93–116.
Edelman, Lee (2004), *No Future: Queer Theory and the Death Drive*, Durham, NC and London: Duke University Press.

Ellis, Robert Richmond (2010), 'Spanish Constitutional Democracy and Cinematic Representations of Queer Sexuality, or, Saving the Family: *Los novios búlgaros*, *Reinas* and *Fuera de carta*', *Revista canadiense de estudios hispánicos* 35:1 (Autumn), 67–80.

Fouz-Hernández, Santiago (2015), 'La mirada homoerótica en el cine de Ventura Pons. De Ocaña a Ignasi M', in Andrés Lema-Hincapié and Conxita Domènech (eds), *Ventura Pons: Una mirada excepcional desde el cine catalán*, Frankfurt and Madrid: Vervuert/ Iberoamericana, pp. 304–27.

Fouz-Hernández, Santiago and Alfredo Martínez-Expósito (2007), *Live Flesh: The Male Body in Contemporary Spanish Cinema*, London and New York: I. B. Tauris.

Fouz-Hernández, Santiago and Chris Perriam (2000), 'Beyond Almodóvar: 'Homosexuality' in Spanish Cinema of the 1990s', in David Alderson and Linda Anderson (eds), *Territories of Desire in Queer Culture: Refiguring Contemporary Boundaries*, Manchester and New York: Manchester University Press, pp. 96–111.

Gras-Velázquez (2013), *Representations of Gay Men in Contemporary Spanish Cinema* (PhD thesis), Durham University.

Gutiérrez-Albilla, Julián Daniel (2013), 'Scratching the Past on the Surface of the Skin: Embodied Intersubjectivity, Prosthetic Memory, and Witnessing in Almodóvar's *La mala educación*', in Marvin D'Lugo and Kathleen M. Vernon (eds), *A Companion to Pedro Almodóvar*, Malden, MA, Oxford and Chichester: Wiley-Blackwell, pp. 322–44.

Halberstam, J. (2011), *The Queer Art of Failure*, Durham, NC and London: Duke University Press.

Hocquenghem, Guy (1993), *Homosexual Desire*, trans. Daniella Dangoor, Durham, NC and London: Duke University Press.

Krzywinska, Tanya (2006), *Sex and the Cinema*, London and New York: Wallflower Press.

Jackson, Earl (1995), *Studies in Gay Male Representation*, Bloomington and Indianapolis: Indiana University Press.

Jagose, Annamarie (2013), *Orgasmology*, Durham, NC and London: Duke University Press.

Levy, Emanuel (2015), *Gay Directors, Gay Films? Pedro Almodóvar, Terence Davis, Todd Haynes, Gus Van Sant, John Waters*, New York: Columbia University Press.

Llamas, Ricardo (1995), 'La reconstrucción del cuerpo homosexual en tiempos de Sida', in Ricardo Llamas (ed.), *Construyendo Sidentidades. Estudios desde el corazón de una pandemia*, Madrid: Siglo Veintiuno, pp. 153–89.

Martínez-Expósito, Alfredo (2015), 'Encarnaciones: cuerpo, clase y nación en el cine gay de Eloy de la Iglesia', in Rafael M. Mérida y Jorge Luis Peralta (eds), *Las masculinidades en la transición*, Barcelona and Madrid: Egales, pp. 157–73.

Melero Salvador, Alejandro (2004), 'New Sexual Politics in the Cinema of the Transition to Democracy: de la Iglesia's *El Diputado*', in Steven Marsh and Parvati Nair (eds), *Gender and Spanish Cinema*, Oxford and New York: Berg, pp. 103–18.

Melero Salvador, Alejandro (2010), *Placeres ocultos. Gays y lesbianas en el cine español de la transición*, Barcelona: Notorious.

Melero Salvador, Alejandro (2011), 'Armas para una narrativa del sexo: transgresión y cine "S"', in Manuel Palacio (ed.), *El cine y la transición política en España (1975–1982)*, Madrid: Biblioteca Nueva, pp. 126–44.

Mira, Alberto (2004), *De Sodoma a Chueca: una historia cultural de la homosexualidad en España en el siglo XX*, Madrid: Egales.

Murray, Raymond (1996), *Images in the Dark. An Encyclopedia of Gay and Lesbian Film and Video*, New York: Plume.

Perriam, Chris (2013), *Spanish Queer Cinema*, Edinburgh: Edinburgh University Press.

Rancière, Jacques (2011 [2008]), *The Emancipated Spectator*, trans. Gregory Elliot, London and New York: Verso.
RTVE (2011), 'Versión Española – *Segunda Piel*': http://www.rtve.es/alacarta/videos/version-espanola/version-espanola-segunda-piel/1238327/ (last accessed 1 August 2016).
Russo, Vito (1987 [1981]), *The Celluloid Closet: Homosexuality in the Movies*, New York: Harper & Row.
Sáez, Javier y Sejo Carrascosa (2011), *Por el culo: políticas anales*, Madrid: Egales.
Smith, Paul Julian (1992), *Laws of Desire: Questions of Homosexuality in Spanish Writing and Film 1960–1990*, Oxford and New York: Clarendon Press.
Smith, Paul Julian (1997), 'Pornography, Masculinity, Homosexuality: Almodóvar's *Matador* and *La ley del Deseo*', in Marsha Kinder (ed.), *Refiguring Spain: Cinema, Media, Representation*, Durham, NC and London: Duke University Press, pp. 178–95.
Tropiano, Stephen (1997), 'Out of the Cinematic Closet: Homosexuality in the Films of Eloy de la Iglesia', in Marsha Kinder (ed.), *Refiguring Spain: Cinema/Media/Representation*, Durham, NC: Duke University Press, pp. 157–77.
Watney, Simon (1987), *Policing Desire: Pornography, AIDS and the Media*, Minneapolis: University of Minnesota Press.
Williams, Linda (1999), *Hard Core: Power, Pleasure and the 'Frenzy of the Visible'*, Berkeley, Los Angeles and London: University of California Press.
Williams, Linda (2008), *Screening Sex*, Durham, NC: Duke University Press.

FILMOGRAPHY

20 centímetros/20 Centimetres, film, directed by Ramón Salazar. Spain/France: Aligator Producciones, Divine Productions, Estudios Picasso, 2005.
Brief Encounter, film, directed by David Lean. United Kingdom: Cineguild, 1945.
Cachorro/Bear Cub, film, directed by Miguel Albaladejo. Spain: Hispanocine Producciones Cinematográficas, Star Line TV Productions, 2004.
Chuecatown/Boystown, film, directed by Juan Flahn. Spain: Canónigo Films, Filmax, 2006.
DiDi Hollywood, film, directed by Josep Joan Bigas Luna. Spain: Audiovisual Aval SGR, Canal + España, Ciudad de la Luz, El Virigili Films, Generalitat de Catalunya, ICO, ICAA, La Canica Films, Malvarrossa Media, TV3 and TVE, 2010.
El diputado/Confessions of a Congressman, film, directed by Eloy de la Iglesia. Spain: Figaro Films, Ufesa, Prozesa, 1978.
El mar/The Sea, film, directed by Agustí Villaronga. Spain: Massa d'Or Productions, 2000.
El sexo de los ángeles/Angels of Sex, film, directed by Xavier Villaverde. Spain/Brazil: Aģencia Nacional do Cinema, Audiovisual Aval SGR, Axenimcia Galega das Industrias Culturais (AGADIC), CCFBR Produções, Canal + España, Consorcio Audiovisual de Galicia, Continental Producciones, Dream Team Concept, Generalitat de Catalunya (ICIC), Ibermedia, Instituto de Crédito Oficial, ICAA, TVG, Xunta de Galicia, 2012.
Fuckbuddies, film, directed by Juanma Carrillo. Spain: Emociones Produce, 2011.
Fuckbuddies, film trailer (for Vimeo On Demand), directed by Juanma Carrillo. Spain: Emociones Produce, 2011: https://vimeo.com/ondemand/fuckbuddies (last accessed 28 July 2016).
Historias del Kronen/Stories from the Kronen, film, directed by Montxo Armendáriz. Spain/France/Germany: Alert Film, Elias Querejeta Producciones Cinematográficas, Victoires Productions, 1995.

Jamón, jamón, film, directed by Josep Joan Bigas Luna. Spain: Lola Films, Ovideo TV S.A., Sogepaq, 1992.
Jóvenes viciosas/Dirty Young Ladies, film, directed by Manuel Iglesias. Spain: Jacinto Santos Parras P.C., 1980.
Kilómetro 0/Kilometre Zero, film, directed by Yolanda García Serrano and Juan Luis Iborra. Spain: Cuarteto Producciones Cinematográficas, Media Park, Universal Pictures Spain, 2000.
Krampack/Nico and Dani, film, directed by Cesc Gay. Spain: Messidor Films, 2000.
La ley del deseo/Law of Desire, film, directed by Pedro Almodóvar. Spain: El Deseo, Laurenfilm, 1987.
La mala educación/Bad Education, film, directed by Pedro Almodóvar. Spain: El Deseo, Canal + España, TVE, 2004.
Laberinto de pasiones/Labyrinths of Passion, film, directed by Pedro Almodóvar. Spain: Alphabille, S.A., 1982.
Los amantes pasajeros/I'm So Excited, film, directed by Pedro Almodóvar. Spain: El Deseo, 2013.
Los novios búlgaros/Bulgarian Lovers, film, directed by Eloy de la Iglesia. Spain: Altube Filmeak, Conexión Sur, Creativos Asociados de Radio y Televisión, TVE, 2003.
Los placeres ocultos/Hidden Pleasures, film, directed by Eloy de la Iglesia. Spain: Aloborada P.C., 1977.
Más que amor frenesí/Not Love, Just Frenzy, film, directed by Albacete, Bardem, Menkes. Spain: Canal + España, Fernando Colomo Producciones Cinematográficas S.L., Películas Frenéticas, TVE, 1996.
Mentiras y gordas/Sex, Party and Lies, film, directed by Albacete and Menkes. Spain: Agrupación de cine 001, Castafiori Films, Tornasol Films, 2009.
Perdona bonita, pero Lucas me quería a mí/Excuse me, Darling, but Lucas Loved Me, film, directed by Dunia Ayaso and Felix Sabroso. Spain: Canal + España, Cristal Producciones Cinematográficas, S.A., Sogetel, Sogepaq, 1997.
Reinas/Queens, film, directed by Manuel Gómez Pereira. Spain/Netherlands/Italy: Warner Bros Films de España, 2005.
Segunda Piel/Second Skin, film, directed by Gerardo Vera. Spain: Antena 3 Televisión, Lolafilms, Vía Digital, 1999.

Index

Note: **bold** signifies illustration

ABC, 76, 81, 84
advertising, 62, 67, 77, 81
aesthetics
   aestheticised violence, 84
   camp aesthetics, 12, 86
   crude aesthetics, 158
   Fascist aesthetics, 48
   hard-core aesthetics, 133
   hyper-real aesthetics, 197
   masochistic aesthetic, 178
   retro-aesthetics, 154
   utopian aesthetics, 183
Africa, 11, 33, 37–50, 50n3, 51n11
   African immigrants, 37
   Hispano-Moroccan brotherhood, 40, 46
   see also colonialism and exoticism
ageing, 13, 204, 208, 211, 214, 215n2
   anti-ageing culture, 203
   affirmative ageing bodies, 211, 215
   affirmative ageing discourses, 14
   ageing female, 14, 202, 207, 215
   patriarchal notions of ageing, 215n3
   successful ageing, 214, 215n3
AIDS, 15in1, 222, 226
Akelarre / Witches' Sabbath, 14, 170, 174–6, 179–8, **181**; *see also* Basque Country, eroticism, masochism and torture
Alas de mariposa / Butterfly Wings, 182
Algo amargo en la boca / Something Bitter in the Mouth, 75, 79
Almodóvar, Pedro, 1, 5, 9, 11, 15, 92, 109, 121, 125, 126, 135n1, 139, 220, 222–3, 228, 232, **233**; *see also* eroticism and 'S' category

Ama Lur / Motherland, 169, 174, 176
amantes pasajeros, Los / I'm So Excited, 15, 92, 224, 230, 232, 234, **233**
¡A mí la Legión! / Follow the Legion, 11, 37, 38–45, 47, 49–50, 51n10; *see also* Africa
Amor a la española / Love Spanish Style, 57
anal sex, 224, 226, 230–1; *see also* penetration
Anderson, Benedict, 174, 177
Angustia / Anguish, 126–8, 133, 135–6n8, 136n19
Antonioni, Michelangelo, 56, 58–9, 64, 71n5
años desnudos (clasificada S) / Rated R, 4, 8, 122n4
apertura, 74–5, 95
Árabe, El / Arab, The, 24
Aranda, Vicente, 1, 5, 79, 139
Arévalo, Carlos, 11, 37, 48, **41**
Armendáriz, Montxo, 14, 34, 37, 187, 224
Arte y cinematografía, 19
asesino de muñecas, El / Killing of the Dolls, 12, 76–7, 80, 83–7, 88n4, **85, 87**
Asignatura pendiente / Unfinished Business, 111, 116, 118
¡Átame! / Tie me up! Tie me down!, 15n1
audience
   Basque audience, 174–6
   bourgeois audiences, 121
   contemporary audiences, 111, 114
   domestic audiences, 76
   GLBT-friendly audiences, 220
   international audiences, 75, 77
   mass audience, 120
   metropolitan audience, 47
   middlebrow audience, 109, 114

audience (*cont.*)
  newly middle-class audience, 114
  queer spectators
  younger audiences, 154
auteurism, 10, 56, 113, 158
  gay auteurs, 120

Bahía de Palma / Bay of Palma, 75
Bakhtin, Mikhail, 99
Balarrasa / Reckless, 43
Banderas, Antonio, 11, 222
Bardem, Javier, 5, 11, 227
Bardem, Juan Antonio, 74, 76, 225
Barker, Jennifer, 155, 159, 160, 162
Barrura Begiratzeko Liehoak / Windows Looking Inward, 173
Barthes, Roland, 71n5, 163
Bartolomé, Cecilia, 14, 204, 205, 215n6, 215–16n7
Basque cinema, 13, 169–70, 174–6, 182–4
  sexlessness of, 169, 171, 176, 182
  see also martyrdom, torture and violence
Basque Country / Euskadi, 169–74, 176, 178–9, 183
Basque imaginary, 171, 169–84
Basque nationalism, 173, 176–8, 182; *see also* ETA
Bataille, Georges, 8, 21, 129, 130, 136nn10,16,17
Baudrillard, Jean, 60, 62, 64, 65, 67, 68, 70, 134
Bazin, André, 156
BDSM (Bondage and Discipline, Dominance and Submission, Sadism and Masochism), 175
Belle de jour, 75
Bersani, Leo, 223, 229, 231, 233
Bésame, monstruo / Kiss Me, Monster, 77
beso de la muerte, El / Kiss of Death, The, 21
beso en un taxi, Un / Kiss in a Taxi, A, 21
beso fatal, El / Deathly Kiss, The, 21
besos, los, 19, 28
¡Bienvenido, Míster Marshall! / Welcome Mr Marshall!, 62
Bigas Luna, Josep Joan, 1, 5, 12, 13, 125–35, 135nn1,2,4,6, 135–6n8, 136nn13,16, 227, 235n10
Bilbao, 13, 125–7, 129, 130–5, 135n1, 136n18, **130, 131, 134**
Board of Classification and Censorship *see* Junta de Clasificación y Censura de Películas Cinematográficas
Boca a boca / Mouth to Mouth, 5
Bodegas, Roberto, 115

body
  as anti-erotic object, 13
  Basque body, 170, 174–9, 182–4
  (de)sexualised body, 68
  erotic body, 23, 55
  female body, 14, 24, 125–8, 132–4, 140, 202, 204, 207–8, 211, 213, 215
  gay male bodies, 219
  homosexual body, 139, 149–50
  male body, 12–14, 24, 47, 77–8, 86–7, 139–40, 143–6, 154, 158, 179, 229
  naked male body, 154
  older body, 202, 203, 214–15
  phallic body, 142
  see also eroticism, Basque Cinema, male and nudity
buen amor, El / Good Love, The, 94
Buñuel, Luis, 1, 75, 114
Bwana, 37
Bypass, 183

Calle Mayor / Main Street, 74
Camino, Jaime, 11, 58, 59, 64–5, 70
camp, 12, 74, 83, 84, 86, 92, 93, 194, 234n5
campana del infierno, La / Bell of Hell, 79, 82
canción de Aixa, La / Song of Aixa, 45
Canciones para después de una Guerra / Songs for the Post-War, 94
Caniche / Poodle, 126–8, 135n5, 136n19
Cantudo, María José, 96, 97, 101
Cara al sol que más calienta / Facing the Warmest Sun, 12, 92, 94, 102
cartas de Alou, Las / Letters from Alou, 34, 37
casa sin fronteras, La / House Without Frontiers, The, 94
Caso, El, 155, 166n2
caso de las dos bellezas, El / Rotte Lippen Sadisterotica, 77
Catholicism, 97, 169
  Catholic Church, 3, 29, 41, 42, 43, 44, 47, 98, 115
  Catholic missionary, 39
  Catholic morality, 81, 87
  Catholic repression, 13
  National Catholicism, 42, 43, 44, 45, 47, 55
  National Catholic rhetoric, 33
  see also Francoism
censorship, 13, 21, 22, 32, 50, 50n2, 77, 82, 87, 88n7, 96, 109–10, 157, 169, 188, 216n8, 219
  abolition of censorship, 3, 4, 12, 110, 115, 125, 139, 204, 219
  after censorship, 127
  creative conditions under censorship, 58

Francoist censorship, 1, 87, 115, 125, 148, 182, 204
liberal censorship, 74, 75
Real Decreto de 1977, 139
relaxed censorship, 94
self-censorship, 81
see also Francoism
child / childhood, 14, 68, 76, 84, 150, 187–97, 198nn1,5,14, 199n20
children of *desarrollismo*, 150
queer child, 188, 189, 190, 191
see also nuevo cine con niño and trauma
Chuecatown / Boystown, 226–8, 231
Cine, El, 19
cine con niño, 11, 187, 198n1; *see also nuevo cine con niño*
Cine Español, 23, 27, 28
Cinegramas, 19
Cine Popular, 19, 23, 24, **31**
cine quinqui, 11, 154–66, 166n1
Cine Revista, 24
Cine S, 126, 140
Cine Sparta, 19, 23
Cold War, 43
Colegas / Pals, 154–6, 159–5
Colomo, Fernando, 5
colonialism
 colonial desire, 39
 colonial films, 37–50
 (neo)-colonialism, 50
 past colonial projects, 37
 paternalistic politics of colonialism, 37
 postcolonial film, 11
 Spanish colonies, 41
 Spanish women, 33, 44
 see also Africa and Francoism
confesor, El / Confesor, The, 21
Consultorio de señoras / Ladies' Appointment, 21
consumer society, 55, 57–8, 65, 67, 68, 71n9, 87; *see also* erotismo de consumo
Contracorriente / Undertow, 121
Coromina, Pepón, 125, 132
corrupción de Chris Miller, La / Corruption of Chris Miller, The, 76, 78, 88n4
Cría cuervos / Raise Ravens, 14, 187, 190–1, 199n15, **192**
crimen de Cuenca, El / Cuenca Crime, The, 170
Cuarenta años sin sexo / Forty Years without Sex, 3, 6

de Beauvoir, Simone, 203, 209, 215n5
de la Iglesia, Eloy, 11, 12, 13, 15, 75, 79, 80, 110–21, 148, 154–66, 166nn1,3, 220–1, 228–9, 232
de la Loma, José Antonio, 156, 166nn1,4
Deleuze, Gilles, 170, 176, 178, 179–80, 182, 183
Delgado, Luis María, 75, 85, 86, 141
Delgrás, Gonzalo, 33
democracy, 12, 13, 33, 50, 57, 61, 87, 92, 93, 96–8, 101, 102, 104, 127, 169, 198n4
 democratic pluralism, 125
 dictatorship to democracy, 50
 European democracies, 12, 61, 100
 neoliberalism on democracy, 60
 new democracy, 110–12, 150
 see also Francoism and Transition
de Orduña, Juan, 11, 37, 38
de Ossorio, Amando, 78, 81
Deprisa, deprisa / Fast, Fast, 156, 166n4
desarrollismo, 11, 55–70, 98
 children of *desarrollismo*, 150
 films of the *desarrollismo*, 65, 150
 neoliberal *desarrollismo*, 62
 see also turism
Deseo carnal / Desire of the Flesh (aka *Carnal Desire*), 13, 139, 143, 146, 147, 150, **144**
desire, 6, 11, 14, 24, 3, 38, 42, 49, 50, 55, 57–8, 62, 64, 68, 70, 74, 83, 86, 131, 134, 189, 195, 203
 aggressive desire, 129
 carnal desires, 98
 democratise desire, 96
 exploration of desires, 77
 heterosexual desire, 203
 homoerotic desire, 213, 223
 individualistic desire, 169
 lesbian desire, 79
 male desire, 74, 132, 148, 227
 male homosexual desire, 116, 117, 148
 mobilisation of desire, 129
 naturalisation of desire, 83
 objetiifcation of desire, 146
 paedophilic desires, 103
 same-sex desire, 190, 193, 196, 199n15, 219, 234n5
 women as objects of desire, 80
 see also sexuality
destape (films), 1, 2, 4, 6, 8, 11–13, 15, 15n2, 92–6, 100–1, 105, 109, 115–16, 122n2, 140, 143, 145, 171, 150, 216n8, 221; *see also* nudity and Transition
De tu ventana a la mía / From Your Window to Mine, 211, 213–15, **214**
Días contados / Running out of Time, 171
DiDi Hollywood, 227

diegetic
    diegetic sounds, 6, 102, 229, 230
    diegetic soundtrack, 6, 232
    extradiegetic, 40, 136, 205, 206
    intradiegetic, 205
    non-diegetic music, 221
Diferente / Different, 75, 85, 86
diputado, El / Confessions of a Congressman, 12–13, 110–21, 122n9, 221–3, 228–9, 234–5n6, **118, 119**
Doane, Mary-Ann, 232
double versions, 3
dubbing, 9, 150, 222
Dulces horas / Sweet Hours, 190, 193

Edelman, Lee, 14, 188, 190, 220, 229
Elena, Alberto, 38, 39, 45, 47
Entre las piernas / Between Your Legs, 5
En un lugar de La Manga / In a Village of La Manga, 57
Equatorial Guinea *see* Spanish Guinea
Erice, Víctor, 14, 187
eróticas vacaciones de Stella, Las / Intimate Confessions of Stella, 140
eroticism
    commercialisation of eroticism, 12
    erotic comedy, 6, 10, 141
    erotic fantasies, 8, 75
    erotic female voice, 9
    erotic frustration, 12
    erotic imagery, 81, 158
    eroticisation of horror cinema, 75
    eroticisation of the terrorist, 175
    eroticism of pornography, 159
    erotic narratives, 5, 14
    erotic-nostalgic comedies, 8
    erotic thrillers, 109
    female eroticism, 202, 203, 210, 211
    instructive eroticism, 82
    self-conscious eroticism, 83, 84
    visual erotics, 13, 155, 159, 163, 165, 166n6
erotismo de consumo (consumerist eroticism), 12, 75, 78, 80–2, 87
erotohistoriography, 14, 190, 196, 197; *see also* eroticism
escopeta nacional, La / National Shotgun, The, 12, 92, 94, 101, 102, 104, 105
espíritu de la colmena, El / Spirit of the Beehive, The, 14, 187, 189, 196, 198n8
Estado de excepción / State of Emergency, 14, 170, 174–82
estanquera de Vallecas, La / Hostages in the Barrio, 154, 166n3

estética de calzoncillo, 13, 158
ETA, 117, 121n1, 170, 172, 173, 177, 179, 183
ethnicity, 28, 30, 120
Evans, Peter, 40, 42, 48, 49
exoticism, 11, 19–34
    Asian exoticism, 24–5
    films exóticos, 24
    foreign bodies, 11
    grammar of exoticism, 24
    see also Africa and postcolonial film

fade to black, 222–4
Falangism, 41, 42–5, 47, 101; *see also* Francoism
familia, bien, gracias, La / Family, Fine, Thanks, The, 150
familia y ... uno más, La / Family Plus One, The, 150
fascism, 42, 43, 112, 118, 119
    Fascist aesthetics, 48
    see also Francoism
Fassbinder, Rainer Werner, 158
felices sesenta, Los / Happy Sixties, The, 11, 58, 63–4, 68–9, 70, 71n10, **69**
female body, 14, 24, 125–35, 140, 202, 204, 207, 208, 211, 213, 215
    female genitals, 134
    older female body, 14, 204, 207, 215
    see also body
female protagonist, 59, 69, 74, 129, 203, 216n8
feminine narcissism, 206
femininity / feminisation, 24, 49, 65, 214
    consecrated femininity, 207
    ideal femininity, 24
    myth of femininity, 203
feminism, 116, 204
fetishism, 7, 9, 10, 25, 33, 47, 67, 68, 80, 86, 125, 127, 129, 132, 134, 141, 176–80, 183, 195, 203
    fetish actor, 38
    fetishisation of the image, 179
    fetishisation of the past, 194
    fetish parties, 15n6
    see also torture
Filigrana / Filigree, 33
Films Selectos, 19
foreignness, 28
Fotogramas, 25, 96, 100, 101, 150, 154, 156; *see also Nuevo Fotogramas*
Fouz-Hernández, Santiago, 1, 6, 11, 13, 100, 148, 169, 222, 225, 226
Fowles, John, 127–9

INDEX 243

Francoism, 79, 97, 101, 102, 112, 117, 179,
    188, 191, 197, 198n5
  elites of Francoism, 104
  Franco-era films, 38, 151n4
  Franco-Falangist iconography, 45
  Francoist censorship, 1, 115, 125
  Francoist classroom, 196
  Franco's cultural revolution, 33
  late Francoist period, 97, 99, 101, 104
  National Movement, 41
  portrayal of Francoism, 119
  post-Franco, 2, 5, 125, 126, 127, 132,
    219–20
  re-evaluation of Francoism, 120
  Regime-friendly films, 55–7, 61, 62
  sexual repression of Francoism, 93, 119
  see also Falangism and Spanish Civil
    War
Franco, Jesús, 75, 77
Freud, Sigmund, 182, 187, 188, 194, 198n2,
    199n15, 203
  Freudian joke, 228
  Freudo-Marxist approach, 80
Fuckbuddies, 15, 230, **231**
Fuentes, Tony, 11, 13, 139, 141, 143, 144,
    146–8, 150–1, 226, 228
fuga de Segovia, La / Escape from Segovia,
    172
Función de noche / Night Function, 207,
    209

García Berlanga, Luis, 57, 62, 92, 101
gay
  gay activist, 221
  gay auteurs, 120
  gay body, 148, 219
  gay couples, 226
  gay liberation, 113
  gay magazine, 154
  gay male directors, 220
  gay male protagonist, 225, 228, 229, 232
  gay male relationships, 219, 222
  gay men, 219
  gay sensibility, 83, 84, 86
  gay sex, 220, 224, 226, 227, 232
  gay-themed, 228
  gay tourism in Spain, 228
  male gay readers, 147
  mature gay man, 149
Gay, Cesc, 15, 224
gaze, 5, 9, 48, 86, 99, 119, 128, 132, 142, 143,
    148, 155, 159, 178, 179, 189, 206, 208,
    210, 229
  desiring gaze, 80

  and female bodies, 4
  gaze of the camera, 203
  historicising gaze, 189
  homoerotic gaze, 234
  masochistic gaze, 179
  see also child and male
gender, 1, 10, 27, 42, 44, 46, 50, 51n8, 57–9,
    62, 63, 65–8, 79, 99, 120, 176, 189, 203,
    208, 229
  cross-gendered, 191
  gender bending, 51n10
  gender-differentiated content, 24
  gendered iconography, 176
  gender equality, 13
  gender identity, 55, 63
  gender politics, 56
  gender roles, 173
  normative gendered, 21, 22
  retrograde gender stereotypes, 93
  societal gender, 59
GLBT, 1, 220, 228; *see also* queer
Goicoechea, Gonzalo, 112, 113, 156, 160,
    166n3
Golfo, El / Scoundrel, The, 21
Gómez Pereira, Manuel, 5, 228
*gota de sangre para morir amando, Una /
    Murder in a Blue World*, 80
gran familia, La / Big Family, The, 150,
    151n4
Grau, Jorge, 11, 12, 58, 59, 64, 66, 70, 92,
    94–101, 105, 105n3, 106n5, 142
Gubern, Román, 2, 45, 48, 76, 81–3, 129,
    130, 132, 136n18
Guerín Hill, Claudio, 79, 82
Gutiérrez, Chus, 5, 15n4, 37
gynocine, 202, 215n1
Gypsy-face, 33

Habitación en Roma / Room in Rome, 5
habitus, 55, 64, 82, 87
  class habitus, 68
haptic, 6, 10, 160, 212, 233–4
  haptic compensation, 19
  haptic eroticism, 212
  haptic images, 159, 203
  haptic quality, 165
  haptic visuality, 159, 163, 210
*Hard Core. Power, Pleasure, and the Frenzy of
    the Visible*, 2
¡Harka!, 11, 37–49, 50–1n4,
    51nn10,12,13,15, **41**
Hayakawa, Sessue, 30, 32
heteroeroticism, 49
heterofuturity, 220

heterosexuality, 9, 116, 143, 149, 188, 189, 211, 220, 226–8, 234nn4,5
  heterosexual bodies, 71n10
  heterosexual erotic scenes, 15
  heterosexual imagery, 84
  heterosexual male desire, 58, 203
  heterosexual masculinity, 175
  heterosexual monogamous, 68
  heterosexual sex, 224–5
  heterosexual women, 225
Historias del Kronen / Stories from the Kronen, 224
hombre llamado flor de otoño, Un / Man Called Autumn Flower, A, 111
homo consumans, 60, 67
homoeroticism, 11, 40, 45, 48–50, 171, 175, 196, 197, 211–13, 222, 224, 227–8, 234n3, 235n10
  homoerotic narrative, 229, 234
homo oeconomicus, 60–1
homophobia, 3, 112, 113, 148
homosexuality
  Good Homosexual, 115
  homosexual desire, 116–17, 148
  homosexual hero, 120
  homosexual lifestyle, 223
  homosexual Others, 175
  homosexual subtext, 50
  illegality of homosexuality, 112
  passive feminine, 46
  representation of homosexuality, 110, 113
  submerged homosexuality, 86
  see also sexuality
homosociality, 49
horror film, 74–87
  erotic horror films, 12
  sexual horror, 79, 84

Ibáñez Serrador, Narciso, 77, 84
identity
  East Asian identity, 28
  female identity, 69
  human identity, 64
  individual and collective identity, 174
  nationalist identities, 13
  sexual identity, 171
  social identity, 62, 64
Iglesias, Manuel, 13, 139, 143–7
Ikuska (series), 171, 177
imaginary
  heteronormative imaginary, 210
  new sexual imaginary, 61
  women's filmic imaginary, 203
  see also Basque Imaginary

imagined community, 170, 173, 174
impotency, 147
impure cinema, 156
incest, 125, 127
  surrealist incest, 194
Indias negras, Las / Indes Noires, Les / Black Indies, The, 24
Interviú, 92, 101, 105n1, 154, 155, 166n5

Japan, 11, 28–33, 46
  Japanese films, 11
  Japanese morality, 33
  Yellow Peril, 28, 29
  see also kiss and racism
Jorza, Diana, 40, 41, 49
Jóvenes viciosas / Dirty Young Ladies, 13, 139, 143, 145, 148, 149, 150, 220
Juana la loca / Mad Love, 5
Julieta, 9, 15n7
Junta de Clasificación y Censura de Películas Cinematográficas, 74
juvenile delinquency, 154, 156, 166n1

Kiki el amor se hace / Quickie, Love is So, 6, 7
Kinder, Marsha, 43, 127, 132, 136nn12,14
kiss
  censorship of kisses, 22
  cinematic kiss, 11, 19, 21, 23, 25, 27, 33
  colour of kisses, 19, 32
  as an erotic object, 21
  impersonal and anonymous kiss, 25
  Japanese prohibition on kissing, 29
  as a technology, 23
  white kisses, 32
  see also censorship, eroticism, Japan and silent cinema
Klimovsky, León, 77, 78
Krampack / Nico and Dani, 224

Labanyi, Jo, 38, 42, 46, 48, 49, 51nn12,13,14
Laberinto de pasiones / Laberynths of Passion, 222
Lacan, Jacques, 129, 173, 174
Ladies' Home Journal, 23
León, Paco, 6, 7, 8, 11, 77, 78
lesbianism, 77–9, 140, 149, 211, 234n5
ley del deseo, La / Law of Desire, 9, 222, 231
Ley de peligrosidad y rehabilitación social, 112; *see also* Francoism and homophobia
López Vázquez, José Luis, 57, 101, 102, 150, 179, 181
L'Origine du monde, 178, 180
Lucía y el sexo / Sex and Lucía, 5
Lys, Ágata, 143

madre muerta, La / Dead Mother, The, 182
Madrid, Miguel *see* Skaife, Michael
mala educación, La / Bad Education, 223, 226
male
  eroticisation of the male body, 77, 80
  male desire, 58, 74
  male-dominated contexts, 40
  male friendships, 11
  male gaze, 4, 128, 204
  male genitals, 147, 211, 222, 223
  male star system, 13
  male voiceover, 4
  male teenagers, 154
Mañá, Laura, 202, 204, 207, 209
Manzano, José Luis, 11, 13, 154–7, 160–5
mar, El / Sea, The, 228–9
Marcelino, pan y vino / Miracle of Marcelino, 43
Marks, Laura, 155, 159, 163, 165, 166n6, 210, 211
Martin-Márquez, Susan, 1, 41, 43, 44, 46, 47, 48, 51n11
Martín Patino, Basilio, 57, 59, 94
martyrdom, 170–9, 182
  nationalist martyrdom, 14
  see also torture
masculinity, 49, 57, 65, 66, 158, 175
  hypermasculine macho, 57
  masculine camaraderie, 42
  masculine mystique, 11, 42
  masculine sexual freedom, 57
masochism, 175, 177, 179
  masochistic imagery, 169
  masochistic nationalism, 169, 173, 179, 182
Más que amor frenesí / Not Love, Just Frenzy, 225
mass immigration, 37
masturbation, 3, 163, 209, 210, 222, 224–5
maternal love, 191
Mayo, Alfredo, 11, 38, 41
Medem, Julio, 5, 13, 14, 139, 169, 172, 182
mediation, 155, 174
  hyper-mediacy, 23
  technological mediation, 11, 23
melancólicas, Las / Exorcism's Daughter, 3
Melero Salvador, Alejandro, 96, 111, 113, 114, 115, 121, 157, 219, 220, 221, 234–5n6
melodrama, 5, 10, 11, 41, 42, 49, 70, 71n3, 83, 109, 115, 122n3, 147, 158, 164
  crime melodrama, 190
  impure melodrama, 40
memory, 25, 187, 191, 193, 198n4, 208
  fabricated memory, 117

historical memory, 195, 199n19
memory of past colonial, 37
memory wars, 187
popular memory, 122n4
remixing memory, 197
see also trauma
menopause, 203, 207, 208, 210, 213, 215n4
Mentiras y gordas / Sex, Party and Lies, 225, 227
middlebrow, 70–1n2, 110, 113, 114–21, 122n7
  middlebrow audience, 109, 114
  middlebrow cinema, 12, 109, 111, 115
  middlebrow erotic, 12, 109
  queer middlebrow, 121
mies es mucha, La / Great is the Harvest, 43, 46
Miró, Pilar, 4, 14, 121, 122n6, 170, 211, 212
  ley Miró, 110, 122n6
mirror image, 174, 178
mise en scène, 85, 86, 112, 116, 117, 143, 146, 157, 162, 180, 222
Misión blanca / White Mission, 11, 37, 38, 40, 41, 42, 44–50, 51n14, **39**
misogyny, 48, 49, 51n13
missionary films, 42, 46, 47, 50; *see also* colonialism
Moix, Terenci, 83
Molina, Josefina, 14, 204, 207, 208
morality
  amorality, 194
  bourgeois morality, 69
  Catholic morality, 87
  Japanese morality, 33
Morena Clara, 33
Morocco, 38–9, 42, 43, 45–6, 50n3, 162
  Spanish Protectorate of, 38
  see also Africa and colonialism
muerte de Mikel, La / Mikel's Death, 171
Muerte de un ciclista / Death of a Cyclist, 74
muerte ronda a Mónica, La / Death Haunts Monica, 145
Mulvey, Laura, 128, 129, 136n12, 143, 180, 205, 206
Munt, Silvia, 11, 179, 181

Nadie oyó gritar / No One Heard the Scream, 80
Nadiuska, 140
nationalism
  conservative nationalism, 42–3
  internationalism, 30
  masochistic nationalism, 173, 175, 179, 182
  patriotic nationalism, 44

nationalism (cont.)
  supranationalism, 44
  see also Basque nationalism
Navajeros / Knifers, 154, 155, 158, 163, 164
negro que tenía el alma blanca, El / Black Man with a White Soul, The (1927), 24
negro que tenía el alma blanca, El / Black Man with a White Soul, The (1934), 32, 33
neoliberalism, 55–60, 214
  neoliberal-*desarrollism*, 61–2
  neoliberal economic policies, 11, 58
  neoliberal societies, 61
  neoliberal unhappiness, 58
  new neoliberal regime, 12
New Wave European cinema, 58
Nieves Conde, José Antonio, 43
noche del terror ciego, La / Tombs of the Blind Dead, 78, 81, 88n11
noche de verano / SummerNight, 11, 58, 63–4, 66, 68–70, 71n10, **66**
noche de Walpurgis, La / Werewolf's Shadow, 77
normative, 21–2, 49, 68, 70, 190
novia ensangrentada, La / Blood Spattered Bride, The, 79
novios búlgaros, Los / Bulgarian Lovers, 228, 229, 232
nudity, 6, 75, 96, 97, 114, 115, 116, 122n2, 139, 140, 145, 146, 147
  female nudity, 96, 141
  frontal nudity, 96
  full nudity, 141
  juvenile nudity, 147
  male nudity, 4, 115, 150, 156, 219
  see also censorship, *destape* (films) and eroticism
Nueve cartas a Berta / Nine Letters to Bertha, 57
nuevo cine con niño, 187, 188, 189; see also cine con niño
Nuevo Fotogramas, 74, 83, 87–8n1
Núñez, Iñaki, 14, 170, 177

obsession, 84, 129, 130, 131, 133, 202
Ocho apellidos vascos / Spanish Affair, 183
Oedipus Complex, 188
ojos azules de la muñeca rota, Los / Blue Eyes of the Broken Doll, 78
Olea, Pedro, 14, 94, 111, 115, 170, 181
Opus Dei, 12, 92–4, 97–105, 106n5; see also Francoism
orgasm
  absence of orgasm, 209
  collective orgasm, 210
  female orgasm, 6, 208, 209, 210
  sexual orgasm, 48
  simultaneous orgasm, 203
orgía de los muertos, La / Terror of the Living Dead, 78
orgía nocturna de los vampiros, La / Vampires Night Orgy, The, 78
Oro y marfil / Gold and Ivory, 33
Ortega y Gasset, José, 33
Other, 120, 174, 196, 203, 215n2
  homosexual Others, 175
  Oriental Other, 29
  otherness, 21
  ultimate Other, 178
Ortíz, Paula, 11, 14, 211, 213, 214

Pagafantas / Friend Zone, 183
pájaro de la felicidad, El / Bird of Happiness, The, 211
Pa negre / Black Bread, 14, 187, 188, 190, 195–7, 199n19
Pantalla, La, 19, 24, 25, 32 20, 26
Party, 147, 154
Pasolini, Pier Paolo, 56, 59, 71n6, 158
pelota vasca: la piel contra la piedra, La / Basque Ball: Skin Against Stone, The, 14, 172, 173
penetrative sex
  anal penetration, 177, 178, 224, 226, 229, 232, 233
  vaginal penetration, 203, 210, 211
penis, 115, 146–7, 203, 210, 211, 222
Peña, Candela, 7, 8, 9
Peña, Julio, 38, 39
Pepi, Luci, Bom y otras chicas del montón / Pepi, Luci, Bom and Other Girls Like Mom, 125, 135n1
Peppermint frappé, 75
Perdona bonita, pero Lucas me quería a mí / Excuse me, Darling, but Lucas Loved Me, 226
Pero, ¿en qué país vivimos? / But In What Kind of a Country Do We Live?, 56, 57
Perojo, Benito, 11, 24, 32, 33
Perriam, Chris, 1, 5, 169, 198n8, 219, 222, 225, 226, 230
Perros callejeros / Street Warriors, 156
Perros callejeros II: Busca y captura / Street Warriors II, 156
Picazo, Miguel, 75, 76
pico, El / Overdose, 154, 155, 157, 159, 160–5, **161**
pico II, El / Overdose II, 154, 157, 163

placeres ocultos, Los / Hidden Pleasures, 113, 148, 150, 151n2, 166n3, 228, 229
playa vacía, La / Deserted Beach, The, 141, 142
Poniente, 37
Popular Film, 19
pornography
  frustration of pornography, 132
  hard-core pornography, 132, 223
  kitsch pornography, 126, 128, 135n2
  minipornography, 75
  non-pornographic realism, 223
  pornographic films, 21, 125, 133, 136n18, 219, 222
  rise of pornography, 115
  soft-core pornography, 87, 109, 115, 120
  ultra-futurist pornography, 29
  X category, 4, 125
  see also destape (films) and eroticism
¿Por qué lo llaman amor cuando quieren decir sexo? / Why do They Call it Love When They Mean Sex?, 5
¿Por qué te engaña tu marido? / Why Does Your Husband Deceive You?, 76
posters, 2, 19, 22, 86, 117–19, 141, 222
precio de un beso, El / Price of a Kiss, The, 21
pregnancy, 165, 194, 207, 208, 210
prensa negra, 155, 166n2
Princesas / Princesses, 8
proceso de Burgos, El / Burgos Trial, The, 173
Profesor Eroticus / Professor Eroticus, 141, 151n1, 142
prohibition, 11, 29, 32, 33, 99; *see also* Japan and kiss
propaganda, 37, 50n2, 113, 117, 183
prostitution, 207, 220
próximo otoño, El / Next Autumn, 57
Proyector, 1, 24

queer, 11, 14, 48, 50, 51n11, 83, 121, 149, 188, 189, 191, 193, 195, 196, 197, 198n10, 228, 234n4
  queer child, 14, 188, 189, 190, 191
  queer cinema, 1, 230
  queer failure, 220
  queerness, 57, 120, 175, 190
  queer politics, 190
  queer sexuality, 120
  queer spectators, 220, 221, 231–4
  tragic queer figure, 225
  see also sexuality
quinqui films (cine *quinqui*), 11, 13, 109, 154–66, 166nn1,3

racism, 21, 22, 25, 27, 28, 33, 37, 44, 46, 47, 51n14, 120
  bio-racial, 33
  ethno-racial diversity, 37
  interracial, 42
  miscegenation, 33, 46, 51n12
  mixed-race, 30, 47
  monoracial, 42
  racially superior, 29
  racial others, 46
  racial politics, 40
  see also colonialism and Japan
Rancière, Jacques, 231
rape, 79, 170, 172, 173, 174, 176, 182, 211, 212, 213, 229; *see also* torture
Raza, 49
realism
  documentary realism, 171
  magnetic realism, 23
  mimetic realism, 47
  non-pornographic realism, 223
Reinas / Queens, 228
repression
  Catholic repression, 13, 87
  censorship and repression, 87, 127, 216n8
  Francoist repression, 136n13
  interior repression, 81
  Opus Dei and repression, 105
  repression in Spain, 177, 188
  self-repression, 81
  sexual repression, 3, 12, 74, 80, 93
  social repression, 81
residencia, La / House That Screamed, The, 77
Rey, Bárbara, 101, 226, 235n9
Rey, Florián, 33, 45
Rivelles, Amparo, 141
Rivero, Jorge, 11, 141, 142, 151n1
Rocha, David, 12, 76, 84–7, 88nn10,12
Romancero marroquí / Moroccan Ballad, 44, 47

Sacristán, José, 11, 111–12, 115, 116–19, 121
Sáenz de Heredia, José Luis, 43, 56
Saïd, 34
Salto al vacío / Jump into the Void, 182
Sánchez, Pedro Mari, 141–3, 150, 163
Saura, Carlos, 14, 75, 113, 135n4, 156, 157, 166nn1,4, 187, 190, 192, 193, 194
'S'classification / films / rating, 120, 121, 125, 126, 139, 140
scopophilia, 128, 203
  male's scopophilia / voyeurism, 180, 206
  passive scopophilia, 133, 206
  see also voyeurism

Second Republic, 22
Second World War, 42, 43
Secretos del corazón / Secrets of the Heart, 14, 187, 188, 196
Segunda piel / Second Skin, 227, 235n10, **227**
semana del asesino, La / Cannibal Man, The, 80, 158
sex and sexuality
   ambiguous sexuality, 221
   casual sex, 225, 228
   clitoral sexuality, 203
   desexualisation, 170, 171, 174, 176, 177, 183
   female sexuality, 77
   heteronormative sexuality, 57
   infantile sexuality, 130
   oral sex, 5, 130, 225
   psycho-sexual, 42
   resexualisation, 170, 171, 174, 176, 177, 183
   sex between men, 14, 219–34, 234n4
   sex education, 4, 209
   sex industry, 9
   sexlessness, 169
   sexual abuse, 144, 172, 178, 183
   sexual austerity, 48
   sexual desire, 9, 83, 116, 117, 148, 189, 195, 203, 206
   sexual frustration, 183, 225, 227, 230, 231
   sexual identity, 171
   sexual imagery, 2, 6, 84
   sexual imagination, 24, 140
   sexualisation of the martyr, 180
   sexualisation of torture, 173
   sexual liberalisation, 12
   sexual obsession, 93
   sexual repression, 3, 12, 74, 80, 93, 105
   sexual stereotypes, 62
   sexual trauma, 182
   sexual violence, 173
   sounds of sex, 221
   violent sex, 229
sexism, 3, 4, 48, 145, 146
sexo de los ángeles, El / Angels of Sex, 227
Sexo oral / Oral Sex, 5
Sexo por compasión / Compassionate Sex, 204, 206, 210
sexploitation movies, 74, 139
siesta, La / siesta, The, 142, 150
silent cinema, 23, 30
Skaife, Michael, 12, 76, 77, 78, 84, 85, 86, 87
skin, 13, 82, 147, 148, 154–66, 196, 203, 211, 212, 221
   dark-skinned, 32, 128

Smith, Paul Julian, 77, 111, 112, 113, 115, 117, 119, 120, 122nn8,9, 148, 235n7
sodomisation, 170, 177
Soler Leal, Amparo, 11, 205
Solos en la madrugada / Alone in the Dark, 112, 116
sound design, 163, 164, 165
Spanish Civil War, 14, 33, 43, 45, 187, 188, 193, 197
   conservative nationalism, 42–3
   post-Civil War films, 45
Spanish Guinea, 38, 44, 45, 47, 51n6; *see also* colonialism and Francoism
Spanish Legion, 38, 40, 41
Spanish New Wave, 55, 70
Stafford, Frederick, 12, 94, 100
Suspiros de España / Sighs of Spain, 33

taboo, 8, 28, 75, 77, 110, 147, 173, 178, 219, 235n13
tactile, 155, 159, 162, 203, 210, 211, 212, 213
Tararí, 19
Tatuaje / Tattoo, 126
technology, 9, 19, 34
   camera and filmic technology, 21, 24
   kiss as a technology, 23, 33
techo de cristal, El / Glass Ceiling, The, 80
temporal drag, 191, 193, 195–6
Terror Fantastic, 76, 82, 83, 121–2n1
terrorism, 79, 117, 171, 175, 182
   activist / soldier / terrorist, 175
   eroticisation of the terrorist, 175
   female terrorists, 173
   see also ETA
tía Tula, La / Aunt Tula, 75
Tigres de papel / Paper Tigers, 5
Todo por la pasta / Everything for the Bread, 182
Tomándote / Two for Tea, 34
Tormento / Torment, 115
Torremolinos 73, 4, 8
Torrent, Ana, 81, 189
torture, 13–14, 169, 170, 171–80, 182, 183
   non-lethal torture, 171
   rape as part of torture, 170, 176
   sexualised torture, 170, 173, 175, 176
   see also eroticism
tourism
   early days of tourism, 65
   European tourism, 15n3
   Francoist tourist cinema, 57
   gay tourism, 228
   mass tourism, 11
   tourist genre, 61

tourist industry, 56
see also desarrollismo
Transition, 1, 2, 4, 8, 12, 13, 93, 96, 101, 102, 105n3, 109, 110, 119, 120, 121–2n1, 126, 134
  169, 220, 221, 222
  democratic Transition, 33, 127
  erotic films of the Transition, 9, 141
  late Transition, 110
  political transition, 125
  post-Transition, 171
  role of TV in the Transition, 114
  and sexual politics, 1
  transition to democracy, 92, 93, 96, 104, 105n1, 109–21, 139, 140, 150, 151n4, 154, 157, 182, 199n20
  see also destape, eroticism and Francoism
trastienda, La / Backroom, The, 12, 92, 94–100, 104–5, **95, 98**
trauma, 14, 84, 170, 171–2, 174, 182, 187, 188, 189, 190, 195
  sexual trauma, 182
  Spain's traumatic past, 188
  trauma of the past, 188, 198n4
  trauma of the Spanish Civil War, 187, 188, 193
Triunfo, 81, 155, 157, 166n3
turismo es un gran invento, El / Tourism is a Fabulous Concoction, 57

último cuplé, El / Last Torch Song, The, 38
últimos golpes del Torete, Los / Torete's Last Blows, 156
underwear, 9, 10, 100, 129, 141, 144, 145
Uribe, Imanol, 37, 171, 172, 173

Vajda, Ladislao, 43
Valentino, Rudolph, 30, 32–3
¡Vámonos, Bárbara! / Let's Go, Barbara!, 204, 216n8, **206**
vampiras, Las / Vampyros Lesbos, 77–8
vamps / vampiresas, 25, 27–8; *see also* kiss
vanguardia española, La, 81, 83
vela para el diablo, Una / Candle for the Devil, A, 76, 78, 88n4

velo de la dicha, El / Veil of Happiness, The, 25
Venenosa, La / Venomous Lady, The, 24
Vera, Gerardo, 15, 227, 235n10
verdugo, El / Executioner, The, 57, 62, 63
vida empieza hoy, La / Life Begins Today, 202, 207, 209, 210
Villalonga, Agustí, 14, 187
violence, 14, 19, 37, 70, 80, 169, 170, 173, 178, 182, 229
  abstract violence, 67
  aestheticised violence, 84
  corporeal violence, 19
  epistemological violence, 63
  sexualised violence, 85, 173
  terrorist violence, 182
  violence against women, 103
  violence of the dictatorship, 63
Volaverunt, 5
voyeurism, 66, 78, 95, 127, 166n6, 180, 205, 206, 221, 230; *see also* scopophilia
Voz, La, 32

Williams, Linda, 2, 6, 10, 94, 145, 155, 158, 162, 164, 219, 221, 233
women
  ageing women, 215
  heterosexual women, 225
  invisible woman, 206
  mature women, 14, 143, 145, 202–5, 207
  middle-aged women, 202, 204, 207, 215n6
  National Catholic values for women, 57
  older women, 14, 194, 202, 204, 211
  one-dimensional models of women, 44
  sexually repressed women, 75
  woman-as-art, 130
  woman as object, 136
  womanhood, 193
  women filmmakers, 14, 202, 203
  see also eroticism and sexuality

Yagüe, Jesús, 12, 92, 102
Yo, El Vaquilla, 156

EU representative:
Easy Access System Europe
Mustamäe tee 50, 10621 Tallinn, Estonia
Gpsr.requests@easproject.com

www.ingramcontent.com/pod-product-compliance
Lightning Source LLC
Chambersburg PA
CBHW062132300426
44115CB00012BA/1893